LOCATION AND STIGMA

ALSO FROM UNWIN HYMAN

Exploring social geography
P. Jackson & S. Smith

Living with chronic illness
R. Anderson & M. Bury (eds)

Mental health social work observed
M. Fisher *et al.*

Mental maps
P. Gould & R. White

The power of geography: how territory shapes social life
J. Wolch & M. Dear (eds)

Race and racism
P. Jackson (ed.)

Risk and society
L. Sjoberg (ed.)

Slums and slum clearance in Victorian London
J. Yelling

The sociology of health and healing
M. Stacey

Urban hospital location
L. Mayhew

LOCATION AND STIGMA

Contemporary Perspectives on Mental Health and Mental Health Care

Edited by

Christopher J. Smith
Department of Geography, State University of New York at Albany

and

John A. Giggs
Department of Geography, University of Nottingham

Boston
UNWIN HYMAN
London   Sydney   Wellington

Allen & Unwin, Inc.,
8 Winchester Place, Winchester, Mass. 01890, USA

Published by the Academic Division of
Unwin Hyman Ltd.
15/17 Broadwick Street, London W1V 1FP, UK

Allen & Unwin (Australia) Ltd,
8 Napier Street, North Sydney, NSW 2060, Australia

Allen & Unwin (New Zealand) Ltd in association with the
Port Nicholson Press Ltd,
60 Cambridge Terrace, Wellington, New Zealand

First published in 1988

Library of Congress Cataloging in Publication Data

Location and stigma.
    Includes bibliographies and index.
1. Mental health. 2. Mental health facilities.
3. Mental health services.   I. Smith, Christopher J.
II. Giggs, John A. [DNLM: 1. Mental Health.
2. Mental Health Services – trends.   WM 30 L795]
RA790.5.L6   1987   362.2   87-17126
ISBN 0-04-614003-4 (alk. paper)

British Library Cataloguing in Publication Data

Location and stigma: contemporary perspectives
    on mental health and mental health care.
1. Mental illness
I. Smith, Christopher J.   II. Giggs, John A.
616.89   RC454
ISBN 0-04-614003-4

Typeset in 10 on 12 point Bembo by Fotographics (Bedford) Ltd
and printed in Great Britain by Biddles of Guildford

Preface

Any study of mental illness or mental health care reveals many paradoxes. For instance, in terms of prevalence mental illness has constituted the most important source of economic loss and social stress in the developed countries for several decades now, yet the causes of its unwelcome pre-eminence among these prosperous nations are still only poorly understood. Although the primacy of mental illness is unmistakeable in its sustained impact on morbidity (less so on mortality), its measurement can only be approximated through such partial or indirect indices as psychiatric service utilization data; mortality statistics for suicide, liver cirrhosis, accidents and homicides; or localized surveys of specific communities, general physician records, and admissions to trauma departments in non-psychiatric hospitals (e.g. for parasuicide cases). For all of these data-sources the bulk of the information is not routinely published, so that research is both expensive and time-consuming. Finally there is still disagreement about what exactly constitutes "mental illness" and its varied (i.e. clinically defined) manifestations. Indeed, mental illness is still regarded by some as a myth!

The resolution of these and other paradoxes will require considerable research effort. Although mental health and mental health-care studies have become increasingly popular in the past 25 years, the published output is still regrettably small in comparison with that produced for mankind's physical ills and related health care systems. Furthermore, to date, mental health studies have been highly specialized. Thus, traditionally books on this subject have been written around a single specialism, notably psychiatry, psychology, sociology, law, political economy, and economics. The dominance of "discipline-bound" perspectives is under-standable, given the increased interest in the subject-matter. Indeed, for most of the disciplines cited above, mental health research still constitutes a novel and minor subfield. However, despite the general preoccupation with narrow, single-disciplinary perspectives, there is some welcome evidence of a trend towards interdisciplinary analyses of both mental health and mental health care.

In planning this book we have attempted to capture the flavor of these integrative developments by commissioning a set of original papers by experts on specific aspects of these phenomena, intending that they would each present their particular topic within a wider view of the whole. The contributors have demonstrated that mental health research is now commonly multilevel in character, ranging from truly macrolevel (i.e. international) perspectives, through the mesolevel (i.e. regional comparisons), down to microlevel studies of such phenomena as the mental health of particular urban neighborhoods and the attitudes of neighborhood residents to the proposed siting of specific kinds of mental health-care facilities. Finally, the contributors address fully the issues of temporal and spatial variations in the specific phenomena under review. Until comparatively recently much research in the mental health field has been both ahistorical and aspatial. We feel that the comprehensive treatment of both the historical and geographical settings of mental health subjects is particularly important.

In conclusion, we hope that this book provides for researchers into mental health a step along the road to achieving the breadth of vision displayed by Hettner, 60 years ago:

> Reality is simultaneously a three dimensional space which we must examine from three different points of view in order to comprehend the whole. From one point of view we see the relations of similar things, from the second the development in time and from the third the arrangement and division in space. Reality as a whole cannot be encompassed entirely in the systematic sciences, sciences defined by the objects they study. Other writers have effectively based the justification for the historical sciences on the necessity of a special conception of development in time. But this leaves science still two-dimensional; we do not perceive it completely unless we consider it also from the third point of view, the division and arrangement in space (Hettner, A. 1927. *Die Geografie, ihre Geschichte, ihre Wessen und ihre Methoden*. Breslau. Cited in Hartshorne, R. 1961. *The Nature of Geography*. Lancaster: The Association of American Geographers, p. 140).

Acknowledgments

It is difficult to know where to start when thanking the people who have helped in the preparation of this book. Obviously our major gratitude goes to the authors of the chapters. They have been patient, which is perhaps the greatest virtue in the case of an edited volume such as this one. They have also been cooperative, responding quickly and efficiently to our demands.

It is customary to offer thanks to spouses and families, although this rarely comes close to making up for all the time stolen from them. Nevertheless, we shall follow suit, and acknowledge the contributions of our significant others, Carolyn Smith and Mavis Giggs. Special thanks also go to Chris Evans for preparing the index of the book. Obviously we owe much to Roger Jones at Unwin Hyman who recognized the potential value of this volume and worked so hard to bring it to fruition.

Contents

List of Tables

List of contributors

JIM BAUMOHL
Medical Research Institute of San Francisco/Alcohol Research Group, Berkeley, California

PHILIP BEAN
School of Social Studies, University of Nottingham

PHIL BROWN
Brown University and Harvard Medical School

TERRY F. BUSS
Center for Urban Studies, Youngstown State University

RALPH CATALANO
Public Policy Research Organization and the Program in Social Ecology, Irvine, California

MICHAEL DEAR
Department of Geography, University of Southern California

DAVID DOOLEY
Public Policy Research Organization and the Program in Social Ecology, Irvine, California

JOHN EYLES
Queen Mary College, University of London

JOHN A. GIGGS
Department of Geography, University of Nottingham

KOSTAS GOUNIS
New York State Office of Mental Health, Albany

GLENDA LAWS
McMaster University

GRAHAM MOON
School of Social and Historical Studies, Portsmouth Polytechnic

JOSEPH P. MORRISSEY
New York State Office of Mental Health, Albany

CYNTHIA A. NELSON
School of Urban and Regional Planning, University of Southern California

F. STEVENS REDBURN
US Department of Housing and Urban Development, Youngstown, Ohio

ANNETTE RUBALCABA
School of Urban and Regional Planning, University of Southern California

STEVEN P. SEGAL
School of Social Welfare, University of California, Berkeley

SETH SERXNER
Public Policy Research Organization and the Program in Social Policy, Irvine, California

ANDREW J. SIXSMITH
Department of Psychiatry, University of Liverpool

CHRISTOPHER J. SMITH
Department of Geography and Regional Planning, State University of New York at Albany

S. MARTIN TAYLOR
Department of Geography, McMaster University

NANCY TOMES
State University of New York at Stony Brook

JENNIFER R. WOLCH
School of Urban and Regional Planning, University of Southern California

Introduction

CHRISTOPHER J. SMITH and JOHN A. GIGGS

During the past few centuries, knowledge about causal factors in human illness has grown at a seemingly exponential rate. As a result, in the developed countries of the world, nearly all of the severely disabling and killing communicable diseases that were commonplace during pre-industrial and industrial times have been eradicated. Since the 1940s the chronic and degenerative diseases have emerged as the most important human health hazards in the more developed nations (Pyle 1979, McKinlay & McKinlay 1986). It is not surprising that the current foci of both clinical and epidemiological research are the cancers and the various heart diseases, since they rank amongst the first five causes of deaths in all countries for which data are available (WHO 1982).

However, it is regrettable that other important aspects of human health have not attracted the attention which they unquestionably deserve. This is particularly true of mental illness. Today, mental illness and mental handicap are probably the leading causes of disability in most developed countries. In the USA, for example, it has been estimated that 29 million people, almost one in five adults, suffer from an identifiable psychiatric disorder (Sharfstein & Biegel 1985). A further (unknown) proportion of undeclared mental illness exists among persons whose behavior is socially "undesirable," including alcoholics, drug abusers, homeless persons, and parasuicides (Smith 1987). In the case of mental handicap, prevalence estimates suggest another 2–3% of the population, although such rates are strongly determined by spatial and cultural variations in case definitions and prevailing public attitudes (Stein & Susser 1974).

The two most obvious concerns about the widespread prevalence of mental illness and handicap involve the adequacy of treatment and the social and economic costs. It appears that only about 20% of the people suffering from mental disorders have ever sought any kind of psychiatric treatment (Mechanic 1980). The implication of this is that the bulk, more than half, of the sufferers receive their only care from general medical practitioners and the rest, perhaps as many as a quarter of them, receive no formal treatment whatsoever (Regier *et al.* 1978).

The economic costs of mental illness and related disorders are enormous. In the USA it has been estimated that the direct and indirect costs generated by mental illness and substance abuse amounted to $191 billion in 1980 (Research Triangle Institute 1980). However, to talk only about the economic costs of mental illness neglects the devastating impact that such illness has on individuals and their families, on the healthy development of children, and on the capacity for people to live a reasonably satisfying life. As Mechanic (1980) has observed, "Examined in this context, psychiatric illness constitutes one of the most compelling problems modern societies face, deserving of the highest priority in social policy considerations . . ." (p. xi). As if to recognize Mechanic's point, in 1975 the UK Secretary of State for Social Services stated that "Mental illness is a major health problem, perhaps the major health problem of our time. It is also a major social problem" (DHSS 1975). However, expenditure by the UK National Health Service on the mentally ill amounted to only 12.5% of the total in that year. Similarly, in the USA only 12% of the nation's health care expenditure was devoted to mental illness in 1980 (Sharfstein & Biegel 1985). Within the medical profession itself, psychiatry is regarded as a relatively unfashionable and low-status speciality. In the UK only 11% of all consultants in the National Health Service (NHS) are psychiatrists, and only 22% of all full-time nurses are employed in psychiatric wards in NHS hospitals. Yet nearly half of the hospital beds are occupied by the mentally ill and mentally handicapped (Ennals 1973, DHSS 1974).

More importantly, perhaps, research into the causes of mental illness is seriously underfunded in most countries. Although the causes of most mental illnesses are still unknown, less than 10% of all expenditure on medical research in England & Wales is devoted to the etiological aspects of these disorders (Ennals 1973). More recently, a review of mental disorder in the UK (*The Times* 1985) showed that the Medical Research Council allocated less than 5% of its annual research budget to mental illness, with 1% going to drug addiction research and less than 0.5% to schizophrenia research. A recent study of schizophrenia in the state of New South Wales, Australia, showed that government support for research into the disorder is grossly inadequate when compared with that for myocardial infarction, and bears no relationship to the overall cost of schizophrenia to the community (Andrews *et al.* 1985). In the United States the problems of research funding for the mental disorders is no less acute. A report of the Institute of Medicine, National Academy of Sciences, to the federal Alcohol, Drug Abuse, and Mental Health Administration (ADAMHA) recommended a substantially increased national commitment to research on mental and addictive disorders (Barchas *et al.* 1985). Although the personal and social costs of these disorders in the USA are similar to those of cancer and cardiovascular disease, they have never received equivalent financial research support. More importantly, since 1966, the inflation-adjusted research funding for the National Institute of Mental Health (NIMH) has declined to roughly half that for 1966 (Barchas *et al.* 1985). This, then, is the ultimate stigma of mental illness, compounding the more widely recognized problem of negative community attitudes (Nieradzik *et al.* 1985). The mentally ill have little prospect of having their problems investigated by adequately funded etiological research.

Given both the comparative novelty of scientific research into the causes of mental illness (e.g., the World Health Organization's first reports on the subject began only 25 years ago), and the chronic underfunding of that research, it is not at all surprising that most mental disorders have not been firmly associated with specific causes. Recent reviews of etiological research into mental illnesses (Giggs 1980, Warner 1985) show that the studies have thus far been dominated by a relatively small number of disciplines, especially medicine, psychiatry, psychology, and sociology. Most of the investigations into causal factors, particularly prior to the 1950s, involved cross-sectional (i.e., nontemporal) analyses of specific potentially etiological factors such as genetic endowments and social class. In contrast, relatively few authors have endeavored to step outside the narrow confines of the perspectives imposed by their specific disciplines, preferring instead to believe that the cures for most mental disorders will come exclusively from advances in neurological research, behavior modification, or the reduction of social inequality. Increasingly, however, it can be argued that the search for causes of mental illness can best be accomplished through interdisciplinary research (Warner 1985). Furthermore, there has been a growing appreciation of the need to conduct research at a variety of spatial scales. Thus the research on life events and mental illness causation amongst individuals and specific population groups is one important example of "microscale" longitudinal research (Dohrenwend & Dohrenwend 1980, Cooke *et al.* 1983, Bebbington *et al.* 1984); whereas the analysis of the impact of broader political, social and economic events shows a developing interest in "macroscale" temporal influences on the levels of mental disorder found in larger populations (Ralph 1983, Brown 1985, Warner 1985).

This volume provides a cross section of recent research that reflects these trends toward interdisciplinary and multilevel analyses of mental health and mental health care. It is recognized that the overall level of mental health within a population is a result of the interactions between a great many factors. For purposes of clarity it has proved useful to distill these factors into four interrelated clusters; namely, individual effects, environmental effects, the characteristics of the service delivery system, and the macrolevel effects of the prevailing social, economic, and political system (Smith 1982). Because of the multiplicity of linkages between these clusters, it is not possible to deal with each of them separately. As an alternative, therefore, the individual chapters are organized into four parts. Part I attempts to put the treatment of mental illness into its historical and political context, adding a geographical–cultural dimension that reflects the backgrounds of the individual authors. Part II looks more specifically at some of the clues about the etiology of mental illness, focusing on the social, environmental, and economic factors that contribute to the incidence of the problems in question. The chapters in Part III deal with the implementation and impacts of recent mental health policies in the UK and the USA. Although this represents a simplification of what has been a complex story, these policies have mainly involved the shifting over from a centralized, institution-based delivery system to a decentralized system provided "in the community." Part IV is an attempt to evaluate the current status, and to speculate on the future, of mental health policy. The focus here is on some of the enduring problems associated with the stigma of mental illness. It is also evident that economic realities will continue to exert a major influence on both mental health and mental health care, by "generating" new cases of mental illness, and also by limiting the scope and effectiveness of treatment and prevention strategies.

References

Andrews, G. *et al*. 1985. The economic costs of schizophrenia. *Archives of General Psychiatry* **42**, 537–43.

Barchas, J. D. *et al*. 1985. The ultimate stigma: inadequate funding for research on mental illness and addictive disorders. *American Journal of Psychiatry* **142**, 838–9.

Bebbington, P. *et al*. 1984. The domain of life events: a comparison of two techniques of description. *Psychological Medicine* **14**, 219–22.

Brown, P. 1985. *The transfer of care: psychiatric deinstitutionalization and its aftermath*. London: Routledge & Kegan Paul.

Cooke, D. J. *et al*. 1983. The aetiological importance of stressful life events. *British Journal of Psychiatry* **143**, 397–400.

DHSS 1974. *Health and personal social service statistics for England*. London: Department of Health and Social Services.

DHSS 1975. *Better services for the mentally ill*. London: Department of Health and Social Services.

Dohrenwend, B. P. & B. P. Dohrenwend (eds.) 1980. *Stressful life events and their contexts*. New York: Prodist.

Ennals, D. 1973. *Out of mind*. London: Arrow.

Giggs, J. A. 1980. Mental health and the environment. In *Environmental medicine*, G. M. Howe & J. A. Loraine (eds.), 281–305. London: Heinemann.

McKinlay, J. B. & S. M. McKinlay 1986. Medical measures and the decline of mortality. In *The sociology of health and illness: critical perspectives*, P. Conrad & R. Kern (eds.), 2nd edn, 10–23. New York: St. Martin's Press.

Mechanic, D. 1980. *Mental health and social policy*, 2nd edn. Englewood Cliffs, NJ: Prentice-Hall.

Nieradzik, K. *et al*. 1985. Public attitudes toward mental illness—the effect of behaviour, roles and psychiatric labels. *International Journal of Social Psychiatry* **31**, 23–33.

Pyle, G. F. 1979. *Applied medical geography*. Washington, DC: V. H. Winston.

Ralph, D. 1983. *Work and madness: The rise of community psychiatry*. Montreal: Black Rose Books.

Regier, D. A., I. D. Goldberg & C. Taube 1978. The de facto US Mental Health Service System: a public health perspective. *Archives of General Psychiatry* **35**, 685–93.

Research Triangle Institute 1980. *The cost to society of alcohol, drug abuse, and mental illness*. Contract 283-79-001. Rockville, Maryland: National Institute of Mental Health (ADAMHA).

Sharfstein, S. S. & A. Biegel (eds.) 1985. *The new economics and psychiatric care*. Washington DC: American Psychiatric Press.

Smith, C. J. 1987. *Public problems: the measurement and management of social disability*. New York: Guilford Press.

Smith, D. M. 1982. Geographical perspectives on health and health care. In *Contemporary perspectives on health and health care*, 1–11. Occasional paper no. 2, Department of Geography, Queen Mary College, University of London.

Stein, Z. A. & M. Susser 1974. The epidemiology of mental retardation. In *American handbook of psychiatry*, vol. 4, S. Arieti (ed.), 464–91. New York: Basic Books.

The Times 1985. Scanning the brain in search of a cure. London, December 16, 1985.

Warner, R. 1985. *Recovery from schizophrenia: psychiatry and political economy*. London: Routledge & Kegan Paul.

World Health Organization (WHO) 1982. *Seventh General Programme of Work (1984–1989)*. Geneva: World Health Organization.

PART I

The history and politics of mental health care: a comparative perspective

1 The Anglo-American asylum in historical perspective

NANCY TOMES

Mental health care is one area of social policy where the burden of history lies heavy and obvious: the institutional parameters of today's policy debates were established over a century ago, when European reformers broke with the long tradition of familial and communal care for the mentally ill and erected a costly, extensive system of state mental institutions. Although its limitations were soon evident, the state mental hospital remained the foundation of public provision for the mentally ill until the 1950s and 1960s. Although the community mental health movement and deinstitutionalization have resulted in considerably more varied therapeutic arrangements, the modern descendant of the 19th-century mental hospital remains an important and seemingly permanent aspect of the mental health care system.

The contemporary debate over the mental hospital has spurred historical interest in its 19th-century origins. Recognizing that many of the contemporary dilemmas concerning the mental health care system have their roots in the past century, historians have looked to the asylum's past for clues to its resilience. Unlike previous historians of psychiatry, who tended to accept the medical legitimation of the mental hospital without question, this new generation of scholars has probed the asylum with a more critical eye to its social control as well as therapeutic functions. While varying in its rejection of psychiatric legitimacy, the new scholarship tends to emphasize the mix of humanitarian and authoritarian goals in the asylum's foundation, the profound tension between individual rights and social needs inherent in the commitment process, and the ultimate failure of the mental hospital's therapeutic mission.

As an introduction to the contemporary studies in this volume, this chapter will review the recent historical literature on the Anglo-American asylum, emphasizing those themes that remain relevant in present-day policy-making: what social needs the 19th-century asylum met; what forces undermined its effectiveness; and what forces conspired to protect it from fundamental change. As we shall see, the broad lines of evolution for English and American mental hospitals were quite similar, yet they show some interesting variations in conception and execution that highlight differences between the social development of the two nations.

Mental illness before the mental hospital

In contemporary discussions of mental health care, one often encounters the assumption that 19th-century psychiatrists "invented" the concept of mental illness to legitimate their control over the mental hospital; that prior to the 1800s, Western Europeans viewed madness solely as a supernatural or spirital affliction and treated its victims as witches or heretics. In fact, traditional concepts of madness were extremely eclectic; natural and supernatural explanations and treatments of mental aberration were not seen as mutually exclusive or contradictory (MacDonald 1981). Drawing on a concept of madness as illness that dated back to the Classical period, physicians in the 1500s and 1600s treated mental maladies as they did other diseases, by using drugs and bleeding to restore the body's internal balance. But the naturalistic approach of early modern medicine did not exclude the possibility of supernatural or spiritual agency in the causation of mental disorder. The cosmology of Tudor England allowed for the direct intervention in human life of both heavenly and satanic forces. Thus depending on its symptoms and context, mental aberration might be interpreted in varied ways. For example, when confronted with a suspected case of possession or bewitchment, local authorities would often ask a physician to examine the victim, and only after he had ruled out epilepsy, hysteria, and melancholy—diseases whose symptoms were regarded as very similar to supernatural afflictions— would the case be treated as supernatural in origin (Walker 1981).

Over the course of the 17th-century and the tumult of the English Civil War, the naturalistic conception of madness gradually gained ascendance in English society. Bruised by the excesses of religious enthusiasm, the Anglican elite suppressed spiritual and magical interpretations of mental disorders. While the latter certainly persisted in English folk society, rationalistic explanations of madness that assigned physicians the primary role in its treatment had become the orthodoxy of the English middle and upper classes by the 18th century (MacDonald 1981).

However, the conviction that madness was an illness that benefited from medical care did not automatically lead to the notion of asylum treatment. Eighteenth century Anglo-Americans firmly believed that home care was the best care for any kind of illness, whether physical or mental. Hospitals offered no medical benefits that could not be more safely prescribed at home; rather, they existed primarily to care for individuals whose families could not care for them. Affluent households supported deranged members out of their own resources, while poor families received financial assistance from the local authorities to keep their insane relations at home. If a poor lunatic had no family, the poor law officials boarded him out at public expense. Confinement in a jail, almshouse, or hospital was an exceptional response reserved for unusually violent or troublesome individuals (Grob 1973, Scull 1979).

While home care remained the most common response to madness, some significant new institutional arrangements for the insane did begin to evolve in the 1700s. The peculiar strains that caring for the mentally ill placed on family and community provided an impetus to search for extrafamilial forms of care. Historians disagree as to whether this impetus reflected a declining tolerance for irrational behavior, or simply the ability of a more affluent society to escape burdens of care that had long been onerous. Whatever the case, a small but growing sector of institutional care emerged in 18th-century England, as wealthier families sought out the services of private madhouses, and public-spirited philanthropists began to expand hospital facilities for the insane poor (Scull 1979, Tomes 1984).

As early as the 1600s, records can be found of individual physicians and clergymen who made a business of caring for lunatic patients in their own homes. By the mid-1700s, the rapid growth of the madhouse trade created concern about possible abuses, especially the confinement of sane individuals. In 1763, the House of Commons appointed a Select Committee to investigate the private madhouses, and in 1774 a Madhouse Act was passed, requiring that they be examined and licensed. The Metropolitan London area had 16 such licensed houses in 1774; a subsequent census in 1802 found 22 provincial madhouses. Although some accepted pauper lunatics, the private madhouses catered primarily to the affluent. Thus the first impetus for expanding institutional provision for the insane came not from public authorities who wanted to control the poor, but from the upper classes who sought extrafamilial care for their own family members (Parry-Jones 1972).

The expansion of hospital provision for the insane occurred as a parallel but independent development from the growth of the private madhouse trade. In contrast to the madhouses, which were at most slightly modified homes, 18th-century hospitals were "purpose-built" structures for the care of the mentally and physically ill. Although by modern standards very small-scale and home-like, hospitals had a distinctive architecture and administration that clearly distinguished them from domestic buildings.

The first hospital set aside exclusively for the insane was London's Bethlem Hospital, popularly known as "Bedlam." As a monastery and priory, Bethlem first began to accept lunatics in the 13th century; in 1547, Henry VIII gave it to the City of London as a hospital for pauper lunatics. Although a favorite target of early 19th-century exposés of patient abuse and neglect, Bethlem did strive for a therapeutic, as opposed to strictly custodial, standard of care. Under the supervision of Edward Tyson (1684–1704), it achieved a reputation for therapeutic efficacy and humane treatment and, for most of the 18th century, confined its services only to patients considered curable (Allderidge 1985).

The 18th-century voluntary hospital movement led to the establishment of additional public hospitals for the insane. The voluntary or subscription hospital, as it was also called, reflected two developments: the rise of a new clinical medicine, which required the cultivation of hospitals as adjuncts to elite medical schools, and the growth of a wealthy merchant class which wanted to create new philanthropic institutions. These two aims—science and enlightened charity—were well served by the voluntary hospital, which combined teaching facilities for elite physicians with medical care for the worthy poor. During the 1700s, voluntary hospitals opened in London and the provincial cities, many with facilities for the insane. London's St. Luke's Hospital was founded in 1751 exclusively for lunatics (Walk 1964).

Compared to England, the North American colonies developed considerably less diverse institutional arrangements. Family care and outdoor relief played the same central role, with almshouses and jails being used primarily for violent cases (Grob 1973). Although it seems likely that clergymen and physicians took in single lunatics, no well developed private madhouse trade ever emerged in the American colonies. The one 18th-century English innovation that did migrate to America was the voluntary hospital. In Philadelphia, the largest and most self-conscious of colonial cities, a group of physicians and merchants founded the Pennsylvania Hospital in 1751 to provide care for the sick and insane. By 1796, demand for its services were so great that the managers opened a separate wing for the insane. Voluntary hospitals operating on similar lines later opened in New York (1971) and Boston (1821) (Tomes 1984).

Curiously, the first hospital for the insane to be built entirely at public expense was not located in the more populous Northern colonies, but in Virginia. Inspired by the same interest in science and charity as the voluntary hospitals, the Williamsburg asylum, which opened in 1773, was paid for entirely out of the colony's own coffers. An unusual practice in the 18th century, this method of financing provision for pauper lunatics would eventually replace private charity as the chief factor in the asylum expansion of the 19th century (Dain 1971).

By the late 1700s, Anglo-American society had developed a variety of arrangements for the insane: home care and boarding out, confinement in general-purpose institutions such as almshouses and jails, and commitment to more specialized facilities such as private madhouses and public hospitals. Yet the vast majority of the insane were still cared for not in institutions, but in households. Moreover, in the two institutions explicitly designated for the insane, the private madhouses and the voluntary hospitals, medical authority was quite limited. Private madhouse proprietors were an eclectic group including clergymen and laymen, and the amount of medical treatment they provided varied greatly (Parry-Jones 1972). Public hospitals had a more clear-cut medical profile, but the resident lay steward often had as much power as the attending physicians (Tomes 1984). The rise of the 19th-century asylum, then, required both the "medicalization" and "hospitalization" of mental illness.

Moral treatment and the asylum movement

The expansion of the mental hospital system was part of a much broader drive to enlarge and reorder institutional responses to disease, poverty, and social disorder. Beginning in the 17th century, a variety of institutions, including jails, almshouses, and hospitals, had arisen as temporary receptacles for homeless or difficult individuals who could not easily be kept in community care. As urban growth and population movement swelled the ranks of such individuals, these institutions grew increasingly larger, more disorderly, and more expensive, and thus fell under the critical eye of late 18th and early 19th century reformers imbued with both utilitarian and humanitarian concerns. If institutions could be run more efficiently and their inmates subjected to more discipline, as utilitarians such as Jeremy Bentham reasoned, the poor and disorderly might be taught more productive habits and be less of a burden on society. Simultaneously, but in more religious terms, evangelicals such as William Wilberforce were inspired by a new conviction of human perfectability to argue for similar changes, stressing the institution's ability to transform souls and thus Christianize the nation (Rothman 1971, Scull 1979).

Late 18th-century asylum reformers employed both utilitarian and humanitarian arguments to critique existing provisions for the insane. While previous reform efforts had been primarily concerned with the illegal confinement of the insane, their focus of complaint broadened to include the lack of adequate food, medicine, and amusements for the asylum inmates. Deploring the assumption that lunatics had lost all human sensibilities, asylum reformers vigorously attacked the physical brutality and neglect so common in many institutions (Grob 1973, Scull 1979).

As part of their critique of existing institutions, late 18th-century reformers began to articulate alternative forms of treatment based on more humane standards. Lunatics could best be restored to human society, they reasoned, by combining kindness with psychological or, as it was then termed, "moral" discipline. No one individual or institution invented this more humane approach, which gradually came to be termed "moral treatment"; it appears to have developed independently in England, Italy, France, and the United States (Deutsch 1949). But one institution did become the chief exemplar of the new treatment philosophy, and did the most to popularize its methods: the York Retreat.

Troubled by abuses at the York asylum, a subscription hospital for the insane, a group of the Society of Friends decided to open an asylum for their own sect in 1796. Skeptical of medical measures, they focused instead on the moral rehabilitation of madness. Employing the shared religious values and practices of the Society of Friends, the York Retreat created a therapeutic "family" that operated according to a gentle system of rewards and punishments. Physical restraint was used very sparingly, and every effort was made to treat the patients as rationally as possible. By appealing to the patients' "inner light", the Retreat's founders claimed that dramatic cures might be obtained in many cases. As publicized in Samuel Tuke's widely read pamphlet, *A description of the Retreat* (1813), the York Retreat's method became a blueprint for asylum reform (Digby 1985).

There was no immediately compelling argument for putting physicians in charge of moral treatment. The Retreat's early managers had the lay steward direct the patients' daily regimen, while the attending physician saw only to their medical ailments (Digby 1985). At other "progressive" institutions such as the Pennsylvania Hospital, lay officers and managers, as well as physicians, took an active role in moral treatment (Tomes 1984). But as the asylum concept gained favor, doctors were quick to assert their superior ability to practice moral treatment, leading to a gradual "medicalization" of the new therapeutic approach (Scull 1979).

The first step in integrating moral treatment into the medical armamentarium required the discovery of a physiological explanation of its efficacy. Frustrated in their efforts to find a physical lesion responsible for insanity, doctors resorted to a functional explanation: insanity was caused by disordered nerve action. From this premise followed a plan of treatment that integrated medical and moral measures: medical therapeutics, chiefly narcotics, would calm the irritated nervous system; then an ordered regimen and gentle discipline would restore healthy nerve action.

This union of medical and moral measures allowed physicians to make their bid to supervise the new "reformed" asylums. If treatment was to be effective, they argued, both its medical and psychological aspects should be under the same man's direction. Since unlike laymen, physicians could both prescribe medical treatment and wield moral authority, they were clearly the best choice for asylum superintendents. Eventually, the medical profession succeeded in promulgating this rationale for "one-man rule", and more eclectic styles of moral management gave way to the plan of having one physician in charge of all aspects of asylum treatment and administration (Scull 1979).

This version of moral treatment became the therapeutic philosophy underlying the asylum expansion that occurred in England and the USA between 1800 and 1860. Impressed by the high cure rates and humane atmosphere achieved by the York Retreat and other progressive institutions, reformers campaigned to make moral treatment available to the poor. State-built and -operated hospitals, they argued, would be both efficacious and economical: the initial outlay on the asylum building and staff would be more than balanced by the savings from rapid cures; pauper patients would no longer languish untreated at the State's expense, but would quickly be rehabilitated and returned to society (Grob 1973, Scull 1979).

While the broad outlines of moral treatment were quite similar in

England and the USA, the timing and context of their institutional reforms differed in significant ways. England's more extensive system of 18th-century asylums, coupled with medical complicity in asylum abuse, gave its reform movement a decidedly more antimedical edge. For the same reasons, England moved toward centralized state regulation of asylums much more quickly than did the Americans. Finally, due in large part to the well developed private madhouse trade, the distinction between public and private modes of care developed much more sharply there than in the USA.

The English reform movement had not only to extend state provisions for the insane, but also improve standards in the private madhouses and voluntary hospitals that had been built in the 18th century. Moreover, the county authorities had already begun to invest in new facilities before moral treatment emerged as a coherent reform philosophy. In 1808, Parliament passed the County Asylum Act, which authorized but did not compel magistrates to erect county asylums at the ratepayers' expense, and by 1827 nine county asylums had been constructed under the permissive Act. Only two of these institutions, the Nottingham and Wakefield asylums, showed much commitment to moral treatment (Walton 1979).

Therefore, the English reformers had to press their case for moral treatment on two fronts: by trying to improve standards through regulation of existing institutions, as well as by expanding reformed facilities for the poor. They set about achieving these goals by systematically exposing conditions in existing institutions. Between 1815 and 1844, three Select Committees appointed by Parliament amassed lengthy reports detailing the therapeutic deficiencies of English asylums. The 1815–16 investigation excoriated Bethlem and the York asylum, amongst others; the 1827 report demonstrated the miserable state of the metropolitan madhouses; and the 1844 committee concluded with an exhaustive, caustic report on the nation's whole system of asylums (Hervey 1985, Scull 1979).

The reform movement necessarily brought about tension between lay and medical men. Physicians were too often associated with abuses in both private and public institutions to have an unambiguous relationship to asylum reform. For example, the profession's failure adequately to regulate the private madhouse trade created doubts about its trustworthiness in the cause of asylum reform. The 1774 Madhouse Act had empowered the Royal College of Physicians to choose five of its members to serve as Metropolitan commissioners, with the power to regulate and license private madhouses. The overwhelming evidence that the medical commissioners had done little to prevent neglect or abuse led to the 1828 Madhouse Act, which provided for as many as 15 laymen to serve on the formerly all-medical Board of Inspection (Hervey 1985).

The influence of evangelical reformers in the asylum movement increased its antimedical thrust. Drawn to the Retreat's model of religiously inspired therapy, the evangelicals remained skeptical of the medical profession's claims to superiority in asylum practice. Lord Shaftesbury, the central figure in the 1844–45 reform effort, frequently expressed his distrust of medical expertise, and aggressively asserted the right of informed lay-men to make asylum policy. Thus from its outset, the English reform movement manifested a pronounced tension between lay and medical viewpoints (Hervey 1985, Scull 1979).

Despite resistance from private madhouse proprietors, physicians, and public officials, all of whom had reason to fear centralized regulation, the asylum reformers finally succeeded in gaining both their goals: in 1845, Parliament passed the Lunacy Acts making construction of county asylums compulsory and setting up a national Lunacy Commission to license and regulate all mental institutions. To be sure, physicians played an important role under the new system, for they and they alone could head the new county asylums. But the evangelicals' skepticism about the medical profes-sion's disinterest carried over into the regulatory machinery; the new board was evenly split between three physicians and three lawyers. In subsequent decades, the Lunacy Commission would prove to be a powerful, although not necessarily hostile, check on medical autonomy[1].

By 1860, virtually all counties in England had built public asylums under either the permissive or compulsory acts. From their inception, these county asylums were intended only for paupers; that is, individuals sup-ported in whole or in part at the ratepayer's expense. Gradually, those private madhouses that specialized in paupers closed down, so that hospital care of poor lunatics was transferred to the county institutions. By the mid-1800s, then, the English asylum system was clearly class-differentiated: the private asylums for the middle and upper classes, and the county asylums for the poor (Scull 1979).

However, this strict class separation did not mean that moral treatment was conceived of as the exclusive privilege of the private asylums. The asylum reformers of the 1830s and 1840s genuinely believed that lunacy reform should bring the benefits of moral treatment to the pauper class. Their concerns were partly economic (moral treatment promised to cure more patients, and thus reduce the cost of their support), but it was also humanitarian in intent. For example, one of the most dramatic innovations of English moral treatment, the nonrestraint system, which did away with mechanical means of confining patients, was developed at two public asylums, Lincoln and Hanwell. Although it proved difficult to maintain, moral treatment was the initial therapeutic premise of the new public institutions built in the mid-1800s (Walton 1979).

Because of America's less advanced level of institutional development, its asylum movement differed in focus and tone from its English counterpart. The American reformers had no entrenched asylum establishment to contend with; rather, moral treatment and institutional expansion occurred almost simultaneously, making the initial course of reform much smoother. Since the medical profession had no prior history of complicity in asylum abuse, lay and medical interests were not opposed in the early reform movement. Finally, due to the dominance of charitable, rather than profit-oriented, private asylums, the sharp distinction between public and private modes of care took much longer to emerge.

As in England, the expansion of the American asylum system first took place in the private sector. However, the early American private asylums differed from their English counterparts in two important respects: first, they were founded on the voluntary hospital plan (that is, as charitable corporations rather than profit-making businesses); and secondly, they were established later, in the first decades of the 19th century, and thus incorporated the new philosophy of moral treatment from their inception. Some of the early corporate asylums developed in conjunction with the old general hospitals; inspired by European developments, the managers of the Massachusetts General, New York and Pennsylvania hospitals all established separate asylums on the moral treatment plan in 1818, 1821, and 1840 respectively. Inspired by the York Retreat, other philanthropists established free-standing asylums, including the Friends' Retreat in 1817 and the Hartford Retreat in 1824 (Grob 1973).

The impressive cure rates and attractive regimens achieved by these small corporate asylums inspired the campaign to extend state care for the insane. Arguing that moral treatment was both economical and humane, reformers turned to the state legislatures to fund progressive asylums for the poor. In making their case for the state asylum, they compiled reports and memorials documenting the inhumane treatment of the insane in the community. However, unlike their English counterparts, the American reformers focused their attack not on existing asylums, whose standards of care tended to be very high, but on nonmedical institutions such as alms-houses and jails (Grob 1973).

The close association between asylums and moral treatment in early 19th-century America meant that the medical profession had no ambiguous attitude toward reform, as was the case in England. American physicians had no cause to be implicated in asylum abuse, nor any reason to resist reform. On the contrary, reform-minded doctors and their state medical societies strongly supported the asylum movement, and lay reformers such as Horace Mann and Dorothea Dix regarded medical men as their best allies in the battle to convince state legislators of the asylum's virtues. Thus the American asylum movement did not manifest the same antagonism between evangelical and medical interests as did English reform.

With the combined backing of the medical profession and prominent lay reformers, the campaign for state mental hospitals proceeded quickly in the mid-1800s. With the exception of four Southern hospitals, which were founded before 1830, the new public institutions were all established under the aegis of moral treatment. The first "reformed" state institution opened at Worcester, Massachusetts, in 1833; between 1850 and 1889, 94 new state hospitals were built in the USA (Grob 1973, 1983).

The influence of the corporate asylums on the planning of these early state hospitals blurred the class distinctions between private and public facilities. While serving primarily an affluent clientele, the corporate asylums did care for pauper patients as part of their charitable mission. Their nonprofit nature and mixed–class clientele made them seem appropriate models for the new state hospitals, despite their patronage by the wealthy. American asylum reformers envisioned the state asylums as less opulent versions of their corporate counterparts and, in architecture and administration, they did not differ dramatically from the private asylums. More importantly, admissions to state hospitals were not limited solely to paupers; many early public asylums took in paying patients, primarily from families of moderate means who could not afford the higher rates of the corporate asylums. This notion of the "mixed" state hospital would prove controversial in the post Civil War period, as overcrowding became a serious issue. But at their inception, American state hospitals were not conceived of solely as institutions for paupers, so that the public–private split so apparent in England was much less evident there (Tomes 1984).

Unlike England, institutional expansion in the USA was not immediately accompanied by a drive toward greater regulation. If, in comparison to other European nations, the English were slow to move toward centralization, the Americans were even more resistant to the concept of governmental regulation. The one 19th-century attempt to involve the federal government in mental health policy failed: after six years of work by Dorothea Dix, a bill providing for a subsidy of federal lands to help the states finance care of the pauper insane passed both houses of Congress in 1854, only to be vetoed by President Franklin Pierce. Well into the 20th century, asylum care remained strictly a state and local concern. The earliest efforts to regulate American asylum practice came from state boards of charities, which were set up in the 1860s and 1870s to monitor welfare expenditures. While not as powerful as the English Lunacy Commission, these lay-dominated boards of control would become among the most vocal critics of moral treatment in late 19th-century America (Grob 1973).

Moral treatment in practice

In both England and the USA, mid 19th-century asylum reformers believed that the institutions they set up would provide sufficient accommodation for some time to come. However, within a few decades, the new hospitals were filled to capacity, while large numbers of the insane remained in alms-houses, jails, and other substandard facilities. This overcrowding, especially of incurable patients, forced painful departures from the original therapeutic goals of the state hospitals. As moral treatment proved to be less efficacious and economical than its proponents had promised, the therapeutic optimism of the asylum movement gradually weakened and eventually disappeared (Grob 1973, Scull 1979).

Both a rising incidence of insanity and an increased willingness to use institutional facilities appear to have contributed to the asylum shortage. Reviewing the English statistics (reliable data are not available for the USA), Scull (1979) found an increase from an estimated 2.26 cases of insanity per 10,000 of the general population in 1807, to 29.6 per 10,000 in 1890. He attributes this rise less to an actual increase in incidence than to a broadening definition of insanity; as institutional facilities expanded, family and community began to widen their conception of insane behavior in order to rationalize the commitment of troublesome individuals to mental institutions.

How conceptions of insanity changed from the 18th to the 19th century is difficult to prove from the extant historical records. Comparison of commitment patterns to the Pennsylvania Hospital from 1751 to 1883 indicates that the range of behaviors thought to benefit from hospital care did indeed widen in this period. But since 18th-century families had relatively few institutions to patronize, their decision to keep relatives at home cannot necessarily be interpreted as evidence of their greater tolerance for insane behavior (Tomes 1984).

That the availability of hospital care encouraged more and more families to use it was obvious even to 19th-century observers. In 1850, an American physician named Edward Jarvis showed, in a study of Massachusetts hospital admissions, that the families and communities closest to an asylum were the most likely to patronize it. Proximity to and awareness of the institution, Jarvis concluded, led families who previously would have kept relatives at home or let them roam the countryside to consider asylum care. To recast his observations in modern terminology, as the asylum system expanded, the "opportunity costs" involved in its use declined, thereby increasing demand for its services (Grob 1978).

However, increased willingness to patronize mental hospitals should not be confused with an uncritical acceptance of its services. Studies of 19th-century commitment patterns show unequivocally that asylums remained heavily stigmatized institutions of last resort for rich and poor alike. Commitment usually came after unsuccessful attempts to care for insane relatives at home, followed by a frantic search for other alternatives. Accounts of precommitment behavior for the affluent clientele of the Pennsylvania Hospital for the Insane and the pauper clientele of the Lancashire asylum show similar patterns: violence, threats of violence, suicide attempts, and other forms of destructive behavior appear to have prompted most hospital admissions. All the evidence suggests, then, that 19th-century families and public authorities used asylums primarily to care for

individuals who, by modern standards, would be considered severely disturbed and disabled (MacKenzie 1985, Tomes 1984, Walton 1985).

Likewise, there is very little evidence to support the popular conception
that asylums arose in the 19th century to confine politically or socially non-
conformist individuals who were not in fact insane. For example, Walton's
study (1985) of pauper admissions to Lancaster asylum in the 1840s found
only a handful of cases that might be construed as victims of political or
sexual repression. As he points out, by the middle of the 19th century there
already existed many, much more straightforward means for controlling
deviant behavior such as physical and legal harassment, without invoking
the complex process of asylum commitment.

Whatever the reality of most asylum admissions, Victorian society
remained very fearful of wrongful confinement, as shown by the popularity
of literature such as Charles Reade's *Hard cash* and Elizabeth Packard's *A
modern persecution* that dramatized the plight of allegedly sane people placed
in mental hospitals by conniving relatives. The ease of 19th-century commitment procedures, which usually required only that the family obtain
one or two medical certificates, did nothing to allay such fears. The use of
asylums for alcoholics and drug addicts, who often seemed quite rational
once the effects of over-indulgence had passed, further compounded controversies over commitment procedures (McCandless 1978, Tomes 1984).

Such controversies reflected the fundamental fact that, as is still the case,
commitment involved a social, primarily familial, judgment on sanity.
Relatives, not doctors or public authorities, usually made the first determination that an individual was insane. Their decision to commit did not
follow from some objective measure of the patient's condition, but rather
from an assessment of the family's financial and emotional resources to deal
with the individual's mental disability. Thus the composition of the 19th-
century asylum population tells us more about the family's response to
insanity than it does the incidence or definition of the condition itself.
Asylum admissions did not reflect the proportion of mental illness in the
population as a whole, but rather the greater or lesser likelihood of certain
individuals to require institutional care (Tomes 1984, Walton 1985).

Obviously, the calculations involved in making the commitment
decision varied according to class. Wealthier families had many more varied
options to pursue, including private medical and nursing care, travel, and
the like, before choosing asylum care; likewise, if a relative proved
incurable, they were better able to remove him from the hospital and make
other provisions (MacKenzie 1985, Tomes 1984). In contrast, insanity,
particularly in its chronic manifestations, posed an almost impossible
burden on working-class families. Walton's study (1985) of admissions to
the Lancashire asylum suggests that when working-class families had the
income to maintain an insane relative at home, they did so; but the exigencies of the industrial economy meant that few households could do so for

very long, and thus were forced to turn over insane relatives to the public authorities. In the USA, the burdens of poverty were compounded by ethnicity and race; since the foreign-born were overrepresented among the working class, the population of urban hospitals in the North tended to be heavily weighted toward Irish and German immigrants; in the South, a system of separate and inferior facilities developed for poor blacks (Grob 1973).

The age of the insane person clearly affected the likelihood of commitment. Unlike their 20th-century counterparts, 19th-century asylums had fewer aged insane patients than existed in the population as a whole. This underrepresentation of the aged seems to have resulted from administrative policy; asylum superintendents strongly discouraged the commitment of the senile aged, on the grounds that cure was unlikely, and they could be better managed at home. Gender appears to have played much less of a role in commitment decisions; one sex was not significantly more likely than the other to be admitted to an asylum[2].

Given that the composition of the asylum population reflected the degree of social need rather than mental disability, it is hardly surprising that its most striking characteristics should be poverty and chronicity. By the late 19th century, roughly 90% of England's asylum population was poor and incurable; comparable data are not available for the USA, but there is little reason to believe that the nature of its institutionalized population would be markedly different (Grob 1983, Scull 1979). Slowly but surely, 19th-century mental hospitals filled with incurable cases needing long-term custodial care. This is not to say that asylums ceased to treat or release any patients; rather, the hospital population at any given time was composed of two groups of inmates: one group who came and went in a year or less, and had a much greater likelihood of being discharged cured or relieved; and another, much larger, group who came virtually for life and never improved. Although never the sole constituency of the 19th-century asylum, this permanent population of chronic patients dominated the asylum's management and strongly undercut its therapeutic profile (MacKenzie 1985, Ray 1981). More than any other factor, the accumulation of the chronic insane contributed to the demise of moral treatment.

The late 19th-century crisis in institutional care

Nineteenth-century asylum superintendents and government officials found it difficult to respond effectively to the problems of overcrowding and chronicity in state institutions. Asylum doctors resisted proposals to return the insane to community care, while welfare authorities proved equally insistent on removing them from almshouses and jails. The unhappy compromise was to expand state hospitals far beyond the size conducive to a therapeutic community. By the early 20th century, the familiar problems of huge custodial state institutions had appeared on both sides of the Atlantic.

In part, the deadlock of the late 19th-century asylum policy stemmed from the professional agenda of asylum doctors who, by the middle of the 19th century, had become a self-conscious and well organized group. In Great Britain, the Association of Medical Officers of Asylums and Hospitals for the Insane (now the Royal College of Psychiatrists) was founded in 1841, and in the USA, the Association of Medical Superintendents of American Institutions for the Insane (now the American Psychiatric Association) was founded in 1844 (three years before the American Medical Association). The shared problems and interests of asylum work created an unusual commonality of viewpoints among the hospital superintendents. Although tensions developed between the men in public and private work, especially in England, asylum doctors had a much more cohesive identity than did the medical profession as a whole (Grob 1973, Scull 1979, Tomes 1984).

From their position of professional strength, 19th-century asylum doctors exercised an influence quite out of proportion to their small numbers. They sustained not only their professional societies, but also published specialized journals, such as the *Journal of Psychological Medicine* (1848) and the *Asylum Journal* (1853) in England, and the *American Journal of Insanity* (1844) in the USA, as well as many scientific monographs and text-books. Despite growing competition for "nervous" patients from the neurologists, asylum doctors firmly established themselves as the medical specialty dealing with insanity. They began to play prominent, if often controversial, roles as expert witnesses in legal cases. Last but not least, the asylum doctors formed a strong lobby on all institutional issues involving the insane, which the state authorities could not afford to ignore (Grob 1973, Scull 1979).

But at the same time as asylum doctors achieved considerable status as experts on insanity, they were unable to prevent the therapeutic decline of their own institutions. The problems of overcrowding and chronicity weighed increasingly heavy on them, both as a managerial problem and as a symbolic indictment of their expertise. By the 1860s and 1870s, the proponents of moral treatment were clearly on the defensive: the therapeutic and economic benefits its early supporters had promised had not materialized. Tied as they were to the asylum, the medical superintendents could not abandon it without losing their claims to expert knowledge. Even as they found themselves in charge of worsening institutional conditions, they proved stubbornly resistant to any reforms that would alter the fundamental premises of asylum treatment (Grob 1973, Scull 1979).

The impetus to rethink institutional provisions for the insane came largely from welfare authorities and physicians outside the ranks of the asylum doctors. Objecting to both the expense and the restrictions on individual freedom characteristic of even the best asylums, critics called for a return to some form of community care. Their most radical proposal for change was the concept of the cottage hospital, loosely based on the Gheel lunatic colony in Belgium, where patients lived in supervised homes and had considerable freedom to move about. More conservative solutions to the problems of overcrowding called for developing separate hospitals for incurables, which could be built and run on less expensive lines than "regular" asylums.

Both English and American asylum doctors proved extremely resistant to both cottage hospitals and separate facilities for the incurable, on the grounds that such measures simply meant a return to the deplorable state of care in the 18th century. Any plans to disperse the insane in the community or to separate acute and chronic cases would inevitably lead to abuse. In weighing the asylum's merits, they believed considerations of safety and social order far outweighed the restrictions on the inmates' freedom. Despite their failure to match early expectations, mental hospitals remained the most humane form of care for the insane, and thus, the superintendents concluded, were worth their considerable expense (Grob 1973, McCandless 1979).

The debate over alternative hospital design was all the more acrimonious in the USA because of the older superintendents' commitment to "mixed"-class state asylums. Working from the premise that private and public hospitals should not have radically different standards, it was all the harder for them to accept propositions such as cottage hospitals or chronic facilities. The adoption of such "European" institutions constituted a tacit admission that America had developed the kind of permanent pauper class that existed in the Old World. The initial ideal of the "classless" state hospital made the widening disparity between public and private hospitals painfully difficult for the American superintendents to accept (Tomes 1984).

Of course, private asylums in England and the USA also faced the problem of chronicity. Like their public counterparts, they underwent a natural aging process in which incurable cases tended to accumulate (Digby 1985, MacKenzie 1985, Tomes 1984). But the critical difference between the two types of facilities was that the private hospitals could regulate their patient populations to preserve a tolerable mix of acute and chronic cases; in other words, their superintendents could refuse to admit new patients who appeared incurable, as well as discharge long-term inmates to make way for more hopeful cases. Thus control over the admission mechanism allowed asylum superintendents to keep the two patient populations, the short-term, acute and the long-term chronic, in a more palatable balance.

It was precisely this discretion over admissions that state hospital men lacked. As part of a larger network of welfare institutions, state hospitals had a clearly defined responsibility to the pauper insane. Their superintendents might complain about the flood of incurables into their institutions, but there was little they could do to resist it. Asylum doctors might differ with the welfare authorities over how to respond to the overcrowding problem, but they accepted the dictum that the chronic patients could not be left in almshouses and jails. So, whatever desire they had to maintain a more therapeutic mix of patients, the state superintendents had little choice but to answer the pressing need for chronic care. As might be expected, given their original conception of "mixed"-class state asylums, the American superintendents struggled more against the growing custodialism in state care; but with the increasing power of the state boards of charity over admission policies in the post Civil War period, the state asylum's responsibility to the chronic poor became paramount (Grob 1973, Scull 1979, Tomes 1984).

Therefore, state regulation in many ways hastened the deterioration of moral treatment of custodialism. The de facto solution of the late 19th-century asylum crisis was to expand provisions in existing asylums. By the 1850s, English asylums had already grown very large; Colney Hatch opened in 1851 with accommodation for over 1000 patients; by 1890, the average size of county and borough asylums was 800 (Scull 1979). American asylums grew at a slower rate; as of 1883, the average number of patients in public institutions was 544. But some American hospitals were beginning to approach the size of their English counterparts (Grob 1973).

Conclusion

With the luxury of historical hindsight, it is easy to fault both the asylum doctors and the welfare authorities for the deterioration of the state hospital system. Asylum reformers had expanded public provision for the insane on the assumption that hospitals would provide more cures at less expense. When this assumption proved false, they were left with an enormous financial and social investment in a system of institutions that did not work effectively. In their determination not to lose their professional prerogatives, the medical superintendents resisted any innovations in asylum design; likewise, governmental authorities easily abandoned the therapeutic potential of the state hospitals and hastened their descent into custodialism. With little improvement, this stalemate would persist long into the present century.

In retrospect, the decline of moral treatment seems virtually inevitable, given the nature of the 19th-century asylum population. There is strong reason to suspect that a substantial number of patients admitted to 19th-century institutions suffered from paresis, Huntingdon's chorea, pellagra, and other organic disorders. For example, when diagnostic tests for syphilis were administered to male admissions to New York state hospitals between

1911 and 1919, fully 20% were found to be paretics (Grob 1983). Such patients could never have been cured by the most exacting medical and moral regimen available to 19th-century physicians.

But the limitations of moral treatment should not obscure the real achievement of the 19th-century asylum. Even though it failed to cure many of its inmates, it still proved quite effective at a very important task: relieving families of the heavy burdens that insanity placed on the family. Then as now, caring for mentally disturbed relatives placed tremendous strains on both the economic and emotional health of the family. The mental hospital offered an institutional alternative to a painful domestic problem. Therein lies the clue to its persistence: custodial care of the chronically ill may have represented a seemingly tragic departure from the asylum's early ideals; yet it filled a very real and compelling social need for 19th-century families, rich and poor alike. So long as the mental hospital served this need, it was destined to remain a permanent fixture of modern social life.

The historical development of the asylum provides a valuable perspective on the contemporary state of mental health policy. The problems associated with the deinstitutionalization movement suggest that, even with the improved forms of drug therapy for chronically ill patients now available, families and communities are reluctant to resume long-term responsibility for disabled relatives and neighbours. At the same time, local and state governments no longer have the motivation or the funds to finance either the expensive solution of institutional care, or the extensive support services necessary to make deinstitutionalization function more effectively. How the current crisis in psychiatric care will be resolved remains to be seen, but given the frustrations and complexities of today's mental health policy, one is inclined to be more charitable toward the imperfect solutions adopted by our historical predecessors.

Notes

1 Scholars disagree over the extent to which the Lunacy Commission developed an independent perspective on asylum policy. Mellet (1981) and Scull (1979) emphasize its collaboration with the public asylum superintendents; Hervey (1975) presents their relationship as more conflicted.

2 The most sophisticated work to date on gender and mental illness in the 19th century, Ellen Dwyer's "Homes for the mad: inside two 19th century lunatic asylums," is still unpublished. Her work suggests that while men and women were not committed in significantly different numbers, their diagnoses and lengths of stay did show some interesting variations.

References

Allderidge, P. 1985. Bedlam: fact or fancy. In *The anatomy of madness*, vol. 2: *Institutions and society*, W. F. Bynum, R. Porter & M. Shepherd (eds.), 17–31. London: Tavistock.

Dain, N. 1971. *Disordered minds: the first century of Eastern State Hospital in Williamsburg, Virginia 1766–1866.* Williamsburg: Colonial Williamsburg Foundation.
Deutsch, A. 1949. *The mentally ill in America*, 2nd edn. New York: Columbia University Press.
Digby, A. 1985. *Madness, morality, and medicine: a study of the York Retreat, 1796–1914.* Cambridge: Cambridge University Press.

Grob, G. 1973. *Mental institutions in America: social policy to 1875.* New York: The Free Press.
Grob, G. 1978. *Edward Jarvis and the medical world of 19th century America.* Knoxville: University of Tennessee Press.
Grob, G. 1983. *Mental illness and American society 1875–1940.* Princeton, N.J.: Princeton University Press.

Hervey, N. 1985. A slavish bowing down: the Lunacy Commission and the psychiatric profession 1845–60. In *The anatomy of madness*, vol. 2: *Institutions and society*, W. F. Bynum, R. Porter & M. Shepherd (eds.), 98–131. London: Tavistock.

McCandless, P. 1978. Liberty and lunacy: the Victorians and wrongful confinement. *Journal of Social History* **11**, 366–86.
McCandless, P. 1979. Build! Build! The controversy over the care of the chronically insane in England, 1855–1870. *Bulletin of the History of Medicine* **53**, 553–74.
MacDonald, M. 1981. *Mystical Bedlam: madness, anxiety and healing in 17th century England.* Cambridge: Cambridge University Press.
MacKenzie, C. 1985. Social factors in the admission, discharge, and continuing stay of patients at Ticehurst asylum, 1845–1917. In *The anatomy of madness*, vol. 2: *Institutions and society*, W. F. Bynum, R. Porter & M. Shepherd (eds.), 147–74. London: Tavistock.
Mellet, D. J. 1981. Bureaucracy and mental illness: the Commissioners in Lunacy 1845–90. *Medical History* **25**, 221–50.

Parry-Jones, W. 1972. *The trade in lunacy.* London: Routledge & Kegan Paul.

Ray, L. 1981. Models of madness in Victorian asylum practice. *Archives Européenes de Sociologie* **22**, 229–64.
Rothman, D. 1971. *The discovery of the asylum.* Boston: Little, Brown.

Scull, A. 1979. *Museums of madness: the social organization of insanity in 19th century England.* London: Allen Lane.

Tomes, N. 1984. *A generous confidence: Thomas Story Kirkbride and the art of asylum keeping.* Cambridge, Cambridge University Press.

Walk, A. 1964. Mental hospitals. In *Evolution of hospitals in Britain*, F. N. L. Poynter (ed.), 123–46. London: Pitman Medical.
Walker, D. P. 1981. *Unclean spirits: possession and exorcism in the late 16th century and early 17th century.* Philadelphia: University of Pennsylvania Press.
Walton, J. K. 1979. Lunacy in the Industrial Revolution: a study of asylum admissions in Lancashire, 1848–50. *Journal of Social History* **13**, 1–22.
Walton, J. K. 1985. Casting out and bringing back in Victorian England: pauper lunatics, 1840–70. In *Anatomy of madness*, vol. 2: *Institutions and society*, W. F. Bynum, R. Porter & M. Shepherd (eds.), 132–46. London: Tavistock.

2 Mental health care in Europe: some recent trends

PHILIP BEAN

It is somewhat misleading to talk about mental health care in Europe in a general way. The cultural variations, levels of development, and socio-political systems proclaim too much diversity. For example, consider the number of psychiatrists; in Portugal in 1982 there were 136 qualified psychiatrists or 1.4 per 100,000 of the population, compared with 2,688 or 4.7 per 100,000 of the population in the Federal Republic of Germany (WHO 1985). But even then such a simple statistic belies greater problems, which involve matters relating to the collection of data or of defining terms. Indeed, in a recent WHO survey of European countries (WHO, 1985), where it was noted that data were largely but not exclusively taken from replies to a questionnaire (in 1982), the following problems were noted: many replies were incomplete; while others were only as good as the national data permitted, and this was sometimes several years old; populations for calculating ratios were also variable, covering six years in some cases; while for some countries it was not clear which year the data actually applied to. Then there was the problem of definition. What is a qualified psychiatrist or a consultant even, or perhaps a psychiatric nurse, an outpatient clinic or a psychiatric hospital? And what constitutes Europe? In the WHO survey, Algeria and Morocco are included (yet few geographers would agree): the WHO gives no reasons for including these countries although they comment on other problems of definition. They say, "inevitably different cultures, different traditions and different administrative structures produce different term usages and traditions and in trying to ally them into sensible categories we end up with rather broad categories of a not-too-specific nature" (WHO 1985: 3). They could have added that political interests also intrude: some countries appear to take every opportunity to advance their political claims or present themselves in the most favorable light, for example, by failing to answer questions which would show defects in existing services, or claiming that certain practices are about to be implemented when there is no intention of doing so.

All comparative studies or, rather, all studies where there is an attempt to interpret data from different countries, are faced with the task of avoiding ethnocentricity (evaluating other cultures according to one's own cultural standards). This is so for WHO studies, just as it is for others. In this respect, it is interesting to note how some social scientists and psychiatrists have recently tried to grapple with the problem (Draguns 1984). Few people can claim to be entirely free of an ethnocentric view, for that is neither possible nor desirable. Nor is it possible to cover all recent and important changes in European mental health systems, for there are too many and they are too diverse to be contained within a single chapter. Therefore, what follows is a selected group of topics relating to a similarly selected group of countries, but perhaps of sufficient scope to show where future trends may lie. The method of presentation places the topics into two main categories; the nature of legislation, and the provision of mental health services. In this the presentation follows recent WHO documents (e.g., WHO 1985).

The nature of legislation

Mental health legislation is often less concerned with promoting mental health than it is with regulating and controlling the activities of those who admit mental patients to forms of psychiatric care, and regulating and controlling the activities of those who provide treatment. The success or failure of such legislation is related to its aims and assumptions, for unless the aims are understood evaluation is likely to miss the mark, or it may permit unjustifiable inferences to be drawn. A proper evaluation of the law would involve going back to a study of the development of each judicial system, and an assessment in the light of contemporary practices.

The modern trend seems to be to provide greater autonomy for the patient, in contrast to earlier legislation which had emphasized the autonomy of the physician. In England & Wales, for example, the 1959 Mental Health Act emphasized the patient's right to receive treatment to the exclusion of almost all else (Bean 1980). It gave the physician the right to determine the amount and extent of that treatment, even if such treatments were irreversible and hazardous. Its modern counterpart, the 1983 Act, has granted patients more rights to refuse treatment, and it has placed obstacles in the path of the physicians. The trend in England & Wales is now towards a form of legalism characterized by a 19th-century view which is concerned with providing and protecting patients' civil rights. On the other hand, some sections of the 1983 Act appear to have brushed patients' rights aside. For example, the Act has granted new and extensive powers to nurses, who are permitted to detain patients who wish to leave the mental hospital against advice. This concession was made in return for an agreement with a trade union, which shows how political trade-offs can affect and determine such legislation (Bean 1986).

Yet, while there may be such a trend in England & Wales toward a particular form of legislation, it is not by any means a common one throughout Europe. This is hardly surprising, given that many European countries are at different stages of development and hold different ideological tenets.

Indeed, some are operating mental health systems according to laws framed in the 19th century: France's 1838 legislation, and the Netherlands' dating back to 1884, are cases in point. Sometimes, as with Belgium, the whole system seems to be overcome by inertia; for example, a mental health reform bill was introduced in the Belgian Parliament as far back as 1969, but a final vote on the bill has still to be taken (in 1987). There is apparently disagreement as to the statuses of the physicians and the courts in authorizing compulsory admissions. One group holds that certification constitutes a deprivation of freedom, and that the exercise of such power should therefore be restricted to the magistrate, while the other holds that diagnosis and decisions relating to that are for the psychiatrist (Baro *et al*. 1985). Indeed, in the WHO 1982 survey, only 17 of the 33 European countries surveyed had legislation dating from 1950 (WHO 1985: 20).

Of course, the date of enactment of legislation provides no certainty about its quality. In France, for example, it is argued that changes in the law are unnecessary, and that it is more important to update methods of practice. But there does seem to be a link between the modernity of the legislation and the type of service provided, as measured by the percentage of compulsory patients and the length of stay in hospital; that is, the older the legislation the higher the percentage of compulsory admissions and the greater the length of stay in the hospital, compulsory or otherwise. There is something odd about a situation in which countries rely on legislation that is over 100 years old, given recent changes that have taken place in the consideration of the provision of patient rights and the type of care offered.

Aside from questions of quality, it is clear that, given the wide range of legislation, we should not be surprised to find a similarly wide range of mental health practices. Compulsory admission provides an example: the WHO survey figures range from 1% for Spain to 85% for Morocco (the former is regarded as being unexpectedly low, and the latter undesirably high). Again, many other countries did not provide data (e.g. the USSR, France, and Germany), but the average percentage of compulsory admissions was about 10%, with countries such as Sweden at 30% rather higher than average (WHO 1985: 48).

As it is likely to be unrewarding, therefore, to concentrate on the wide sweep of the debate and talk of Europe as a whole, or even of a European view, it is more useful to concentrate on specific countries. In this respect, there can be no doubt that the most radical, innovative and truly modern piece of legislation in Europe—or elsewhere for that matter—is the now famous Law 180 of the 1978 Act in Italy. This is found in its most dramatic form in Trieste, for throughout Italy there are variations in practice. Law 180 abolished psychiatric hospitals in Italy and established community based nonsegregated and demedicalized care. Up to January 1981, Law 180 prevented admission of all new patients to public mental hospitals and permitted voluntary readmission only. It also prohibited the construction of new psychiatric hospitals. Psychiatric wards in general hospitals are allowed, but they can have no more than 15 beds, and wards must work together with community mental health centers. These community-based facilities are responsible for a prescribed geographical area, and facilities will be staffed by existing mental health personnel (Maste 1982). The law also prohibits the use of compulsory treatment except in emergencies, or in cases where mental disorders are such that urgent therapeutic measures are needed even if they are not accepted by the patient, and if there are no conditions or circumstances that allow the adoption of rapid and effective out-patient medical measures (Law 180, Article 34, Para. 4).

One of the most important features of the Italian legislation is that the law-makers argued that treatment can and should be the only reason for compulsory admission; in other words, a person regarded as dangerous or who has committed offenses should be the responsibility of the judicial system, not the psychiatric system. In this way, Italian law separates the judiciary from the mental health care system, although psychiatric teams continue to work closely with the legal profession when patients are deemed to be ill and dangerous. Therefore, Law 180 departs from the type of legislation found in other countries where mental health care is mixed with penal matters. In the UK, for example, civil patients, whether they be compulsorily admitted or not, can be mixed with criminal patients of varying levels of dangerousness.

Secondly, under the new Italian law there is an attempt to move away from the hospital setting toward a system of community mental health centers (CMHCs). In this, of course, the Italian law is not so different, because there are similar shifts in such countries as the UK, Sweden, and the Netherlands. However, in Italy, the change is more positive. CMHCs are said to be preferred to hospitals because they can be more informally maintained, and their use is thought less stigmatizing for clients (Ramon 1985). The movement towards community-based facilities also produces a corresponding reduction in psychiatric influence and control, for the mental hospital represents the psychiatrist's power base. Moreover, the community mental health centers largely remove the set roles contained within the mental hospital and the specific forms of division of labor contained therein, although, in the CMHCs, the physician alone is responsible for prescribing drugs to the patient and the social worker is responsible for such matters of financial assistance.

Thirdly, on matters of treatment, Law 180 requires treatment to consist mainly of clinical advice and counselling (Ramon 1985). Psychotropic drugs are used in very small doses, whereas ECT and psychosurgery are not offered at all: and with the breakdown of traditional roles associated with the structure of the mental hospital, contacts between patients and staff (especially senior medical staff) take on new meanings—they are more informal and, some would say, of greater value to the patient than hitherto.

The social distance created by the traditional doctor–patient relationship has been replaced by a more egalitarian situation in which the power of the physician has been greatly reduced.

Inevitably, such radical legislation attracts staunch supporters and critics. For some, the "Psichiatria Democratia" movement has become a way of life; for others, a dreadful experiment gone wrong. To its supporters, the movement is seen to enter a new era in which the basic terms and the relationships between patients and psychiatric staff are redefined. To its opponents, the lack of a correct diagnostic approach and of effective treatment will, it is said, contribute to a progressive increase in chronic patients, so creating once again a need for institutions and long-term inpatient treatment. It will, such critics say, complete a vicious circle that progress in psychiatry has led us to imagine had been broken (Sarteschi *et al.* 1985). Moreover, the 1978 Act has, it is argued, created a new class of patients, namely those neglected and untreated who are denied the basic right of psychiatric care. And so the argument goes on.

Whatever the merits of the various points of view, their relative strength or weaknesses have to be set against the manner in which some parts of Italy seem to have gone further along the path of Law 180 than others. The spatial impact of the change is somewhat patchy, with Trieste, for example, being at the center of things. But the full story has yet to unfold, and there will be many twists and turns to the argument before matters are settled. Law 180 was the result of a special series of political and social processes, uniquely Italian, which makes copying elsewhere difficult, if not impossible. Ramon describes it thus:

> After more than a decade of largely successful experiments with mental health reform in several parts of Italy, those closely involved with these experiments began an energetic campaign for a mandatory policy of nationwide reform. Their case was taken up by the Radical Party, one of the small left of centre parties which on its own did not carry sufficient political weight to bring about legislation. However, the Italian constitution provides for a public referendum for any proposal supported by the signatures of more than 500,000 citizens. Once the number of signatures has been collected the ruling coalition headed by the Christian-Democratic party felt that it might become a political embarrassment to allow the Law to be proposed via a referendum rather than by the government. The coalition government therefore adopted the proposal as its own piece of legislation and it was comfortably passed by Parliament since it attracted opposition support (Ramon 1985).

The opponents of the law remain hopeful that things will change. They hope for "new legislation" to provide "a better balanced framework based on a clear and pragmatic view of mental illness . . . providing for the development of a truly scientific and human approach to psychiatric care" (Sarteschi *et al.* 1985). My own view, for what it is worth, is that the voices of the critics will grow, and new legislation will be provided introducing that so-called "better balanced framework."

Set against the Italian experience, legislative changes elsewhere appear commonplace, yet there have been some recent solid achievements which ought not to go unnoticed. Consider the 1983 Mental Health Act in England & Wales, as well as legislation in Scotland and Northern Ireland (in the latter, the provision that a compulsory admission to a mental hospital will no longer be recorded after a certain length of time is of great importance). In England & Wales, the 1983 Act created a new Mental Health Act Commission whose task it is to oversee and protect patients' rights. Scotland has had a superior commission and for a long period of time—superior in the sense of being more vigorous. The consent to treatment provisions in the 1983 Act (Italy has consent provisions also) may lead to a lasting achievement for they *inter alia* imply that mentally disordered patients are capable of making important decisions about their own welfare. But these provisions go beyond the straightforward matters of providing consent, for they reopen questions relating to the nature of mental disorder and the responsibility of the mentally disordered, questions that have remained submerged for decades. Hopefully, the debate will not remain within the confines of mental health but will be extended to other areas of medicine (Bean 1986).

The provision of mental health services

To emphasize some of the points made above, particularly about the variety of practices and methods, there can be no better illustration of the range of service provisions in Europe than that which exists in Greece. Regional inequalities are greater than almost anywhere else, with half of all psychiatric beds being located in the largest cities. Sixty percent of all Greek psychiatrists practise in Athens. Three large hospitals account for 60% of all available beds; outpatient and community services are of very recent origin with the first day hospital being established as late as 1977. Services are now implemented by the community mental health centers (Mangen 1985: 30). In Greece problems exist at a more basic level; there is an urgent need for even the most rudimentary of services in large areas of the country.

If we concentrate on countries where service provision is advanced, some important trends can be identified. First, and as a general rule, there has been a shift away from the larger mental hospitals of the 19th century. These changes have occurred perhaps as a result of a consensus of opinion that very large institutions are unlikely to promote satisfactory treatment. In the WHO

1982 survey, for example, in the 21 countries providing information (bearing in mind that France, the Federal Republic of Germany, and the USSR did not answer the relevant part of the WHO questionnaire), there were 202 large mental hospitals in 1972, but this number had fallen to 96 a decade later, "large" meaning over 1,000 beds (WHO 1985: 30). According to the survey, the corollary, in service development, of a reduction in the number of beds in large psychiatric hospitals is that smaller units will be favored or other settings developed. This turns out to be the case, for a further and important change has been in the increase in psychiatric units in general hospitals where, according to the WHO, "the main virtue is to bring psychiatry and the treatment of psychiatric illness into the same arena as other specialists treating other illnesses" (WHO 1985: 31).

Similarly, there has been a general trend towards the development of community care, or rather care taking place within the community. This is so for outpatient clinics and day-care centers. Also, changes in the extent of these community care facilities have had repercussions, it is suspected, on other matters. Take, for example, the length of hospital inpatient stay: in the UK the great majority of patients now stay for less than three weeks, only about 5% staying for one year or more (WHO 1985: 47). This reduction is due in part to the development of community care facilities of the types mentioned above. European countries are, of course, keen to develop community care facilities (or so they say), for reasons of cost and efficiency. But again one must be careful not to draw too many conclusions from the available data: for example, only 11 countries provided the WHO with information on outpatient attendances, with two of these countries showing fewer outpatient attendances than 10 years ago. Again there may be serious problems of definition at work here, with some countries defining outpatient attendances as being only those in which the patient actually attends the hospital, while others may define outpatients as being treated in a health center. Similarly, the figures for day care are poor: only 12 countries reported day care facilities to the WHO, compared with 14 a decade earlier. The results are startling—the Netherlands seems to have experienced a dramatic reduction—but this too may be a problem of definitions which, incidentally, lead the WHO to suggest that a major new study is worth undertaking to find out the true position (WHO 1985: 55).

It is clear, then, that interpretations or inferences based on this type of national data are limited. Yet to understand the provision of services we can do more than simply list the service provisions. Services can also be interpreted as including the quality of relationships, which involves the *structure* of those relationships and the corresponding balance of power between the patients and physicians. Seen in this way, and being the argument on the evidence taken from a small number of countries, the doctor–patient relationship is being slowly transformed, as the balance of power is being shifted towards the patient.

The implications of such a change are important. In the short term, there will be changes in the structure of the mental hospital and in the type of treatment provided. In the long term, there will be changes in the status of psychiatry—perhaps other branches of medicine may be affected too. Why have such changes occurred? In part, they have been brought about by an increasingly strong and vociferous critique of psychiatry and all it stands for. Consider, for example, those organizations calling themselves "psychiatric resistance groups" (*Asylum* 1986): these are groups whose aim it is to express deep dissatisfaction with the current psychiatric systems. The influence of such groups is, of course, difficult to assess and the movement, if it can indeed yet be called a movement, is patchy and lacks co-ordination. But the intention is clear; it is to reduce the influence of psychiatry and of psychiatrists, and of the whole superstructure that goes with the practice of psychiatric medicine. It is to demonstrate that the multimillion-pound industry associated with psychiatry is based on a series of questionable premises—a situation in which the Emperor has neither clothes nor supportive ideology—and in which the term "patient" is seen as entirely inappropriate. Supporters of such groups say there are no patients, for there is no medicine as such to practise. Typical of such groups is the British Network, part of the so-called International Network for Alternatives to Psychiatry "aimed at a fundamental debate in psychiatry and the promotion of alternatives to the existing system" (*Asylum* 1986). More specifically, the British Network accepts the view that mental distress exists but "firmly rejects the nature of mental disease as a disease which afflicts the individual; partly because that masks the social reasons for such distress, partly because it serves to stigmatize and segregate people and diminish personal autonomy" (ibid.). It comes as no surprise to know that the British Network is ". . . opposed to involuntary incarceration of psychiatric patients. Individuals should have the right to refuse any psychiatric intervention as well as the right to receive the best help possible" (ibid.).

Alternatively, consider the more flamboyantly titled "Campaign against Psychiatric Oppression" (CAPO), which seems to offer little that is different from the British Network, except that there is a stronger socialist component. CAPO's aims involve an interpretation of psychiatry which is conflict-based in a traditional Marxian style. Psychiatry is seen as a form of class oppression in which the mental patient is the scapegoat of capitalism. So ". . . the big guns of psychiatry are held to the heads of the working class in order to control them. Statistics show the disproportionate admissions to psychiatric institutions from areas of poverty, bad housing, high unemployment and heavy industry—in short, working-class areas" (CAPO 1986). Therefore, what psychiatry calls "delusions" are, according to CAPO, "accurate perceptions of a working person's oppressive reality," and the use of drug treatment interpreted as "poisons that deform the central nervous system to create passive addicts" (ibid.). CAPO's solution is to promote collective action through class struggle alongside other working-class groups that are similarly persecuted by the class system and capitalism.

What is extraordinary, and to some extent paradoxical, about these groups is not that they exist or that they are flourishing, but that their ideological heritage is derived from the influential work of Thomas Szasz, an altogether different political animal. Indeed, in CAPO's case one sometimes sees their socialist interpretation as of less importance than the attack on psychiatry, which could have been lifted wholesale from Szasz (1961). Szasz's arguments are there, writ large: mental illness is a myth; there is no physiological basis to that condition, although this is not to deny mental disease; compulsory psychiatry is a political sham; the presence of involuntary incarceration removes all possibilities of voluntary admission for the threat can always encourage or promote specious agreements; and so one. Of course, CAPO wants to relate all this to class domination but, up to that point, CAPO's views are directly attributable to a supporter of capitalism. It may be that fringe organizations such as the British Network or CAPO will always remain on the sidelines, except that their message is now often being put across by highly articulate "users," either ex-patients or current patients whose personal horror stories are recounted as chilling reminders of the extent of medical psychiatric power. The organizations they promote may not be successful in the sense that they achieve political control, but their more personal message may be accepted. One effect, intended or otherwise, is to push earlier radical organizations such as MIND (National Association for Mental Health) into a more conservative stance, creating the impression that MIND is tied to a psychiatric system which others are trying to break.

There are other movements, less overtly ideological but nevertheless capable of changing, if not transforming, the doctor–patient relationship. The best example is the patients' councils movement in the Netherlands (and its parallel in the UK's "Advocacy Alliance": Sang 1985). The background to the Dutch movement is itself interesting. In 1970, a patients' committee was formed in a large Dutch psychiatric hospital. The committee was based on the patients' initiative and at the time was mainly concerned with leisure pursuits. Later on, another committee which was concerned with hospital administration (in this case, poor food) formed elsewhere. Both groups began to consider further matters regarding the management of their respective institutions. By 1975 the movement was sufficiently developed to organize its first national meeting, at which representatives from eight patients' councils, as well as patients from another four hospitals, came together to discuss mutual problems and aspirations. By 1977 there were 35 such councils and by 1980 a national umbrella organization of patients' councils was established, which is now supported with funds from the Dutch government. It has two aims: to influence legislation, and provide support and advice to individual councils.

In the first of its aims, that is to influence legislation, the movement can claim partial success. Legislation is proposed for 1987, though there may still be some delay. Such legislation will require all Dutch psychiatric hospitals to provide patient councils with a defined organizational position within the hospital (even though 40 out of 44 such hospitals already have councils). Some of the councils have negotiated formal contracts with the hospital management board, granting rights to representation and access to documents including patients' records. In others, the nature of the contract is such that the patients' council has the power to veto management decisions, and can insist that management takes the council's advice on certain matters (for example, on issues relating to house rules and the like). Should there be conflict or a dispute between the patients' council and the management board, arbitration is available.

Councils on the Dutch model are spreading to other European countries. They were first introduced to the UK in 1986 (Barker 1986, Peck & Barker 1986). They represent a forceful example of patients taking power within the mental health system. However, their implementation in the UK, or indeed elsewhere, is likely to be a fragile affair, for to flourish they need firm structural support. A number of factors militate against patients (or whatever term is used to refer to mental health service users) having any real power. The credibility of patients is assumed to be in question especially when behavior, and particularly that which is vigorously opposed to the health care professionals, can easily be interpreted as being symptomatic of their illness. The fear of compulsory detention and of hazardous forms of treatment can all too easily discourage patients, except the most tenacious, from voicing complaints. When patients complain there is often no effective channel for them to use except the hospital administration, who more often than not find it convenient to refer the complaints back to the consultant psychiatrist.

But who else is there to act for the patients? Social workers sometimes appear as if they were able to deal with such complaints, but they are too close and too dependent on the system to be able to help. Other groups, such as the Community Health Councils (CHCs), are supposed to provide a voice for the patients, but they are unlikely to do so. Unlike social workers, CHCs are remote and marginal to the system. In the UK at least it seems that the structure and the trappings of professional controls are in place, but there are ways of emasculating those structures. CHCs are a case in point. In the UK, and probably elsewhere, the medical profession retains the real power, and a shift in power towards the patient is therefore a shift of some substance. Patient councils are offering ways of doing that (Bean 1986).

Yet, while the Dutch have been moving in the direction of patients' councils, Sweden and Denmark (and to some extent the Netherlands and the UK also) have been concerned with systems of advocacy. In the same way that patients' councils can be defined in free or restricted terms, so too can advocacy groups. At their lowest levels, professionals and users of mental health services refer to advocacy as "raising a fuss" and sometimes of "meeting clients' needs". These definitions lead many social workers and nurses to define their role as advocates, even though only part of their work involves advocacy. At a higher level, advocacy involves transferring power to certain groups of people with disabilities. These people are denied power, either collectively or individually, yet they wish to exercise increased levels of autonomy.

It is possible to classify advocacy in a number of different ways; the classification perhaps being made according to either the client, the methods used, or the method of representation. In the latter there is citizen advocacy in which a patient is represented by a concerned and informed citizen, self-advocacy in which the patient represents himself, and legal advocacy in which the patient is represented by a professional lawyer.

However, definitions of advocacy do not answer the basic question which is: Why is advocacy required at all? For this there must be consideration of the position of law. In mental health matters law is, I suggest, concerned with: (a) regulating and controlling the activities of those who admit and detain patients in hospitals; and (b) regulating and controlling the activities of those who treat such patients and decide on discharge. But in mental health law these two aims have not always been realized, and some would argue that they can never be unless and until greater attention is paid to the position of the legal system as it meets and interacts with psychiatry. Be that as it may, advocacy arises when people are deprived of the opportunity to represent themselves. Advocacy can, therefore, be defined as a form of representation for people who are highly dependent on others.

Yet why is advocacy still required? Is it not ironic that demands for patient power should develop and grow out of an institutional setting in which there is a moral and legal obligation to cater for the patient? Is it not true that mental hospitals are giving way to community health centers and that multidisciplinary teams are being established, and more and more psychiatrists recruited and employed? Is it not also true that buildings have been renovated and new noninstitutional care programs established? (a trend which seems to be constant throughout Europe: WHO 1985). In spite of such changes, there is a growing realization that, in some respects, nothing changes at all. Few patients possess the necessary powers to influence decisions taken about them, and attempts to redress the balance are long overdue.

It is interesting to note that changes which encourage advocacy are part of a greater series of changes worldwide. For example, in the United Nations Declaration of Rights of Mentally Retarded Persons, adopted in 1971, advocacy was expected to be enlarged and developed. That Declaration embodied principles of policy and protection from abuse, and provided proper legal safeguards against unwarranted restriction of rights. Moreover, the Declaration of the Rights of Disabled Persons (Article 2) recognizes the rights of such persons to avail themselves of qualified legal aid, while the International League of Societies of Persons with Mental Handicap produced guidelines on the implementation of the UN Declaration. This too recognized advocacy as a basic support service to ensure appropriate access to services and facilities.

The European country which seems to have gone furthest along this road is Sweden, where Swedish law on Guardianship and Trusteeship provides severely mentally ill and handicapped people with graded assistance for a paid and independent spokesman. The Swedish position is that compulsory care is seen as a serious infringement of personal privacy even if its purpose is to provide a patient with necessary care which he would not otherwise receive. This makes it important for legal security to be augmented. In addition, Swedish law allows a patient to appeal against certain decisions made by the consultant, e.g., decisions concerning admission and refusal to discharge him. Furthermore, every district must have at least one politically appointed supervisory board charged with keeping compulsory care under observation. This board is charged with visiting institutions and consulting patients and nursing staff, as well as others involved in the patient's treatment. The supervisory board must also appoint a support person for a patient whenever continuing compulsory care arises (Swedish Mental Health Law, summary in English 1986: 475).

Advocacy, then, is another method of transforming the doctor–patient relationship and of shifting power toward the patient. Moreover, it is a movement with full international support, notably from the United Nations. However, there is a price to pay, as there is for the councils discussed earlier. It also seems that some specific social conditions need to be satisfied before advocacy schemes can get off the ground. This can best be illustrated in the case of citizen advocacy. Bob Sang, who was Britain's first full-time citizen advocate with Advocacy Alliance, notes that citizen advocacy is a most difficult concept to implement (Sang 1985). He gives three major reasons. First, the authorities continually attempt to block, modify, or control the activities of citizen advocates. Secondly, ordinary people are often unwilling or unable to commit themselves to a fellow citizen who is excluded from daily life, especially if their label is itself interpreted as a barrier to any relationship. Finally, within the relationship itself, the individual runs the risk of being dominated as the advocate slips into professional or paternal attitudes and behavior.

There are also limitations inherent in the working conditions under which advocates operate. Consider accountability: can advocates be made answerable to any authority, or are they to remain outside traditional or established lines of authority? And what about treatment? Should advocates concern themselves with treatment? Advocates tend to argue that treatment must always be within their province for it is central to their task. Relationships with staff and relatives are also a problem. In the former case, is there not a possibility that relationships will degenerate into arguments about who knows best for the patient? And with relatives cannot advocacy easily slip into a display of expertise which results in the advocate usurping the relatives' position? All of these eventualities are likely when roles are unclear.

Patients' councils and advocacy schemes share similar aims, namely that of shifting power towards the patients. The movement poses new and interesting questions and its success will (if success is to be achieved) involve considerable change in the structure of the mental hospital and the practice of psychiatry. Councils and advocacy are of a piece, producing new tensions in an earlier well established conventional setting.

Finally, when discussing the provision of services and likely future trends, one comment by the WHO stands out as worthy of greater attention; it concerns the ratio of psychiatrists to patients (assuming, that is, we are clear about what is meant by these terms). Many countries have now increased the ratio of psychiatrists to the population, and in the absence of other comparable developments in trained staff and community-based service provisions, this may present several dangers:

> Psychiatrists take a high proportion of the limited mental health budget yet often pay little attention to chronically sick or disabled patients, long-stay institutional residents or the mentally infirm who constitute the great bulk of psychiatric need. Neither do they necessarily involve themselves in service development work. Indeed if trained in traditional patterns of work they may represent a great force of inertia in traditional patterns of care and therefore a constraint on the development of comprehensive community based services (WHO 1985: 71).

This is a strong statement, especially from such an august body as the World Health Organization, and bearing in mind that those writing the report were eminent psychiatrists in their own right. It is, therefore, one of the most singeing set of publicly made self-criticisms. It does two things. First, it compares psychiatrists to other physicians and notes how psychiatrists compete for limited resources in the mental health budgets, yet fail to devote appropriate time and skills to the chronic patients; in the case of psychiatry, patients suffering from senile dementia clearly being a neglected category (Bean 1986). Secondly, it makes rather straightforward reference to the way psychiatrists "fail to involve themselves in service department work" and the way "they represent a great force of inertia" and "a constraint on the development of comprehensive community-based services". This argument can be illustrated by the current situation in the UK, where psychiatrists are moving from the mental hospitals and becoming attached to general-practice clinics (Tyrer 1984; see also Eyles, this volume). General practitioners offer a first form of defense in primary health care settings, and many psychiatrically ill patients attend the GP's surgery but are never referred to a psychiatrist. It was hoped that the psychiatrist attached to the GP's surgery could thereby offer assistance to both physician and patient. Unfortunately, where GP attachments have occurred, the movement has not always been an unqualified success, for the psychiatrists, not the GPs, have tended not to adapt to their new role. The psychiatrists have attempted to reproduce the hospital setting, and have tried to turn the surgery into a sort of mini-hospital dealing with a few selected patients. At the same time, they have expected the nursing and other comparable staff to offer back-up services. The net effect is that community facilities are not used to their full effect and resources are wasted. This is an example of what the WHO authors had in mind when they spoke of psychiatrists being a "great force of inertia".

In spite of what psychiatrists or anybody else might think, the problem for psychiatry in the immediate future is the problem of the chronic patient (which mainly means the chronic, elderly patient). It is not a problem for psychiatry alone but it is one that will increasingly involve psychiatrists. The changing socio-demographic structure of advanced Western societies is testimony to that (Bean 1986; Post 1983; see also Sixsmith, this volume). Yet psychiatry seems ill-prepared to deal with such patients, preferring the more glamorous acute patients who need immediate treatment. In contrast, the chronic patient needs long-term care. Sir Aubrey Lewis made the point as long ago as 1945 when he said, "We must regard the mental disorders of the elderly as likely to be responsible within the next 30 years for the bulk of patients admitted to mental hospitals" (Post 1983). In a study reported by Post, "In the course of their lives, out of every 1,000 males only 8 will be admitted for schizophrenia, 8 for manic depressive conditions, but 21 for psychosis of old age. The figures for females are rather higher: out of 1,000 there will be 10 for schizophrenia, 14 for effective psychosis, and 28 for senile dementia" (Post 1983: 280). To say that most observers know this, are aware of this and still do little about it, is only part of the problem. The other part is to convince psychiatrists and others to provide appropriate resources, for this is what the provision of mental health services is all about.

References

Asylum 1986. Editorial: The British Network for Alternative Systems in Psychiatry. *Asylum* **1** (1), 8.

Barker, I. 1986. Dutch lessons. *Headlines*, vol. 2.
Baro, F., A. Prims & P. de Schouwer 1985. Belgium psychiatric care; a pluralistic system. In *Mental Health Care in the European Community*, S. Mangen (ed.), 42–54. London: Croom Helm.

Bean, P. T. 1980. *Compulsory admissions to mental hospitals*. Chichester: Wiley.
Bean, P. T. 1986. *Mental disorder and legal control*. Cambridge: Cambridge University Press.

CAPO 1986. *Campaign against psychiatric oppression*. Mimeo.

Draguns, S. G. 1984. Assessing mental health and disorder across cultures. In *Mental Health Services*, S. B. Penderson, N. Sartorious & A. J. Marsella (eds.), 31–58. London: Sage.

Mangen, S. P. 1985. Psychiatric policies—development and constraints. In *Mental Health Care in the European Community*, S. P. Mangen (ed.), 1–33. London: Croom Helm.
Maste, L. 1982. Italy's revolutionary mental health law: an assessment. *American Journal of Psychiatry* **139** (2), 199–203.

Peck, E. & I. Barker 1986. Power to the patients. *Health Source Journal* (April 3), 437.
Post, F. 1983, Psychogeriatrics as a specialism. In *Mental illness: change and trends*, P. T. Bean (ed.), 279–97. Chichester, Wiley.

Ramon, S. 1985. The Italian psychiatric reform. In *Mental Health Care in the European Community*, S. P. Mangen (ed.), 170–203. London: Croom Helm.

Sang, R. 1985. A question of power. *Openmind* **17**, 12.
Sarteschi, P. *et al*. 1985. The Italian Psychiatric Care Act of 1978. In *Psychiatry, human rights and the law*, Sir M. Roth & R. Buglass (eds.), 32–42. Cambridge: Cambridge University Press.
Szasz, T. 1961. *The myth of mental illness*. London: Paladin.

Tyrer, P. 1984. Psychiatric clinics in general practice: an extension of community care. *British Journal of Psychiatry* **145,** 9–14.

WHO 1985. *Mental health services in Europe: 10 years on*. Geneva: World Health Organization.

3 Mental health services, the restructuring of care, and the fiscal crisis of the state: the United Kingdom case study

JOHN EYLES

An historical overview

The main purpose of this chapter is to provide an overview of the nature of mental health services in the contemporary UK. Because such services are not provided in a vacuum, the historical as well as the societal context of this provision will be examined. The evidence suggests that services for the mentally handicapped (defined as those with "general intellectual functioning at a level significantly below average combined with problems in adapting to normal behavior patterns and achieving social skills": DHSS 1971), and for the mentally ill (defined as those with "a disorder of the mind at every level of intelligence": House of Commons Social Service Committee 1985) are in a state of flux, and that more is known about intentions and plans than practice and reality. In such circumstances it is only possible to draw on selected examples of the care and treatment of those with psychiatric problems. However, it is possible to conclude that much care and treatment depend on the definitions employed as well as the context of provision.

This has always been the case. Rosen (1968) has shown how the definitions and care of illness have always been based on what society defines, interprets and classifies as deviant. Depressive and violent individuals who acted in impulsive, uncontrolled and socially unreasonable ways were always seen as mad. While they were few in number, they were tolerated and allowed to roam in their localities. Social and economic changes, first in agriculture and then in industry, altered that as they created a large pauper class of dispossessed people. In fact, it was the industrial era in particular that saw the rise in "lunacy," coincidental with the movement off the land and the increase in riots over many aspects of social change (see Parry-Jones 1972). Indeed, under the provisions of the 1744 Vagrancy Act, each county was permitted to establish an asylum for both criminal and pauper lunatics, with local magistrates rather than doctors determining who was lunatic. The social need to incarcerate the "lunatic" and the excesses discovered in the private madhouses in the early 19th century (Henderson 1964, Levine 1981, Morgan *et al*. 1985) resulted in great pressure to construct and regulate public asylums. The 1845 Lunatics Act made the construction of county asylums mandatory, and within ten years all English counties had complied. With the pressure to admit more in-patients, and the failure of the increasingly involved medical profession to find cures for many conditions, overcrowding resulted. Scull (1979) estimates that in the 1820s there were six public asylums with an average of 116 inmates; this had risen to 60, averaging 650 patients, by 1880. This rise in the asylum population continued to the early 1930s (see Scull 1983), although changes were initiated by the 1890 Lunacy Act which was concerned with the proper process of admission, the subsequent creation of a Central Board of Control, the eventual need to treat the victims of shell-shock from World War I, and European ideas on mental hygiene and the importance of outpatient facilities (Mangen & Rao 1985). Thus the custodial function of the psychiatric hospital (exacerbated by over-crowding in large institutions) became less important, and the therapeutic possibilities of the hospital setting were explored. (For a detailed historical account of the development of the lunatic asylum, see Tomes, this volume.)

The Mental Treatment Act of 1930, which heralded the domination of doctors over lawyers on questions of admission, encouraged the develop-ment of observation wards, outpatient clinics, and aftercare facilities. Psychiatric social work and occupational therapy were developed, and the late 1940s saw the availability of new drugs and social therapies, as well as the instigation of open-door policies. This period also witnessed, therefore, the construction of the first day hospital to allow the mentally ill to live in the community and yet be treated in a medical setting. Jones (1972), in her history of mental health services, cites new drug therapy and this open-door movement as two of the three revolutions to shake service provision in the post-1945 period. The third, the Mental Health Act of 1959, is really the legislative culmination of much of the debate on treatment from the 1930s onwards. Drugs to control the symptoms of mental illness, the establish-ment of the welfare state with its free health care at the point of delivery, and minimum levels of income maintenance and security, reduced the need for hospitalization. The 1959 Mental Health Act suggested this return to, or retention in, the community for the mentally ill and handicapped, while the hospitals were to reduce their inpatient populations and concentrate on voluntary admissions. The Act saw compulsory admissions as the last resort. It established patients' rights and interests as legitimate concerns through mental health review tribunals (these rights were later strengthened by the 1983 Mental Health Act).

The 1959 Act has been seen as the first official support for community care, although it did not establish such care as a statutory responsibility. Nor did it provide financial support. In many ways it provided a model for later exercises in cutting one type of service (hospital beds), advocating another form of care (community care), while at the same time failing to provide sufficient resources to move successfully from one type of treatment to another. In addition, the 1959 Act may be seen as belated governmental recognition of the declining inpatient population, which peaked at 148,000 in 1954—in other words, legislation had caught up with medical and social practice. As we shall see, the 1959 Act put community care at the center of the debate on mental health services, but it is not clear whether attitudes about the mentally ill changed as a result. It seems that although alternative attitudes exist, many people still view the mentally ill as unpredictable and dangerous (Walkey *et al.* 1981, Dear &. Taylor 1982, Eyles 1986). If the majority of the public sees some form of custody as necessary for those with mental disorders, does the 1959 Act show that government is willing to lead the public to a more enlightened view? Although this may be the case, there is also an economic motive to consider. This has been highlighted by Scull (1977), who argues that modern treatments are not very effective, that inpatient numbers were being reduced before such treatments appeared in the late 1950s, and that the detrimental consequences of prolonged hospitalization were known in the 1870s but did not stimulate policy until the 1950s and 1960s. The real reason for community care, according to Scull, is economic. The welfare state, with its provision of drugs, day- and outpatient facilities, and social security entitlements, is a cost-effective form of social control. Hospital care is only one possible means of treatment and control while, overall, the relative costs of different social control strategies shape the incarceration and decarceration of the mentally ill. Community care appears to be humane as it allows for the normalization of the lives of those affected by mental illness and handicap but, for many, the care they receive in the community remains custodial.

The emergence of community care, and fiscal crisis

Throughout the early 1960s, the economic rationale for community care was evident. In 1961, the UK Minister of Health talked of the need to reduce the number of hospital beds from over 150,000 in 1961 to 80,000 16 years later. The Regional Hospital Boards (RHBs) were asked to spend no more money than was necessary for upgrading hospitals not likely to be required in the future. The 1962 Hospital Plan confirmed the decision on hospital closure (Ministry of Health 1962), while a document a year later argued for the desirability of community care even if it failed to establish its firm rationale (Ministry of Health 1963). Throughout the 1960s policy changed little, although a series of inquiries into the ill-treatment of mental patients (see Watkin 1978) and academic reports on the effects of institutionalization (see Goffman 1961, Wing & Brown 1970) gave further support to the emergence of the community care concept.

If the thrust of policy was clear, its implementation was not. The evidence from hospital surveys as to who should be discharged into the community was variable (Cooper & Early 1964, Hassall & Hellon 1964). And, as a survey in Leeds (Gore *et al*. 1964) noted, administrative decisions may result in the discharge of patients and the emptying of beds, but only at the cost of hardship to patients and their families. Thus, while community care does usually mean treatment in the community in the form of day hospitals, psychiatric nurses, meals-on-wheels services, home helps and so on, it also implies a burden on the discharged patient and his or her family. Despite evidence to demonstrate that the mentally ill are less burdensome or costly to their families in hospital as opposed to home settings (Grad & Sainsbury 1968, Miles 1981), this fact has been widely and conscientiously ignored by government policy statements, as has the need for additional resources to support community services.

Two White Papers appearing in the early 1970s outlined the future directions of UK mental health policy (DHSS 1971, 1975). The White Paper on services for mentally handicapped (1971) suggested reducing hospital beds from 51,000 to 22,000, and increasing the number of residential places almost sixfold, to around 29,000 by 1991. No new policies were formulated for increasing community services at the local authority level. It was hoped that faster progress would overcome present deficiencies in this area but, as Tyne (1978) estimated, on the basis of the rate of change achieved between 1971 and 1976, it would take 46 years to reach the desired level of service provision. The White Paper on services for the mentally ill (DHSS 1975) firmly pushed the planning horizon into the 21st century. It stressed that people should be able to use the service with a minimum of formality and delay, and that the service philosophy would be one of integration rather than isolation. While cautious about the run-down of existing mental hospitals, it put forward the long-term aim of the creation of a compre-hensive, locally based service system.

The objectives of the 1971 and 1975 White Papers were confirmed in the 1976 priorities document (DHSS 1976a). Between 1975/76 and 1979/80, current expenditure on health and personal social services would grow by just over 2%, with services for the mentally ill increasing by an extra 1.8%, and those for the mentally handicapped by an extra 2%. However, reviews of these policy statements indicate that such progress has not been achieved. Personal social-service expenditure on community care actually declined from 22.7% of all expenditure to 21.1% between 1974/5 and 1977/8. Residential care expenditure (which should have declined) actually increased from 49.6% to 50.6% (DHSS 1980a, Eyles & Woods 1983). Further, having spelt out the need for greater expenditure on personal social services in 1976, that year marked the end of growth in expenditure on these services. In 1973/4 expenditure grew by 15%. In 1976/7 and 1977/8 it actually declined by 1.3% and 1.6% respectively. From 1979/80 to 1984/5 expenditure again increased by about 12%, after discounting for inflation (CSO 1986); in other words, by just over 2% p.a. in real tearms. The proportion of the health and personal social services budget spent on personal social services has declined from around 17% in 1979/80 to a planned 11% for 1985/6.

In reality, then, the priorities policy was abandoned before it was begun. The 1976 document pointed to the need to examine the cost-effectiveness of curative medicine, and to direct resources to the more economical primary care sector. It also highlighted the importance of prevention and the responsibility of the individual for his or her own health. The context of resource constraint began seriously to affect the NHS and, within it, the services for the mentally ill and the mentally handicapped. The fiscal crisis of the mid-1970s allowed for the restructuring of care in the guise of individual responsibility and normalization, so that community care became not care *in* but *by* the community. After the Conservative electoral victory of 1979, this restructuring was given a rigorous philosophical underpinning in terms of individual freedom and freedom of choice.

In fact, for most of the period from 1951 to 1979, the UK enjoyed rapid economic growth and high increases in public expenditure. Between 1951 and 1979 this expenditure increased by 15%, with social expenditure growing by 250% (Judge 1982). However, while the average annual growth of social expenditure was 6.3% between 1970 and 1974, it fell to 2% between 1974 and 1979, a period which saw the UK experiencing high levels of inflation, economic recession, and high unemployment. The increase in public spending during the post-war years had resulted in a continual rise in public-sector borrowing (Gamble & Walton 1976, Doyal 1979). Both Labour and Conservative parties saw this spending and borrowing (and the social expenditures that they supported) as public burdens. In an influential publication, Bacon & Eltis (1976) argued that high levels of taxation and public borrowing had pre-empted investment in the private sector, from which, in a mixed economy such as that of the UK, "real" wealth springs. Public expenditure has thus been reduced in an attempt to transfer resources from the "unproductive" to the "productive" sectors of the economy.

These expenditure reductions were initiated by the Labour government in the face of recession and of mounting budget deficits (Gough 1979). The Conservatives have, as Mishra (1984) points out, continued rather than accelerated this trend. Change is, of necessity, slow in a democracy where government is by consent, honoring the role of law and heeding the influence of organized interest groups. Mishra further suggests that three decades of the welfare state have created a social climate—a diffuse framework of values—in which drastic service reductions could strain the social order. But the Conservatives, if they have not succeeded in reducing public expenditure, have made significant transfers between sectors. The most recent government expenditure plans (HM Treasury 1986) show that total spending has increased by 8.9% between 1979 and 1986. Housing expenditures declined by 59% in that period, and this has had serious consequences for a policy of deinstitutionalization of the mentally ill and handicapped. The major "gains" are in employment strategies (+67.2%), agricultural support (+62.6%), law and order (+40.7%), social security payments (+33.7%), defense (+29.8%) and the health service (+19.7%). (However, for the health service, the annual increase of around 2.5% gives little real growth after taking the UK's ageing population, technological developments, and wage increases into account.) Expenditure on personal social services depends primarily on the local authorities, which are subject to rigorous cash-limitation, with rate-capping as the ultimate penalty. The Conservatives now appear to be creating their own social climate, which may have become a potent force in UK social life. It is a view which emphasizes the limits of governmental activity, good housekeeping, self-provision and self-help, and individual responsibility and freedom. The need to live within the nation's means has been linked to the reduction of state activity. Rolling back the state, especially in the field of welfare, has become a policy priority, enabling individual enterprises, initiative, and commitment to flourish. The individual is to be given the freedom to choose the level of welfare he or she needs, with the state sector reduced to the function of providing a safety net for those lacking the necessary income or intelligence to care for themselves. The safety net will itself be rigorously means-tested. In pursuit of these (admittedly long-term) aims, the Conservative government has put forward ideas on health maintenance organizations and vouchers for primary health care, and has encouraged private health care provision (Eyles 1987). It has fostered a particular view of and approach to community care for all dependent groups, including the mentally handicapped and ill.

Community care in the 1980s

At the beginning of the 1980s, some statement about the policy for dependent groups appeared to be necessary. The Royal Commission on the NHS (1979) declared itself mystified as to how resources were allocated to such groups, suggesting a cloudiness in departmental thinking on such matters. But a series of reports and documents in the late 1970s and early 1980s began to shape intentions. The importance of locally and community-based services was emphasized (DHSS 1979) and the shift to the community was documented (DHSS 1981a). This documentation high-lighted the rise in the numbers of GPs and community nurses, as well as day centers and home helps. However, it must be noted that the sharpest increase in these facilities and personnel came in the 1967–71 period, before the priorities documents. Further, in 1979 there were still ten nurses in the hospital compared to every one in the community. A report on mental handicap noted that many patients remained in hospital because there was no alternative community provision (DHSS 1980b). With regard to the increase in community services, it remains unclear whether they have kept pace with demographic and social change, or if the manpower growth means more effective care for dependent groups. A study of the elderly, including psychogeriatrics, suggests that community care has not kept pace with demand (Webb & Wistow 1982).

It is perhaps the 1981 document *Care in action* (DHSS 1981b) which emphasized the importance and context of community care best of all. It stressed that most people who need long-term care can and should be looked after in the community, because that is what they want for themselves and what those responsible for their care believe to be best. While the priority groups remained the same (the elderly, the mentally ill, and the mentally and physically handicapped) the priority services were seen as primary care, the voluntary sector, and informal care-givers. It is in these services that we see most clearly the context of community care and the break with the policies of the past. The 1981 document no longer expressed its priorities in terms of norms or financial targets: no additional resources were to be found for such priorities, except in efficiency savings. As Klein (1983) notes, if the implementation of priorities policy implied tightened rationing in other sectors, responsibility was firmly delegated to the peripheral authorities. Klein's point was tellingly clarified by a ministerial response in the House of Commons which stated that there were no targets for the provision of long-stay hostel places, day centers, or community psychiatric facilities, as the level of local need could only be fully appreciated and determined locally. Furthermore, authorities must fund all services within existing cash allocations and from resources generated by greater efficiency (*Hansard* 1286, col. 59–61, October 1983). The context was spelled out clearly by the Secretary of State in the foreword to *Care in action*: "I'm sure you do not need reminding that the Government's top priority must be to get the economy right; for that reason, it cannot be assumed that more money will always be available to be spent on health care." Priorities are, therefore, to be achieved by exhortation, but spending on priorities (such as most public services) is restricted by cash-limiting or rate-capping.

What has, therefore, been achieved? Community care for the mentally ill and mentally handicapped is probably the greatest change in the nature of care and treatment since the early 19th century. In the summary to their report, the Social Services Committee noted the great commitment of money, staff and buildings represented by the asylums. It questioned whether the commitment was being matched in community care (House of

Commons 1985). Such commitment is difficult when there is no clear definition of community care to be found in DHSS documents and circulars. As a result, as the National Association of Health Authorities (NAHA) pointed out, community care has come to mean different things to different people, which has led to some confusion and delays in planning and implementing community services (House of Commons Social Service Committee 1985). The health authorities have been keen to release patients from long-stay hospitals into local-authority-provided residential care, while many local authorities have taken community care to mean the development of services to allow people to stay at home. The extent of provision of health care in the community and residential provision by local authorities has not been clarified, although the mechanism of joint finance does exist to facilitate the transfer of people from mental hospitals to the community.

The possibilities of collaboration between the health and local authorities were first explored in the early 1970s (DHSS 1973). An overall aim was to set up joint planning from the initial stages of project and planning formulation and, to this end, Joint Consultative Committees (JCCs) were established. The National Health Service Act of 1977 laid a statutory duty on health and local authorities to cooperate in order to secure and advance the health and welfare of the population. Joint Care Planning Teams (JCPTs) were established and joint finance became available (DHSS 1977). Joint finance is the mechanism for reallocating health service resources to fund local social service spending to increase the quantity of care available to the community. Each year part of the health budget is set aside for projects in the personal social services. Initially, the health authorities provided finance for up to 7 years. This has now been increased through DHSS *Circular* HC83(6) to 13 years, with the health budget subsidy being available for all the costs for 10 years in exceptional circumstances. In the past, local authorities have used joint finance for additional day care, domiciliary, and social work, rather than alternative residential accommodation for patients discharged from mental hospitals. Since 1983, subsidies have been tied more closely to the movement of patients from hospitals (Mangen & Rao 1985), and DHSS *Circular* HC84(9) extended joint financing arrangements to educational and housing authorities, both municipal and voluntary.

Although 95% of the available funds have been taken up, the overall amounts available are small. It is estimated that the first 5 years of joint finances added 0.5% annual growth to the total social services budget (Wistow 1984). For 1983/4 the total available for joint finance was in fact £96 million, representing 0.8% of the health service budget and 4.5% of the personal social services budget (Walker 1984). Furthermore, NAHA noted an increasing reluctance on the part of local authorities to participate in joint finance schemes which commit them to future financial outlays. Their survey indicated that four authorities had discontinued joint finance projects, 13 were refusing to participate in future schemes, and 24 were renegotiating arrangements to extend financial support (House of Commons Social Services Committee 1985).

The Social Services Committee has recorded that around one-third of joint finance has been spent on mental handicap services, but only around 5% on mental illness (House of Commons Social Services Committee 1985). But, even with respect to mental handicap services, progress has been slow. The situation in England has been much worse than in Wales, where £26 million was available for mental handicap community care alone (Wistow 1985). In England, some £15 million of joint finance is centrally reserved over the next 4 years for care in the community initiatives for trans-ferring patients from hospitals to the community (in other words, under £4 million p.a.). This figure amply demonstrates the parsimonious nature of community care. Joint finance can be no more than seed money, especially when a typical Regional Health Authority (RHA) receives only about £6–7 million p.a. (House of Commons Social Services Committee 1985). It is also likely to encourage capital or short-term revenue projects rather than long-term expenditure on staff. This is particularly unfortunate, given the labor-intensive nature of much community care. Moreover, 20% of joint finance is now retained within the NHS, and the whole scheme has the appearance of being a short-term expedient rather than a coherent policy. However, the importance of joint finance cannot be overestimated. For example, without funding from the DHSS and the North Western RHA, no patients would have been released from Brockhall Hospital in the Bolton area (House of Commons Social Services Committee 1985).

The policy shift to reduction of the hospital population through joint finance has brought some other monetary difficulties to the fore. The transition from hospital to the community requires extra short-term finance, sometimes referred to as bridging finance, but more graphically called a dowry payment, a financial entitlement to pay for the services that replace hospital care. Wistow & Hardy (1986) have investigated three RHAs which have evolved different bridging and dowry strategies. North Western and Trent RHAs have established regional pools of bridging funds from which dowries are paid. However, the Trent RHA will only pay maximum allowances to health authorities, militating against community services provided by local and voluntary authorities, and it deducts social security entitlements from transfer payments. North Western RHA allows all authorities the maximum allowance, and allows social security monies to be added to the sums available, insisting on a close link to the specified needs of individual patients. North East Thames RHA is similar to Trent on allowances, but does not have a regional pool, preferring to adjust district revenues to create a priority services growth pool.

Even with the NHS, therefore, there are different perceptions and policies. Different perceptions between health and local authorities (Booth 1981) have, in fact, tended to hinder effective collaboration. It has also been hindered by insufficient funding, which is not helped by the fact that the movement of patients from hospitals does not increase available funds greatly because of the low marginal cost—and therefore saving—of each patient. Additional hindrances have been the differences in organizational and financial structure, in professional attitudes and practices, and in the lack of coterminosity in administrative boundaries between health and local authorities. Where there is such coterminosity, in Wales and Northern Ireland, the resultant practice is mixed. The Welsh Office, through its plans, has succeeded in putting significant extra resources into community care for the mentally handicapped (Welsh Office 1983), while the integrated services of Northern Ireland, because of financial constraints and administrative upheavals, have failed to provide better treatment and care for the priority groups (Connolly 1985).

Joint finance is a microcosm of community care, both being funded parsimoniously and subject to variability in definitions and perceptions. This variability is reflected in care strategies and, while it is impossible to describe the spatial patterning of care for the entire UK, attention can be drawn to particular examples. While commitment to the nebulous concept of "community care" is universal among health authorities, the bases of that commitment and hence the type of care are extremely variable. Thus, for example, in their regional strategy, Oxford RHA (1984) suggests that the current emphasis on hospital care for the mentally handicapped will be shifted to community support, including greater collaboration with local authorities. It further requests that large mental hospitals be replaced by new local facilities. But only a year or so before, it had suggested the closure of mental handicap and illness hospitals, without waiting for the local authorities to make alternative provision for those living in them (reported in Iliffe 1983). The private sector could, in fact, provide more facilities. The backdrop of this move to "community care" is zero growth in funds, and a growing and ageing population.

Other authorities have tried to provide facilities outside hospitals for psychiatric patients. For example, in Southampton, a hostel for long-term chronically ill patients has been established in Cranbury Terrace, near the city center and the Royal South Hampshire hospital (Vousden 1985). This facility has, however, been made possible by a DHSS grant towards capital costs and the full amount of the first four years' revenue costs. Cranbury Terrace is one of only three such units in the country, and others are not likely to be opened until full evaluations have been carried out. Therefore, it is very much an experiment and, as such, fits the model of caution and parsimony of much UK social and urban policy (Eyles 1979). In the field of mental health there are other such experimental examples, such as the collaboration of voluntary and public authorities in day centers, as in Warrington (Murray 1981), and the Worcester development project (Hall

& Gillard 1982), the latter being an attempt to provide enough community services to allow the closing of the one remaining mental hospital.

A similar problem remains in Exeter, which has become a DHSS showcase (House of Commons Social Services Committee 1985). Exeter District Health Authority (DHA) has led the drive to community care, being willing to close hospitals and transfer services and resources to other authorities. Exeter has so far managed all bridging finance, while the South West RHA has guaranteed reserve bridging support. Thus far, a hostel for the chronically mentally ill has been opened in North Devon, mental health community teams with day hospital bases have been established in Exmouth and Tiverton, and a day center and hostel have been set up in Exeter. For mental handicap, resource transfers have led to the establishment of community based services in Torbay, Plymouth and North Devon, and sheltered housing in Exeter. The commitment to community care cannot be doubted (Hyde 1985), including the closure of Exminster hospital to release resources. But, as the Select Committee found for themselves on their visit in 1984, 150 patients remained in the hospital at that time. There may thus be a limit to deinstitutionalization, because some mentally ill people benefit more from hospital care than from being in the community. For such patients, the closure of facilities may mean the transfer to other, perhaps less suitable, institutions. This process of trans-institutionalization has certainly become manifest in the USA (see Brown and Wolch *et al.*, this volume).

The experiments demonstrate, first, the costly nature of a community care which, on a small-scale, does not replicate institutional care; and secondly, that housing is one of the key problems in deinstitutionalization. There has been some transfer to residential homes and hostels run by local and voluntary authorities. In fact, local authorities provide two-thirds of the registered accommodation for the mentally ill and handicapped. For the former group, by 1983, local authorities provided only 4,200 beds compared with an estimated need of 12,100 places (Scott 1986). In the late 1970s less than one-half of English local authorities provided residential accommodation (see Mangen & Rao 1985). This situation has certainly improved throughout the 1980s, but by 1983, 11 local authorities still had no residential places (*Hansard* 1289, cols. 10–14, November 1983). Expenditure on such accommodation has certainly increased from its low base, as the Association of Metropolitan Authorities submission to the Select Committee shows (House of Commons Social Services Committee 1985). Expenditure on residential care for the mentally ill increased from £11.4 million in 1975/6 to £16.7 million in 1981/2, and from £46.5 million to £87 million for mentally handicapped adults and children (figures in average 1981/2 prices).

The accommodation that is provided in the community is of a variable nature. Most hostels are of reasonable standard, but some long-stay ones are no better than the worst of the old wards (Ryan 1979, Brandon 1985). Insufficient support services mean that some dischargees are forced to live in boarding houses and unsuitable bed-and-breakfast accommodation (Conway & Kemp 1985, Heptinstall 1985). The decanting of patients without sufficient support services can also mean the retention of institutional attitudes and practices (Bennett & Morris 1983). These problems, along with those of cash limits and the need to make efficiency savings, have produced a variety of responses on the part of health and local authorities. Some, like Bristol and Weston DHA, have encouraged the establishment of housing associations, such as the one in South Avon which caters for the mentally handicapped (Ward 1986). Others, such as East Sussex, have set up hostels for psychiatric patients, with the major aim of cost saving as well as community-based care (Raafat 1986) while, more controversially, Frenchay DHA has given funds to the private sector to look after mentally handicapped people (Anderson 1986). It is only possible to provide such snapshots of the attempts to restructure care under conditions of financial exigency, because no national monitoring occurs. This lack may be particularly glaring with respect to the private sector which, in such towns as Northampton, is setting up unregistered residential homes (see Eyles 1986).

Although we have considered community care for the mentally ill and handicapped in some detail, it must be recognized that it is but one dimension of care for this group. Further, it is a dimension which must be seen in the context of the other types of care provided. But before turning to general questions of provision and policy in the 1980s, we may use the memorandum of the Royal College of General Practitioners (RCGP) to the Select Committee (House of Commons Social Services Committee 1985) to highlight some of the problems of community care, and to demonstrate how these relate to other aspects of health policy. The RCGP notes that care in the community is set against predominantly urban culture, from which the extended family has largely disappeared. Materialistic attitudes, political stress, and an ageing population have conspired to sap the caring capacity of the general population (see also Barnes 1981). As a result, community care requires investment in professionals and facilities. It cannot mean home care, although the government's Chief Medical Officer admits that this is exactly what many people mean by the term "community care" (Acheson 1985). The investment required for community care has been impossible with static budgets and poor lines of responsibility and cooperation. These difficulties have been compounded by other developments. Resource reallocations under the government formulae (DHSS 1976b) have tended to discriminate against inner-city areas to which the mentally ill may gravitate. Wage settlements have largely been met out of existing budgets, making the deployment of further community psychiatric nurses very difficult. In financially austere times, the competition for resources to treat life-threatening and non-life-threatening illnesses is usually resolved to benefit the former. Acute services outbid those of, say, psychiatry because it is easier for them to demonstrate their effectiveness. This competition, under the resource allocation formulae which allocate funds on the basis of bed costs with respect to need defined in terms of Standardised Mobility Ratios (SMRs), means that additional resources for community services are seldom forthcoming. It also means that the regional variations identified by Maynard (1972) for 1969 cannot seriously be addressed (for example, psychiatric nurses varied from a low of 27.6 per 1,000 mentally ill patients in East Anglia to a high of 39.3 in Oxford RHB, and from a low of 23.16 per 1,000 mentally handicapped patients in South Eastern RHB to 41.51 in Liverpool).

There is also competition within social services budgets and between local authority departments. An ageing population and increased public awareness of child abuse have meant that mental illness and handicap are fairly low priorities. In 1979 one-quarter of English social services departments had no day-care provision, and only 30% of staff had any qualification (Vaughan 1983). By 1980, only five local authorities had reached the 1975 guidelines for day-care places, all of them London boroughs (*Hansard* 1210, col. 402–5, June 1981); and, in 1981, 9 local authorities still had no day-care place at all (*Hansard* 1289, cols. 610–14, November 1983). The organization of psychiatric services, in which movement from one type of treatment to another is difficult because of local "zoning"; the difficulty of setting up primary care teams for casework purposes; and drug availability, which seems to provide a ready solution to an immediate problem at the expense of counseling skills, can be cited as other obstacles to community care.

Provision and planning in the 1980s

Community care has become the dominant option, at least at the level of policy intention, because of its apparent cost-effectiveness, which is in large measure ensured by not putting a financial value on the contributions of informal care-givers, who, it is recognized, shoulder considerable social, emotional and financial burdens (DHSS 1981a). Even if these informal providers are ignored, the relative costs of different kinds of treatment remain a question of debate. Thus Mangen (1983) suggests that the cost of treating neurotic patients are comparable whether community psychiatric nurses or outpatient facilities are employed. The costs and benefits of the psychiatric unit attached to a general hospital, a strategy much favored by the DHSS (to such an extent that the proportion of psychiatric beds in such facilities almost trebled between 1970 and 1981: DHSS 1984), are also the subject of controversy (Goldberg & Jones 1980, Baruch & Treacher 1978). In addition, there is some question about the efficacy of the move to the community for treating the mentally ill and handicapped (Laurance 1985). There is no guarantee that it will necessarily lead to lower levels of symptoms or better standards of living.

It is difficult to obtain data on expenditure on community care as opposed to hospital care because of different views about what services constitute such care. Evidence presented by the DHSS to the Social Services Committee shows that in 1982/3 a total of £1.56 billion was spent on services for the mentally ill and handicapped but, of this figure, £1.23 billion went to inpatient services. A further £55.9 million was spent on outpatient services, and £121.7 million on local-authority residential care. There is a distinction to be made between the two groups. Although more is spent on hospital care than on personal social services for both groups, for the mentally handicapped there is twice as much of the former, while for the mentally ill there is 30 times as much, which reflects the hospital legacy and difference in public attitudes towards the groups. Although hospital expenditure dominates, it is minute when set against all hospital expenditure. Looking at the slightly different hospital revenue expenditure figures, £1.13 billion was spent on mental illness and handicap hospitals in 1982/3 compared with £25.5 billion on acute ones (DHSS 1985). Thus mental hospital expenditure represents some 1.5% of the total hospital expenditure, compared with 2.25% in 1958/9. The relative reduction in such expenditure may be said to demonstrate the move to community care: but we may calculate from the official sources (House of Commons Social Services Committee 1985) that the expenditure on services for the mentally ill and handicapped remained at about 14% of the total health and personal social services budget between 1976/7 and 1982/3. There has been a small rise in personal social service expenditure, accounted for largely by residential care expenditure, which rose from 47 to 54% of the total between those years.

The progress to residential places outside institutions has been slow, whether those places take the form of hostels, sheltered accommodation or residential homes. This slowness is a function of the lack of finance and the time it takes to plan facilities and to train staff. The growth in availability was rapid during the mid-1970s but, since 1978, the increase in places in staffed and unstaffed homes has been slight (CSO 1985a, 1986; House of Commons Social Services Committee 1985). Because of the increasing number of demands on static social service budgets, this situation is unlikely to improve. Indeed, the Association of Metropolitan Authorities informed the Social Services Committee that it was not politically possible to guarantee priority for the mentally ill and handicapped (House of Commons Social Services Committee 1985). This may mean that those discharged from hospital must increasingly rely on family practitioner services, informal care, and perhaps, the private sector for accommodation. Whether such uncoordinated and largely unplanned responses can cope is open to question.

The question is open because of the scale of the problem. While there have been progressive reductions in the numbers of people in mental hospitals (Fry *et al*. 1984, Scottish Home and Health Department 1985, DHSS 1985), there remains the question of adequate care and treatment. There are some 120,000 severely mentally handicapped people (including about 50,000 children) in the UK, of which 42,000 are in hospital, although it has been estimated that 15,000 could be discharged immediately if facilities were available. While the scale and annual increase of mental handicap problems can be calculated, it is more difficult with mental illness. There are around 69,000 patients in mental illness hospitals in England, a decline of nearly 30% since 1972: but, using symptom inventories, it has been estimated that there are around 250 per 1,000 people in the community with some kind of psychological problem (Goldberg & Huxley 1980). Of these, 230 will go to a GP, who will identify 140 as having a diagnosable problem; but only 17 will be referred to psychiatric services. Herein lies the difficulty for the services provided. It is only possible to say that provision is adequate or inadequate in relation to need and demand. Such prevalence rates add greatly to the workloads of GPs. In fact, Goldberg & Huxley (1980) estimate that 9–39% of GP workload is devoted to mental illness, although this may of course reflect recognition rates (Goldberg & Blackwell 1970). Family practitioner services (FPS) are not cash-limited but are demand-generated, so they have provided much of the care not forthcoming from the other sectors. Thus, in Scotland, the cost of the hospital service increased in total by 14% between 1981 and 1983, while payments to doctors increased in total by 21% in the same period (CSO 1985b). In the UK, between 1981/2 and 1984/5, current expenditure on hospital and community health services increased by a total of 21%, but expenditure on FPS grew by 37% (CSO 1986). This type of care may become more important, because the pressure to close mental illness and handicap hospitals may become more intense as the management reforms of the mid-1980s (DHSS 1983) require unit managers in charge of mental health services to seek efficiency and cost-effectiveness. Suggestions have been made to restrict FPS by voucher schemes which entitle patients to only so much state-provided treatment (Eyles 1987).

Given the scale of mental health problems, provision does appear to be inadequate. Community care exhorts informal care-givers to provide, and allows for the development of a network of privately run but social-security-funded boarding houses and residential homes. Where formal medical treatment is required, that need will appear where it is allowed to appear. If funds are denied to hospitals and day-care treatments, more people receive care from FPS. Furthermore, as government strategy is geared toward the cost-saving potential of community care, it concentrates on the removal of patients from hospitals. Those retained in the community are left to fend for themselves with the assistance of the informal sector and FPS—these are very much the forgotten cases.

However, it is this government strategy that is reflected in many reviews of present provision and plans for the future. Thus, in the Hereford area, the strategic plan is to create a network of community services with day centers in Hereford, Ross-on-Wye, and Leominster. The plan must be financed from existing resources, and it is therefore necessary to close wards at the main psychiatric hospital, St. Mary's. The plan also requires the co-operation of social service departments and GPs (Harbridge 1984).

The financially straitened circumstances in which strategic plans are derived, and the need to make efficiency savings of closures to facilitate new ventures, are reflected in the long timescales envisaged for improvements in provision. For example, the North Western RHA recognizes that it has a shortfall of over 2,450 mental illness day places, providing only 1,667 against a norm of 4,118. Its capital plans show that it has budgeted to provide under two-thirds of this shortfall by 1991, assuming that there is no increase in demand for such places (figures from House of Commons Social Services Committee 1985). With respect to mental illness beds, there are several deficiencies in some districts, notably Bury, Trafford, and Blackburn, and large hospitals elsewhere, e.g., Prestwich in North Manchester. The RHA intends to remedy the situation in part by reducing bed norms in line with a community-oriented service and review, and to replace large hospitals over the next 10 years as part of a planned develop-ment of district-based services, taking account of local authority and voluntary services. For the mentally handicapped, the RHA intends to develop "model district services" in which ordinary housing, day-care services, and a run-down of large hospitals and the resettlement of long-stay hospital patients are envisaged. Although total revenue allocated to mental handicap services rose from 4.6% in 1979/80 to 5.25% in 1982/3, the region recognized that the pattern of services has not changed dramatically. It is left with the intention of funding a doctor-and-nurse team to visit each district to inform on good practice. Its long-term objectives of community mental handicap teams for each district, the provision of new purpose-built, small-scale, long-term residential places, and relief care provision for informal care-givers, must await additional resources.

London is particularly affected by the policy shifts to locally- and community-based care. Of London's mental illness beds, 88% are housed in 15 hospitals, each with over 1,000 beds, located on the fringe of the metropolitan area (LHPC 1981). Of the 31 DHAs, 11 have no district general hospital inpatient facilities. Between 1978 and 1981 the use of the large hospitals actually increased (GLC 1985). Community services are particularly underdeveloped. The provision for the mentally handicapped also remains below the standards put forward by the government (Woods 1983). Day care and residential provisions are inadequate in over 80% of the London boroughs. This means that after-care for those discharged from psychiatric inpatient treatment remains largely concentrated in the NHS sector. This is particularly problematic given that the four Thames RHAs are losing funding under the resource allocation formulae (Mohan & Woods 1985). Thus the attempts to develop local, comprehensive, psychiatric services remain at the preliminary planning stages. Even then, there is variety in the approaches adopted by the four RHAs, with South East and South West Thames recognizing the value of primary-care services (and South West Thames intending to reallocate resources to community services) and North West and North East Thames looking first to the hospital service to provide both inpatient and day and community services (GLC 1985). At the district level, reduced funding means, for example, that even in the City and Hackney districts, which have a longstanding commitment to community provision, it is impossible to meet NHS targets for day places for the mentally ill and handicapped by 1991 (City and Hackney DHA 1983). Reductions in local-authority expenditure also make the development of locally based services difficult. Furthermore, the number of authorities in London makes effective collaboration and coordination difficult. MIND's (1983) view that different planning cycles, management structures, conditions of employment, and preoccupations of the authorities discourage effective coordination is particularly pertinent for London; and the Greater London Council painted a bleak picture of inadequate funding and poor coordination which, in the present societal context, bode ill for mental health services in London (GLC 1985).

Conclusions

Mental health services in the UK have, particularly over the past 25 years or so, changed radically in form and rationale. The move from hospital to community care is now well established, despite the nebulous nature of the definition of community care and the re-emergence of institutional attitudes and practices in many community settings. Community care represents the most important development in the treatment of mental illness and handicap since the construction and supervision of the public asylums in the early 19th century. This development may be based on a humanitarian rationale in that living in noninstitutional settings may increase the possibilities of a "normal" style of living for the people concerned. Even if based on such a rationale, however, it must be recognized that there is a limit to deinstitutionalization in that some people, because of their afflictions, isolation or frailty, may require a hospital or clinical setting. There is also an economic rationale in that community care, especially if seen solely or predominantly in terms of the removal of patients from institutions, appears to be a less costly form of treatment than hospital care. This is particularly the case if community support services are not adequately developed to ease the transfer into the noninstitutional world. It must be noted that both rationales tend to ignore the mentally ill and handicapped who are retained in the community, and it is among these groups that reliance on informal care and FPS is perhaps at its greatest.

It is, to say the least, a misfortune of timing that the desire to develop community care strategies coincided with the fiscal crisis of the British state and perhaps, more importantly, with the emergence of a government that wanted to use the crisis to reshape the nature of British life. The "living within our means," "value for money," "individual responsibility" arguments sat well with a cost–effective strategy that appeared at the same time humanitarian. But the lack of clarity over the purposes of community care, and the unwillingness to release more than parsimonious bridging and support finance, have resulted in some unfortunate consequences. The UK mental health services are increasingly becoming similar to those in the USA (Greer *et al.* 1983, Brown 1985). The Social Services Committee noted the appearance of transinstitutionalization, as those unable to cope in a non-hospital setting are moved to other institutions following closures. There is increasing reliance on informal and voluntary care and, for accommodation, the private sector. In fact, as Robinson (1986) argues, the health and personal social services have an incentive to transfer all those needing long-term care from their own cash-limited budgets to the private sector, where they become eligible for assistance via noncash-limited social security payments.

As we have seen, the "living within our means" and "putting the economy first" argument did not result in reductions in public expenditure or, except through some creative accounting, public borrowing. Since 1979 there has been a change in the composition of public expenditure between sectors, much of which has resulted in widening economic inequalities between groups (see CSO 1986), while the oil revenues and public asset sales have allowed expenditure to increase and borrowing to be reduced. The fiscal crisis, an accurate description of the late-1970s UK economic position is now given little prominence. While this crisis, through the introduction of cash limits, helped to inaugurate a financially restricted restructuring of care, it was the social aims and philosophical rationale of the New Right that ensured that the restructuring would occur in the form and way it did. Despite the New Right's desire to "roll back the state," its government, initially fueled by a welfare backlash which in the UK never reached the proportions of that found in the USA, has been directive. The state's roles are no longer simply those of crisis avoidance and management, damage limitation and ensuring mass loyalty (Habermas 1976; Offe 1976, 1984). It is now more directive, although the New Right would argue that the state can only enable. Through its monetary and fiscal policies, it directs not only to provide the conditions to ensure continued capitalist accumulation, but also to create the conditions for a more individualistic, capitalist society. Some of these changes are recognized in the recapitalization-of-capitalism argument (Gough 1979, Szelenyi 1984) which see the state as encouraging the purchase of privately produced services. But we also need to recognize that a particular form of consciousness supports, and is supported by, this recapitalization. The disappearance of many extended family and neighborhood bonds, and the increasing recognition of the primacy of individual interest in a materialistic world, are significant in the creation of a more capitalistic society. In such a context, community care for the mentally ill and handicapped makes sense. Community care is cost-effective and appears humanitarian. If the character of mental health services is to change, it will require not only inputs of resources but also challenges to the ways we see and act in the world, because it is on these that our definitions of care are based.

References

Acheson, D. 1985. That overworked word community! *Health Trends* **17**, 3.
Anderson, F. 1986. Severn storm as mentally handicapped go private. *Health Services Journal* March 6, 308.

Bacon, R. & W. Eltis 1976. *Britain's economic problems*. London: Macmillan.
Barnes, R. 1981. The careless community. *Health and Social Services Journal* **91** (4762), 1083.
Baruch, G. & A. Treacher 1978. *Psychiatry observed*. London: Routledge & Kegan Paul.
Bennett, D. & I. Morris 1983. Deinstitutionalisation in the UK. *International Journal of Mental Health* **2**, 5–23.
Booth, T. A. 1981. Collaboration between health and social services. *Policy Politics* **9**.
Brandon, D. 1985. Four principles to guide community care plans. *Community Care* **584**, October 24, 10–11.
Brown, P. 1985. *The transfer of care*. London: Routledge & Kegan Paul.

CSO (Central Statistical Office) 1985a. *Social Trends* 15. London: HMSO.
CSO 1985b. *Annual Abstract of Statistics* 121. London: HMSO.
CSO 1986. *Social Trends* 16. London: HMSO.
City and Hackney DHA 1983. *Strategic plan 1983–93*. London: City and Hackney DHA.
Connolly, M. 1985. Has integration worked? The health and personal social services in Northern Ireland. In *Health care UK 1985*, A. Harrison & J. Gretton (eds.). Policy Journals.
Conway, J. & P. Kemp 1985. *Bed and breakfast*. London: SHAC.
Cooper, A. B. & D. F. Early 1964. Survey of a long-stay population in a psychiatric hospital. *British Medical Journal* June 3, 1600–3.

Dear, M. J. & S. M. Taylor 1982. *Not on our street*. London: Pion.
DHSS (Department of Health and Social Security) 1971. *Better services for the mentally handicapped* (Cmnd 4683). London: HMSO.
DHSS 1973. *Report of the working party on collaboration between the NHS and local government*. London: HMSO.

DHSS 1975. *Better services for the mentally ill* (Cmnd 6233). London: HMSO.
DHSS 1976. *Priorities for health and personal social services in England*. London: HMSO.
DHSS 1976b. *Sharing resources for health in England*. London: HMSO.
DHSS 1977. *The way forward*. London: HMSO.
DHSS 1979. *Patients first*. London: HMSO.
DHSS 1980a. *Inequalities in health*. London: DHSS.
DHSS 1980b. *Mental handicap: progress, problems and priorities*. London: HMSO.
DHSS 1981a. *Report of a study on community care*. London. HMSO.
DHSS 1981b. *Care in action*. London: HMSO.
DHSS 1983. *NHS management inquiry report*. London: HMSO.
DHSS 1984. *Inpatient statistics from the mental health enquiry 1981*. London: HMSO.
DHSS 1985. *Health and personal social services statistics for England*. London: HMSO.
Doyal, L. 1979. *The political economy of health*. London: Pluto Press.

Eyles, J. 1979. Area-based policies for the inner city. In *Social problems and the city*, D. T. Herbert & D. M. Smith (eds.). Oxford: Oxford University Press.
Eyles, J. 1986. Images of care, realities of provision and location. *East Midlands Geographer* 9, 53–60.
Eyles, J. 1987. *The geography of the national health*. London: Croom Helm.
Eyles, J. & K. J. Woods 1983. *The social geography of medicine and health*. London: Croom Helm.

Fry, J., D. Brooks & I. McColl 1984. *The NHS data book*. Lancaster: MTP Press.

Gamble, A. & P. Walton 1976. *Capitalism in crisis*. London: Macmillan.
Goffman, E. 1961. *Asylums*. Harmondsworth: Penguin.
Goldberg, D. P. & B. Blackwell 1970. Psychiatric illness in general practice. *British Medical Journal* 2, 439–43.
Goldberg, D. P. & P. Huxley 1980. *Mental illness in the community*. London: Tavistock.
Goldberg, D. P. & R. Jones 1980. The costs and benefits of psychiatric care. In *The social consequences of psychiatric illness*, L. N. Robins, P. J. Clayton & J. K. Wing (eds.). New York: Brunner-Mazel.
Gore, C. P., K. Jones, W. Taylor & B. Ward 1964. Needs and beds. *Lancet* August 29, 457–60.
Gough, I. 1979. *The political economy of the welfare state*. London: Macmillan.
Grad, J. & P. Sainsbury 1968. The effects that patients have on their families in a community care and a control psychiatric service. *British Journal of Psychiatry* 114, 265–78.
GLC (Greater London Council) 1985. *Mental health services in London*. London: GLC.
Greer, A. L., S. Greer & T. Anderson 1983. The city's weakest dependents. In *Cities and sickness*, A. L. Greer & S. Greer (eds.). Beverly Hills: Sage.

Habermas, J. 1976. *Legitimation crisis*. London: Heinemann.
Hall, P. & R. Gillard 1982. The Worcester development project. *International Journal of Social Psychiatry* 28, 163–72.
Harbridge, E. 1984. Getting in touch with rural needs. *Remedial Therapist* 7, no. 21, June 29, 6.
Hassall, C. & C. F. Hellon 1964. Survey of a long-stay population in a psychiatric hospital. *British Journal of Psychiatry* 110, 183–5.
Henderson, D. K. 1964. *The evolution of psychiatry in Scotland*. Edinburgh: Livingstone.
Heptinstall, D. 1985. The great illusion? *Community Care* 583, October 17, 223.

HM Treasury 1986. *Government expenditure plans to 1988–9*. London: HMSO.

House of Commons Social Service Committee 1985. *Community care, with special reference to adult mentally ill and mentally handicapped people*. Social Services Committee Second Report (3 vols). London: HMSO.

Hyde, A. 1985. How much will we tolerate? *Health and Social Services Journal* **94** (4959), 949.

Iliffe, S. 1983. *The NHS: a picture of health?* London: Lawrence & Wishart.

Jones, K. 1972. *A history of the mental health services*. London: Routledge & Kegan Paul.

Judge, K. 1982. The growth and decline of public expenditure. In *Public expenditure and social policy*, A. Walker (ed.). London: Heinemann.

Klein, R. 1983. *The politics of the NHS*. London: Longman.

Laurance, J. 1985. The care no one knows how to give. *New Society* **74** (1194), November 15, 287.

Levine, M. 1981. *The history and politics of community mental health*. New York: Oxford University Press.

LHPC (London Health Planning Consortium) 1981. *Profile of services for the mentally ill in London*. London: HMSO.

Mangen, S. P. 1983. Cost effectiveness of community psychiatric nurse and out-patient psychiatrist care of neurotic patients. *Psychological Medicine* **13**, 407–16.

Mangen, S. P. & B. Rao 1985. United Kingdom: socialised system—better service? In *Mental health care in the European Community*, S. P. Mangen (ed.). London: Croom Helm.

Maynard, A. 1972. Inequalities in psychiatric care in England and Wales. *Social Science and Medicine* **6**, 221–7.

Miles, A. 1981. *The mentally ill in contemporary society*. Oxford: Martin Robertson.

MIND 1983. *Community concern*. London: MIND.

Ministry of Health 1962. *Hospital plan for England*. London: HMSO.

Ministry of Health 1963. *Health and welfare: the development of community care*. London: HMSO.

Mishra, R. 1984. *The welfare state in crisis*. Brighton: Wheatsheaf Books.

Mohan, J. & K. J. Woods 1985. Restructuring health care. *International Journal of Health Services* **15**, 197–217.

Morgan, M., M. Calnan & N. Manning 1985. *Sociological approaches to health and medicine*. London: Croom Helm.

Murray, N. 1981. Working together in Warrington. *Community Care* **392**, December 24, 9.

Offe, C. 1976. Political authority and class structures. In *Critical sociology*, P. Connerton (ed.). Harmondsworth: Penguin.

Offe, C. 1984. *Contradictions of the welfare state*. London: Heinemann.

Oxford RHA 1984. *Regional strategy 1984–94*. Oxford: Oxford RHA.

Parry-Jones, W. L. 1972. *The trade in lunacy*. London: Routledge & Kegan Paul.

Raafat, I. 1986. From hospital care to hostel residency. *Health Services Journal* May 22, 701.

Robinson, R. 1986. Restructuring the welfare state. *Journal of Social Policy* **15**, 1–21.

Rosen, G. 1968. *Madness in society*. Chicago: University of Chicago Press.

Royal Commission on the NHS 1979. *Report of the Royal Commission on the NHS* (Cmnd 7615). London: HMSO.

Ryan, P. 1979. Residential care for the mentally disabled. In *Community care for the mentally disabled*, J. K. Wing & R. Olsen (eds.). Oxford: Oxford University Press.

Scott, H. J. 1986. Accommodation for mentally ill people. *Housing Review* **35**, 10–13.

Scottish Home and Health Department 1985. *Mental health in focus*. Edinburgh: HMSO.

Scull, A. T. 1977. *Decarceration*. Englewood Cliffs, NJ: Prentice-Hall.

Scull, A. T. 1979. *Museums of madness*. London: Allen Lane.

Scull, A. T. 1983. The asylum as community and the community as asylum. In *Mental illness: changes and trends*, P. Bean (ed.). Chichester: Wiley.

Szelenyi, I. 1984. *Cities in recession*. Beverly Hills: Sage.

Tyne, A. 1978. *Review of progress in provision for mentally handicapped people*. London: MENCAP.

Vaughan, P. J. 1983. The disordered development of day care in psychiatry. *Health Trends* **15**, 91–4.

Vousden, M. 1985. Caring on the coast. *Nursing Mirror* **160** (6), February 6, 20–5.

Walker, A. 1984. *Social planning*. Oxford: Basil Blackwell & Martin Robertson.

Walkey, F. H., D. E. Green & A. J. W. Taylor 1981. Community attitudes to mental health. *Social Science & Medicine*, **15E**, 139–44.

Ward, L. 1986. From hospital to ordinary houses, ordinary streets. *Health Services Journal*, May 1, 601.

Watkin, B. 1978. *The NHS: the first phase*. London: Allen & Unwin.

Webb, A. & G. Wistow 1982. The personal social services: incrementalism, expediency or systematic social planning. In *Public expenditure and social policy*, A. Walker (ed.). London: Heinemann.

Welsh Office 1983. *All Wales strategy for the development of services for mentally handicapped people*. Cardiff: HMSO.

Wing, J. K. & G. W. Brown 1970. *Institutionalism and schizophrenia*. Cambridge: Cambridge University Press.

Wistow, G. 1984. Joint finance and community care. In *Health care UK 1984*, A. Harrison & J. Gretton (eds.). London: Chartered Institute of Public Finance and Accountancy.

Wistow, G. 1985. Community care for the mentally handicapped. In *Health care UK 1985*, A. Harrison & J. Gretton (eds.). Policy Journals.

Wistow, G. & B. Hardy 1986. Transferring care: do financial incentives work? In *Health care UK 1986*, A. Harrison & J. Gretton (eds.). Policy Journals.

Woods, K. J. 1983. The NHS in London. *London Journal* **9**, 165–83.

4 Recent trends in the political economy of mental health

PHIL BROWN

Mental health care in the past 25 years can best be conceptualized as various forms of transfer of care (Brown 1985). During the period, the traditional state-hospital inpatient wards ceased to be the primary location of mental health care. Community mental health centers (CMHCs), general hospitals, outpatient clinics, private psychiatric hospitals, and nursing and boarding homes grew in importance. What was once a clear-cut two-class system of public and private care also became less distinct, as public funds and private insurance opened up private facilities to a wider range of persons, and as new forms of government health planning intervened to coordinate a new *public–private allied sector*.

Chronic patient care has been transferred from the mental health system to other social service systems and to nonsystem settings. State-hospital deinstitutionalization represents an attempted transfer of financial responsibility from state to federal budgets. The relocation of chronic patients to nursing homes, boarding homes, homeless shelters, and the street is a transfer of social responsibility from professional psychiatric providers to low-quality, nonpsychiatric facilities. This relocation is also a transfer of responsibility from public to private authority. Further, it is a transfer of responsibility from state mental health departments to public health and public welfare departments. This transfer results in less attention to the psychiatric and psychological needs of patients. There has also been a transformation of the public perception of clients from mental patients to welfare cases, thus further devaluing them. As is most evident in nursing and boarding homes, the transfer of care often involves a shift of location, while keeping traditional forms of personal control and institutional rigidity. Within the mental health system, there has been the growth of private-sector care (especially general hospital psychiatric care) to replace or augment public services, especially for acute care. Even though this has largely centered around a new public–private alliance, it is a transfer of power and authority to a private sector which is less accountable to government and public scrutiny.

The details of this process have been traced in terms of three structural factors: political economy, professionalism, and institutional structures (Brown 1985). This chapter concentrates on a narrower slice, the political–

economic structure of mental health care, although it is often hard to isolate the three factors. In order to set the stage, there will be a brief discussion of the paucity of political–economic analysis of mental health care. Next will come a description of the well-known trends in state-hospital deinstitutionalization, the growth of community mental health centers, and the rise of nursing and boarding homes. Following that, the more recent developments in the public–private allied sector will be examined, especially with regard to general hospital psychiatric units and private psychiatric hospitals. Particular emphasis will be placed on the rationalizing and monopolizing tendencies in the mental health field, most noticeably evidenced in the prospective payment approach and in the spread of for-profit hospital chains in the psychiatric sector.

The paucity of political–economic analysis of the mental health system

The notion of a medical–industrial complex has been around for quite some time, beginning with radical, conflict analysts (Ehrenreich & Ehrenreich 1970, Kotelchuck 1975, Navarro 1976, Doyal 1981). Later, liberals adopted this theme, most notably Starr (1982) and Relman (1980). Currently, there is much concern among many practitioners that the monopolizing and rationalizing tendencies of the medical world will impinge on psychiatric practice styles and patient outcome. Interestingly, though, there has been very little application of political–economic analysis to the psychiatric sector (cf. Castel *et al*. 1982, Kovel 1980, Scull 1984, 1985).

This lag has been due in part to the fact that the mental health system previously was far less subject to the monopolizing and rationalizing forces which dominate health care. The public sector in psychiatry is far larger than in medicine; the service delivery is less amenable to capital-intensive, high-technology applications; there is far less of a medical supply market; and so much of mental health care is decentralized. The medical sector has far more surplus wealth than the mental health system, thus making it easier to institute rationalizing tendencies, such as prospective payment, in medicine. Mental health facilities lack the medical sector's ability to cut back on certain areas such as supplies and laboratory tests. Also, given the full occupancy typical of private-sector psychiatric beds, there has been less of the competitive marketing strategies seen in voluntary hospitals. In related fashion, there has been no regulatory drive to close down private-sector psychiatric beds. On the contrary, additional psychiatric beds have been created in recent years as a trade-off for closing down medical or surgical beds.

Health planning and regulation have had far less impact on mental health than on medical services. Until recently, mental health services were not so directly tied to the medical sector. Also, many mentally ill persons are cared for in nursing and boarding homes and welfare hotels, which fall under social welfare agencies. Mental health planning has been weak itself, and has been poorly integrated with health planning. Compared to health services, it is difficult to accurately break down the cost of psychiatric services. This especially holds true for chronic patients who move between many medical, psychiatric, and social-service agencies, as well as urban jails.

It is striking that, unlike medical services, mental health service planning is often concerned with the situation of chronic patients for whom little can be done. This is not to say that chronic patients are well served, for indeed they usually are not. But the mental health needs of the "normal" population are typically absent from planning discussions. This is markedly different from medicine, where chronic care is rarely addressed, and where most planning involves acute services (even though many acute services are in fact acute care for chronically ill persons). This may be due in part to the different levels on which planning takes place. Most planning involves *public-service provision*, as well as some *private-source regulation*. For the public services, medical care is typically organized at city or county levels. But for psychiatry, the state level is more typical, and the federal level is far more powerful (e.g., in CMHs) than in medicine (e.g., Neighborhood Health Centers).

Recent changes in the mental health system have made it harder to ignore political–economic forces. Mental health services are increasingly provided by and integrated with health facilities. Also, the monopolizing process has overtaken psychiatry, most notably in the expansion of for-profit hospital chains in psychiatric hospitals and general-hospital psychiatric beds. In tandem with this, both governmental and private third-party payers have sought to apply to mental health care some of the cutbacks and the rationalizing and cost–benefit approaches which are being employed in the health care sector. This is aided by the serious flaws in deinstitutionalization, and the subsequent legislative and public backlash.

Recently, psychiatric discussion has begun to deal with such issues, with articles appearing in psychiatry journals on topics such as "The industrialization of American psychiatry" (Bittker 1985) and "The medical industrial complex" (Rome 1985). It is not clear how widespread this awareness is, although professional literature is very concerned with diagnosis-related groups (DRGs), which reimburse hospitals prospectively on an average-cost basis. Also, mental health professionals have long been critical of cutbacks and retrenchments, while still being unaware of the structures underlying the psychiatric system's operations. In order to examine the trends which may be finally setting off these alarms, it is best to look at an overview of political–economic currents during the past quarter-century era of mental health policy.

An overview of trends in the post World War II era

In the past 25 years, the mental health system has changed in such facets as location of treatment, type of treatment, length of stay, and number of admissions. Following the introduction of psychotropic drugs in 1955, the state-hospital population showed its first decline ever in the century-long constant rise in census (though factors other than drugs laid the foundation for that change). In 1955, 77% of all psychiatric episodes were inpatient, and the remainder were outpatient. By 1975, inpatient episodes were only 27%, outpatient episodes 70%, and day treatment 3%; this breakdown has remained stable since (Witkin 1980).

State hospitals are no longer the major location of total psychiatric episodes, or even of inpatient episodes, as they were in 1955 when they accounted for 49% of all episodes. By 1971, they were down to 19%, and the new CMHCs continued their climb to provide for 29% of total episodes while state hospitals fell to 9%. In 1977, CMHCs accounted for almost one-third of all episodes (Witkin 1980). If we count only inpatient episodes, we see that public and private general hospitals combined, including both psychiatric and nonpsychiatric units, account for 60% of episodes, and state hospitals only 19% (Kiesler & Sibulkin 1982).

Much of the background to these alterations is economic. Although anti-custodial beliefs and new treatment advances played important roles, the bottom line of mental health care was also the bottom line of the ledger. State hospitals, the old mainstay of the system, were far too costly. The National Association of State Mental Health Program Directors (NASMHPD) considers that the state mental health departments have a "$6 billion industry." State governments provide $4.6 billion of these funds, Medicaid $1 billion, and federal block grants for CMHCs $463 million (Jennings 1983). If we look at all sources of direct costs for 1980, the low estimate is $19.2 billion, and the high estimate $22 billion; the latter figure equals 7.7% of all health costs (Frank & Kamlet 1985). Given these high expenditures, states attempted to reduce their censuses and to use other types of services. Much of the cost savings represented a transfer of costs from state budgets to local and federal ones. An additional set of economic forces is the power of entrepreneurial segments, especially nursing homes, boarding homes, and for-profit private psychiatric hospitals. These facilities were able to gain by providing services which had only become recently reimbursable, and which were not being provided by the public sector. In addition, nonprofit facilities such as general hospitals and residential community facilities also filled the cracks left by a retreating and retrenching public sector. General hospitals have also grown in importance by opening up psychiatric beds in exchange for the closing down of excess medical or surgical beds which grew out of rampant hospital expansion.

GROWTH OF NURSING AND BOARDING HOMES IN MENTAL HEALTH CARE

Nursing homes, boarding homes, and single-room occupancies (SROs) are the largest locus of mental health "care" and expenditure. This is one of the principal legacies of the national mental health policy, and a clear sign of that policy's failure. Close to one million mentally disabled persons live in nursing and boarding homes, compared to the 1980 state-hospital inpatient census of under 138,000. This is the major transinstitutionalization in the psychiatric delivery systems, and represents the most dramatic transfer of care for the mental health system to the public welfare and public health systems. Whereas in 1963, 53% of elderly mentally ill persons were in homes and 47% in state hospitals, by 1969 the ratio had changed dramatically, with 75% of elderly mentally ill in homes and only 25% in state hospitals (NIMH 1977).

The magnitude of nursing home expenditure is clear as early as 1971, with nursing homes making up 28% of total direct care costs at that time, and a slightly higher 29.2% in 1974. This form of transinstitutionalization has been going on since the 1960s, although it is only in the past five or ten years that the phenomenon has been clearly noticed. The $4.24 billion spent in 1974 on nursing-home care outpaced the $2.75 billion spent on state-hospital care. The bar graph in Figure 4.1 provides an excellent visual representation of this data. By 1978, Medicare and Medicaid together paid for $8.4 billion of the $15.8 billion nursing-home costs. Medicaid has paid for a growing portion of the nursing-home costs, and such costs have also become a larger percentage of all Medicaid costs. In 1972, nursing-home bills took 23% of all Medicaid spending, in 1976 33%, and in 1978 34% (Lerman 1982: 184–8). Table 4.1 shows Medicaid expenditure for mental health services.

Table 4.1 Medicaid expenditures for mental health services, 1977/8 fiscal year (in millions of dollars).

public and private psychiatric hospitals	558
general hospital (inpatient and outpatient) and emergency services	185
Community Mental Health Centers (CMHCs)	100
private free-standing clinics	25
private practitioners	82
nursing homes	2,189
residential treatment centers and children's programs	110
drugs	110
total	3,389

Source: President's Commission on Mental Health (1978), Vol. 11: 520.

Note: $720 million for nursing homes serving primarily mentally retarded people is not included in this table.

As pointed out earlier, precipitous discharge and stringent admissions practices were largely attempts to transfer state costs to federal Medicaid,

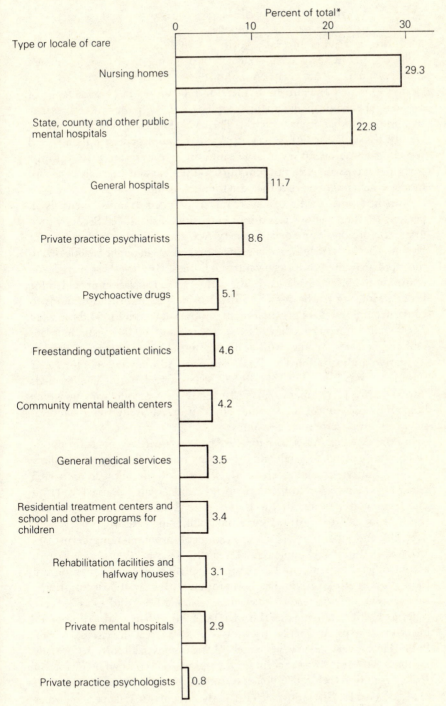

Percent of total*

Type or locale of care

Nursing homes — 29.3

State, county and other public mental hospitals — 22.8

General hospitals — 11.7

Private practice psychiatrists — 8.6

Psychoactive drugs — 5.1

Freestanding outpatient clinics — 4.6

Community mental health centers — 4.2

General medical services — 3.5

Residential treatment centers and school and other programs for children — 3.4

Rehabilitation facilities and halfway houses — 3.1

Private mental hospitals — 2.9

Private practice psychologists — 0.8

*Estimated total expenditures for direct care were $14.5 billion

Figure 4.1   Percent distribution of expenditures for direct care of the mentally ill by type or locale of care, United States, 1974

Source: Levine and Willner (1976).

Medicare, and Supplemental Security Income funding, and also to local welfare spending. As a result of a lack of planning and foresight, mental health planners did not create enough alternative care facilities to provide a choice other than the nursing home: nor did CMHCs offer a wide range of services for chronic mental patients which might keep them in less restrictive and custodial environments. The availability of federal payment, largely through Medicaid, has attracted the enterprising nursing- and boarding-home operators. At the same time, federal and private third-party payers usually will not reimburse outpatient and alternative service modes which might obviate the need for nursing-home care.

Nursing homes in the USA were never intended to house mentally ill persons. Rather, they were a minor extension of the Social Security program. Before the 1935 Social Security Act, there were very few nursing homes. The Act's exclusion of benefits for recipients in public facilities led to the rapid growth of proprietary nursing homes. By 1939 there were 1,200 homes with 25,000 residents. In the early 1950s, legislation provided for Federal Housing Authority and Small Business Administration funds to construct and renovate private nursing homes. Thus, by 1954 there were 7,000 skilled nursing facilities (SNFs), containing 180,000 beds. In 1956, lobbying efforts by the American Nursing Homes Association won legislative authorization for Small Business Administration mortgages (Lerman 1982: 214). By 1961, 9,582 SNFs existed, with 330,981 beds (Stotsky 1969: 12; Kramer 1977). These figures only account for SNFs which hold about 65% of the total homes population. Also important is federal financing support for nursing homes.

In 1960, Medical Assistance for the Aged provided payments for public and private general hospitals and for nursing homes. Two years later, new Health, Education and Welfare (HEW) regulations allowed under-65 persons to receive Aid to the Permanently and Totally disabled (APTD) if they were convalescing after a hospital stay (Lerman 1982: 89–90). As a result, from 1960 to 1970 nursing home facilities increased by 1400%, beds by 232%, and patients by 210% (Senate Subcommittee on Long Term Care 1976: xiii). In 1972, Supplemental Security Income (SSI) was initiated; among other things, it would absorb APTD benefit categories. This program took effect in 1974, providing a boon for entrepreneurial boarding-home owners who did not need to meet more exacting Medicaid and Medicare criteria for skilled nursing care (Lerman 1982: 94). Adequate data for boarding homes are sparse, since licensing laws are so lax, if at all existent. A 1965 Public Health Service survey counted 18,958 homes of all sorts nationwide (Stotsky 1969: 10). A more recent survey (NIMH 1977) counted a 1973 total of 15,737 facilities with 1,075,900 residents, excluding the lowest level of boarding homes. Glasscote et al. (1976: 23–5) report 16,150 nursing homes and 7,000 boarding homes, for a total of 23,150 facilities.

According to governmental reports (Senate Subcommittee on Long

Term Care 1976) and health service researchers (Glasscote *et al.* 1976), the profitability of the nursing-home industry is obtained by low quality of care, understaffing, brutality, and widespread use of psychoactive drugs. As a result, nursing and boarding homes have come to be considered a prime example of inhumane treatment of the socially undesirable population. In studying 46 California nursing homes, Fottler *et al.* (1981) found that there was an inverse relationship between profitability and quality of care. To date, there has been only one controlled prospective study of the outcomes of psychiatric patients who are randomly assigned to nursing homes on continued hospitalization. In an eight-hospital Veterans Administration study, Linn *et al.* (1985) found significant deterioration among nursing-home placements in the areas of self-care behavior, mental confusion, depression, and satisfaction with care. While the nursing-home annual cost per patient is about $10,000 less than in hospitalization, the detrimental outcomes are a poor exchange.

CREATION OF A PUBLIC–PRIVATE ALLIED SECTOR
Two decades ago, when the CMHC program was developed, there was a clear demarcation of public and private mental health sectors. Public-sector patients were cared for in state hospitals, in some psychiatric wards of municipal hospitals, and in the remnants of the few urban psycopathic hospitals. Private-sector patients were cared for in private psychiatric hospitals and a very few general-hospital psychiatric units; those not requiring hospitalization were seen as outpatients in office psychiatry. A patient could either afford private care, or was forced to rely on low-cost or free public care. Health insurance was not generally available for psychiatric coverage, and federal reimbursements were not yet in place. Little, if any, crossover existed between the public and private sectors.

This separation has been changed in the past two decades, both consciously and inadvertently, leading to a complex public–private mix in which private facilities tend to care for the acutely ill and public facilities for the chronically ill. The private sector is no longer composed primarily of more well-to-do persons. One reason for this is the growth of private and governmental reimbursements. Secondly, CMHCs often have collaborative structures, in which public CMHCs contract out to private facilities for some services, especially inpatient care. Thirdly, state health-planning agencies have allowed bed "trade-offs," whereby surplus medical–surgical beds are closed in exchange for the opening of more psychiatric beds. While these factors have increased the number of private facilities, they have also boosted utilization of these private facilities by the less well-to-do. When one looks at the overall national cost of psychiatric care, it is evident that public expenditures have not declined, but that they have shifted the range of public and private facilities which they support (Brown 1985: 47–73).

Reimbursement biases played a large role in this new system. Medicaid excludes CMHCs and many mental health clinic services. Further, for recipients between 21 and 65, Medicaid covers care in private general-hospital psychiatric units but not in private psychiatric hospitals. Similarly, Medicare limits psychiatric hospital inpatient care to a lifetime maximum of 190 days, but covers 90 days for each illness in a general-hospital service. Again, no CMHC outpatient or partial treatment is covered. Thus, the two major federal health programs favor general-hospital psychiatric wards. Private commercial and Blue Cross insurance favor both private psychiatric hospitals and general-hospital psychiatric wards (Comptroller General 1977).

To see how these practices have favored the growth of the private sector, it is necessary to look at recent increases in these facilities. From 1968 to 1972 the only private psychiatric hospitals that opened were for-profit institutions, which increased by 34%, while nonprofit hospitals declined by 3%. Of the 42 new profit-making facilities, all but one were corporate (as opposed to individual or partnership structures) and half of those were part of multihospital chains (Taube & Redick 1976). Over the 1970–80 period, the total of private hospitals rose from 150 to 184, an increase of 22% (NIMH 1982). Two-thirds of these are proprietary, and two-thirds of these proprietaries are part of chains. From 1980 to 1982, chain-owned hospitals rose from 25% to 43% of all private hospitals (Levenson 1983). In one year alone, 1982–3, investor-owned psychiatric hospitals increased from 106 to 151, a 42.5% growth, with a 28.4% increase in beds, from 11,201 to 14,384 (Gaylin 1985). Eighty-three percent of the chain facilities are in the hands of the four largest chains (Levenson 1983). Health Corporation of America, the largest hospital chain (with a 1984 income of $4.2 billion), owns 25 psychiatric hospitals. National Medical Enterprises owns 22, with Community Psychiatric Centers and Charter Medical Corporation slightly behind. The chains have been particularly aggressive in obtaining mental hospitals. When chain-owned mental hospitals are added to psychiatric beds in chain-owned general hospitals, those multihospital firms own over 50% of nongovernment psychiatric beds in the nation, which is far greater than the 15% of nongovernmental acute general hospital beds owned by the chains (Salmon 1985). Psychiatric hospitals are pursued by hospital corporations since they have good profit margins, and their investment costs average $60,000 per bed, compared to $140,000 per bed in medicine (Gaylin 1985).

General-hospital psychiatric wards have increased markedly during the community mental health era. From 1964 to 1970 they increased from 538 to 766 wards nationwide, a 42.4% increase. From 1970 to 1980 they grew to 923 wards, a slower increase of 19% (NIMH 1972, 1982). If we add to this figure the general-hospital units in Veterans Administration (VA) hospitals and those which serve as CMHC affiliates, the number rises to 1,010 units, according to the American Hospital Association's 1978 survey (Flamm 1981). This growth has been all in the private sector. From 1971 to 1977, inpatient additions in private hospitals jumped 36.8% while they fell 37.0% in public ones. In 1977 there were nearly three times as many inpatients in private general-hospital psychiatric wards as in public ones, almost double the public : private ratio in 1971 (NIMH 1972, Witkin 1981). Further, most of the patients treated in general hospitals are cared for in hospitals without separate psychiatric units: this is a rapidly growing location of mental health care in recent years (Kiesler & Sibulkin 1982).

Apart from CMHC affiliations for their own inpatient care, the early growth of general-hospital psychiatry appears to have been planned more by general hospitals than by mental health planners. Then, mental health administrators were often confronted with the fact that these private institutions provided more reliable care, without many of the bureaucratic entanglements of the public system. The state officials began to look at private facilities as services with which to contract for state-paid services. This enabled the state mental health departments to provide certain programs without having to start them from scratch, a strategy well in place from years of CMHC affiliation agreements. State governments also were attracted by the opportunity to reduce the state's permanent payroll and its future pension costs, and to deal with what are in many states largely non-union private facilities.

Another factor in the expansion of private psychiatric facility use by state Departments of Mental Health is the crisis in general-hospital overbedding. As health policy analysts have understood for some time, hospital competition for physicians and patients has resulted in overbedding. State "determination of need" programs came too late and could only stem future bed expansion. In Massachusetts in 1979, for instance, there were 3,500–5,000 surplus acute medical–surgical beds, and yet approximately 800 beds in psychiatric units of 36 general hospitals and 770 beds in seven psychiatric hospitals had long waiting lists. Conversion of medical beds to psychiatric beds has thus begun in earnest. Here we see how a major mental health development stems from the political-economic forces in the health sector which produced overbedding.

The alliance of public and private sectors in general-hospital psychiatric wards allows for some indigent, working-class and lower-middle-class persons to benefit from the more dynamic treatments offered in private general hospitals. But the public general hospitals remain overcrowded with the poorer elements of society, many of whom are recent state-hospital discharges. Even with the current alterations in the mental health system, public general hospitals have poorer, more disturbed patients, with an evenly distributed male : female ratio, and paid for largely by Medicare and Medicaid. However, private general hospitals serve less disturbed, more well-off persons, with a higher proportion of women, and are largely paid by Blue Cross and commercial insurance (Heimann 1980, Bachrach 1981).

Another important trend is the care of mentally ill persons in non-psychiatric settings. We have already discussed this in terms of the major role of nursing and boarding homes. As mentioned earlier, general hospitals *without* psychiatric wards serve twice as many inpatients as general hospitals *with* psychiatric units (Regier *et al.* 1978). Also, general-hospital emergency rooms are taking on a significant psychiatric burden, as de-institutionalization and related policies lead to less service provision by the specialty mental health sector (Bassuk 1980).

Given the huge number of psychiatric episodes seen outside regular psychiatric facilities, the public–private mix is even more salient. Third-party payments to the general medical sector by Medicare, Medicaid, and by local, state, and federal employees' insurance plans play a major role in the expansion of treatment in nonpsychiatric facilities.

New trends in the 1980s

In the 1980s, existing trends in mental health policy continue. Most notably, the proprietization of psychiatric hospitals and general-hospital psychiatric beds has become one of the most prominent features; but there has been a qualitative change associated with the Reagan administration's cutbacks, particularly involving block grants, DRGs, and with new waves of cutbacks in private insurance and governmental programs. Further, corporations are increasingly fashioning their approaches to mental health on cost-cutting models.

GOVERNMENT LIMITATONS AND CUTBACKS

Mental health cutbacks have threatened the major national effort at providing mental health care; the community mental health centers. CMHCs had finally begun to move towards fulfilling their mandate of serving all mental health needs in their areas. After their first decade of rather selective client service, centers began to better serve more chronic, seriously ill patients, under prodding by the 1975 CMHC amendments and by widespread public, professional, and governmental criticism. Unfortunately, as soon as that trend got under way, new fiscal policies threatened its continuation. This stemmed from state and federal cutbacks resulting from the so-called fiscal crisis, and from the specific action of the 1981 Omnibus Budget Reconciliation Act (OBRA), which repealed the original 1963 CMHC Act, its various amendments, and the 1980 Mental Health Systems Act.

The OBRA instituted block grants to replace categorical funding, and reduced alcohol, drug abuse, and mental health funding by 21% in the first fiscal year (1982/83), a 30% cut if inflation is taken into account (Estes & Wood 1984). It is difficult to assess the impact of block grants as a cutback mechanism, since the federal government no longer funds specific services such as CMHCs; nor does it collect appropriate national data, or require states to collect uniform data. This makes it difficult for the public and professions to gauge needs and services, and represents a severe relinquishing of federal responsibility (Okin 1984).

The best data therefore come not from NIMH but from surveys of CMHCs: one by the American Psychological Association of 223 centers; one by the National Council of Community Mental Health Centers (NCCMHC) of 104 centers; one by Estes & Wood (1984) of 32 centers; and a two-wave study of 71 centers by Jerrell & Larsen (1985). CMHCs have been hurt financially—nearly half suffered deterioration in the first two block grant years. For 38% of centers, clinical services have been negatively affected, as smaller staffs dealt with larger caseloads and fewer service modes. Most staff attrition occurred in 1982, and by 1983 staffing leveled off at a 15% reduction. The remaining workers have been subject to higher workloads and increased productivity demands. More services for chronic patients have been offered, since states exercise more control over center operations and can therefore pressure centers to meet this pressing state mandate. But once they made some shifts in this direction, centers' increase in outpatient services have targeted privately paying clients. Many centers have altered their legal corporate structure to create a two-class system of public and private care. This is particularly striking in light of the great emphasis in 1960s planning to abolish the old two-class system. Access declined as centers closed satellite clinics. Consultation, education, and prevention programs have been reduced as well. Rather than concentrate on clinical issues, many CMHCs have focused on management innovations and stricter billing and collection. Centers have sought caseloads of clients who can pay out of pocket or through insurance, have increased fees, and have become entrepreneurial in such activities as selling employee-assistance programs to private firms and specialty services to other agencies. Center directors do not totally disparage the changes resulting from block grants. Many support efficiency moves, entrepreneurial directions, and increased staff commitment (Estes & Wood 1984, Okin 1984, Jerrell & Larsen 1985).

Interestingly, a survey of all state mental health authorities finds that those bodies assess the problems far less severely (Logan *et al.* 1985). This is perhaps a function of their different vantage points, since the DMHs are in charge of serving all mental health facilities in the state and are therefore less sensitive to specific cuts. Further, states are able to reassert much of the state control previously lost to the federal government (NIMH). This may be appealing to many state officials, for whom state federal relations can be equally or more salient than specific service issues (Estes & Wood 1984, Okin 1984, Jerrell & Larsen 1985).

In addition to direct reductions in mental health funding, other cutbacks have hurt. The end of the Comprehensive Employment and Training Act (CETA) removed many job prospects for CMHC patients. Not only did this harm clients' needs for training, work, and income, but it reduced fees that employed persons might otherwise pay to centers. States have failed to make up the missing federal CMHC funds, and have themselves made cuts in Medicaid which have reduced services and increased copayments (Estes & Wood 1984).

Medicaid cutbacks for many medical services have accelerated in recent years. In psychiatry, there are two main forms of this in general-hospital psychiatric care: maximum length of stay per admission, and maximum daily charge. Frank & Kessler (1984) expect that this will lead to premature discharge, or to keeping some patients in the hospitals where they will run up bad debts. A further likelihood is that hospitals will share financial risks by spreading charges with Blue Cross and commercial insurance payments, thus leading to the situation whereby insured patients subsidize Medicaid patients. In addition, hospitals may develop criteria to screen out those patients with a high probability of longer stay. Once the selective admissions and dumping become evident, CMHCs and other agencies will probably triage patients away from Medicaid-reimbursable settings and into state hospitals. This will shift costs back to the state, reversing a long-term trend in the other direction. As Frank & Kessler (1984) write, "The recent Medicaid changes are likely to produce a movement of patients resembling reinstitutionalization. This probable outcome conflicts with the state and federal policy of the past 30 years that has deemphasized the role of the mental hospital." This will be, they continue, an incentive to return to the two-class system from which mental health care had only just begun to emerge.

For chronic patients, government cutbacks have been attempted through blatantly inappropriate curtailment of SSI benefits. In a one-month period in 1981, the Social Security Administration reviewed 436,308 cases and terminated 40% of them. Half of the terminated cases appealed against the rulings and, of those, 67.2% were reinstated. Many recipients were quite obviously severely disabled. Of New York State terminations, 42% were persons with mental troubles (Kihss 1982). Mental health advocates have opposed this policy, and, in one jurisdiction, have been successful. Federal District Judge Earl Larson in Minneapolis ordered the Social Security Administration to restore benefits to mentally ill persons who had been denied payments since March 1981, and to pay retroactive benefits. He also ordered the SSA to cease using strict guidelines for eligibility which violated constitutional due process (*New York Times* December 25, 1982). In response to tremendous objections and much litigation, the Department of Health and Human Services announced that 200,000 recipients would be exempt from eligibility review. Among this number are 135,000 persons diagnosed as psychotic (*Mental Disability Law Reporter* 1983).

Underlying these cutbacks are several trends. First, the federal government is trying to reverse the earlier transfer of care from state to federal funds. Secondly, the government seeks to reduce social spending across the board, and mentally disabled people are perhaps the least likely to protest. Thirdly, the policy-makers hold a low opinion of the chronically mentally ill, seeing them as a welfare burden and largely undeserving group (Scull 1985).

INSURANCE LIMITATIONS AND CUTBACKS

There has been a recent reversal of past expansion in insurance coverage through Blue Cross or Blue Shield and commercial insurers. A 1980 survey by the Health Insurance Association of America showed that, of persons covered for mental health care, 65% were insured in full for hospital charges in 1980, as compared with 80% insured in full in 1975 (Ruby 1984). Massachusetts Blue Shield filed an amicus brief in the US Supreme Court seeking to overturn a state's power to mandate mental health coverage. The same Blue Shield was overruled by the state insurance commissioner when it tried to withhold benefits from certain diagnostic categories such as "uncomplicated bereavement" and "marital problems." The insurer believed that Massachusetts residents are "aberrant" in using too much therapy, and that Blue Shield's reliance on DSM III categories is merely in keeping with what the mental health field sees as a standard consensus (Foreman 1985).

Reductions in the Federal Employees Health Plan (FEHB) have been significant as well, particularly since the FEHB was once considered a standard of good psychiatric coverage. In the 1980–83 period, mental illness cutbacks were far larger than those for physical illness, according to a survey of the 16 major plans in the federal system. Hustead et al. (1985) report that Blue Cross and Blue Shield reduced coverage of inpatient care to 60 days (high-option plan) or 30 days (low-option plan), and reduced outpatient benefits to 70% of up to 50 visits (high-option) or 75% of up to 25 visits (low-option). The letter carrier's plan reduced outpatient benefits from 80% of up to $5,000 to 50% of up to $1,250. In a hypothetical calculation of reimbursement for $10,000 of care, there would be up to a four-fold disparity between physical and psychiatric reimbursement; for $100,000 of care, the disparity could reach 30-fold (Hustead et al. 1985).

Insurers balk at attempts to increase the mandated minimum coverage for outpatient mental health benefits. They argue that costs will increase by the same factor as the increased mandates; thus, they assume a doubling of the mandated minimum from $500 to $1,000 (as is proposed in Massachusetts) would double the insurers' outlay. However, health economists estimate that the insurance firms would only increase their outlay by 65%. Further, more appropriate treatment under a raised mandate can replace use of other medical facilities or inpatient psychiatric services (Frisman et al. 1985). This logic of an offset phenomenon is crucial to expansion in mental health coverage, and has been frequently raised in recent years.

A further element of these cutbacks is that they are aided, though probably not impelled, by a devaluation of the importance of mental health care. For chronically ill people, this devaluation involves their being recasted as welfare cases, since much of their support comes from the welfare sector. For acutely ill persons, treatment is seen as only valuable for those who can afford it by virtue of their better benefits which accrue from a more important position in society. And for persons seeking psychotherapy for nonserious problems, treatment is seen as a frill or a personal indulgence in an era when such things are frowned upon.

Whereas direct governmental and insurance cutbacks are more obviously unfair and even punitive, there are other forms of retrenchment which stem from a pseudoscientific attempt to rationalize the financing and delivery of health care. The rationalizing approach is found in health maintenance organizations (HMOs), employee-assistance programs (EAPs), and prospective payments systems such as Medicare's diagnosis-related groups (DRGs).

MENTAL HEALTH CARE IN HMOs

A key factor in providing mental health coverage in HMOs is the "offset" phenomenon, whereby mental health services reduce medical utilization and even medical costs. HMOs can provide low-cost mental health care since staff are usually salaried and have no vested interest in continued treatment. Management can force professionals to ration care, treatment goals are oriented to "return to function" rather than "personality reconstruction," many nonmedical staff are used, much group therapy is used, and management can make plans based on the relatively known homogeneity of the group plan's population (McGuire 1981). While HMOs have proven that they can reduce medical utilization (Jones & Vischi 1979) it is not yet clear if their low-cost mental health services still cost less than the medical care which would otherwise be provided. A positive cost "offset" has been found for certain chronic medical conditions in the Blue Cross/Blue Shield Federal Employees Plan. Mental health care of 7–20 visits reduced the amount and cost of medical care to persons with airflow limitation disease, diabetes, ischemic heart disease, and hypertension, by the third year following diagnosis (Schlesinger et al. 1983). But offset studies have typically failed to take into account the cost of the mental health care itself. Even if psychiatric care reduces both medical utilization and medical charges, when mental health charges are included, the offset gain is wiped out and the treated patients' overall charges are greater (Borus et al. 1985).

An interesting point about the rash of offset studies is that they are concerned solely with utilization and cost. Nothing is said about the appropriateness or quality of care, with one important exception. The HMO reliance on short-term therapy has led to an ideological stance which argues that such brief treatment is in fact more therapeutic to most patients than is long-term psychotherapy. This is important to note, since it demonstrates how the power of third-party reimbursement can alter what is considered good practice.

The HMOs, like other insurers, have been reluctant to expand their range of covered services: HMOs are commonly understood to limit access to care in order to spend less of their capitation premiums. They may be limiting services to people who really need care, and therefore working against better mental health. Federal regulations for federally-qualified HMOs require the plans to provide up to 20 outpatient mental health visits, but not inpatient care. Some 20 states add their own requirements, such as a $500 outpatient mandate and a 30-day inpatient benefit (Levin & Glasser 1984). In fact, only 23% of all HMOs offer more than the 20-visit minimum (Cheifetz & Salloway 1984).

Despite the manner in which HMOs have rationalized and streamlined their mandated psychiatric care, the Reagan administration has nevertheless argued that the 1973 HMO Act requirements for mental health services should be retracted, since they increase utilization and cost (Chiefetz & Salloway 1984).

EMPLOYEE-ASSISTANCE PROGRAMS AND OTHER CORPORATE MENTAL HEALTH PLANS

Employee-assistance programs (EAPs) and other corporate mental health plans, such as HMO mental health services, are based on a cost–effectiveness model. As one variety of industrial psychology and psychiatry, EAPs seek to reduce corporate and governmental loss of time, material, productivity, and personnel, while providing counseling and referral services. More recently, firms are pursuing the HMO medical offset phenomonen. On their own or with state Blue Cross or Blue Shield organziations, companies are expanding mental health benefits and "wellness" programs to cut health costs (Mervis 1985). While largely concerned with alcoholism, a good number of EAPs provide mental health services as well. Financially, EAPs may provide some hospitals and CMHCs with marketable services to sell to the private sector. Further, there is a growing number of private concerns who sell their services to companies which cannot or do not wish to set up their own EAPs. There is the possibility that this may provide a new mental health growth industry. As EAPs proliferate, there are two major concerns. First, confidentiality is clearly an issue since the professional helper works for the firm, not the client. Secondly, the professional's loyalty to the firm makes him or her less able to ally with the client, particularly since part of the EAP's mission is to ensure smooth corporate operation and efficiency.

THE IMPACT OF DRGs

Diagnosis-related groups (DRGs) for Medicare reimbursement have had more of an impact on medicine than on psychiatry[1]. Psychiatric hospitals are all exempt, and most general-hospital psychiatric units apply for exemptions, which they usually receive. However, there is much worry that DRGs will become standard practice in the near future. At the end of 1985, the Health Care Financing Administration will report to Congress on whether the psychiatric exemption should be maintained. Much discussion is taking place in the mental health fields concerning this threat. Further, prospective reimbursement will probably be extended to other third-party payers in the future, and the DRG challenge is thus perceived as the forefront of a thrust to curtail mental health care.

The DRG approach seeks to standardize and rationalize the manner in which patients are admitted and treated. This is hard enough to do with medical care, and even harder with mental health care. Much of the appeal of DRG models is that costs can be cut in an administratively easy fashion which has scientific overtones, and which pits hospital against hospital.

Much has been written and spoken of the fact that DRGs were developed out of a single database which might not be sufficient for generalization. In terms of psychiatry this involves an important feature: the DRG database did not differentiate between general hospitals with and without psychiatric units. There are more episodes in general hospitals without such specialty units, a ratio of 1.6 : 1. Since the actual length of stay in hospitals with units (16.7 days) is 31% higher than in nonunit hospitals (12.7 days), the DRG system is inequitable, perhaps providing a windfall to nonunit institutions and a financial burden to those with units. This may also cause clinical problems, since patients in unit hospitals are more seriously ill and require more care; yet the DRG system would force them out prematurely. Indeed, there is already evidence of early transfer to state hospitals (Taube et al. 1985, English et al. 1986).

While DRGs account for only 30% of the variance in length of stay across all 467 DRG categories, the 15 DRGs for alcoholism, drug abuse, and mental health (ADM) categories explain an even lower 7.6% of the variance. This is because the diagnostic groups are not sufficiently homogeneous within categories and not sufficiently heterogeneous between categories. Even when psychiatric biometricians used a national probability sample to re-calculate a set of unofficial DRGs for the ADM categories, they were only able to explain 12% of variance. As Taube et al. (1984) note, there are simply too many unmeasured variables, such as differing practice style, treatment philosophy, patient characteristics, and local demand for beds. In the American Psychiatric Association Task Force on Prospective Payment Study (English et al. 1986), only 5.6% of the variance in length of stay was explained by the nine psychiatric DRGs. This can be understood by looking at the coefficient of variation, which measures homogeneity. None of the psychiatric DRGs had a coefficient of variation less than 0.94, and 55% had coefficients in excess of 1.00. When all psychiatric DRGs are grouped together, the coefficient is 1.019, compared to 0.954 for medical and 0.808 for surgical cases (English et al. 1986).

Mental health providers fear for the detrimental effects of DRGs. While most of those fears are based on logical intuition and forecasting, there is some actual related evidence from New Jersey's DRG system and from Medicaid limitations. In New Jersey's statewide DRG plan, psychiatry has been included. While length of stay and costs are down, hospitals have had to make staff reductions in nursing, psychotherapy, recreational therapy and art therapy (Ruby 1984). Medicaid limitations on the number of days covered per episode has been found to result in increased discharge from general-hospital psychiatric units to state hospitals (Frank & Lave 1985). Planners and providers believe that more of such dumping will occur. Restrictive practices may, in fact, start at the other end, as hospitals practise patient-skimming. General hospitals and psychiatric hospitals would be likely to refuse admission to patients who appear to need more resources, leaving these sicker, less "profitable" patients to the state hospital system. Hospitals will also probably try to shift costs from Medicare patients to other patients by raising their fees. Finally, quality of care is likely to suffer as hospitals curtail more expensive services (Widem *et al.* 1984). Some observers predict that providers will set more modest treatment goals and will encourage more electro-convulsive therapy (ECT) (Fogel & Slaby 1985).

Although DRGs are largely perceived as detrimental, hospitals may be forced to improve certain aspects of their work. For example, they may elect to fully staff wards seven days a week, may establish their own nursing home or halfway house, or at least consult to such local after-care facilities (Fogel & Slaby 1985). Such possibilities are perhaps desirable, but probably not plausible, given the general tendency of nongrowth in mental health services. Despite any indirect benefits, such as mentioned above, prospective payment systems threaten to severely curtail appropriate treatment for many patients. Particularly for chronically ill patients, DRGs represent much abandonment of care.

EFFECTS ON PROVIDERS AND PATIENTS
It is true that new third-party payer systems have strong effects on admission and treatment decisions, and clinicians are wise to point out the negative effects. But this debate should not be so one-sided, since clinicians and administrators have a history of selective practices. "Creaming" of less disturbed patients occurred before any significant third-party payments existed. This makes it even harder for clinicians to fight the new trend, since they themselves operated previously in similar fashion: and it makes even more clear the reason why matters of political economy cannot be discussed in isolation from issues of professionalism.

A very clear connection between professional practice and political economy can be seen in the matter of licensing, and of the intraprofessional and interprofessional rivalry concerning it. Licensing is completely a creature of third-party payments, since it would not be required otherwise. Psychologists and social workers have, in various states, obtained the legal right to bill directly for mental health services. This process leads to intra-professional rivalry between licensed and unlicensed providers. It also leads to interprofessional rivalry, as each professional tries to restrict others further down the hierarchy from becoming reimbursable. Because of re-imbursement practices, providers are encouraged to develop a false consciousness concerning what is proper professional ability, and the disciplines are further set against each other. Such developments are bound to reduce the time and energy expended on patient care. Professionals will also be increasingly caught in cross-pressures between proper practice and business practice. Incentives for shorter length of stay may lead to precipi-tous discharge. In psychiatry, this is of particular interest, since a prior policy—deinstitutionalization—so easily led to inappropriate discharge.

For patients, proprietarization and rationalization can limit access for Medicaid patients and other indigent persons. Services which do not generate enough surplus can be discontinued, and more seriously ill patients may be denied care (Kennedy 1985). It has always been hard to measure actual psychiatric outcomes, and no data presently inform us of specific problems areas. But the growing concern of mental health providers, such as those mentioned earlier in the CMHC surveys, indicate the likelihood of diminished care.

Conclusions

This chapter has examined the political economy of mental health care, focusing on three main areas: (1) increasing absorption into the health sector; (2) corporatization of mental health care, and (3) maintenance and/or acceleration of already existing transfers of care away from traditional set-tings and responsibilities. For those familiar with trends in the political economy of the health care sector, this discussion on the mental health care sector will not be very surprising. Nonetheless, little effort has been put into applying medical–political economy to mental health, and such efforts are long overdue. For those unfamiliar with the general medical–political economy framework, it is hoped that the analysis put forth here will explain what might otherwise seem a random and unconnected set of features of the system.

It is important to understand that the mental health field is being pulled more and more into the health care mainstream, and that it is undergoing the same sorts of corporate rationalizing pressures as the health sector. As a result we can expect to see major shifts in locations of care, structures of facilities and agencies, and professional beliefs and practices. There is much room for concern about these developments, especially as they affect the ways in which providers work, the manner in which clients are served, and the payment mechanisms for services. Mental health care in the past several decades has been largely designed to end the traditional two-class system of care. Whatever progress has been made in that direction is currently subject to revision and retrenchment.

Acknowledgment

Christopher J. Smith read the manuscript and provided valuable comments.

Note

1 Medicine categorizes all hospital stays as belonging in 467 diagnostic categories, and reimburses hospitals prospectively on the basis of the average cost of the past treatment expenses for that category. This replaces the prior system of retrospective payment, whereby the hospital billed for all the services it chose to provide. The federal government seeks to save money on its extensive Medicare costs by thus getting hospitals to limit length of stay, extra tests, and other discretionary expenses. While Medicare only covers the care of elderly persons, DRGs are expected to be applied in the future to other federal programs (Medicaid) as well as to private insurance.

References

Bachrach, L. 1981. The effects of deinstitutionalization on general hospital psychiatry. *Hospital and Community Psychiatry* **32**, 786–90.

Bassuk, E. L. 1980. The impact of deinstitutionalization on the general hospital emergency ward. *Hospital and Community Psychiatry* **31**, 623–7.

Bittker, T. E. 1985. The industrialization of American psychiatry. *American Journal of Psychiatry* **142**, 149–54.

Borus, J. F., M. Olendzki, L. Kessler, B. J. Burns, U. C. Brandt, C. A. Broverman & P. R. Henderson 1985. The "offset effect" of mental health treatment on ambulatory medical care utilization and changes: month-by-month and grouped-month analyses of a five-year study. *Archives of General Psychiatry* **42**, 573–80.

Brown, P. 1985, *The Transfer of Care: Psychiatric Deinstitutionalization and its Aftermath*. Boston: Routledge & Kegan Paul.

Castel, R., F. Castel & A. Lovell 1982. *The Psychiatric Society*. New York: Columbia University Press.

Cheifetz, D. I. & J. C. Salloway 1984. Patterns of mental health services provided in HMOs. *American Psychologist* **39**, 495–502.

Comptroller General 1977. *Returning the mentally disabled to the community: government needs to do more*. Washington, D.C.: US Government Printing Office.

Doyal, L. 1981. *The political economy of health*. Boston: South End Press.

Ehrenreich, B. & J. Ehrenreich 1970. *The American health empire: power, profits, and politics*. New York: Vintage.

English, J. T., S. S. Sharfstein, D. J. Scherl, B. Astrachan & I. L. Muszynski 1986. Diagnosis-related groups and general hospital psychiatry: the APA study. *American Journal of Psychiatry* **143**, 131–9.

Estes, C. L. & J. B. Wood 1984. A preliminary assessment of the impact of block grants on Community Mental Health Centers. *Hospital and Community Psychiatry* **35**, 1125–9.

Flamm, G. H. 1981. General hospital psychiatry: structure or concept? *General Hospital Psychiatry* **3**, 315–19.

Fogel, B. S. & A. E. Slaby 1985. Beyond gamesmanship: strategies for coping with prospective payment. *Hospital and Community Psychiatry* **36**, 760–3.

Foreman, J. 1985. Mental health coverage curb. *Boston Globe*, November 20th 1984.

Fottler, M. D., H. L. Smith & W. L. James 1981. Profits and patient care quality in nursing homes: are they compatible? *The Gerontologist* **5**, 532–8.

Frank, R. G. & M. S. Kamlet 1985. Direct costs and expenditures for mental health care in the United States in 1980. *Hospital and Community Psychiatry* **36**, 165–8.

Frank, R. G. & L. G. Kessler 1984. State Medicaid limitations for mental health services. *Hospital and Community Psychiatry* **35**, 213–15.

Frank, R. G. & J. R. Lave 1985. The impact of medicaid benefit design on length of hospital stay and patient transfers. *Hospital and Community Psychiatry* **36**, 749–53.

Frisman, L. K., T. G. McGuire & M. L. Rosenbach 1985, Costs of mandates for outpatient mental health care in private health insurance. *Archives of General Psychiatry* **42**, 558–61.

Gaylin, S. 1985. The coming of the corporation and the marketing of psychiatry. *Hospital and Community Psychiatry* **36**, 154–9.

Glasscote, R. M. *et al.* 1976. *Old folks at homes: a field study of nursing and board-and-care homes.* Washington, D.C.: Joint Information Service.

Heimann, E. M. 1980. CMHC inpatient unit: private hospital for the poor? *Hospital and Community Psychiatry* **31**, 476–9.

Hustead, E., S. Sharfstein, S. Muszynksi, J. Brady & J. Cahill 1985. Reductions in coverage for mental and nervous illness in the Federal Employees Health Benefits Program, 1980–1984. *American Journal of Psychiatry* **142**, 181–6.

Jennings, J. 1983. *State mental health financing.* Denver: National Conference of State Legislature.

Jerrell, J. M. & J. K. Larsen 1985. How community mental health centers deal with cutbacks and competition. *Hospital and Community Psychiatry* **36**, 1169–79.

Jones, K. R. & T. R. Vischi 1979. Impact of alcohol, drug abuse, and mental health treatment on medical care utilization: a review of the research literature. *Medical Care* (suppl.) **17**, 1–82.

Kennedy, L. 1985. The losses in profits: how proprietaries affect public and voluntary hospitals. *Health PAC Bulletin* **15** B (6), 5–13.

Kiesler, C. A. & A. E. Sibulkin 1982. Episodic length of hospital stay for mental disorders. In *Progress in applied social psychology*, G. M. Stephenson & J. H. Davis (eds.). Unpublished.

Kihss, P. 1982. Disabled seek welfare after cutoff of U.S. aid. *New York Times*, May 19.

Kotelchuck, D. (ed.) 1975. *Prognosis negative: crisis in the health care system.* New York: Vintage.

Kovel, J. 1980. The American mental health industry. In *Critical Psychiatry*, D. Ingleby (ed.). New York: Pantheon.

Kramer, M. 1977. *Psychiatric services and the changing institutional scene, 1950–1985.* NIMH Report Series 13, No. 12. Rockville, M.D.: NIMH.

Lerman, P. 1982. *Deinstitutionalization and the welfare state*. New Brunswick, N.J.: Ruttgers University Press.

Levenson, A. I. 1983. Issues surrounding the ownership of private psychiatric hospitals by investor-owned hospital chains. *Hospital and Community Psychiatry* **34**, 1127–31.

Linn, M. W., L. Gurel, W. O. Williford, J. Overall, B. Gurland, P. Laughlin & A. Barchiesi 1985. Nursing home care as an alternative to psychiatric hospitalization: a Veterans' Administration comparative study. *Archives of General Psychiatry* **42**, 544–51.

Logan, B. M., D. A. Rochefort & E. W. Cook 1985. Block grants for mental health: elements of the state response. *Journal of Public Health Policy*, December, 476–92.

McGuire, T. G. 1981. Financing and demand for mental health services. *Journal of Human Resources* **16**, 501-22.

Mental Disability Law Reporter 1983. HHS alters disability review process, no 7, 241.

Mervis, J. 1985. The psychological route to cutting costs. *New York Times*, November 24.

Navarro, V. 1976. *Medicine under capitalism*. New York: Prodist.

New York Times 1982. Judge orders benefits restored to mentally ill. December 25, New York.

NIMH 1972 *Psychiatric services in general hospitals*. NIMH Report Series A, No. 11. Rockville, M.D.: NIMH.

NIMH 1977. *1973 survey of 15,737 nursing care homes and personal care homes with nursing*. Memo. Rockville, M.D.: NIMH.

NIMH 1982. *Number and percent distribution of mental health facilities by type of facility: United States, selected years 1970–1980*. Unpubl. data. Rockville, M.D.: NIMH.

Okin, R. L. 1984. How community mental health centers are coping. *Hospital and Community Psychiatry* **35**, 1118–25.

Regier, D. A., I. O. Goldberg & C. A. Taube 1978. The de facto U.S. mental health services system. *Archives of General Psychiatry* **35**, 685–93.

Relman, A. 1980. The new medical-industrial complex. *New England Journal of Medicine* **303**, 963–70.

Rome, H. P. 1985. The medical industrial complex. *Psychiatric Annals* **15**, 475–6.

Ruby, G. 1984. The policy implications of insurance coverage for psychiatric services. *International Journal of Law and Psychiatry* **7**, 269–84.

Salmon, J. W. 1985. Profit and health care: trends in corporatization and proprietization. *International Journal of Health Services* **15**, 394–418.

Schlesinger, H. J., E. Mumford, G. V. Glass, C. Patrick & S. Sharfstein 1983. Mental health treatment and medical care utilization in a fee for service system: outpatient mental health treatment following the onset of a chronic disease. *American Journal of Public Health* **73**, 422–9.

Scull, A. 1984. *Declaration: community treatment and the deviant: a radical view*. New Brunswick, N.J.: Rutgers University Press.

Scull, A. 1985. Deinstitutionalization and public policy. *Social Science and Medicine* **20**, 545–52.

Senate Subommittee on Long Term Care 1976. *The role of nursing homes in caring for discharged mental patients and the birth of a for-profit boarding home industry*. Supporting paper no. 7 of the series "Nursing Homes Care in the United States and Failure in Public Policy," Washington, D.C.: US Government Printing Office.

Starr, P. 1982. *The social transformation of American medicine.* New York: Basic.
Stotsky, B. A. 1969. *Psychiatric patients in nursing homes.* Rockville, M.D.: NIMH.

Taube, C. A. & R. W. Redick 1976. *Provisional data on patient care episodes in mental health facilities, 1973.* NIMH statistical note no. 127. Rockville, M.D.: NIMH.
Taube, C. A., J. W. Thompson, B. J. Burns, P. Widem & C. Prevost 1985. Prospective payment and psychiatric discharges from general hospitals with and without psychiatric units. *Hospital and Community Psychiatry* **36**, 754–60.

Widem, P., H. A. Pincus, H. H. Goldman & S. Jencks 1984. Prospective payment for psychiatric hospitalization: context and background. *Hospital and Community Psychiatry* **35.**
Witkin, M. J. 1980. *Trends in patient care episodes in mental health facilities, 1955–1977.* NIMH statistical note no. 154. Rockville, M.D.: NIMH.
Witkin, M. J. 1981. *Changes in numbers of additions to mental health facilities, by modality, United States, 1971, 1975, and 1977.* NIMH statistical note no. 157. Rockville, M.D.: NIMH.

PART II

Some clues about etiology: the social and environmental context of mental illness

5 Coping in the community: a review of factors influencing the lives of deinstitutionalized ex-psychiatric patients

GLENDA LAWS and MICHAEL DEAR

When you first get out of hospital everything seemed rosy for a few days. Then the novelty wore off and you saw how bleak your life looked and you lost all your confidence. It doesn't seem possible to be sufficiently prepared in the hospital for the stresses you have to withstand shortly after leaving. The final days on the ward are directed toward encouraging you to feel strong and confident enough to sever your ties with the hospital community. A realistic appraisal of what lies ahead might very well be incompatible with that goal and might critically reduce the momentum needed to move out. If you knew what you were getting into, you just wouldn't have the courage to leave (Bachmann 1971).

Introduction

Between 1955 and 1977 the population of mental hospitals in the USA declined from 500,000 to 190,000 (Ashbaugh & Bradley 1979). In Ontario the number of psychiatric beds was reduced from 16,000 to 4,600 between 1963 and 1978, a drop of almost 75%. This process has been called *deinstitutionalization*, "a shifting of care for the mentally handicapped and the emotionally disturbed or ill into the community, wherever possible, with the goal to be what has been called rehabilitation or normalization" (Marshall 1982). Halpern *et al.* (1980) have identified three fundamental objectives of deinstitutionalization. It should provide clients with: (1) treatment in an environment less restrictive than an institution; (2) low-cost treatment; and (3) support services necessary to their adjustment to community living.

In the USA deinstitutionalization gained political acceptance and support with the passing of the Kennedy administration's Mental Retardation Facilities and Community Health Centers Construction Act (1963).

Socially, such a philosophy was in keeping with the civil rights movement of the 1960s; and professionally, it was seen to be favorable for ex-patients because it countered the debilitating effects of institutions (Test & Stein 1975). In theory, deinstitutionalization sounds desirable, but how much is merely political rhetoric? One author has suggested that the release of psychiatric patients may be "prompted more by political and economic considerations than by any planned treatment strategy" (Jones, cited in Fowler 1980). Historically, the treatment of the mentally ill "has always been shaped by the social, economic, religious and philosophical temper of the times" (Bassuk & Gerson 1978). The present pattern of service delivery is no exception. The fact that deinstitutionalization gained credence with the passing of legislation, and that it is funded by various agencies of the state's welfare program points to its political nature. This is further accentuated by the drastic implications of "Hand-me-down financing" and the ever-present threat of cutbacks (Bradley 1978, Marshall 1982).

Clearly, if the state, in conjunction with professionals and others, has decided that a program of deinstitutionalization is the most attractive means of treating and accommodating the mentally ill, there is a real need for long-term planning, both temporally and spatially, beyond the term of one budget or political party. Given that, often, such planning has not been implemented successfully, one must ask how the patients who have been subjected to this procedure have been able to adjust to, and cope with, life in the community? Such a question provides for an assessment of the success, or failure of the deinstitutionalization program.

This chapter identifies four dimensions of an individual's ability to cope within the community; these are the *individual*, the *institutional* experience, the *community*, and the *built environment*. Particular attention is given first to the individual, because we are trying to assess an individual's ability to cope. This does not mean that we do not think that more macroscale issues are not of critical importance. Indeed, the analytical framework which we then present explicitly focuses on the links between micro- and macroscale factors that influence the lives of discharge psychiatric patients. Finally, we present some thoughts on the implications of the discussion for the future research agenda.

Dimensions of coping

What factors are responsible for an individual's success or failure in community living after release from a psychiatric institution? A problem immediately arises in defining "success". Almost without exception, success is measured as an individual's ability to stay out of hospital, rather than the ability to function within, and as part of, the wider society. Therefore, it would seem that a patient may be judged as successful if he or she stays in a house all day, is unable to find employment or does not participate in any social activities.

THE INDIVIDUAL

The most obvious and immediate concern in "coping" is the individual patient. Very little research has concentrated on the ex-patients' perceptions of how well they are adjusting. The literature has considered how various characteristics of the patient may influence his or her post-discharge performance in the community. Four variables are important: (1) demographic characteristics, including age, sex, marital status, etc.; (2) attendance at aftercare facilities; (3) personal social networks; and (4) the patient's daily activity patterns.

(1)   The literature covering the relationship between a person's *demographic profile* and the ability to cope in a community setting suggests no consistent relationship. For example, the research surveyed by Buell & Anthony (1975) and Braff & Lefkowitz (1979) reveals a variety of findings with regard to age as a predictor of success in community living. Some studies found that younger people were more likely to be readmitted (Weinstein *et al.* 1973, Marks 1977, Woogh *et al.* 1977) while others suggest that there may be higher readmission rates among the elderly (Weinstein *et al.* 1973, Viesselman *et al.* 1975). Other considerations associated with aging (e.g., physical deterioration) mean that elderly patients may not appear on psychiatric-hospital readmission records because they are being cared for in some other institutional setting (e.g., a nursing home). Similarly, it is difficult to conclude from the literature whether a person's marital status will affect the likelihood of remaining within the community on discharge. Several studies suggest that unmarried persons are more likely to be readmitted than those who are married (Rawls 1971, Franklin *et al.* 1975, Viesselman *et al.* 1975, Marks 1977). Other studies provide evidence to suggest that it is not always the case (Wessler & Iven 1970, Woogh *et al.* 1977). In general, researchers appear to have concluded that ethnicity is not a reliable predictor of community tenure (Braff & Lefkowitz 1979, Rosen *et al.* 1980, Marks 1977). However, race may be significant when combined with unemployment (Wexler & Iven 1970). Finally, relatively little attention has been given to whether a person's sex is important in determining the outcomes of community placement. When gender is mentioned, it is often in conjunction with some other variable (e.g., age or marital status). Those studies that do report on sex differences suggest that it is not a reliable predictor of the likelihood of rehospitalization (McCarver & Craig 1974, Kirk 1976, Woogh *et al.* 1977, Bowden *et al.* 1980).

(2)   A second consideration in coping is the individual's *attendance at after-*

care programs. Again, there are contradictory research findings (Franklin *et al.* 1975, Kirk 1976, Winston *et al.* 1977, Bene-Kociemba *et al.* 1979, Bowden *et al.* 1980). Involvement in aftercare is not in itself enough to prevent the readmission of a patient. Byers *et al.* (1978) found that the quality and quantity of post-discharge service was of primary importance.

(3) As might be expected, fewer patients who do not develop extensive *networks* of contacts and supportive interpersonal relationships are more likely to end up being readmitted to institutional care (Rawls 1971, Peretti 1974, Cohen & Sokolovsky 1979, Smith & Smith 1979). Family networks are not always the most appropriate source of contacts (Brown 1959). Table 5.1 shows that the mentally ill patients' social network tends to be more limited than that of the general population. The inability to cope with community living might therefore be a function of the absence of familial and extrafamilial support networks (see Mannino & Shore 1974, Cohen & Sokolovsky 1979, Wellman 1979).

Table 5.1 Characteristics of mentally ill patients' social network, as compared to the general population.

smaller in size
fewer ties with kin
fewer members living far away
fewer different sources of friends (i.e., work, school, etc.)
fewer long-term friends
less interaction with family, friends, and relatives
fewer friends who know family members
greater degree of change in terms of moves, deaths, etc.
greater feelings of loss of help from relationships

Source: Froland *et al.* (1979).

(4) With fewer interpersonal contacts, it might be expected that the former psychiatric patient has a somewhat limited pattern of *daily activities*. From the relatively sparse literature that is available, this assumption is shown to be valid (Cheadle *et al.* 1978, Christenfeld & Haveliwala 1978, Dear *et al.* 1980, Anglin 1981). Limited financial resources and lack of contacts clearly limit the ability of the ex-psychiatric patients to venture far beyond their residence; and the poverty of appropriate community resources further restricts opportunities to expand social networks or to introduce any diversity into the rather mundane pattern of activities (Gollay *et al.* 1978, *New York Times* 1978, *The Spectator* 1982).

In summary, the clear implication of the literature on individual coping skills is that it is difficult to predict the success or failure of community tenure by considering the sociodemographic profile of the individual. This is because the ex-psychiatric patient interacts with a variety of social institutions and practices which will also determine his or her success in the community. We now turn our attention to these broader concerns.

THE INSTITUTIONAL EXPERIENCE

Because of the existence of an extremely thorough review of the literature concerning this topic (see McCarver & Craig 1974), a detailed discussion will not be presented here. Rather, it will suffice to present a summary of those variables most commonly examined.

McCarver & Craig have identified six variables from the literature which they reviewed: reasons for admission; age at admission; institutional behavior; institutional training; institutional work experience; and length of institutionalization. To this must be added the number of previous admissions. The following is a brief summary of McCarver & Craig's findings, without reference to the original sources they cited:

(a) One study reported that community adjustment could not be predicted by the type of admission, be it court order, voluntary admission, or transfer.

(b) While most studies did not find any significant relationship between age at admission and post-discharge success, there tends to be a greater chance of success with younger admissions. Several studies reported particular success with those admitted before the age of 12.

(c) Several studies have claimed that institutional behavior has at least some relationship with community adjustment. Others have pointed to the unreal setting of the institution as not indicative of the community: institutional conformity may not be the type of behavior needed to cope with the social demands of the community.

(d) There is little strong evidence either to support or to refute claims that work experience within the institution may influence later adjustment.

(e) Although many studies have identified longer hospitalization as being important in post-discharge community tenure, there is no concordance on this matter.

Rosenblatt & Mayer's (1974) literature review found that the number of previous admissions was a consistent predictor of recidivism. Likewise, Braff & Lefkowitz (1979) reported a positive relationship between rehospitalization and previous stays. Such findings are supported by Kirk (1976) and Buell & Anthony (1975), although the latter authors cite one study which cannot support such claims (see also Weinstein et al. 1973).

THE COMMUNITY

How does the community assist or resist integration of the formerly mentally ill? The community experience of these people can be examined from a number of perspectives. First, we can examine the role of community attitudes toward the mentally ill. Aviram & Segal (1978) and Dear & Taylor (1982) have made contributions in this area. Other studies noting the importance of attitude structures, be they of the community, professionals or patients, include Barahal (1971), Aviram & Segal (1973), Allen (1974), Bachrach (1979), Colom (1981), Walkey et al. (1981), Marshall (1982), and the Conference Report of The National Association of Private Psychiatric Hospitals (1981). Secondly, a close look at the patients' perceptions of how well they are performing within the community would provide insight into problems which exist. Unfortunately, there has been little systematic research into this area, but what there is makes a substantial contribution (e.g. Allen 1974, Colom 1981, Winberg & Wilson 1981, Bogdan & Taylor 1982). Generally, such reports are not encouraging; dissatisfaction with community attitudes, accommodation, job opportunities, financial prospects and social life punctuate the writings of the mentally ill. Thirdly, it is important whether or not the needs of ex-patients are being met by the community. Such information would be invaluable to professionals and planners and, if acted upon positively, to the patients. Table 5.2 is a list of services deemed to be necessary for patients to be able to function within the community. Other suggestions have included categories of housing, financial assistance, employment, medical, and leisure and social activities (Bene-Kociemba et al. 1979, Dear et al. 1980, Parker & Rosborough 1982). These needs are similar in many ways to those of the general population, and success in community living must depend at least partly on access to services which satisfy these needs. Unfortunately, little research has sought to identify the relationships between the degree to which these needs are met and the community adjustment of the patient.

There is a fuller discussion on employment and community tenure in the literature. Franklin et al. (1975) were unable to find any support for the idea that employment would prevent readmission. But they found that the source of income could be influential: those with the lower chance of re-admission were probably receiving money from their own employment, or the employment of someoebody else in the same house. Income from other sources, and unemployment, were associated with recidivism. On discharge, certain groups have more chance of finding a job. Woolley & Kane (1977) found that lower status groups (such as the semi-skilled, laborers, and agricultural workers) were more successful in gaining employment than higher status workers (clerical, professional–managerial). This could be due to the stigma associated with the label of "ex-mental patient"; there exist "definite prejudices against hiring mental patients and no work opportunities [are] made available to them" (Solitar 1982). However, Buell &

Anthony (1975) concluded that whether a person is an ex-patient or not does not matter; what is important is that the applicant is "married, white, younger and possesses a more stable employment history and job skills."

Table 5.2   Essential services for retarded and other handicapped persons.

development programs	day activity
	education
	training
residential services	domiciliary
	special living arrangements
employment services	preparation
	sheltered (including work activity)
	competitive
identification services	diagnosis
	evaluation
facilitating services	information and referral
	counseling
	protective and sociological
	follow-along
	case management
treatment services	medical
	dental
transportation	
leisure and recreation	

Source: Bruininks & Warfield (1978), as cited in Bruininks *et al.* (1980).

Many problems associated with deinstitutionalization are partly due to the unpreparedness of the community to accommodate the demands of the mentally ill (Parker & Rosborough 1982). The provision of services in the community requires a coordinated system of planning and implementation (Bachrach 1979). But, as Bradley (1978) has observed, problems will continue to plague efforts at reform "until the entire context in which these changes must take place is taken into consideration." Until then, community tenure will remain an "illusion," with the new residences being little more than "small long-term state hospital wards isolated from the community" (Lamb & Goertzel 1971; see also Allen 1974, Murphy & Santiestevan 1976).

THE BUILT ENVIRONMENT
How much the physical constraints existing within the urban environment influence an individual's level of community adjustment is not explicit from the literature. However, descriptions of physical conditions often tolerated make it clear that integration has not been achieved.

Within a block are the major shopping areas of Fifth Avenue and Herald Square. The benches of tiny Herald Square Park, often inhabited by a derelict population, provide the closest public area for free relaxation outside the hotel. It is within a three to four block radius of the Needham that most of the tenants with a psychiatric history spend the majority of their waking hours. Despite the high mobility and potential isolation engendered by the nature of the area, the hotel's location has one major advantage for the schizophrenic tenants: There is no permanent residential population that could serve as a stigmatizing force against them. In this way, their comparatively high levels of bizarre behaviour, e.g. unprovoked verbal tirades, inappropriate motor activities, generally are tolerated and often go unnoticed among the passing crowds of shoppers (Sokolovsky *et al*. 1978, p.6).

This is the sort of environment in which the discharged must often live. The creation of such areas is a function of several social and political processes which are yet to be explained in detail. However, the mentally ill are often without choice in location of accommodation: planning, lack of financial resources and the need for certain services often restricts the options available to them.

Several authors have provided taxonomies of the types of residential facilities available to patients who have been placed in the community (see McCarver & Craig 1974, Bruininks *et al*. 1980). Potentially, there exists a continuum of residences from the hospital with 24-hour supervision to independent living arrangements. Generally, such facilities can be found concentrated either in downtown areas or close to mental hospitals. Dear *et al*. (1980) have pointed to the fact that the downtown core provides the services and agencies needed by the patient, and so it would seem logical (in some sense) for the residents to cluster around such agencies. Mechanic (1979) suggests that these "colonies" of patients find the inner city the most appropriate, if not desirable, location, because of its access to transport, its social support, and the greater tolerance of core-area residents. Such an environment is part of the classic "zone of transition" (Burgess 1925) characterized by blight, mixed land use, a highly transient population, higher than average crime rates, and little chance to be free of a community of service-dependent individuals. Mechanic (1979) has questioned whether integration is really possible under such conditions, and Smith (1978) found that former mentally ill patients living in such an environment were more likely to be readmitted.

Attempts to introduce residential facilities which may be conducive to integration often meet with community opposition (see the preceding section). This may take the form of what Aviram & Segal (1973) called society's "new method of excluding their mentally ill," including legal or group pressures, zoning regulations, and bureaucratic maneuvering. Chase

(1973) has demonstrated the existence of such exclusion mechanisms in California, where "normal" neighbors have complained about the behavior of residents of a board-and-care home and some residences "are 'zoned into' low rent, high crime areas, such as in the core city of San Jose."

The availability of suitable housing for the mentally ill is critical if successful integration is to be achieved. The literature specifically addressed to the problem of the provision of housing for the mentally ill is minimal, even though several authors have expressed concern over the problem (Lamb & Goertzel 1971, Aviram & Segal 1973, Mannino & Shore 1974, Bachrach 1976, Bruininks et al. 1980). Scott & Scott (1978) sought "to estimate the capacity of communities, regions, and states to absorb individuals who are clients of community-based programs" by determining the vacancy of rental accommodation in New Jersey, identifying the location of such, and attempting to see how such information may be used in the planning and implementation of deinstitutionalization programs. After finding that housing available for rent is often unsuitable for the deinstitutionalized, they concluded that "there simply is not enough room in the community to receive all of the people . . . for whom either deinstitutionalization and/or community care programs exist or are planned."

It is not only the physical availability of housing which needs to be considered. The deinstitutionalized suffer from particular problems because of their limited financial resources, making it all but impossible for them to buy their own home. The bureaucratic and legal necessities involved in obtaining housing would also often exclude an ex-patient from the buyers' market.

Not unrelated to the housing question is that of mobility. Transport is often a major, but overlooked problem in the process of community placement. When available, transport provides accessibility to other social services and facilities necessary to community integration (Bruininks et al. 1980). Lamb (1979) found that the use of an aftercare facility declined when the availability of transportation for residents of a board-and-care home was reduced to public transport only. Cohen (1975) has briefly discussed the problems associated with defining the agencies responsible for the delivery of transportation services. Christenfeld & Haveliwala (1978) found that one of the patients' complaints was the lack of transport available to them. This could partly account for another of the complaints—boredom. The paucity of literature referring to the problems associated with transport experienced by the mentally ill makes it essential that such an issue be fully investigated. Increasing the physical mobility of these people may assist in alleviating their concentration in the inner city, and would be a positive step in helping them to cope with life in our society.

DISCUSSION

The usual dichotomous method of measuring a former patient's success within the community (readmission/nonreadmission) tells us little of the experience of the individual *in* the community. Aviram & Segal (1973) observed that "physical existence in a certain community, however, does not necessarily lead to social inclusion". Researchers, with a few notable exceptions (e.g., Gollay *et al.* 1978, Bogdan & Taylor 1980, Dear *et al.* 1980, Winberg & Wilson 1981), have failed to give their subjects the opportunity to express their opinions as to how well they are adjusting in the community, and what they see as problem areas. Too often families or "significant others" are interviewed.

It would therefore seem important to turn more attention to the interests of the mentally ill themselves. Writings by mental patients about their experiences are becoming increasingly accessible, and seem to fall into three major groups. There are those autobiographical accounts which have been deemed worthy of publication as books. Secondly, periodicals published by mental patients' associations such as *In a Nutshell: Mental Patients Association Newsletter* from Vancouver, or *Madness Network News* from California contain a "strong psychiatric inmate bias" (see Frank 1980). A third, but extremely small, body of literature by former patients is those articles which occasionally appear in professional journals (e.g. Allen 1974, Colom 1981). More detailed examination of reports contained in such sources would provide potentially invaluable information to supplement that provided by the "professional" literature.

The problems associated with the inadequate nature of the readmission criteria used in most studies are obvious. There is now a need for the development of a set of indicators which would allow a realistic assessment of how the ex-patients are coping with the demands of everyday life. Examples of such indicators include: unemployment rates; crime rates (both crimes committed by the mentally ill and those committed against them); suicide rates; legal problems; difficulties in obtaining insurance coverage, bank loans, etc.; and the extent and quality of their social networks. A major problem in developing a valid set of indicators is deciding on the most appropriate control group. 'Should it be the wider population? Or should it be other service-dependent groups such as the unemployed, elderly, and physically handicapped? Or should it be other formerly mentally ill individuals who have successfully reintegrated into the community?

Toward an analytical framework

So far, we have highlighted those variables which have some effect on the reintegration of mentally ill patients to the community. These variables operate within society and its structures. In order to understand the interaction of the discharged patient with the set of wider social forces, we focus first on the *individual*, whose lifestyle necessarily involves functioning in several environments on varying scales. First, the individual is placed in some kind of *institutional situation*. This environment provides a formalized treatment program in order to "normalize" the individual's behavior. The fact that an individual has been institutionalized implies a degree of removal from the *community*. Even though the institution is part of, and located in, the community, the "patient" is often excluded from any semblance of community living. The community here is a localized territory and is defined, at least partly, by the *built environment*, or physical environment in which the community, institution and individual meet. It is impossible to ignore the fact that the problem of mental health care is embedded within wider *societal structures*. The evolution of any social formation subsumes changes in the nature of any other of the variables. This can be seen in histories of the development of asylums and associated treatment programs (see, e.g., Foucalt 1967, Bassuk & Gerson 1978). The model immediately implies several levels of analysis, each of which invites a variety of potential research agendas.

The operational model (Fig. 5.1) examines three sets of factors which interact to produce a particular deinstitutionalization outcome. These are *personal*, *social*, and *contextual* factors which incorporate the individual, community, and societal dimensions identified in the above. The outcome of deinstitutionalization is viewed in the context of the prevailing social formation, which intersects with the more everyday concerns via a network of institutional and contextual factors. Upon deinstitutionalization, personal and social concerns become the most influential in determining an individual's fate. Contextual factors continually operate to maintain or modify the influence that such factors have on the eventual outcome. "Outcome" is measured as three possible alternatives: first, community tenure; secondly, hospital readmission; and thirdly, the death of the ex-patient. (Suicide, for example, would be an extreme indication of an inability to adjust. Other forms of premature death may suggest that the individual was unable to take advantage of community resources such as health services.)

PERSONAL FACTORS
The degree of social integration of any individual may be gauged by looking at social networks and activity patterns. There are three elements of the former patient's social network: contacts with family and friends, with medical and welfare professionals (whether private or state agents) and informal contacts with, for example, absentee landlords, staff at frequently visited stores, etc. The amount of time spent with these contacts, frequency of interaction, the kind of assistance obtained, the manner of contact (group or individual), who was the instigator of the meeting, whether it was a voluntary meeting, and the perceived usefulness of the interaction are examples of the types of issues which need to be considered.

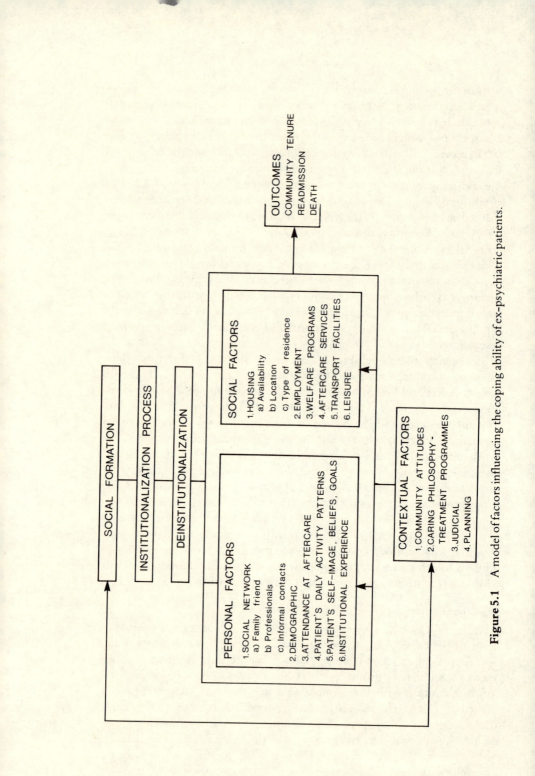

Figure 5.1 A model of factors influencing the coping ability of ex-psychiatric patients.

Associated with the nature of these contacts are the daily activity patterns of these people. One could assume that a day with little variety in terms of the types of activities engaged in, the location and timing of relevant events, or the composition of the groups involved would provide minimal stimulation and suggest a lower degree of integration than a more diverse timetable.

Differing approaches to treatment and pre-release training in an institutional environment may lead to variable levels of preparedness for community living. Some idea of the types of training needs to be gained, and whether the patient sees these as being beneficial or not needs to be addressed. Whether the length of training program is influential should also be assessed. Other factors such as the length of institutionalization and the type of institutional experience (type of ward, the degree of supervision) must be examined. The continuance of contact with an "institution" via aftercare facilities should be looked at in similar terms (e.g., length of attendance, frequency of visits, and type of assistance).

Finally, the patient's own perception of his or her position and responsibilities cannot be ignored. Self images may influence decisions, for example, to participate in particular activities, approach certain people for assistance, or seek employment. This requires that the individual be given the opportunity to express his or her own opinion, rather than relying on reports of "significant others." Patients' expectations, behavior, and ultimate success may be seen also to be influenced, to some extent, by demographic characteristics.

SOCIAL FACTORS
Certain needs of the individual can be expected to be provided by society, via either private or public bodies. Generally, the provision of services required by the mentally ill population is left to government agencies because of their unprofitable nature. Housing is one of the most fundamental needs of any individual, along with food and clothing. Service-dependent groups rely on welfare programs to ensure that these needs are satisfied. Obviously, if employment opportunities were forthcoming, this welfare dependency would be reduced significantly. It is possible to identify six areas in which society could be of assistance to the former patient: the supply of suitable housing; the creation of job opportunities; assistance via welfare programs; continuing professional support from aftercare services; provision of appropriate transport services; and leisure activities.

Questions of the accessibility of housing cannot be ignored. A residence may be accessible in terms of distance but out of the financial reach of a particular group. Conversely, an affordable house may be in an "undesirable" location, such as the decaying older industrial sections of a city, or too distant from transport and other necessary services. Rented accommodation has obvious problems in the lack of any permanency; the landlord has the "right" to turn over his or her property to a higher-paying group. Unfortunately, there is little chance of these people being able to aspire to the buyers' market, because of the absence of any financial or employment security. Subsidized housing is one potential source of accommodation, but demand continually exceeds supply and the former patient is placed in a position of competition with other low-income groups. Appropriate housing and security of tenure would no doubt benefit the discharged patient.

Employment is almost a necessity for survival beyond bare subsistence. Ex-psychiatric patients are prone to difficulties in finding jobs because of a lack of skills and, more particularly, because of the stigma associated with the "mentally ill" label. Prejudice in the job market consequently reduces opportunities. Eventually, the former patients may come to believe that they are unsuitable for employment. Simple possession of a job is, however, not the full story. It may be important to establish the degree of job satisfaction in order to assess successful community tenure.

The needs of the deinstitutionalized individual can be met, at least partly, by welfare programs. A number of agencies are involved, including health, housing, and social security. An assessment of the role of the welfare apparatus in coping would consider two related areas; first, an identification of the services sought by these people, including the level of assistance required and the duration of dependency on that service; and secondly, an examination of the administration of the program and the ways this influences any external sources of assistance.

Not entirely divorced from the welfare programs are aftercare facilities, such as community-based mental health clinics and drop-in centers. These services offer support to the patient who has returned to the community, and are seen as a mandatory component of the deinstitutionalization process. Where these centers are located with respect to their client population will influence the level of patronage. The types of programs offered will be reflected in the people who take advantage of their availability. A comparison of those who attend and those who fail to use these facilities may point to the success of the aftercare program.

Two final areas which make life somewhat easier for the former mental patient are the related issues of leisure activities and the provision of transportation. These are important considerations since they are able to encourage diversity in the daily lives of these people, and the responsibilities can be shared among the family, and private and public bodies.

CONTEXTUAL FACTORS

Everyday individual and social concerns do not operate in a vacuum. They are continually being modified by contextual factors, which include the role of community attitudes, the dominant caring philosophy and associated treatment programs, and the roles of the judicial and planning apparatuses.

These factors act as the link with the prevailing social formation and its ideologies. The factors are subtle in their influence on the ability of an individual to contend with the community setting, but it can be argued that they are the most significant since they strongly constrain the operation of the other factors.

Community attitudes are important in that they are related to prejudice, stigma, and the acceptance or rejection of the former patient. Community members may, after some resistance, come to accept the treatment of the mentally ill within the community rather than removing them from it. These attitudes evolve over time, and so we need to know why particular attitudes emerge as dominant over time. The evolution of attitudes is not separable from the influence exerted by caring philosophies; for example, the community's acceptance of deinstitutionalization may result from the medical profession's belief that this is the most humane and useful treatment presently available.

There are two major reasons for emphasizing the role of the judiciary. First, many patients are admitted to an institution only after a legal decision. Legal (and medical) definitions of what constitutes mental illness and its treatment strongly determine who will be institutionalized. Secondly, acts of legislation have been responsible for the implementation of many of the phases of deinstitutionalization. The legal machinery offers an illustration of the ways in which forces operating at the level of the society intersect with an individual's life. For example, a person's behavior is judged to be "abnormal" and so legal action recommends incarceration until the "proper" behavior returns.

Finally, the influence of planning can be seen in two forms. There is (1) the planning of the delivery of health care, and (2) the planning of the physical environment. Planning of health services affects, for example, the institutional experience, contacts with medical professionals, and the provision of aftercare facilities. In terms of the built environment, planning is important because it places controls on where these people can find suitable accommodation, during or after institutionalization. In conjunction with other processes, it has been responsible for the concentration of service–dependent people within the inner city.

The model identifies those factors which interact to produce a range of possible outcomes for a person who has been discharged from a psychiatric institution and returned to the community. The emphasis in the model is on the dynamics of this process. Ideologies, caring philosophies and planning practices are not static constraints. They are continually changing products of an evolving social formation. As such, it is necessary to look at how combinations of the social, personal, and contextual factors operate to influence the life of each individual. We need to acknowledge the role of macrohistorical forces in shaping the immediate environment and available alternatives. It is only then that we can look at the state and private mechanisms which act to link such forces with the everyday actions of the ex-psychiatric patient.

Summary and conclusions

This chapter has presented an overview of those factors influential in the life of an individual after discharge from a psychiatric institution. The review has revealed a focus of attention on characteristics of the individual and the role of the institutional experience. Also seen to be important are community attitudes and (to a lesser extent) elements of the built environment. Research has tended to concentrate on readmission as an indicator of "success" or "failure" in community adjustment: hence there has been little examination of how the patient operates within the community, how they are coping with everyday tasks of satisfying their needs for housing, entertainment, friendship, etc.

A framework has been proposed for the examination of ex-patients' coping. It emphasizes that ability to cope is related to the condition of existing societal structures. Our model shows that contextual factors act as the link between social and personal factors and the social formation.

A model of this type has several implications for future research. Five tasks emerge as particularly important points of departure. First, there is the need to define those social structures which exert an immediate influence on the mentally ill. Secondly, it is necessary to explain how such structures have evolved to their present status. Thirdly, the ways in which social structures intersect with the everyday lives of psychiatric patients needs to be clarified. Fourthly, what is the outcome of this intersection for the individual ex-patient? And, finally, there is a need to examine the many ways in which the individual reacts in coping with the restrictions and alternatives presented. Only when these issues are addressed can we begin to assess the effects of deinstitutionalization properly.

Acknowledgments

Thanks are due to Martin Taylor for his valuable input into the writing of this chapter. This research was supported by a grant from the Social Science & Humanities Research Council of Canada.

References

Allen, P. 1974. A consumer's view of California's mental health care system. *Psychiatric Quarterly* **48** (1), 1–13.
Anglin, B. 1981. *They never asked for help*. Maple, Ontario: Belsten.

Ashbaugh, J. W. & V. J. Bradley 1979. Linking deinstitutionalization of patients with hospital phase-down: the difference between success and failure. *Hospital and Community Psychiatry* **30** (2), 105-10.

Aviram, U. & S. P. Segal 1973. Exclusion of the mentally ill: reflection on an old problem in a new context. *Archives of General Psychiatry* **29,** 126–31.

Aviram, U. & S. P. Segal 1978. *The mentally ill in community-based sheltered care: a study of community care and social integration*, New York: Wiley.

Bachmann, B. J. 1971. Re-entering the community: a former patient's view. *Hospital and Community Psychiatry* **22** (4), 119–22.

Bachrach, L. 1976. A note on some recent studies of released mental hospital patients in the community. *American Journal of Psychiatry* **133** (1), 73–5.

Bachrach, L. 1979. Planning mental health services for chronic patients. *Hospital and Community Psychiatry* **30** (6), 387–92.

Barahal, H. S. 1971. Resistances to community psychiatry. *Psychiatric Quarterly* **45,** 333–43.

Bassuk, E. & S. Gerson 1978. Deinstitutionalization and mental health services. *Scientific American* **238** (2), 46–53.

Bene-Kociemba, A., P. G. Cotton & A. Frank 1979. Predictors of community tenure of discharged state hospital patients. *American Journal of Psychiatry* **136** (December), 1556-61.

Bogdan, R. & S. J. Taylor 1982. *Inside out.* Toronto: University of Toronto Press.

Bowden, C. I., L. S. Shoenfeld & R. L. Adams 1980. A correlation between dropout status and improvement in a psychiatric clinic. *Hospital and Community Psychiatry* **31** (3), 192–5.

Bradley, V. J. 1978. *Deinstitutionalization of developmentally disabled persons: a conceptual analysis and guide.* Baltimore, M.D.: University Park Press.

Braff, J. & M. Lefkowitz 1979. Community mental health treatments: what works for whom? *Psychiatric Quarterly* **51** (2), 119–34.

Brown, G. W. 1959. Experiences of discharged chronic schizophrenic patients in various types of living group. *The Milbank Memorial Fund Quarterly* **37** (2), 105–31.

Bruininks, R. H., M. L. Thurlow, K. Thurman & J. S. Fiorelli 1980. Deinstitutionalization and community services. *Mental Retardation and Developmental Disabilities* **XI**, 55–101.

Buell, G. J. & W. Anthony 1975. The relationship between patient demographic characteristics and psychiatric rehabilitation outcome. *Community Mental Health Journal* **11** (2), 208–14.

Burgess, E. W. 1925. The growth of the city. In *The City*, R. E. Park *et al.* (eds). Chicago: University of Chicago Press.

Byers, S., S. Cohen & D. D. Harshbarger 1978. Impact of aftercare services on recidivism of mental hospital patients. *Community Mental Health Journal* **14** (1), 26–34.

Chase, J. 1973. Where have all the patients gone? *Human Behaviour*, October, 14–21.

Cheadle, A. J., H. L. Freeman & J. Korer 1978. Chronic schizophrenic patients in the community. *British Journal of Psychiatry* **132**, 221–7.

Christenfeld, R. & Y. A. Haveliwala 1978. Patients' views of placement facilities: a participant–observer study. *American Journal of Psychiatry* **135** (3), 329-32.

Cohen, C. I. & J. Sokolovsky 1979. Clinical use of network analysis for psychiatric and aged populations. *Community Mental Health Journal* **15** (3), 203–13.

Cohen, H. J. 1975. Obstacles to developing community services for the mentally retarded. In *The mentally retarded and society: a social science perspective*, M. J. Begab & S. A. Richardson (eds.), 401–22, Baltimore: University Park Press.

Colom, E. 1981. Reaction of an angry consumer. *Community Mental Health Journal* **17** (1), 92–7.

Dear, M. & S. M. Taylor 1982. *Not on our street*. London: Pion.

Dear, M., L. Bayne, G. Boyd, E. Callaghan & E. Goldstein 1980. *Coping in the community: the needs of ex-psychiatric patients*. A Mental Health/Hamilton Project funded by Young Canada Works.

Foucault, M. 1967. *Madness and civilization: a history of insanity in the Age of Reason*. New York: Mentor.

Fowler, G. 1980. A needs-assessment method for planning alternatives to hospitalization. *Hospital and Community Psychiatry* **31** (1), 41–5.

Frank, K. P. 1980. *The anti-psychiatry bibliography and resources guide*. Vancouver: Press Gang.

Franklin, J., L. Kittredge, J. Thrasher 1975. A survey of factors related to mental hospital readmissions. *Hospital and Community Psychiatry* **26** (11), 749–51.

Froland, C., G. Brodsky, M. Olson & L. Stewart 1979. Social support and social adjustment: implications for mental health professionals. *Community Mental Health Journal* **15** (2), 82–93.

Gollay, E., R. Freedman, M. Wyngaarden & N. R. Kurtz 1978. *Coming back: the community experiences of deinstitutionalized mentally retarded people*. Cambridge, Mass.: Abt Books.

Halpern, J., K. Sackett, P. Binner & C. Mohr 1980. *The myths of deinstitutionalization: policies for the mentally disabled*. Boulder, Col.: Westview Press.

Kirk, S. 1976, Effectiveness of community services for discharged mental hospital patients. *American Journal of Orthopsychiatry* **46** (4), 646–59.

Lamb, H. R. 1979. The new asylums in the community. *Archives of General Psychiatry* **36**, 129–34.

Lamb, H. R. & V. Goertzel 1971. Discharged mental patients—are they really in the community? *Archives of General Psychiatry* **24**, 29–34.

McCarver, R. B. & E. M. Craig 1974. Placement of the retarded in the community: prognosis and outcome. *International Review of Research in Mental Retardation* **7**, 45–207.

Mannino, F. & M. Shore 1974. Family structure, aftercare, and post-hospital adjustment. *American Journal of Orthopsychiatry* **44** (1), 76–85.

Marks, F. M. 1977. The characteristics of psychiatric patients readmitted within a month of discharge. *Psychological Medicine* **7**, 345–52.

Marshall, J. (ed.) 1982. *Madness: an indictment of the mental health care system in Ontario*. Toronto: Ontario Public Service Employees Union.

Mechanic, D. 1979. *Future issues in health care: social policy and the rationing of medical services*. New York: The Free Press.

Murphy, H. B. M., B. Penee & D. Luchins 1972. Foster homes: the new back wards? *CMH* Suppl. no. 71, September–October.

National Association of Private Psychiatric Hospitals 1981. Patient re-entry into the community. *Hospital and Community Psychiatry* **31**, 52–6.

New York Times 1978. The problem that can't be tranquilized. May 21.

Parker, A. L. & L. Rosborough 1982. *A matter of urgency: the psychiatrically disabled in the Ottawa–Carleton community*. Ottawa: Canadian Mental Health Association.

Peretti, P. O. 1974. Precipitating factors of readmission of psychiatric patients. *Community Mental Health Journal* **10** (1), 89–92.

Rawls, J. R. 1971. Toward the identification of readmissions and non-readmissions to mental hospitals. *Social Psychology* **6**, 58–61.

Rosen, A., S. Olarte & R. Masnik 1980. Utilization patterns of a CM in an urban ghetto area. *Hospital and Community Psychiatry* **31** (10), 702–70.

Rosenblatt, A. & J. Mayer 1974. The recidivism of mental patients: a review of past studies. *American Journal of Orthopsychiatry* **44** (5), 697–706.

Santiestevan, H. 1976. *Deinstitutionalization: out of their beds and into the streets*. Washington, D.C.: American Federation of State, County and Municipal Employees.

Scott, N. J. & R. A. Scott 1980. The impact of housing markets on deinstitutionalization. *Administration in Mental Health* **7** (3), 210–22.

Smith, C. J. 1978. Recidivism and community adjustment amongst former mental patients. *Social Science and Medicine* **12**, 17–27.

Smith, C. J. & C. A. Smith 1979. Evaluating outcome measures for deinstitutionalization programs. *Social Work Research and Abstracts* **15**, 23–30.

Sokolovsky, J., C. Cohen, D. Berger & J. Geiger 1978. Personal networks of ex-mental patients in a Manhattan SRO hotel. *Human Organization* **37** (1), 5–15.

Solitar, F. 1982. Summary of research studies on mental health. In *Madness: an indictment of the mental health care system in Ontario*, J. Marshall (ed.), 164–77. Toronto: Ontario Public Services Employees Union.

The Spectator 1982. Madness in South Parkdale. March 6.

Test, M. A. & L. Stein 1975. The clinical rationale for community treatment: a review of the literature. In *Alternatives to mental hospital treatment*, L. I. Stein & M. A. Test (eds.), 3–22. New York: Plenum Press.

Viesselman, J. O., L. H. Spalt & V. B. Tuason 1975. Psychiatric disorders in a community mental health center: II. Who gets readmitted? *Comprehensive Psychiatry* **16** (5), 485–94.

Walkey, F. H., D. E. Green & A. J. W. Taylor 1981. Community attitudes to mental health: a comparative study. *Social Science and Medicine* **15E**, 139–44.

Weinstein, A. S., D. Dipasquale & F. Winsor 1973. Relationship between length of stay in and out of the New York State mental hospitals. *American Journal of Psychiatry* **130** (8), 904–9.

Wellman, B. 1979. The community question: the intimate networks of East Yorkers. *American Journal of Sociology* **84**, 1201–31.

Wessler, R. L. & D. Iven 1970. Social characteristics of patients readmitted to a community mental health center. *Community Mental Health Journal* **6** (1), 69–74.

Winberg, E. & T. Wilson 1981. *Single rooms: stories of an urban subculture*. Cambridge, Mass.: Schenkuan.

Winston, A., M. Pardes, D. Papernik & L. Breslin 1977. Aftercare of psychiatric patients and its relation to rehospitalization. *Hospital and Community Psychiatry* **28** (2), 118–21.

Woogh, C. M., H. M. R. Meier & M. R. Eastwood 1977. Psychiatric hospitalization in Ontario: the revolving door in perspective. *Canadian Medical Association
Journal* **116**, 876–81.
Woolley, E. R. & R. L. Kane 1977. Community aftercare of patients discharged
from Utah State Hospital: a follow-up study. *Hospital and community psychiatry*
28 (2), 114–18.

6 *The spatial ecology of mental illness*

JOHN A. GIGGS

Introduction

Historical research has shown that the mentally ill have always been with us. The earliest written evidence, derived from Egyptian and Mesopotamian sources in the third millennium BC, confirms that mental illnesses were recognized and that they were attributed to a variety of natural and social causes (Alexander & Selesnick 1966). Since the middle of the 19th century, researchers from many disciplines have concerned themselves with the tasks of identifying and classifying mental disorders, studying their distributions in time and space, and trying to determine their causes (Cooper & Morgan 1973). Of all the disciplinary perspectives involved in the analysis of mental illness incidence and causation, the spatial viewpoint is unquestionably the most weakly represented. This is extremely regrettable for, as Hettner (1927) cogently argued, exactly 60 years ago:

> Reality is simultaneously a three-dimensional space which we must examine from three points of view in order to comprehend the whole. From one point of view we see the relations of similar things, from the second the development in time and from the third the arrangement and division in space. Reality as a whole cannot be encompassed entirely in the systematic sciences, sciences defined by the objects they study. Other writers have effectively based the justification for the historical sciences on the necessity of a special conception of development in time. But this leaves science still two-dimensional; we do not perceive it completely unless we consider it also from the third point of view, the division and arrangement in space.

Only one discipline, namely geography, can justifiably claim that the spatial dimension is its central concern. However, although medical geography has long been a distinct specialty within the discipline, attention has been devoted almost exclusively to the analysis of the spatial distribution and environmental correlates of *physical* illnesses in man. Thus the authors of the three major textbooks in medical geography published to 1980 completely ignored the subject of mental illness (McGlashan 1972,

Learmouth 1978, Pyle 1979). Geographers have only recently begun to evince an interest in both mental illness and mental health research (Timms 1965, Giggs 1973a, b, Taylor 1974, Smith 1977). Among nongeographers, though, there has been a concern—albeit modest and intermittent—with the spatial patterning and environmental correlates of mental disorders for at least a hundred years (Levy & Rowitz 1973). Several reviews of the ecological studies produced by geographers and others were published during the late 1970s (Giggs 1979, 1980, Freeman 1978, Schwab & Schwab 1978, Smith 1980). Fortunately, interest in the field has burgeoned during the past decade. This chapter attempts to provide a tentative conceptual framework for existing ecological work, give a few illustrative examples, and outline possibilities for future research.

Conceptual framework and data problems

The major concerns of "ecological psychiatry" are summarized in Figures 6.1 and 6.2. Figure 6.1 is reproduced from a recent study by Smith (1982). In the present context, the level of health (i.e. mental health) in any given

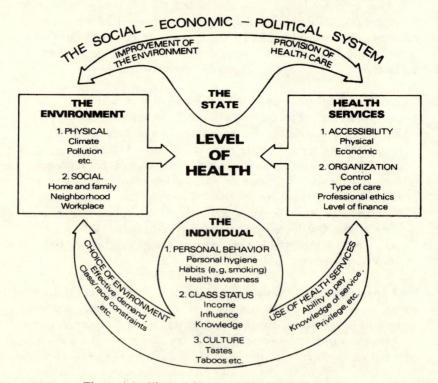

Figure 6.1   The social context of health and health care.

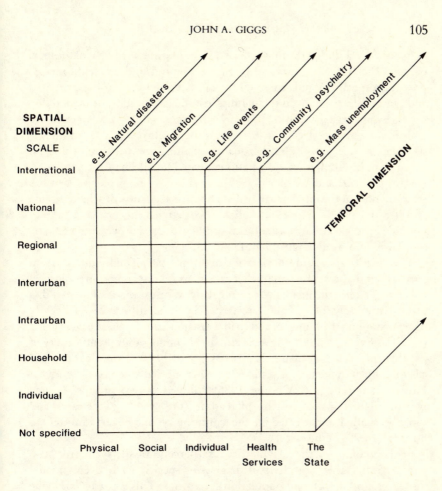

SPATIAL DIMENSION

SCALE

- International
- National
- Regional
- Interurban
- Intraurban
- Household
- Individual
- Not specified

e.g. Natural disasters e.g. Migration e.g. Life events e.g. Community psychiatry e.g. Mass unemployment

TEMPORAL DIMENSION

Physical Social Individual Health Services The State

ENVIRONMENTAL DIMENSION

Figure 6.2 The distribution of schizophrenic movers in Nottingham's social space.

population/area is represented as being the outcome of four interacting sets of factors, namely the individual, the environment, the health services, and the broader social–economic–political system (i.e., the state). Figure 6.2 shows that, in ecological studies, one (or more) of these environmental influences can be examined at a specific spatial scale. Thus Ineichen *et al.* (1984) adopted the intra-urban scale in their cross-sectional analysis (1978–81 inpatient admissions) of the ethnic (i.e. social environment) factor in psychiatric hospital admissions in Bristol. Warner (1985), in contrast, reviewed the literature on national and international variations in the prevalence of schizophrenia. Furthermore, he also adopted a *temporal* perspective, invoking macrolevel variables (chiefly aspects of the state and the mental health services) to develop his model of schizophrenia causation.

In ecological studies the first task is the accurate measurement of the level of mental health (or, more typically, the degrees and kinds of mental illness) present in specific populations. Unfortunately, there are still great spatial and temporal variations in the definition and classification of mental disorders by psychiatrists (WHO 1973, 1979; Kramer *et al.* 1983; Warner 1985). This *health services* effect (Fig. 6.1) upon the levels of all types of mental disorder seriously degrades the quality of most comparative ecological research at the international and national spatial scales (Fig. 6.2), as reviews by Giggs (1977) and Warner (1985) have shown. The problem even has repercussions at the intra-urban scale. Thus a recent study of schizophrenia and affective psychosis in Nottingham revealed that the incidence rates of both disorders varied markedly according to the particular diagnostic standards employed (Giggs 1986b).

The identification and enumeration of the mentally ill individuals within specific populations presents further problems for researchers in ecological psychiatry. The true incidence or prevalence of most kinds of mental disorder can rarely be gauged precisely. Their identification is heavily dependent upon the numbers and spatial distribution of trained psychiatrists (i.e., a *health services effect*, Fig. 6.1) and the changing volume and variety of psychiatric services available (Giggs 1977, WHO 1985). Thus the total (i.e., *administrative*) incidence of schizophrenia identified in a recent study of Nottingham (Giggs & Cooper 1986) comprised two groups of new patients, namely psychiatric hospital admissions (83.8% of the cases) and those identified and treated in the community but never admitted to hospital (16.2% of the cases).

In many countries, the social and cultural perceptions of psychiatrists also appear to affect their objectivity in diagnosing specific (even severe) mental disorders among different population subgroups. This is particularly true of important ethnic minorities (Gaw 1982, Littlewood & Lipsedge 1982, Rack 1982). Thus, in the UK, many ethnic patients have been diagnosed as schizophrenic although ".. . . it [i.e., the diagnosis] often conveyed the doctor's lack of understanding rather than the presence of the 'key symptoms' by which this reaction is conventionally recognised by British psychiatrists" (Littlewood & Lipsedge 1982: 7). Three studies of the first–contact schizophrenics in Nottingham have shown that, for three cohorts of cases (i.e., 1963–9, 1969–73, and 1978–80) the disorder has consistently appeared to be much more common among ethnic immigrant groups than among native-born residents (Giggs 1973b, 1983, 1986a). These intergroup variations in incidence rates are also attributable, at least in part, to important individual and social–ethnic group variations in personal behavior (Fig. 6.1) and differential use of the available psychiatric health care services (Cole *et al.* 1980, Gaw 1982, Littlewood & Lipsedge 1982, Rack 1982, Hall *et al.* 1985, Liu & Yu 1985).

Psychiatric service statistics are the principal source of data on the incidence and prevalence of mental disorders. For most countries their publication is effected by the combined efforts of the appropriate departments of the state (e.g., the Department of Health and Social Security for England & Wales) in collaboration with the record departments of all the individual psychiatric service areas (Fig. 6.1). Unfortunately, in many countries, both psychiatric morbidity and mortality records are either not produced or published, or are published only intermittently and in highly aggregated form. Precise comparative international and national analyses of mental disorder incidence rates (Fig. 6.2) are consequently severely handicapped by these constraints (Giggs 1977, WHO 1985). Even in the UK, where mental health care is provided almost exclusively by the National Health Service, there are still marked local (i.e. service area based) variations in the quality, range and continuity of the statistics recorded. Thus Cochrane (1977), in a study of psychiatric hospital admissions in England & Wales, found that information on country of birth was missing for 30% of all patients. Only eight psychiatric register areas in the UK currently have centralized, computerized, psychiatric case registers (i.e., Aberdeen, Camberwell, Cardiff, Nottingham, Oxford, Salford, Southampton, and Worcester). Although these cover only 5% of the total population of England, Wales, and Scotland, they are used to provide comparative statistics on specialist psychiatric care in Britain (Jennings 1983). Only the Nottingham Register area (1981 population, 380,023) has a computerized file which matches psychiatric case register records with the national population census (1971 and 1981) small-area boundaries (i.e., enumeration districts) and census data (Giggs & Cooper 1986). From 1975 onwards it is thus possible to select cases quickly from the large patient *characteristics* and *event* files (Table 6.1), assign them to appropriate spatial units and calculate both incidence (or prevalence) rates and the relevant demographic and social–environmental variables. Matched systems of this kind are essential requirements if workers in psychiatric ecology in particular, and psychiatric epidemiology in general, are to make significant advances over existing research.

The final important requirement for ecological psychiatric research is adequate population census data. Ideally, researchers require readily accessible detailed census statistics, since these constitute the denominators for the calculation of precise mental illness incidence or prevalence rates for the appropriate spatial framework. Yet again, in practice, these requirements are rarely fully satisfied. A review of international variations in the incidence of several mental disorders (Giggs 1977) showed that, during the early 1960s, many countries lacked adequate population census data. Even in Europe, nearly 25 years later (WHO 1985), the problem persists. Similarly, in those countries where population censuses are quite detailed, published regularly, and are readily accessible, many kinds of ecological studies of mental disorders are still constrained by inadequacies in the data recorded in those censuses (Giggs 1979). Thus, in the UK, the analysis of the incidence of mental disorder by ethnic status and marital status is severely restricted by the crude categorization of these important groups in the population census (Giggs 1983, 1986a).

The spatial patterning of mental disorders

For spatial ecologists, the first important stage in their analyses is the identification of spatial variations in the incidence or prevalence of mental disorder at some desired spatial scale (Fig. 6.2). However, few geographers would agree with Shepherd's (1984a) sweeping assertion that, among epidemiological approaches, "The simplest demographic level is that of medical geography." It is certainly true that most spatial studies of mental disorders have been produced by nongeographers, and that their methodological sophistication has rarely advanced beyond the techniques employed by the founding fathers of ecological psychiatry (e.g., Faris & Dunham 1939). During the past 25 years, however, geography has witnessed enormous advances in the fields of statistical and spatial analysis (Wrigley & Bennett 1980). Although medical geography has participated in these developments (Pyle 1979, Greenberg 1983, McGlashan & Blunden 1983) it is true that almost all of the research to date has been devoted to the mapping of *physical* illnesses and mortality. The adequate mapping of mental disorders has barely begun and is a matter of considerable urgency (Giggs 1979).

Inspection of the existing studies confirms that there is marked variation in terms of the spatial scales employed in ecological research. The international, national, and regional scales (Fig. 6.2) are comparatively poorly represented. Researchers working at these "macro" spatial levels have used either the routinely published national morbidity and mortality statistics for administrative areas, with all their attendant disadvantages (Giggs 1977) or compared the mental illness prevalence rates identified in detailed community surveys of selected places (e.g. towns or villages), scattered around the world. Warner (1985) has employed both strategies in a detailed comparative analysis of the prevalence of schizophrenia in both the developed and Third World countries. Although the results are interesting, they must be interpreted with caution. Thus Warner's analysis of global spatial variations in the prevalence of schizophrenia is based upon the findings of only 68 prevalence studies. Meaningful statistical analysis and interpretation of spatial variations in the world distribution of mental disorders will require a much larger set of study areas than this. King *et al.* (1982) adopted quite a different approach in their study of Northern Ireland. Instead of mapping regional variations in the levels of mental illness in this socially disturbed province, they analysed psychotropic drug use. Analysis of the psychotopic drug prescribing data for the region's 17 health districts in 1978 revealed that there were marked spatial variations, with the highest rate of tranquillizer and hypnotic drug prescribing located in the eastern, pre-dominantly urban, districts. In contrast, the highest rates of neuroleptic and antidepressant use were found in the western and southern rural parts of the province.

Although disease mapping has been poorly served at the macroregional scales, there is better evidence for the existence of substantial (and generally consistent) spatial variations in the levels of mental illness morbidity and mortality at the intra-urban scale, and also along the urban–rural con-tinuum. Existing reviews of the ecological literature (Giggs 1980, Rutter 1981, Freeman 1984, Shepherd 1984a) generally confirm the fact that there are consistent variations both between urban areas (differentiated by such variables as population size, social class and economic "health") and between rural and urban areas. These findings apply for mental disorders of all levels of severity, ranging from the psychoses, through minor psychiatric illnesses to subclinical disorders, and measures of psychological distress and expressed dissatisfaction (Shepherd 1984a).

It has been suggested that these differences between big cities, smaller towns, and rural areas might simply be due to the fact that the cities have disproportionately larger (and more accessible) shares of the psychiatric services. Certainly, similar significant differences still persist between urban and rural areas in access to other forms of health service (Palen & Johnson 1983). However, control for these effects in several urban–rural comparative studies has still produced significant excesses of cases in the cities (Lavik 1977, Rutter 1981, Adebimpe et al. 1982, Burvill et al. 1982a, Blazer et al. 1985). Many more studies are required, though, to confirm the generality of these findings.

When a temporal dimension is added to these studies the results are considerably improved. Several sets of national statistics for mental dis-orders have recently been analysed by Warner (1985). He argues that the fluctuations in mental disorders can be linked with parallel changes in such macrolevel influences as industrialization, urbanization, and unemploy-ment (see also Ch. 7). Several workers have also commented upon the apparent worldwide increase in mental disorders over time (Kramer 1983, Hafner 1985). The utility of the temporal perspective has also been demonstrated at lower spatial scales (Fig. 6.2). Thus Krupinski has analysed changes in suicide, drug abuse, violence and mental illness in Victoria State, Australia (1976, 1979). The issues of diagnostic stability and hospital size are clearly very influential in temporal research (Krupinski et al. 1983). More recently, Hunter et al. (1986) have shown that, for large mental hospitals in 18 US states and two Canadian provinces during the first half of the 19th century, "frictions of distance inexorably reduced admission rates." Dur-ing that period, therefore, the limitations of contemporary transportation technology had a direct effect upon admission rates to mental hospitals. At a still more localized scale (i.e., the inter-urban level), several workers have shown that the rates for several mental disorders now appear to be increasing (e.g. Hagnell *et al.*1982).

Much of the attention in ecological psychiatry has been focused upon the intra-urban spatial patterning of mental disorders (Fig. 6.2). This interest can be attributed to three factors: first, the bulk of the populations of developed countries live in large urban areas; secondly, the pioneering research of urban sociologists in the USA (Park & Burgess 1925) revealed that each big city constituted a mosaic of widely contrasted social, demographic and environmental subareas; thirdly, for psychiatric epidemiological research the problems of variation in diagnostic reliability and of case finding were considerably reduced, since the administrative boundaries of cities usually coincided with those of psychiatric service areas (e.g., psychiatric registers).

Although quite a large number of intra-urban studies now exist, it is not possible to make *precise* generalizations concerning their findings. Inspection of the available studies shows that there is considerable methodological variation. Thus, for schizophrenia, most authors have used only psychiatric hospital admissions to calculate rates (e.g., Faris & Dunham 1939, Levy & Rowitz 1973). Relatively few workers have identified the total cases in contact with *all* the psychiatric services located within their study areas (e.g., Taylor 1974; Giggs 1973a, 1983, 1986b). Secondly, there are marked variations in the kinds of rates used by authors. Thus, for schizophrenia, Faris & Dunham (1939) and Levy & Rowitz (1973) used both first admissions (i.e., incidence) and unduplicated first and subsequent admissions (i.e., prevalence). In other studies the total first-admission schizophrenia group has been disaggregated into subsets by gender and by ethnic, family, and marital status (Giggs 1973a, 1983, 1986a) and by levels of diagnostic precision (Giggs 1986b). The third source of variation in intra-urban ecological studies of mental disorders arises from the use of widely different areal units as spatial frameworks. These have ranged in size from enumeration districts (average population size 500), through census tracts and electoral wards (population range, 5,000–15,000) to entire metropolitan boroughs in London (Giggs 1979). The effects of using spatial frameworks of contrasting size have never been measured in psychiatric ecological studies, although the influences of size and numbers of areal units are known to be important (Dever 1972a, b; Stimson 1983).

Despite these methodological differences, simple visual comparison of the spatial patterning of the various mental disorders which have been mapped reveals a remarkable stability both across national boundaries and through time. For most mental disorders, ranging from the psychoses to minor subclinical complaints, there is a gradient pattern (Taylor 1974, Daiches 1981). Typically, the highest rates are found in inner city neighborhoods and the lowest in suburban areas. However, several British studies have also shown that important secondary high-rate tracts are to be found in suburban areas (Bagley *et al.* 1973; Taylor 1974; Giggs 1983, 1986b). Thus the distribution of high-rate schizophrenia areas in Nottingham (Fig. 6.3a) is typically bipolar (Giggs 1986b). An important exception appears to be affective psychosis (i.e., manic depression), for virtually every study has shown that its spatial distribution is random in character (Giggs 1980). The spatially diffuse distribution of high-rate affective psychoses areas in Nottingham (Fig. 6.3b) is typically representative in this respect (Giggs 1986b). Furthermore, analysis of two separate cohorts of affective psychotics, differentiated by diagnostic attributes, produced virtually identical spatial results in Nottingham (Giggs 1986b). However, a word of caution needs to be added here. Virtually all the intra-urban analyses have been based on entire diagnostic categories, e.g., schizophrenia. When these cohorts are disaggregated by gender, family, marital, and ethnic status, the spatial distributions become more complex (Giggs 1983, 1986a). These findings suggest that further research is needed on this particular subject. Moreover, the significance of the observed spatial variations in the incidence of most mental disorders needs to be tested statistically, not simply mapped and discussed descriptively (Giggs 1983, 1986a, b). Thus Poisson probability analysis and mapping can identify those areas in which the numbers of cases of specific mental disorders are significantly greater, or smaller, than could be expected by chance (Fig. 6.3c, d).

Considerable scope still exists for several other important developments in mapping mental disorders, particularly at the intra-urban scale. Thus several mental disorders have received very little attention from ecological researchers. This is particularly true of the depressive illnesses. Some writers suggest that we may now be entering an "age of melancholy" (Fried 1982, Hagnell *et al.* 1982). In Nottingham, 20% of all the admissions at the District Hospital Accident and Emergency Unit every year are parasuicides (i.e., attempted suicides). Similar rates have been reported for other cities in the UK (Burston 1970, Griffin 1983), and yet the spatial analysis of this phenomenon (and also of suicide) has been undertaken in only a few localities, notably Brighton (Bagley *et al.* 1973, Bagley & Jacobson 1976), Bristol (Morgan *et al.* 1975, Griffin 1983) and, especially, in Edinburgh (Holding *et al.* 1974, Buglass & Duffy 1978, Platt & Kreitman 1985).

The range of psychiatric ecological analysis could also be usefully extended by focusing upon specific population groups, rather than simply upon diagnostic groups. Sociologists (Bastide 1972) and psychiatric epidemiologists (Cooper & Morgan 1973) have long recognized that both the incidence and prevalence of mental disorders vary significantly among subgroups of given populations, defined by such variables as gender, age, family status, socioeconomic status, and ethnicity. However, specifically ecological (i.e., spatial) analyses of these subgroups are quite rare. Thus

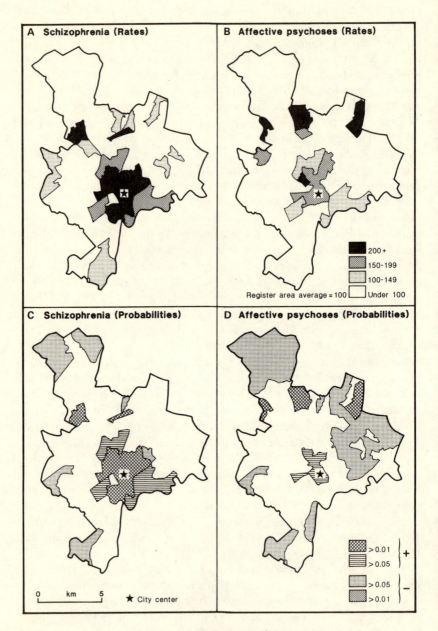

Figure 6.3 The distribution of schizophrenia and the affective psychoses in Nottingham.

virtually all ecological analyses have been limited to consideration of mental disorders among the *adult* population; children have been virtually ignored. Although child psychiatry is a relatively young discipline (Rutter 1986) it is clear that many forms of psychopathology have their roots in the early years of life (Rutter 1985), that they have important implications for the adult years, and that there is considerable scope for both mapping and ecological analysis (Rutter 1981, 1985; Garfunkel *et al*. 1982; Stein & Susser 1985).

The incidence and spatial patterning of mental disorders among apparently vulnerable immigrant ethnic communities has received considerable attention in countries where they have long constituted significant proportions of the total population, notably the USA (Levy & Rowitz 1973, Gaw 1982) and Australia (Krupinski 1975, Burvill *et al*. 1982b). In the UK, however, the influx of large numbers of immigrants has been a very recent phenomenon (rising from 2.0% of the total population of England & Wales in 1951 to 6.6% in 1981). Ecological analyses of these diverse newcomers are therefore quite rare (Giggs 1986a). The worldwide onset of economic recession in the mid-1970s has revived concern about the likely links between changes in the macro-economy and morbidity and mortality (see Ch. 7). The specifically psychologically harmful effects of unemployment have been well documented in numerous recent papers (e.g., Kasl 1982, Warr 1982, Hagen 1983, Stokes *et al*. 1984, Linn *et al*. 1985, Ullah *et al*. 1985). Even so, the spatial aspects of the incidence of mental illness and distress among the unemployed have been addressed by very few researchers. There are several aggregate cross-sectional ecological studies which show significant associations between mental illness rates and unemployment (e.g., Bagley *et al*. 1973, Faris & Dunham 1973, Buglass & Duffy 1978), but virtually no comparative ecological analyses of the incidence of mental disorders among the employed and unemployed sectors of the workforce. The study of parasuicide among employed and unemployed men in Edinburgh (Platt & Kreitman 1985) is an important recent exception. They have calculated parasuicide rates for the two groups, using the 23 electoral wards for 1971 (1970–72 data) and the 31 regional electoral districts (REDs) for 1981 (1980–82). Unfortunately, the rates are presented only in tabular form, but there are clearly massive spatial variations, and these certainly deserve further analysis.

Among the various population groups which merit further ecological analysis, however, unquestionably the most important are the elderly (i.e., those over 65 years old). The worldwide increase in the proportion of the elderly population has been widely documented (Warnes 1982, Post 1983, Shepherd 1984b). Thus the total population of England & Wales rose by only 29% between 1921 and 1971, compared with 163% for the elderly. This massive increase has important mental health implications for, despite the substantial problems involved in determining their prevalence (e.g., Cooper & Bickel 1984, Henderson & Huppert 1984), mental illnesses are markedly more common among the elderly than any other age group. Only a small proportion of the mentally ill elderly population receives psychiatric care: even so, the 1980 point prevalence rates for psychiatric contacts in Nottingham rose from 178 and 180 per 100,000 population respectively for males and females aged 15–24, to 1,123 and 1,624 for males and females aged 75 and over. Moreover, the massive increases in the numbers of elderly mentally ill are compounded by the fact that these illnesses tend to be chronic and progressive. Thus Winn (1985) found that 58.4% of the elderly first contacts with Nottingham's psychiatric services during 1979–81 had organic psychoses, and a further 15.6% had other psychoses.

There are very few explicitly spatial studies of the mental disorders of old age. In US cities a gradient has been identified, with the highest incidence and prevalence rates for senile psychoses occurring in city-center neighborhoods (Faris & Dunham 1939, Queen 1940, Schroeder 1942, Gruenberg 1954, Levy & Rowitz 1973). For English cities, however, the spatial patterns for the senile psychoses are more diffuse (Hare 1956, Bagley et al. 1973, Taylor 1974, Winn 1985). Winn's study of Nottingham is the most comprehensive analysis to date, for she has analysed all elderly first contacts with local psychiatric services during 1979–81. Furthermore, the cohort is subsequently disaggregated into important diagnostic subgroups (i.e., organic and nonorganic psychoses, and neurotics) by gender and marital status.

The spatial analysis of mental disorders could also be further advanced by a sustained and systematic interest in the question of temporal stability. All of the existing spatial research is essentially cross-sectional, or "period picture," in character. Furthermore, for most cities, the distribution of mental disorder has been studied only once. In relatively few cases do we have the opportunity to compare two or more successive "snapshots" showing distributions at successive points of time. Thus it is possible to compare two dates for Chicago (Faris & Dunham 1939, Levy & Rowitz 1973), three for Edinburgh (Buglass & Duffy 1979, Platt & Kreitman 1985), Liverpool (see Giggs 1979) and Nottingham (Giggs 1973a, 1983, 1986b), and eight for London (Sainsbury 1955, Whitlock 1973, Farmer et al. 1977, Howe 1979). Unfortunately, it is generally possible only to compare the distributions visually, because of variations in research design between the different studies. Nevertheless, the findings suggest that there is frequently considerable stability in the distribution of many mental disorders over quite long periods of time. These facts raise questions concerning the mechanisms generating consistently high (or low) rates in specific neighborhoods within large cities (Buglass & Duffy 1978). Thus the three studies of schizophrenia in Nottingham showed that the inner-city neighborhoods had the highest incidence rates over the period 1969–80 (Giggs 1973a, 1983, 1986b). This is quite remarkable for, during this period, most of the 19th-century housing stock in the city centre was completely cleared and replaced by new public housing estates and deck-access blocks of flats. Moreover, most of the former residents were rehoused in suburban public housing estates. Of 12,068 households rehoused from only two of these clearance and redevelopment areas, only 2,847 (23.6%) were rehoused back into their redeveloped neighborhoods.

Environment – mental health relationships

For more than a century, therefore, it has been demonstrated that there are marked variations in the spatial distribution of most mental disorders (Deas 1875). Furthermore, these variations have been mapped at a variety of geographical scales (Fig. 6.2). It is only at the intra-urban level, though, that we have sufficiently numerous studies to enable us to make reasonably firm statements concerning the spatial regularity of patterns of mental disorder distribution and of their temporal stability.

The identification of spatial variations in the distribution of mental disorders have invariably prompted the familiar geographical question "Why there?". Most researchers have therefore endeavored to analyse the relationships between mental disorder distribution and specific elements drawn from a host of potentially "causal" environmental factors (Fig. 6.1). Several comprehensive reviews of this ecological research (and of its conceptual and methodological limitations) have been published during the past decade (Giggs 1979, 1980; Smith 1980, 1984; Freeman 1984). These show that many efforts have been made to attribute various mental disorders to specific causes. These range in scale from individual and family genetic factors, physical, psychological and psychosocial attributes, through such mesoscale (i.e., ecological level) factors as the social and built environmental attributes of neighborhoods, to the macroscale effects exerted by national social, economic, and political systems (i.e., the state), and the "gatekeeper" attributes of the mental health care system (Fig. 6.2). However, most of the available evidence appears to suggest that mental illnesses result from multiple determinants. Thus Strauss & Carpenter (1981) proposed an interactive conceptual model incorporating many factors which appear to influence the development and course of schizophrenia. Their model embraces both temporal and scale components. An individual may therefore become predisposed to schizophrenia during the prenatal and perinatal period (e.g., via genetic predisposition), vulnerable to schizophrenia during childhood (e.g., via physical injuries, infections, learning defects, or family problems), and then have a schizophrenic episode precipitated by stressful life events, or by family, neighborhood, or work environments. The sequential and interrelated nature of the many factors affecting the levels of mental health in a given population has also been modelled by Hill (1982).

It seems likely, therefore, that significant advances in the study of mental illness causation will come from interdisciplinary, multiscale, longitudinal investigations. It is certain that geographers can make important contributions to this research. However, they will need to demonstrate more often (and effectively) the importance of the spatial dimension in psychiatric epidemiology, particularly by improving the statistical methods employed in disorder—environmental analysis at the ecological level. Furthermore, it will also be necessary to incorporate into these mesolevel analyses the findings of other researchers, working at both the micro- and macrolevels (e.g., geneticists, psychologists, and sociologists). Equally importantly, investigation of the causation, course and outcome of mental disorders will require increased geographical involvement in longitudinal analyses. These suggestions can be supported by evidence drawn from recent research.

It is generally accepted that the aggregative and cross-sectional attributes of ecological analyses of mental disorder severely constrain their power in "explaining" observed spatial variations in the distributions of those mental disorders (Giggs 1979, 1980; Smith 1980, 1984). Nevertheless, they have identified strong and systematic statistical relationships with many aspects of the social and built environment, particularly at the intra-urban scale. Despite these methodological limitations, their continued use is still widely advocated, both in the search for neighborhood effects on mental health and as a means of determining needs for psychiatric services among well recognized vulnerable client groups (Dohrenwend & Dohrenwend 1982, Gordon 1982, Morgenstern 1982, Wilkinson & O'Connor 1982). In addition, further ecological analysis of many disorders (e.g., depressive illnesses and attempted suicide) and important subgroups of the total population (e.g., children, ethnic minorities, the unemployed, and the elderly) is required, since they are poorly represented in the literature. Furthermore, the burgeoning literature on the mental health effects of natural and man-made disasters rarely contains any explicit analysis of the spatial–ecological dimensions (Giggs 1980, Sims 1984).

Recent geographical contributions have focused upon using better statistical methods. Thus factor analysis and nonhierarchical cluster analysis have been used to identify optimum sets of neighborhoods as a prelude to analysing the spatial distribution and ecological correlates of schizophrenia (Giggs 1983, 1986b) and the mental disorders of old age (Winn 1985). Furthermore, these two researchers have disaggregated these broad groups into significant diagnostic and social subsets, thus revealing important variations in both their distributions and ecological correlates. In addition, the relationships between these variables have been measured by means of generalized linear models (GLMs) and the newer Generalized Linear Interactive Modelling (GLIM: Griffin 1983, Winn 1985). Psychiatric epidemiologists have also used multivariate statistical methods to good effect. Thus Buglass & Duffy (1978) used both multiple regression analysis and canonical correlation analysis in their study of the ecological pattern of suicide and parasuicide in Edinburgh. For those studies in which the numbers of new cases emerging in a given population are relatively low (e.g., puerperal psychosis and schizophrenia) it would appear that newly developed Poisson regression techniques (Lovett et al. 1986) offer exciting possibilities. This concern for methodology is echoed in the wider debate about the role of statistics in psychiatry and psychiatric epidemiology (Knuiman & Burvill 1984, Hand 1985, Veiel 1985).

The interpretive problems inherent in ecological analysis need to be addressed more seriously and systematically in future research. One way of doing this would be to test the stability and strength of mental disorder, environmental correlations for a range of different spatial scales. Pioneering research on this topic by Dever (1972a, b) has yet to be fully explored by psychiatric epidemiologists. Bagley et al. (1973) used both electoral wards and enumeration districts in their ecological analysis of mental illness, suicide and delinquency in Brighton, but provided no statistical analysis of the relationship between the two sets of results. Another useful research strategy would involve combining both the ecological and behavioral approaches in a single study. This approach is currently best exemplified by three linked analyses of clinical, social, and ecological data for completed suicides in Brighton (Jacobson et al. 1976, Bagley et al. 1976, Bagley & Jacobson 1976).

Many researchers have also attempted to overcome the specifically cross-sectional limitations of traditional ecological analysis by invoking particular processes to explain observed spatial variations in the incidence of mental disorder. Thus, Faris & Dunham (1939) tried to explain the massive concentrations of mental disorders in central Chicago in terms of both the "breeder" (i.e., the stress, or social causation) hypothesis and the residential "drift" (i.e., the social selection) hypothesis. Unfortunately, both they and many other workers were unable to test the relative importance of these two mechanisms because they lacked data relating to the actual residential movements of the mentally ill population (see Giggs 1984). Other analysts have suggested that the inner-city concentration of high rates of mental disorder might be attributed to additional processes, notably the genetic and social "pooling" of vulnerable populations in the inner city (Lei et al. 1974, Irving 1975), and the selective outward movement of the mentally healthy individuals who are both willing and able to do so, leaving the relatively less competent behind (i.e., the social residue hypothesis, see Freeman 1984).

In order to be able to test these hypotheses properly one would require the full record of the residential histories of mentally ill individuals during the pre-morbid phase. This information is, of course, extremely difficult to acquire. However, several researchers have explored the residential movements of psychiatric patients after their first contact (e.g., Dunham

1965, Daiches 1981, Giggs & Cooper 1986). Even here there are difficulties, due to erosion of the initial survey populations. Thus Daiches (1981) reports that only 48% of the respondents first interviewed in Chicago in 1972 could be reinterviewed in 1976–7. In contrast, Giggs & Cooper (1986) found that 81 out of 90 schizophrenics were still living in Nottingham 5 years after first contact. Of the 1,106 persons reinterviewed in the Chicago study, 268 (24.2%) had changed addresses. Of these, only 13% had moved closer to the city center and most were more psychologically distressed than when first interviewed. In contrast, over 48% of the movers were living further away from Chicago's center in 1976–7 than when first interviewed. More-over, few of these outmigrants displayed increased distress. In the Nottingham study only 14 (17.3%) of the schizophrenics changed address within 5 years of first contact. Of these movers, only six (four of them with their families) had "drifted" inwards to poorer central-city neighborhoods. In these two particular studies, therefore, the residential drift hypothesis appears to find little supportive evidence.

Further scope also exists for ecological investigation and interdisciplinary research which incorporates "causal" strands other than the familiar social and physical (especially built) environments shown in Figures 6.1 and 6.2. The environmental roles played by the individual, the mental health services, and the state *vis-à-vis* the spatial distribution of mental disorders, all deserve greater attention than they have received to date. The possible biological and psychological antecedents of mental disorder in individuals have long attracted the attention of psychiatrists. Thus the question of the role of genetics in the etiology of schizophrenia has concerned psychiatrists and neurologists for decades (Stevens 1982, Abrams & Taylor 1983, Crow 1983, Lidz & Blatt 1983, Kety 1983, McGuffin 1984, Sturt & McGuffin 1985, Warner 1985). Despite a considerable number of disappointments, there do appear to be a few instances in which links between some biological factors and some mental disorders have been established. Thus mental retardation due to Down's syndrome results from a defect in one of the chromosomes (trisomy 21). Similarly, the notion of viral infection as a major etiological factor in several mental disorders, has received fresh impetus from recent research findings (Morozov 1983, Bruce 1984, Ridley *et al.* 1986). The possibility that some mental disorders are contagious suggests that hypotheses about spatial contagion and diffusion could be tested, using methods long familiar to medical geographers (Pyle 1979). Explicitly spatial studies of genetic factors in mental disorders and mental subnormality are poorly represented in the literature (Penrose 1958, WHO 1979) and clearly deserve greater attention.

The contributions of psychologists and psychiatrists to the classification of personality and personality disorders in individuals (Eysenck 1970, Eysenck & Eysenck 1976, Blashfield 1984, Widiger & Frances 1985) have also been neglected by geographers. The relationships between several mental disorders and the major dimensions of personality are now well known and could be profitably incorporated into ecological analyses. In one rare example, Lynn & Hampson (1975) have attempted to extend personality theory as formulated for individuals to the analysis of national personality differences. They used the national prevalence rates for 12 variables (including suicide, alcoholism, and chronic psychosis) as measures of the levels of extroversion and neuroticism in the populations of the world's 18 most economically advanced countries. Principal components analysis yielded two major axes which were labelled as extroversion and neuroticism. The component scores indicated that the most extrovert nation was the USA, and the most introvert was Japan. The most neurotic nation was Austria and the least neurotic was Ireland. A subsequent analysis of fluctuations in national levels of neuroticism and extroversion in these 18 nations between 1935 and 1970 (Lynn & Hampson 1977) showed that levels of neuroticism rose significantly in the nine nations that experienced military defeat and occupation in World War II. Thereafter, neuroticism rates declined to present levels. Among the nine undefeated nations, levels of neuroticism remained fairly constant. For extroversion, the picture was quite different, for all the nations showed increases in levels. These correlated very strongly with increased affluence, indexed by per capita income. The nature of this relationship was considered to be a matter for speculation.

The findings of such macrolevel studies need to be treated with caution, given the substantial problems of data comparability and aggregation for nations of very different sizes. Even so, the identified links between two major dimensions of personality and measures of mental disorders deserve to be tested further, using smaller spatial units. Most of the relevant research has been conducted by environmental psychologists (Moos 1976, Freeman 1984). However, their attention has largely been restricted to community surveys of individual neighborhoods and such specialized residential settings as tower blocks and university campuses. Irving (1975), in contrast, has measured the two major dimensions of personality (i.e., extroversion and neuroticism) among samples of female respondents drawn from six socially, environmentally, and spatially disparate neighborhoods in the city of Hull. His exploratory investigation identified significant variations in these traits between the neighborhoods. These findings raise interesting questions concerning the genetic aspects of personality variation and the influence of the social and built environments upon personality development, notably with reference to the genesis of maladaptive behavioral patterns, mental disorder and mental subnormality. Unfortunately, this solitary geographical contribution has not been replicated elsewhere.

Although ecological analysis has been much criticized, it has nevertheless provided insights into the precipitants of mental disorder which have not been indentified via the traditional, aspatial, methodology employed in most psychiatric epidemiological research. These have shown, via detailed surveys of individuals and social groups, that, for example, rates of mental disorder, stress and expressed dissatisfaction within life circumstances tend to be higher among blacks than whites (Lawrence 1974, Gaw 1982, Little-wood & Lipsedge 1982, Smith 1984). These facts require qualification when the spatial context is considered, for several ecological studies have shown that the apparently inimical effects of ethnicity (and, indeed, of other important sociodemographic attributes, see Giggs 1980) vary markedly according to community setting within cities (Smith 1984, Giggs 1986a). First-admission rates for all ethnic groups tend to be higher where they constitute a minority of a neighborhood population than where they form the majority. To date, however, this important finding has raised more questions than it has answered (Smith 1984). Thus these high rates have been variously attributed to the fact that these particular individuals are mostly relatively "high achievers" (and are therefore more prone to stress and mental illness), socially and geographically isolated from the major, inner-city concentrations of their own folk; they are more willing to seek psychiatric care than their inner-city counterparts, or simply that such care is more readily available in the suburbs than in the central-city neighbor-hoods. Further research is required in order to determine whether one (or all) of these individual, social–environmental, or health services effects (Fig. 6.1) are involved.

The possibilities for linked behavioral–ecological research into the relationship between mental health and the individual are therefore con-siderable. Similar opportunities exist for examining the various influences exerted by the mental health services (Fig. 6.1). Most of the other contribu-tors in this book have demonstrated that the kind, volume, organization, operational methods, and distribution of psychiatric services have profound effects on the client populations. However, virtually all the research cited concerns service-related effects upon established cohorts of the mentally ill. In other words they relate primarily to the mental health careers of patients *after* the critical stage of first contact. In contrast, relatively few ecological studies show evidence of concern with measuring the effects which mental health services exert upon the *etiology* of mental disorder.

The major "gatekeeper" effects upon entry into psychiatric services were reviewed above (pp. 106–7), and therefore do not require further discussion here. However, several elements discussed therein merit ecologically orientated research. Thus the effects of diagnostic precision upon both the spatial patterning and ecological correlates of specific mental divisions need to be measured. Giggs (1986b) explored this topic in an analysis of two diagnostically discrete categories each for schizophrenia and affective psychoses in Nottingham. Mapping and Pearson correlation analysis revealed that the spatial distributions of the two cohorts for both mental disorders were virtually identical. Regression analyses of disorder – social–environmental precipitants also yielded stable results across the diagnostic groups.

The detailed data collected for new contacts with modern psychiatric services (e.g., Table 6.1) would permit the researcher to test for other important health service effects. Thus it would be possible to determine, say, whether there were significant differences in mode of entry into contact with local psychiatric services (e.g., via compulsory admission, the police, consultants, family referrals) between specific subsets of the population (e.g., diagnostic groups, occupational groups) and for different neighborhoods within the psychiatric services catchment area. For many psychiatric service catchment areas there is likely to be considerable diversity, because relatively few mentally ill people are now admitted to mental hospitals (Jennings 1983). In Nottingham, for example, only 695 (6.1%) of 11,358 first contacts with local psychiatric services during 1975–80 entered hospital within the first six months of treatment (Kontny 1981). Tyrer *et al.* (1984) have used the Nottingham Psychiatric Register to measure the impact of devolving outpatient care to five new general practice (GP) psychiatric clinics, by comparing the frequency of contact with different psychiatric services in practices with and without psychiatric clinics. Over a two-year period, 20.5% of the patients referred to the new practices were first contacts (Tyrer 1984). Detailed discussion of the results of these two studies is not possible here. However, both the aggregate and spatial effects of such service developments clearly have important repercussions for etiological and ecological research.

Of the four main sets of influences which have been invoked to account for spatial variations in levels of mental health, the elements subsumed under the heading "the state" (Fig. 6.1) have probably received the most attention during the past 20 years. In consequence, there now exists quite a substantial body of research which examines the impact of pervasive social, economic, and political forces upon the spatial distribution and treatment patterns of the mentally ill at a variety of spatial scales (Smith 1984, Warner 1985). However, most of this research effort has focused upon the spatio-temporal effects of these predominantly macrolevel forces for established populations of the mentally ill, rather than upon their (potentially) illness-inducing attributes. Moreover, in some studies it is evident that prevalence data have been used, so that the effects for first contacts (i.e., incidence, or illness inception) cannot be isolated. In the Atlantic Provinces of Canada, for example, Richman *et al.* (1984) examined the interrelations of provincial policy, psychiatric service resource factors, and sociodemographic variables with standardized measures of short-term psychiatric bed use. Preliminary analysis identified substantial variations in the number of bed-days per capita (age–sex standardised) among the 42 counties of the region. Regression analyses of the policy, resource, and sociodemographic

Table 6.1   Data format on magnetic tapes, Nottingham Psychiatric Case Register. Each patient record consists of two parts, patient characteristics and event details. It is preceded by a "header," a four-digit number specifying record length. The "header" takes values such as 44, 50, 56, and 62, comprising 1–38 patient characteristics plux $6 \times n$ patient events, where $n = 1, 2, 3 \ldots \infty$.

---

(1) Patient characteristics

This is a fixed-length section describing patient characteristics. Allowance is made for the fact that some items, such as addresses, can change with time. The format used for the file is: [I6, I1, 2I6, I1, 2(I1, I6), 2I4, 2(2I4, I6), 4I1, 6I4, 2I3, 2(I3, I6), I2, 2I1] and the following data is recorded.

(1) Patient identity number	(20) Social service area (current), I1
(2) Sex, I1	(21) Social service area 2, I1
(3) Date of birth, I6	(22) Social service area 3, I1
(4) Date of first psychiatric contact, I1 (in Mapperley Group of hospitals)	(23) Previous psychiatric contact elsewhere, I1
(5) Marital status (current), I1	(24) Diagnosis—primary, I4
(6) Marital status 2, I1	(25) Diagnosis—secondary, I4
(7) Date of change, I6	(26) Diagnosis—physical, I4
(8) Marital status 3, I1	(27)
(9) Date of change, I6	(28) } Supplementary diagnoses, I4
(10) Marital status 4, I1	(29)
(11) Date of change, I6	(30) Occupation, I3
(12) House number (current), I4	(31) GP (current), I3
(13) Street code (current), I4	(32) GP 2, I3
(14) House number 2, I4	(33) Date of change, I6
(15) Street code 2, I4	(34) GP 3, I3
(16) Date of change, I6	(35) Date of change, I6
(17) House number 3, I4	(36) Number of pre-1975 admissions, I2
(18) Street code 3, I4	(37) Previous day-care pre-1975 (yes/no), I1
(19) Date of change, I6	(38) Previous outpatient care pre-1975 (yes/no), I1

(2) Event information

This is a variable-length section containing the psychiatric events which are cumulative over time and are stored chronologically. The format is (I6, 3I2, I1, I2) and records the following data.

(1) Date of contact, I6
(2) Place of contact, I2
(3) Type of contact, I2
(4) Consultant, I2
(5) Source of referral, I2
(6) Legal status, I2

The complete file is terminated by a header value: 9999. All records in unit number order. The filename NCRV where *wm* is used where *nn* is an identifying code. NCR stands for Nottingham Case Register. The tapes used are standard nine-track tapes containing patient records stored in serial mode in patient number order.

factors accounted for 61% of the total variation in use among males and 47% among females. The provincial policy variable was the single most important factor, explaining two-thirds of the total variability for males and nearly half that for females. Although the study was based on prevalence data, it nevertheless provides a valuable example of the ways in which the mental health effects of several social factors (i.e., the state, the mental health service, and aspects of the environment; see Fig. 6.1) can be examined simultaneously.

There is now a real need for specifically etiological analyses, at a variety of spatial scales, which incorporate much greater consideration of the various macrolevel forces subsumed under the heading of "the state" (Fig. 6.1). These should include analyses of the political impacts (e.g., legislative and financial) of the recent profound changes which have occurred in the provision of mental health services for the newly mentally ill in many Western countries (see especially the chapters in Parts I and III). In addition, the spatial aspects of mental illness and the criminal law (e.g., likelihood of being arrested, responsibility for a crime, being compulsorily admitted to a mental hospital) require further examination (Bean 1980, Morris, 1983, Teplin 1983, Teplin et al. 1985, Borzecki et al. 1985). An ecological analysis of psychiatric hospital admissions in Bristol (Ineichen et al. 1984) found that the proportion of admissions which were compulsorily admitted varied considerably from one part of the city to another. In the central-city wards compulsory admissions exceeded one in ten, but in the suburban middle-class wards the compulsory admissions were fewer than one in 30. Four central-city wards accounted for nearly 46% of all the city's New Commonwealth and Pakistan-born residents. Of the white UK-born residents in these four wards, 28% were admitted compulsorily; for nonwhite residents the rate was 51.6%, rising to 62.8% for West Indians. In addition, recent regional and intra-urban studies of political violence and mental illness in Northern Ireland (e.g., Lyons 1971, King et al. 1982, Cairns & Wilson 1984), and of the inimical mental health effects of apartheid in South Africa (Burke 1985, Dommisse 1985), highlight the importance of these phenomena and the need for further, more rigorous, ecological analyses.

The substantial body of research on the stressful effects of past and present fluctuations in the fortunes of national economies (Warner 1985, see also Ch. 7) also needs to be more effectively incorporated into ecological analyses of mental disorder. Some authors (e.g., Kasl 1982) argue that the results provided by macrolevel analyses are incomplete and sometimes contradictory. However, several microlevel and ecological investigations have confirmed the existence of a strong relationship between unemployment and several kinds of mental ill health (Bagley et al. 1973, Buglass & Duffy 1978, Banks & Jackson 1982, Melville et al. 1985, Platt & Kreitman 1985, Warr & Jackson 1985). Platt & Kreitman's (1985) analysis of parasuicide and unemployment among men in Edinburgh is particularly valuable because it incorporates both cross-sectional and longitudinal evidence. They found that the parasuicide rate among the unemployed was nearly always more than 10 times higher than among the employed. Among the unemployed the rates were highest among the long-term un-employed, followed by the most recently unemployed. Moreover, the ecological correlation between male unemployment and parasuicide was very strong across the city's 23 electoral wards in 1971 ($r = 0.76$) and 31 regional electoral divisions in 1981 ($r = 0.95$).

This brief and selective review of the existing ecological literature has shown that the state exerts considerable influence upon the mental health of the nation. These effects are the products of its social, political, and economic policies, and of its involvement in the funding, provision, and disposition of mental health services. However, as Figure 6.1 demonstrates, there is a further direction of research—into the effects of state involvement in the improvement of the environment. Since the early 19th century, it has been recognized that many determinants of human health are environ-mental and, therefore, susceptible to control. In the industrialized countries in particular, there has been a long tradition of governmental and legislative policies to control environmental health hazards and to promote health. Even so, inspection of the relevant literature reveals that most of the re-search which has established firmly convincing links between morbidity, mortality, and specific environmental factors (and thus prompted state intervention) relates to man's physical health (Holland *et al.* 1984, 1985). In contrast, for almost all mental illnesses, absolutely unequivocal evidence for specific environmental precipitants is still lacking. Therefore, it is perhaps scarcely surprising that governmental and legislative policies have been addressed almost exclusively to producing environmental improve-ments which were primarily intended to minimize physical illnesses.

Unwittingly, however, many of these governmental interventions in environmental issues also appear to have had considerable impact upon the mental health of large segments of the population. This has been most convincingly demonstrated in large urban areas, which now contain the majority of the population. Freeman (1984) has provided the most recent comprehensive review of the literature, much of which is ecological in terms of research design. This shows that since the 1950s, urban govern-ments have increasingly implemented programs designed to alleviate the inimical effects of 19th-century urban–industrial growth (e.g., pollution, high population densities, bad housing, and urban sprawl). Ironically, many of these entirely laudable activities have had unforseen adverse effects upon the mental health of some of the populations affected. Thus inner-city slum clearance programs, the building of high-rise flats, new public hous-ing estates, and new towns have frequently resulted in increased levels of mental disorder and psychological distress in newly created communities. Much of this illness appears to be comparatively mild and transitory in character, although high rates of schizophrenia and affective psychosis have been identified in both new suburban housing tracts and inner-city council estates in Nottingham (Giggs 1986b). Nevertheless, these findings demonstrate the need both for further research and for careful consideration of the likely mental health implications of environmental improvement programs by the responsible agencies.

In the USA there is evidence of a growing awareness among government agencies of the mental health implications of some of their environmental policies. In part this has been prompted by isolated, but potentially serious episodes, such as the nuclear accident at Three Mile Island (Fabrikant 1983, Fienberg *et al.* 1985). More importantly, though less dramatically, this attitudinal shift has been brought about by an increasing concern with the issues of preventive intervention and mental *health*, as opposed to the traditional concern with mental *illness* and its treatment. Research by psychiatrists and social scientists has helped to prompt this change in attitude (Weiss *et al.* 1981, Albee 1982, Philips 1983, Spaulding *et al.* 1983, Cahill 1984). Much of this research has been explicitly environmental and ecological in character (Brogan 1980, Andrews 1982, Sandler 1985). The notion that explicitly preventive psychiatric services should be established within the community has a comparatively long history in the USA. In 1963, the Community Mental Health Centre (CMHC) Act provided federal funds for this purpose as part of the first formal attempt to establish a national policy of comprehensive community mental health care. However, as Smith's (1984) review of the subsequent evaluative research has shown, the spread of this innovation has been both very limited and geographically uneven.

Conclusions

Although mental illnesses have long represented major social problems, their precise etiologies have yet to be determined exactly. Nevertheless, considerable progress has been made in the search for critical variables involved in the causation of mental illnesses. The growth of knowledge has been characterized by two features. First, development has proceeded via the emergence of largely separate bodies of literature on specific parts of the causal spectrum—biological, social and environmental. Secondly, the contributions made by the relevant scientific disciplines have varied markedly, in a fashion which scarcely reflects their relative importance. Thus medical geographers, who specialize in identifying both spatial variations in disease distribution and their aggregate (i.e., ecological) social–environmental correlates, have contributed only recently to the epidemiological analysis of mental disorders. This is regrettable for, as Lilienfeld (1957) observed over 30 years ago, epidemiology is "the study of the distribution of disease in time and space, and of the factors that influence this distribution."

This chapter has attempted to redress the balance by identifying both the past and likely future contributions of the spatial–ecological perspective. It has also involved the use of a conceptual model designed to synthesize and integrate the hitherto separate sets of literature relating to the causes of mental disorders. To date, the search for knowledge about the etiology of mental disorders has largely proceeded via in-depth analyses of individual components of the causal spectrum. Ultimately, however, the gains made by this reductionist approach are limited. The conceptual model presented here is intended to provide a framework for future recognition and exploration of the broader etiological system which generates mental disorders. Although the employment of an integrated perspective is likely to benefit future research, all the available evidence suggests that progress is unlikely to be rapid and spectacular. Etiological investigations of all the critical variables involved in the causation of mental disorders will be difficult to mount and accomplish, not least because of the chronic and long-term underfunding of research by both governments and medical research agencies.

References

Abrams, R. & M. A. Taylor 1983. The genetics of schizophrenia: a reassessment using modern criteria. *American Journal of Psychiatry* **140**, 171–5.

Adebimpe, M. D., C. Chung-Chou, H. E. Klein & M. H. Lange 1982. Racial and geographical differences in the psychopathology of schizophrenia. *American Journal of Psychiatry* **139**, 888–91.

Albee, G. W. 1982. Preventing psychopathology and promoting human potential. *American Psychologist* **37**, 1043–50.

Alexander, F. G. & S. T. Selesnick 1966. *The history of psychiatry*. New York: Harper & Row.

Andrews, H. F. 1982. *Preventive intervention for the health and well-being of urban children*. Child in the city: report no. 17. Toronto: University of Toronto, Center for Urban and Community Studies.

Bagley, C., S. Jacobson & C. Palmer 1973. Social structure and the ecological distribution of mental illness, suicide and delinquency. *Psychological Medicine* **3**, 177–87.

Bagley, C. & S. Jacobson 1976. Ecological variation of three types of suicide. *Psychological Medicine* **6**, 423–7.

Bagley, C., S. Jacobson & A. Rehin 1976. Clinical and social variables which differentiate suicide, open and accident verdicts. *Psychological Medicine* **6**, 417–21.

Banks, M. H. & P. R. Jackson 1982. Unemployment and risk of minor psychiatric disorder in young people: cross-sectional and longitudinal evidence. *Psychological Medicine* **12**, 789–98.

Bastide, R. 1972. *The sociology of mental disorder*. London: Routledge & Kegan Paul.

Bean, P. T. 1980. *Compulsory admissions to mental hospitals*. Chichester: Wiley.

Blashfield, R. 1984. *The classification of psychopathology: neo-Kraepelinian and quantitative approaches.* New York: Plenum Press.

Blazer, D. *et al.* 1985. Psychiatric disorders: a rural/urban comparison. *Archives of General Psychiatry* **42**, 651–6.

Borzecki, M. *et al.* 1985. The criminalisation of psychiatrically ill people: a review with a Canadian perspective. *Psychiatric Journal of the University of Ottawa* **10**, 241–7.

Brogan, D. R. 1980. Physical environment correlates of psychosocial health among urban residents. *American Journal of Community Psychology* **8**, 507–22.

Bruce, M. E. 1984. Scrapie and Alzheimer's disease. *Psychological Medicine* **14**, 497–500.

Buglass, D. & J. C. Duffy 1978. The ecological pattern of suicide and parasuicide in Edinburgh. *Social Science and Medicine* **12**, 241–53.

Burke, A. W. 1985. Mental health and apartheid: World Psychiatric Association conference report. *International Journal of Social Psychiatry* **31**, 144–8.

Burston, G. R. 1970. *Self-poisoning*, London: Llody-Luke.

Burvill, P. W., H. Stampfer, J. Reymond & J. Carlson 1982a. Comparison of psychiatric admissions between city and country residents in Western Australia. *Australian and New Zealand Journal of Psychiatry* **16** (4), 253–8.

Burvill, P. W., J. Reymond, H. Stampfer & J. Carlson 1982b. Relation between country of birth and psychiatric admissions in Western Australia. *Acta Psychiatrica Scandinavica* **66**, 322–35.

Cahill, J. 1984. Structural characteristics of the macroeconomy and mental health: implications for primary prevention research. *American Journal of Community Psychology* **11**, 553–71.

Cairns, E. & R. Wilson 1984. The impact of political violence on mild psychiatric morbidity in Northern Ireland. *British Journal of Psychiatry* **145**, 631–5.

Cochrane, R. 1977. Mental illness in immigrants to England and Wales: an analysis of mental hospital admissions, 1971. *Social Psychiatry* **12**, 25–35.

Coie, J. D., P. R. Constanzo & G. B. Cox 1980. Behavioral determinants of mental illness concerns: a comparison of community subcultures. *American Journal of Community Psychology* **8**, 537–53.

Cooper, B. & H. Bickel 1984, Population screening and the early detection of dementing disorders in old age: a review. *Psychological Medicine* **14**, 81–95.

Cooper, B. & H. G. Morgan 1973. *Epidemiological psychiatry.* Springfield, Ill.: Thomas.

Crow, T. 1983. Is schizophrenia an infectious disease? *Lancet* **8317**, 173–5.

Daiches, S. 1981. *People in distress: a geographical perspective on psychological well-being.* Research Paper no. 197, Department of Geography, University of Chicago.

Deas, P. M. 1875. An illustration of local differences in the distribution of insanity. *Journal of Mental Science* **21**, 61–7.

Dever, G. E. A. 1972a. Leukemia in Atlanta, Georgia. *Southeastern Geographer* **12**, 91–100.

Dever, G. E. A. 1972b. Leukemia and housing: an intra-urban analysis. In *Medical geography: techniques and field studies*, N. D. McGlashan (ed.), 233–46. London: Methuen.

Dohrenwend, B. P. & B. S. Dohrenwend 1982. Perspectives on the past and future of psychiatric epidemiology. *American Journal of Public Health* **72**, 1271–8.

Dommisse, J. 1985. Apartheid as a public mental health issue. *International Journal of Health Services* **15**, 501–10.

Dunham, H. W. 1965. *Community and schizophrenia.* Detroit: Wayne State University Press.

Eysenck, H. J. 1971. *The structure of human personality.* London: Methuen.
Eysenck, H. J. & S. B. G. Eysenck 1976. *Psychoticism as a dimension of personality.* London: Hodder & Stoughton.

Fabrikant, J. I. 1983. The effects of the accident at Three Mile Island on the mental health and behavioural responses of the general population and nuclear workers. *Health Physics* **45**, 579–86.
Faris, R. E. & H. W. Dunham 1939. *Mental disorders in urban areas.* Chicago: University of Chicago Press.
Farmer, R. T. D., T. D. Preston & S. E. M. O'Brien 1977. Suicide mortality in Greater London: changes during the past 25 years. *British Journal of Preventive and Social Medicine* **31**, 171-7.
Fienberg, S. E., E. J. Bromet, D. Follman, D. Lambert & S. M. May 1985. Longitudinal analysis of categorical epidemiological data: a study of Three Mile Island. *Environmental Health Perspectives* **63**, 241–8.
Freeman, H. L. 1978. Mental health and the environment. *British Journal of Psychiatry* **132**, 113—24.
Freeman, H. L. (ed.) 1984. *Mental health and the environment.* London: Churchill Livingstone.
Fried, M. 1982. Endemic stress: the psychology of resignation and the politics of scarcity. *American Journal of Orthopsychiatry* **52**, 4–19.

Garfunkel, B. D., A. Froese & J. Hood 1982. Suicide attempts in children and adolescents. *American Journal of Psychiatry* **139**, 1257–61.
Gaw, A. (ed.) 1982. *Cross-cultural psychiatry.* Boston: John Wright.
Giggs, J. A. 1973a. The distribution of schizophrenics in Nottingham. *Transactions, Institute of British Geographers* **59**, 55–76.
Giggs, J. A. 1973b. High rates of schizophrenia among immigrants in Nottingham. *Nursing Times* 1210–12.
Giggs, J. A. 1977. Mental disorders and subnormality. In *A World geography of human diseases*, G. M. Howe (ed.), 477–506. London: Academic Press.
Giggs, J. A. 1979. Human health problems in urban areas. In *Social problems and the city: geographical perspectives*, D. T. Herbert & D. M. Smith (eds.), 84–116. London: Oxford University Press.
Giggs, J. A. 1980. Mental health and the environment. In *Environmental Medicine*, G. M. Howe & J. A. Loraine (eds.), 281–305. London: Heinemann.
Giggs, J. A. 1983. Schizophrenia and ecological structure in Nottingham. In *Geographical aspects of health*, N. D. McGlashan & J. R. Blunden (eds.), 197–222. London: Academic Press.
Giggs, J. A. 1984. Residential mobility and mental health. In *Mental health and the environment*, H. T. Freeman (ed.), 327–54. London: Churchill Livingstone.
Giggs, J. A. 1986a. Ethnic status and mental illness in urban areas. In *Health, race and ethnicity*, T. Rathwell & D. Phillips (eds.), 137–74. London: Croom Helm.
Giggs, J. A. 1986b. Schizophrenia and affective psychosis in Nottingham. *Social Science and Medicine* **23**, 945–61.
Giggs, J. A. and J. E. Cooper 1986. Mental disorders and human ecological structure: a case study of schizophrenia and affective psychosis in Nottingham. *Cambria* **13** (1), 151–80.
Gordon, E. W. 1982. Human ecology and the mental health professions. *American Journal of Orthopsychiatrics* **51**, 109–10.

Griffin, L. R. 1983. *The utility of log-linear models in the analysis of the geography of mental health*. PhD thesis, University of Bristol.

Greenberg, M. 1983. *Urbanization and cancer mortality*. Oxford: Oxford University Press.

Gruenberg, E. M. 1954. Community conditions and psychoses of the elderly. *American Journal of Psychiatry* **110**, 888–96.

Hafner, H. 1985. Are mental disorders increasing over time? *Psychopathology* **18**, 66–81.

Hagen, D. Q. 1983. The relationship between job loss and physical and mental illness. *Hospital and Community Psychiatry* **34**, 438–41.

Hagnell, O., J. Lanke, B. Rorsman & L. Öjesjö 1982. Are we entering an age of melancholy? Depressive ilnesses in a prospective epidemiological study over 25 years: the Lundby Study, Sweden. *Psychological Medicine* **12**, 279–89.

Hall, L. E. & C. M. Tucker 1985. Relationships between ethnicity, conceptions of mental illness, and attitudes associated with seeking psychological help. *Psychological Reports* **57**, 907–16.

Hand, D. J. 1985. The role of statistics in psychiatry. *Psychological Medicine* **15**, 471–6.

Hare, E. H. 1956. Mental illnesses and social conditions in Bristol. *Journal of Mental Science* **102**, 349–57.

Henderson, A. S. & F. A. Huppert 1984. The problem of mild dementia. *Psychological Medicine* **14**, 5–11.

Hettner, A. 1927. *Die geographie, ihre gesicht, ihr wessen und ihr methoden*, Breslau, 1927. Cited in Hartshorne, R. 1961. *The nature of geography*, 140. Lancaster, Pennsylvania: The Association of American Geographers.

Hill, J. 1982. Reasons and causes: the nature of explanations in psychology and psychiatry. *Psychological Medicine* **12**, 501–14.

Holding, T. A., D. Buglass, J. C. Duffy & N. Kreitman 1974. Parasuicide in Edinburgh—a seven year review. *British Journal of Psychiatry* **130**, 534–43.

Holland, W. W., R. Detels & G. Knox (eds.) 1984. *Oxford textbook of public health. Vol. 1*. Oxford: Oxford University Press.

Holland, W. W., R. Detels & G. Knox (eds.) 1985. *Oxford textbook of public health. Vol. 2*. Oxford: Oxford University Press.

Howe, G. M. 1979. Death in London. *Geographical Magazine* **LI** (4), 284.

Hunter, J. M., G. W. Shannon & S. L. Sambrook 1986. Rings of madness: service areas of 19th century asylums in North America. *Social Science and Medicine* **23**, 1033–50.

Ineichen, B., G. Harrison & H. G. Morgan 1984. Psychiatric hospital admissions in Bristol, I. Geographical and ethnic factors. *British Journal of Psychiatry* **145**, 600–11.

Irving, H. W. 1975. A geographer looks at personality. *Area* **7** (3), 207–12.

Jacobson, S., C. Bagley & A. Rehin 1976. Completed suicide: a taxonomic analysis of clinical and social data. *Psychological Medicine* **6**, 429–38.

Jennings, C. 1983. *Psychiatric care in Britain: statistics from the Psychiatric Care Registers: 1976–81*. Mimeo paper, Knowle Hospital, Fareham, Southampton.

Kasl, S. V. 1982. Strategies of research on economic instability and health. *Psychological Medicine* **12**, 637–49.

Kety, S. S. 1983. Mental illness in the biological and adaptive relatives of schizophrenic adoptees: findings relevant to genetic and environmental factors in etiology. *American Journal of Psychiatry* **140**, 720–7.

King, D. J., K. Griffiths, P. M. Reilly & J. D. Merrett 1982. Psychotropic drug use in Northern Ireland 1966–80: prescribing trends, inter- and intra-regional comparison and relationship to demographic and socioeconomic variables. *Psychological Medicine* **12**, 819–33.

Knuiman, M. W. & P. W. Burvill 1984. A statistical modelling approach to community prevalence data. *Psychological Medicine* **14**, 167–73.

Kontny, E. L. A. 1981. *Nottingham case register report to the DHSS* (mimeo). Nottingham: Mapperley Hospital.

Kramer, M. 1983. The increasing prevalence of mental disorders: a pandemic threat. *Psychiatric Quarterly* **55**, 115–43.

Kramer, M. & J. Anthony 1983. Review of differences in mental health indicators used in national publications. Recommendations for their standardisation. *World Health Statistical Quarterly* **36**, 256–338.

Krupinski, J. 1975. Psychological maladaption in ethnic concentrations in Victoria, Australia. In *Cultures in collision*, I. Pilowsky (ed.). Adelaide: Australian National Association for Mental Health.

Krupinski, J. & L. Alexander 1983. Patterns of psychiatric morbidity in Victoria, Australia, in relation to changes in diagnostic criteria 1848–1978. *Social Psychiatry* **18**, 61–7.

Lavik, N. 1977. Urban–rural differences in rates of disorder: a comparative psychiatric population study of Norwegian adolescents. In *Epidemiological approaches in child psychiatry*, P. Graham (ed.), 223–51. London: Academic Press.

Lawrence, D. 1974. *Black migrants: white natives*. Cambridge: Cambridge University Press.

Learmonth, A. T. A. 1978. *Patterns of disease and hunger*. Newton Abbot, Devon: David & Charles.

Lei, T. J. *et al.* 1974. An ecological analysis of agency labelled retardates. *American Journal of Mental Deficiency* **79**, 22–31.

Levy, L. & L. Rowitz 1973. *The ecology of mental disorder*, New York: Behavioral Publications.

Lidz, T. & S. Blatt 1983. Critique of the Danish–American studies of the biological and adoptive relatives of adoptees who became schizophrenic. *American Journal of Psychiatry* **140**, 426–35.

Lilienfeld, A. M. 1957. Epidemiological methods and influences in studies of noninfectious diseases. *Public Health Reports* **72**, 51.

Linn, M. W., R. Sandifer & S. Stein 1985. Effects of unemployment on mental and physical health. *American Journal of Public Health* **75**, 502–6.

Littlewood, R. & M. Lipsedge 1982. *Aliens and alienists: ethnic minorities and psychiatry*. Harmondsworth: Penguin.

Liu, W. T. & E. S. H. Yu 1985. Ethnicity, mental health, and the urban delivery system. In *Urban ethnicity in the United States*, L. Maldonado & J. Moore (eds.), 211–47. Beverly Hills: Sage.

Lovett, A. A., C. G. Bentham & R. Flowerdew 1986. Analysing geographic variations in mortality using Poisson regression: the example of ischaemic heart disease in England and Wales. *Social Science and Medicine* **23**, 935–44.

Lynn, R. & S. L. Hampson 1975. National differences in extraversion and neuroticism. *British Journal of Social and Clinical Psychology* **14**, 223–40.

Lynn, R. & S. L. Hampson 1977. Fluctuations in national levels of neuroticism and extraversion. *British Journal of Social and Clinical Psychology* **16**, 131–7.

Lyons, H. A. 1971. Psychiatric sequelae of the Belfast riots. *British Journal of Psychiatry* **118**, 265–73.

McGlashan, N. D. (ed.) 1972. *Medical geography: techniques and field studies*. London: Methuen.
McGlashan, N. D. & J. R. Blunden (eds.) 1983. *Geographical aspects of health*. London: Academic Press.
McGuffin, P. 1984. Biological markers and psychosis. *Psychological Medicine* **14**, 255–8.
Melville, D. I., D. Hope, D. Bennison & B. Barraclough 1985. Depression among men involuntarily made redundant. *Psychological Medicine* **15**, 789–93.
Moos, R. R. 1976. *The human context: environmental determinants of behavior*. New York: Wiley.
Morgan, H. G., H. Pocock & S. Pottle 1975. The urban distribution of non-fatal deliberate self-harm. *British Journal of Psychiatry* **126**, 319–28.
Morgenstern, H. 1982. Uses of ecologic analysis in epidemiologic research. *American Journal of Public Health* **72**, 1336–44.
Morozov, P. V. (ed.) 1983. *Research on the viral hypothesis of mental disorders*. Basle: Karger.
Morris, N. 1983. Mental illness and the criminal law. In *Mental illness: changes and trends*, P. T. Bean (ed.), 1–25. Chichester: Wiley.

Palen, J. J. & D. M. Johnson 1983. Urbanization and health status. In *Cities and sickness: health care in urban America*, A. L. Greer & S. Greer (eds.), 25–54, Beverly Hills: Sage.
Park, R. E. & E. W. Burgess 1925. *The city*. Chicago: University of Chicago Press.
Penrose, L. S. 1958. Genetics of anencephaly. *Journal of Mental Deficiency Research* **1**, 4–15.
Philips, I. 1983. Opportunities for prevention in the practice of psychiatry. *American Journal of Psychiatry* **140**, 389–95.
Platt, S. & N. Kreitman 1985. Parasuicide and unemployment among men in Edinburgh 1968–82. *Psychological Medicine* **15**, 113–23.
Post, F. 1983. Psychogenatrics as a speciality. In *Mental illness: changes and trends*, P. Bean (ed.), 279–96. Chichester: Wiley.
Pyle, G. F. 1979. *Applied medical geography*. Washington, D.C.: Winston.

Queen, S. A. 1940. The ecological study of mental disorders. *American Social Review* **5**, 201–9.

Rack, P. 1982. *Race, culture and mental disorder*. London: Tavistock.
Richman, A., C. Boutilier & P. Harris 1984. The relevance of socio-demographic and resource factors in the use of acute psychiatric in-patient care in the Atlantic Provinces of Canada. *Psychological Medicine* **14**, 175–82.
Ridley, R. M., H. F. Baker & T. J. Crow 1986. Transmissible and non-transmissible neurodegenerative disease: similarities in age of onset and genetics in relation to aetiology. *Psychological Medicine* **16**, 199–207.
Rutter, M. 1981. The city and the child. *American Journal of Orthopsychiatry* **51**, 610–25.
Rutter, M. L. 1985. Resilience in the face of adversity: protective factors and resistance to psychiatric disorder. *British Journal of Psychiatry* **147**, 598–611.
Rutter, M. L. 1986. Child psychiatry: the interface between clinical and developmental research. *Psychological Medicine* **16**, 151–69.

Sainsbury, P. 1955. *Suicide in London*. London: Chapman & Hall.

Sandler, I. 1985. Children's environments and mental health: opportunity and responsibility. *American Journal of Community Psychology* **13**, 467–86.

Schroeder, C. W. 1942. Mental disorders in cities. *American Journal of Sociology* **48**, 40–7.

Schwab, J. L. & M. E. Schwab 1978. *Sociocultural roots of mental illness: an epidemiologic survey*. New York: Plenum Press.

Shepherd, M. 1984a. Urban factors in mental disorders—an epidemiological approach. *British Medical Bulletin* **40**, 401–4.

Shepherd, M. 1984b. Psychogeriatrics and the neo-epidemiologists. *Psychological Medicine* **14**, 1–4.

Sims, A. C. L. 1984. Mental illness and urban disorder. In *Mental health and the environment*, H. L. Freeman (ed.), 271–92. London: Churchill Livingstone.

Smith, C. J. 1977. *The geography of mental health*. Resource Paper no. 76–4. Washington, D.C.: Association of American Geographers.

Smith, C. J. 1980. Neighbourhood effects on mental health. In *Geography and the urban environment: progress in research and applications*, R. J. Johnson & D. T. Herbert (eds.), 363–415. Chichester: Wiley.

Smith, C. J. 1984. Geographical approaches to mental health. In *Mental health and the environment*, H. L. Freeman (ed.), 121–68. London: Churchill Livingstone.

Smith, D. M. 1982. Geographical perspectives on health and health care. In *Contemporary perspectives on health and health care*, 1–11. Occasional paper no. 20, Department of Geography, Queen Mary College, University of London.

Spaulding, J. & P. Baulch 1983. A brief history of primary prevention in the twentieth century: 1908 to 1980. *American Journal of Community Psychology* **11**, 59–80.

Stein, Z. & M. Susser 1985. Effects of early nutrition on neurological and mental competence in human beings. *Psychological Medicine* **15**, 717–26.

Stevens, J. R. 1982. The neuropathology of schizophrenia. *Psychological Medicine* **12**, 695–700.

Stimson, R. J. 1983. Research design and methodological problems in the geography of health. In *Geographical aspects of health*, N. D. McGlashan & J. R. Blunden (eds.), 321–34. London: Academic Press.

Stokes, G. & R. Cochrane 1984. The relationship between national levels of unemployment and the rate of admission to mental hospitals in England and Wales, 1950–76. *Social Psychiatry* **19**, 117–25.

Strauss, J. S. & W. T. Carpenter 1981. *Schizophrenia*. New York: Plenum Press.

Sturt, E. & P. McGuffin 1985. Can linkage and marker associations resolve the genetic aetiology of psychiatric disorders? Review and argument. *Psychological Medicine* **15**, 455–62.

Taylor, S. D. 1974. *The geography and epidemiology of psychiatric illness in Southampton*. PhD thesis, University of Southampton.

Teplin, L. A. 1983. The criminalization of the mentally ill: speculation in search of data. *Psychological Bulletin* **94**, 54–7.

Teplin, L. A. 1985. The criminality of the mentally ill: a dangerous misconception. *American Journal of Psychiatry* **142**, 593–9.

Timms, D. W. G. 1965. The spatial distribution of social deviants in Luton, England. *Australian and New Zealand Journal of Sociology* **1**, 38–52.

Tyrer, P. 1984. Psychiatric clinics in general practice: an extension of community care. *British Journal of Psychiatry* **145**, 9–14.

Tyrer, P., N. Seivewright & S. Wollerton 1984. General practice clinics: impact on psychiatric services. *British Journal of Psychiatry* **145**, 15–19.

Ullah, P., M. Banks & P. Warr 1985. Social support, social pressures and psychological distress during unemployment. *Psychological Medicine* **15**, 283–95.

Veiel, H. O. 1985. Psychopathology and Boolean factor analysis: a mismatch. *Psychological Medicine* **15**, 623–8.

Warner, R. 1985. *Recovery from schizophrenia: psychiatry and political economy.* London: Routledge & Kegan Paul.

Warnes, A. M. (ed.) 1982. *Geographical perspectives on the elderly.* Chichester: Wiley.

Warr, P. 1982. Psychological aspects of employment and unemployment. *Psychological Medicine* **12**, 7–11.

Warr, P. & P. Jackson 1985. Factors influencing the psychological impact of prolonged unemployment and re-employment. *Psychological Medicine* **15**, 795–807.

Weiss, J. A. & C. H. Weiss 1981. Social scientists and decision makers look at the usefulness of mental health research. *American Psychologist* **36**, 837–47.

Whitlock, F. A. 1973. Suicide in England and Wales, Part 2: London. *Psychological Medicine* **3**, 411–20.

Widiger, T. A. & A. Frances 1985. The DSM-III personality disorders. *Archives of General Psychiatry* **42**, 615–23.

Wilkinson, C. B. & W. A. O'Connor 1982. Human ecology and mental illness. *American Journal of Psychiatry* **139**, 985–90.

Winn, S. 1985. *The geography of old age mental disorders in Nottingham.* PhD thesis, University of Nottingham.

WHO 1973. *The international pilot study of schizophrenia.* Geneva: World Health Organization.

WHO 1979. *Schizophrenia: an international follow-up study.* Chichester: Wiley.

WHO 1985. *Mental health services in Europe: 10 years on.* Geneva: World Health Organization.

Wrigley, N. & R. J. Bennett (eds.) 1980. *Quantitative geography: a British view.* London: Routledge & Kegan Paul.

7 The economy as stressor

DAVID DOOLEY, RALPH CATALANO, and SETH SERXNER

Introduction

Economists have been aware of the social costs of change in the system of collection, production, and distribution since at least the 18th century (Steuart 1767). These costs have traditionally been considered low compared to benefits accrued through long-term economic development. The object of post World War II public policy regarding these costs in the USA has been to provide a system of income supplements and subsidized treatment services to reduce pain and suffering to a politically acceptable level. Societal concern over inflicting such pain and suffering has apparently increased over the past two decades and the "safety net" systems have become more extensive and expensive. The increased sensitivity to adverse effects and the growing costs of reducing them have intensified the continuing debate over the prudence of existing safety net policies (Thurow 1980). Those holding the traditional view that increased productivity always enhances the quality of life see the human costs of change as inevitable, and the further extension of the safety net as a costly brake on productivity. Those who see mobile capital and labor as sources of pain and suffering contend that the benefits of added productivity are small and accrued by few, while the human costs are underestimated and widespread.

Attempts to contribute to the above debate through empirical analyses would begin by identifying the mechanisms that theory and existing research suggest may connect mobile capital and labor to phenomena previously implicated in the etiology of health and behavioral disorder. The hypothesis that these mechanisms exist could then be tested, and estimates made of the magnitude of the health and behavioral costs, if any, caused by economic change.

STRESS MODELS OF ILLNESS AND BEHAVIORAL DISORDER

Most claims that economic change affects health and behavior are based on the stress model. Theories of how physiological and psychological stressors affect health and behavior are numerous, and a comprehensive review of them would be repetitive and beyond the scope of this chapter (see Dohrenwend & Dohrenwend 1974). Reducing these theories to a simple statement may not do justice to their profundity, but will suffice to demonstrate the plausibility of the connection between economic dislocation and behavioral disorder.

Stress models of physiological illness in humans are based on the long-standing observation that environmental threats to the equilibria among internal systems evoke an ordered, involuntary set of adaptation responses (Selye 1946, 1962). These responses include such measurable phenomena as changes in blood pressure and galvanic skin response, as well as increased production of corticoids (Theorell 1974). Two types of illnesses are assumed to follow from the adaptation to environmental stressors. The first type, or diseases of adaptation, are manifestations of the adaptation response itself and are not specific to a particular stressor. Ulcers of the digestive system, for example, can be caused by processes triggered by the presence of corticoids. Stressor-elicited corticoids have also been implicated in cardiovascular-renal disease (Rahe & Paasikivi 1971, Theorell & Rahe 1971).

Other illnesses assumed to follow from adaptation to stress are often called diseases of exhaustion. Typical of these illnesses are those assumed to be specific to ubiquitous micro-organisms that are necessary, but not sufficient, to becoming ill. The stress model implies that the ability to cope with those micro-organisms can be diminished when a person is subjected to another, more taxing stressor. The capacity to cope with stressors is assumed to be limited, and responding to a sudden environmental demand may leave the system with insufficient reserve to deal with previously resisted microbes. The respiratory infections often suffered by elderly persons who have been subjected to acute physiological stressors, such as burns or trauma from falls, are often cited as examples of diseases of exhaustion. The degree to which the "disease of exhaustion" concept has been extended is demonstrated by the suggestion that the common cold is caused by succumbing to ubiquitous microbes, which are no longer resistable because adaptive capacity has been depleted by coping with stressors such as extreme weather (Cassell & Tyroler 1961).

The stress model also has been applied to accident injuries by assuming that coping with stressors can affect manual dexterity and response time (Selzer & Vinokur 1974). The stress-to-accident connection also has been attributed to the intervening variables of alcohol and drug abuse (Selzer 1969).

All explanations of behavioral disorder imply that we develop behavioral equilibria with our environments; that is, we adapt to the demands and opportunities in our environment in such a way that most observers would agree is functional. As our environments change we adapt or change behaviors so that a new equilibrium is achieved. Disordered behavior is that which is not functional in, or predictable from, the changed environment. Individuals are assumed to be normally distributed in the ability to adapt behaviorally to change. Poor adapters are supposedly at higher risk of being diagnosed as disordered than are good adapters. The traditional task of abnormal psychology has been to identify the causes of the variation in adaptability across individuals.

The stress model of behavioral disorder does not attempt to replace the more traditional person–based theories of abnormal behavior, in that it assumes that variation in adaptive capacity can be a function of biological factors, psychodynamic processes, or conditioning. It complements the traditional theories by emphasizing the role of the adaptation demand in the process by which individuals are diagnosed as abnormal. The logic for shifting the emphasis to the adaptation demand, or stressor, is best explained through probability models. The probabilities of a good adaptor making an unexpected or nonfunctional response to an environmental change may be low compared to a poor adaptor. However, the good adaptor could be subjected to many changes in a given time period, and therefore be as likely to be diagnosed as disordered during that period as the poor adaptor with few changes with which to cope. A corollary to this principle is that a population with an adaptation distribution that remains constant will yield more diagnoses of disorder during periods of relatively greater environmental change than during periods of stability.

The stress theories of abnormal behavior also imply that the type as well as number of experienced stressors predicts the likelihood of exhibiting an unexpected or nonfunctional response. The death of a spouse, for example, is assumed to be more difficult to adapt to than is an increase in income (Holmes & Rahe 1967).

The shift to studying stressors rather than determinants of adaptive capacity does not mean that stress models ignore the latter. Most stress theories assume, for example, that adaptive capacity is limited and that the number and intensity of stressors experienced in the recent past will affect ability to deal with acute or chronic stressors.

THE ECONOMY AS A SOURCE OF STRESSORS

Perhaps the most visible of the stress literature has been that which attempts to make the concept of the stressor more operational (Holmes & Rahe 1967). This work has led to the "stressful life events" literature, and the standard inventories of environmental changes, which are assumed to play a role in the etiology of behavioral and physiological disorder (Dohrenwend & Dohrenwend 1974). While much work has been done on identifying these events and on assessing whether characteristics such as controllability or desirability account for their effect, or lack of it, relatively little research has focused on their origins. That is, most life-event research assumes, implicitly or explicitly, that the occurrence of life events is random. The exceptions to this observation (e.g., Catalano 1979a, Ruch 1977) have noted that the standard life-event items conceptually and empirically cluster into groups such as life-cycle events (e.g., graduation from school, retirement) and, more importantly for this chapter, economic and employment events (e.g., changes in work hours, trouble with boss, loss of income, loss of job).

The concept of an economic life-event cluster inevitably suggests the hypothesis that the incidence of such events varies with the status of the economy (Catalano & Dooley 1977, 1979a). The hypothesis has also been suggested by decades of economic studies. The literature that began by modeling local economies as a mix of basic and dependent industries (Hoyt & Weimer 1939) and has developed into "regional science" (e.g., Isard 1976) is laden with conceptual and empirical demonstrations of how shifts in investment from one region or industry to another reverberate throughout a community's spatial, employment and sociopolitical structure (Berry 1972). An obvious, but until recently overlooked, extension of this work was the hypothesis that these reverberations yield stressors to which individuals and families must physiologically and behaviorally adapt.

A review of empirical findings

The intuitively attractive hypothesis that the performance of the economy can affect mental health has been tested in many ways. The following is a summary of the epidemiologic research concerned with the mental health effects of economic contraction. This summary is evaluative rather than descriptive; that is, we attempt to infer which effects hypothesized by the research can be assumed to be probable, possible, or only suggested.

The term "economic contraction" was chosen because it subsumes the various economic phenomena that the existing research implies are risk factors for psychological distress. As will be discussed in greater detail later, research in the field has used several independent variables to gauge the undesirable nature of bad economic times. Several studies have, for example, used the unemployment rate which is the number of "unemployed" persons (i.e., those who are looking for a job but cannot find one) divided by the sum of the unemployed and the employed. The "unemployed" include those who have lost jobs, who are entering the job market for the first time, or who are returning to the job market after voluntary withdrawal (see Buss & Redburn, this volume). Other studies have been concerned only with those who have lost jobs, while yet other research has focused on the mental health effects of undesirable experiences associated with bad economic times (e.g., loss of overtime hours and attendant income, business failure, financial losses, inability to pay bills, and the fear of job loss). We believe all these risk factors are important and subsume them under the heading "economic contraction."

The remainder of this section is divided into two parts. The first is a description of the decision rules we devised to infer which effects are probable, possible, or suggested. The application of the decision rules to the research is described in the second subsection, as are several caveats concerning how general the inferred effects may be.

DECISION RULES

The following assessment of the published research is intended to be as objective and replicable as possible. The assessment is based on decision rules that lead to characterizing a suspected mental health effect of economic contraction as probable, possible, or suggested. The decision rules have a conservative bias. That is, the effects that are inferred are probably the minimal impacts that can be expected from economic contraction.

The decision rules are based on an organization of the research shown in Table 7.1. The matrix is formed by two constructs. The first construct is how economic contraction, or the independent variable, is measured. One way the research has measured economic contraction is with a population-level indicator such as the unemployment rate for metropolitan areas, states, counties, or even nations. Other population-level indicators have included inflation rates, total employment, and measures of absolute economic change which imply that either expansion or contraction is equally likely to elicit problems.

The second way economic contraction has been measured is as the undesirable job or financial experiences of individuals. Losing a job, losing overtime income, or being unable to pay one's bills are examples of individual experiences that are assumed to be "driven" by the economy and to be risk factors for disorder.

The third way the economic variable has been measured is "cross-level," that is a combination of individual experiences and economic climate in which those experiences occur. For example, losing a job in an expanding economy may have a different meaning and effect compared with losing one in a contracting economy.

The second construct that defines Table 7.1 is how the dependent variable, or indicator of psychological disorder, is measured. One way is as symptoms of disorder gauged by standard epidemiologic questionnaires. These questionnaires are administered either face-to-face or by telephone, and are intended to measure either the likelihood of being clinically disordered or of experiencing discomfort that may not conform to clinical syndromes but that can disrupt normal functioning (e.g., "demoralization").

A second type of dependent measure that frequently appears in the research is admissions to specialty mental health treatment. This measure is for a population per unit of time (e.g., admissions per year for a state) in cell 2 and for individuals in cells 7 and 12. A third measure is suicide, measured either as incidence in a population or as an act by an individual. A fourth dependent variable that has been empirically linked to economic contraction is child abuse. The fifth dependent variable is "psychogenic" illness, or physiological syndromes believed to be associated with stress.

Table 7.1 lists research representative of each cell. We have tried to list the most rigorous examples in each cell when there are more than a few published studies. Most of the studies in cells 6–10, for example, attempt to control for "reverse causation" or the possibility that psychologically disordered persons may have undesirable job and financial experiences due to their disorder, rather than vice versa. The studies in cells 1–5, which are all aggregate time-series studies, have attempted to control for autocorrelation among error terms that make estimates of confidence intervals impossible.

The rule used to designate a "probable" effect is that there must be at least two supporting studies in each of the three cells of a column. This means that the effect has been found and replicated at the population and individual level, and that the interaction of the individual experience and economic climate has been tested at least twice. A "possible" effect is one for which there are at least two supporting studies in two cells. A "suggested" effect is one for which there are at least two converging studies in one cell and at least one study in another.

The reason for adopting such conservative rules is that findings in any one cell of a column can, even if replicated by other studies in that cell, be explained by "rival hypotheses," or in ways that do not require the economy to have an effect on mental health. However, a finding across all three cells in a column is very difficult to attribute to other than an effect of the economy, because none of the plausible rival hypotheses can survive all three tests. Since an effect of the economy can logically survive all three tests, it becomes the most likely, or parsimonious, explanation.

APPLYING THE DECISION RULES

The best-documented effect appears to be that job loss (not necessarily the inability to find a first job or unsuccessful return to the labor market after a voluntary withdrawal) is a significant risk factor for reporting symptoms of psychological disorder. This effect has been found and replicated in all three cells of column one. There are, however, at least three caveats regarding this work that should be heeded. One is that the seriousness of the disorder measured by self-reported symptoms is not clear. While the survey instruments used to measure disorder have been diverse, they are not universally accepted as sufficiently developed to allow diagnoses. The most conservative inference is that losing a job is a significant risk factor for psychological distress that does not necessarily reach the level generally believed to require clinical intervention.

The second issue concerns the strength of the effect of losing a job on psychological wellbeing. Individual-level research in the field suggests that experiencing an undesirable job event doubles the odds of reporting symptoms of disorder (Dooley & Catalano 1984a,b). While this is an

Table 7.1 Research on economics and mental health.

Independent variables	Dependent variables				
	Psychiatric symptoms 1	Psychiatric admissions and help-seeking 2	Suicide 3	Child abuse 4	Psychogenic illness 5
Population-level economic indicator (aggregate time-series)	Catalano & Dooley 1977, 1979a,b Catalano et al. 1981 Dooley & Catalano 1979 Dooley et al. 1981	Ahr et al. 1981 Banziger et al. 1982 Barling & Handal 1980[a] Brenner 1973, 1976 Catalano & Dooley 1979a,b Catalano et al. 1981, 1983, 1985 Dear et al. 1979 Frank 1981 Marshall & Funch 1979 Sclar & Hoffman 1978 Stokes & Cochrane 1982	Brenner 1976 Catalano et al. 1983 Cook et al. 1980 Hammermesh & Soss 1974 Mark 1979 Marshall 1978 Marshall & Hodge 1981 Pierce 1967 Stack 1981 Vigderhous & Fishman 1978	Steinberg et al. 1981	Brenner 1976 Bunn 1979

	6	7	8	9	10
Job and financial events experienced by individual	Aldwin & Revenson 1984 Banks & Jackson 1982[b] Brenner et al. 1982 Buss & Redburn 1983 Cobb & Kasl 1977 Dooley & Catalano 1984a,b Feather & Davenport 1981 Ferman & Gardner 1979 Gurney 1980[b] Hartley 1980 Hepworth 1980 Liem & Rayman 1982 Parnes & King 1977 Pearlin et al. 1981 Stokes 1981	Banziger & Foos 1983 Dooley & Catalano 1984b Theorell et al. 1975	Theorell et al. 1975	Garbarino & Crouter 1978 Gil 1971 Light 1973 Watkins & Bradbard 1983	Catalano & Dooley 1983 Cobb & Kasl 1977

	11	12	13	14	15
Cross-level	Cohn 1978[b] Dooley & Catalano 1984a,b Dooley et al. 1982	Dooley & Catalano 1984b Korper 1976			Catalano & Dooley 1983

[a] No check on serial correlation.
[b] Ecological correlation.

important effect, it must be put in perspective. For example, smoking increases the odds of lung cancer by 20 to 30 times.

The third caveat concerns the population to which these findings can be generalized. The labor force, for our purposes, can be separated into several groups defined by the perceived security and desirability of their jobs (Buss & Redburn, this volume). Most of the research concerning job loss has been concerned with the short-term effect of job loss on individuals who had secure jobs in the "primary labor market," or that dominated by historically stable industries. These jobs were often protected by unions and conferred good benefit packages. Relatively little research has focused on the long-term effects of job loss or on the effects of job loss on the remainder of the labor force. Limited research (Ferman & Gardner 1979) suggests that those who have lost secure, desirable jobs often become "skidders" or move into the secondary labor market of less secure and desirable jobs. This "skidding" appears to have adverse psychological effects beyond those of losing the original job in the primary labor market. Research based on representative population samples (Dooley & Catalano 1984a,b) also suggests that the effects of undesirable job or financial events have at least as great an impact on lower- as on middle- and upper-income people. While these findings suggest that the existing research will generalize to all segments of the labor force, broader-based research is necessary. For example, no published research focuses on the psychological effect of economic contraction on laborers who move in and out of marginal jobs that offer no security or benefits. Moreover, there is very little published research concerned with the effects of economic contraction on the psychological status of the chronically mentally ill population including, but not limited to, "deinstitionalized" persons.

A possible effect involving symptoms of psychological disorder is that the inability to find work for the first time or after a voluntary withdrawal from the labor force may increase symptoms. This effect has been reported at the individual and cross-level but not at the aggregate level: it could move soon into the "probable effect" category. The two issues (those of seriousness and strength of effect) described under the probable effect of job loss on symptoms apply to this literature as well.

The division of the population at risk into those who have lost jobs in the primary or secondary labor market, those who are entering the labor market for the first time or after a voluntary withdrawal, and those who have unstable work histories due to chronic psychological problems is useful for reasons beyond noting gaps in the research. These groups also present very different opportunities for mounting prevention and treatment programs.

HELP-SEEKING FOR PSYCHOLOGICAL DISORDER

A second probable effect is that economic contraction increases the likelihood of seeking help for psychological disorder. This effect is due, in part, to the fact that economic contraction increases the incidence of psychological distress, as noted above. The effect is also due to the fact that individuals whose symptom levels do not change are more likely to seek help when they have undesirable job experiences (Dooley & Catalano 1984b). In other words, the number of persons in a community who seek mental health services will increase when the economy of that community contracts. This appears to be true, because there are newly symptomatic persons, and because others whose symptom levels do not change also seek help when they experience undesirable job and financial events.

The research on help-seeking has raised several issues, two of which should be described. The first is that it is as yet unclear as to which undesirable job and financial events have the greatest impact. Work on this issue continues but progress has been slow because these events occur as clusters, making it difficult to test the effect of one while controlling others. The second issue concerns the strength of the connection between changes in the economy (i.e., the system of producing and distributing goods and services) and the individual risk of experiencing undesirable job and financial events. The limited, existing research suggests that the middle class is most likely to experience undesirable job and financial events when the economy contracts (Catalano & Dooley 1983). This finding should not be confused with that noted above, that the mental health *effect* of experiencing such events does not vary across socioeconomic groups.

SUICIDE

The "suggested" effect that has historically received the most attention is that on suicide. Aggregate time-series research has frequently reported an association between economic contraction and the incidence of suicide. There have, however, been exceptions to this finding (e.g. Pierce 1967). Moreover, the only individual-level finding has not been replicated, and no "cross-level" research has appeared. Prospective individual-level research on suicide is, of course, difficult to conduct, given the low incidence of the behavior.

CHILD ABUSE

There is a suggested effect of economic contraction on child abuse. Research at the individual level consistently finds that job loss and inability to find work are more common among known abusers than expected by chance (Garbarino & Crouter 1978, Gil 1971, Light 1973, Watkins & Bradbard 1982). One rigorous aggregate time-series analysis also reports that job loss (not unemployment) is associated with child abuse (Steinberg *et al.* 1981).

While the effect of economic contraction on child abuse could, by our decision rules, move to the "possible" category with additional aggregate time-series research, it should be noted that the existing individual-level research is not as rigorous as many of the studies in row two of Table 7.1. There is little research that attempts to control for reverse-causation, because prospective studies of a low-frequency, criminal behavior are difficult to conduct.

PSYCHOGENIC PHYSIOLOGICAL ILLNESS
It is widely believed that psychological disorder is related to physiological disease processes. If this is so, a reasonable hypothesis would be that economic contraction may affect physical health through psychological processes. By the rules used above, we believe the current research suggests a possible effect. Research at the individual and cross-levels has reported a connection between undesirable job and financial events, and episodes of illness controlling for age, sex, socioeconomic status, and other stressors (Catalano & Dooley 1983). Aggregate-level research also reports association between economic contraction and psychosomatic illness (Brenner 1976, Bunn 1979). However, cross-level research needs to be replicated before this effect can be judged "probable."

Discussion

NOTES ON THE RESEARCH BASE
We would like to make several points concerning the research summarized above. The first is that we do not believe the epidemiologic research has reached the point at which we can estimate how many cases of a particular outcome will occur if the unemployment rate increases by a given percentage. This is true for several reasons, only two of which need to be noted here. The temptation to predict from historical time-series data should be resisted, because the existing analyses all control for unspecified confounding variables by removing "trends and cycles" (Catalano 1981). Therefore, prediction must always be prefaced with "if all other things remain equal." This is a reasonable assumption for statistical modeling of historic data but is not, in our opinion, appropriate for predictions that will be taken literally rather than as condition statements. The second reason is that the unemployment rate is a composite measure of many different kinds of individual experiences (e.g., job loss, inability to find first job, inability to find work after voluntary withdrawal) that probably have very different "risk effects." We cannot use risk ratios based on specific, individual experiences to derive an overall effect for the unemployment rate, because we do not know the relative incidence of the experiences among the unemployed. Moreover, changes in the unemployment rate do not necessarily gauge the incidence of undesirable financial experiences associated with economic contraction.

A second fact that should be noted is that there is research that suggests that rapid economic expansion in a community also has health costs. These costs are believed to include accidental injuries (Catalano 1979b), and many include other less well studied outcomes (Eyer 1977). We should be careful to recognize that the underlying theory of much of the research alluded to above is that disruption of the social ecology of communities will be manifested by health and behavioral problems. Intuitively good economic occurrences, such as rapid economic expansion, can be disruptive.

A third point is that much of the aggregate time-series research in row one of Table 7.1 has value beyond its contribution to epidemiologic knowledge. The techniques that have emerged from this research make it possible to forecast changes in the demand for mental health services by geographically defined populations (Catalano *et al.* 1983, 1985). These forecasting methods should be developed further because of their potential usefulness in the management of mental health services.

POLICY AND SERVICE IMPLICATIONS
The economic policies recently adopted at the federal level are intended to increase productivity by accelerating the shift of capital and labor away from less efficient industries and regions to those that promise higher returns and wages. Regulations have been cut back to reduce the amount of capital that flows into nonproductive activities. Social programs have been curtailed to reduce the proportion of national product diverted to the public sector. This package of programs was supposedly chosen after a full, fair and sincere debate of the costs and benefits of the available alternatives. The implicit ratio of benefits to costs assumed by the majority who supported the adopted policies may or may not have included a fair estimation of the health and behavioral outcomes of impending economic shifts. Assuming the best circumstances, that these costs were sincerely estimated and considered, the research reviewed above still raises questions that should be considered by state and national policy makers. These questions arise from the fact that the national, aggregate benefit-to-cost ratio assumed by policy makers probably will not be experienced by any region.

Regional differences   Some regions, probably those in the west and southwest, will experience most of the economic benefits of the national drive for productivity. Other regions, probably the middle Atlantic and industrially based middle west, will experience most of the economic costs (Sternlieb & Hughes 1977). The health and behavioral costs, however, will not be distributed identically to the more traditionally accounted economic costs and benefits. The fastest growing and fastest declining communities will both bear the health and behavioral costs of their dynamism. Several large metropolitan regions, the economic bases of which include both declining and expanding industries, will experience the health and behavioral costs associated with both types of change. The implication of this distribution of costs and benefits is that if the new, smaller version of the safety net programs is "sized" to meet the national benefit-to-cost ratio, few if any regions will be appropriately served. Even if the safety-net programs were "paid" directly to needy individuals in an attempt to avoid public bureaucracies, the effect would be to under-serve regions with high concentrations of needy persons. The reason is that the cost of providing services often increases nonlinearly with the number of persons needing services. For example, the capital costs of the health facilities needed to effectively serve large concentrations of needy raises the *per-patient* cost over that needed for smaller populations requiring care.

Given the likely mismatch of safety net to need, several states and localities likely to experience the costs of growth may be forced to use their land-use control and taxing powers to phase growth and to raise funds, to ensure that the health and behavioral costs of economic growth do not become politically destabilizing. States and localities experiencing the economic as well as health and behavioral costs of decline will be in very precarious positions. They will not be able to increase local taxes to raise the funds needed to augment the federally supported safety net, because these taxes would only accelerate the movement of capital investment out of their jurisdictions. It would appear prudent of the federal government to be prepared to offer geographically targeted supplements to social programs. These supplements could be triggered by a mix of indicators measuring capital attractiveness and the incidence of health and behavioral problems in excess of that expected by socioeconomic and demographic composition.

Care providers The implications of the research reviewed above are potentially greater for the providers of health and behavioral services than for those who make public policy. Prudent assumptions, given current political realities, are that safety-net programs will be smaller in the near future than in the recent past, and that the geographically defined supplements suggested above will not be forthcoming. These assumptions, coupled with the economic dislocations that seem imminent, lead to the inference that there will be fewer resources to deal with more problems. State and local, public and private providers of health and mental health services will have to find ways to deploy their resources cost-effectively. Among the ways to improve cost-effectiveness is to anticipate where and when services most likely are to be needed. The fact that economic phenomena have been linked to both the demand for service and the incidence of symptoms raises the possibility that econometric modeling might allow the identification of populations and communities at risk of economic stress. As noted above, regional science has developed techniques for modeling the effects of shifts in the economic structure of communities. While the dependent variable in existing models is typically demand for infrastructure (e.g., transportation systems, schools, water facilities) or for housing, there is no conceptual reason why the procedures could not be extended to include aggregate measures of demand for health and mental health services.

If such modeling were successful, it would allow the targeting of preventive and remedial programs to populations that appear to be at risk of economic stress. Preventive programs could be based on "stress inoculation" techniques that have appeared in recent years (Michenbaum & Jaremko 1983). A recently suggested program, tailored to economic stressors, would include three components (Catalano & Dooley 1979b). The first would be an educational effort designed to inform individuals of the adaptation demands they and their communities are likely to experience and of the potentially positive and adverse effects of these demands. The second component, cognitive restructuring, could help individuals to avoid maladaptive cognitive responses such as self-blame and paralyzing anxiety. The restructuring would involve improving the logic by which individuals attribute causation and forecast experiences. The third component, behavioral training, would introduce individuals to techniques that have been found to reduce the adverse effects of stressors. These techniques include relaxation routines to reduce the physiological costs of stressors, as well as more proactive behaviors intended to decrease the individual's exposure to stressors. Examples of these more proactive techniques are improving interpersonal skills to enhance self-confidence in the ability to find and keep employment, and learning new job skills that will enhance the likelihood of maintaining employment in a shifting labor market.

Programs such as that outlined above are costly and most likely to be successful when the participants are motivated to take the experience seriously. It would not therefore be cost-effective to offer these programs to the general population. However, if a subpopulation, defined either geographically or by participation in a particular industry, could be identified as at risk of experiencing relatively many economic stressors, the cost-effectiveness of preventive programs could be maximized. When the population at risk is defined geographically, the organizational vehicle for delivering the program could be churches or similar organizations, or mental and public health agencies. When the population is industry-defined and likely to be dispersed over many communities, labor unions could be used.

The fact that economic phenomena predictably influence the incidence of illness and the demand for mental health services is important to service providers even if preventive programs are not possible. Remedial services for those who have not adapted successfully to economic changes will be most cost-effective when deployed to those areas and groups most likely to yield "casualties." Formulae used by state governments for the allocation of public and mental health funds therefore should be revised to reflect the likely effect of economic change in communities the economies of which are heavily based on either or both declining or growth industries.

While the short-run effect of shifting economic activity may not be as dramatic as has been argued in the recent past (e.g., Brenner 1973), the connection of the economy and disorder appears real. That connection is made particularly important by the fact that we have adopted economic policies intended to accelerate the mobility of capital and labor. While the benefits of this mobility may far outweigh the health and psychological costs, it must be acknowledged that we have the ability, if not the duty, to reduce these costs. Extending the line of research described above could enhance the effectiveness of the effort to reduce these costs, and therefore should be considered an integral part of the nation's research agenda for the next decade.

References

Ahr, P. R., M. J. Gorodezky & D. W. Cho 1981. Measuring the relationships of public psychiatric admissions to rising unemployment. *Hospital and Community Psychiatry* **32**, 398–401.

Aldwin, C. & T. Revenson n.d. *Vulnerability to economic stress.*

Banks, M. H. & P. R. Jackson 1982. Unemployment and risk of minor psychiatric disorder in young people: cross-sectional and longitudinal evidence. *Psychological Medicine* **12**, 789–98.

Banziger, G. & D. Foos 1983. The relationship of personal finance status to the utilization of community mental health centers in rural Appalachia. *American Journal of Community Psychology* **11**, 543–52.

Banziger, G., A. Smith & D. Foos 1982. Economic indicators of mental health service utilization in rural Appalachia. *American Journal of Community Psychology* **10**, 669–86.

Barling, P. & P. Handal 1980. Incidence of utilization of public mental health facilities as a function of short term economic decline. *American Journal of Community Psychology* **8**, 31–9.

Berry, B. J. (ed.) 1972. *City classification handbook: methods and applications.* New York: Wiley.

Brenner, M. H. 1973. *Mental illness and the economy.* Cambridge, Mass.: Harvard University Press.

Brenner, M. H. 1976. *Estimating the social costs of economic policy: implications for mental and physical health, and criminal aggression.* Report to the Congressional Research Service of the Library of Congress and Joint Economic Committee of Congress. Washington, D.C.: US Government Printing Office.

Brenner, S. O., L. Levi, H. E. Salovaara, T. Arevstedt, R. Hjelm, D. Sorbom & S. Tellenbach 1985. Job insecurity and unemployment: effects on health and well-being, and an evaluation of coping measures. In *Health Policy Implications of Unemployment*, G. Westcott, P. G. Svensson & H. F. K. Zöllner (eds), 325–34. Copenhagen: World Health Organization.

Bunn, A. R. 1979. Ischaemic heart disease mortality and the business cycle in Australia. *American Journal of Public Health* **69**, 772–81.

Buss, T. F. & F. Stevens Redburn 1983. *Shutdown at Youngstown: public policy for mass unemployment*. Albany, New York: State University of New York Press.

Cassell, J. & H. Tyroler 1961. Epidemiological studies of culture change, I: health status and recency of industrialization. *Archives of Environmental Health* 3, 31–8.

Catalano, R. 1979a. *Health, behavior, and the community*. New York: Pergamon.

Catalano, R. 1979b. Health costs of economic expansion: the case of manufacturing accident injuries. *American Journal of Public Health* 69, 789–94.

Catalano, R. 1981. Contending with rival hypotheses in correlation of aggregate time-series (CATS): an overview for community psychologists. *American Journal of Community Psychology* 9, 667–79.

Catalano, R. & D. Dooley 1977. Economic predictors of depressed mood and stressful life events in a metropolitan community. *Journal of Health and Social Behavior* 18, 292–307.

Catalano, R. & D. Dooley 1979a. Does economic change provoke or uncover behavior disorder: a preliminary test. In *Mental health and the economy*, L. Ferman & J. Gordus (eds.), 321–46. Kalamazoo, Mich.: Upjohn Institute.

Catalano, R. & D. Dooley 1979b. The economy as a stressor: a sectoral analysis. *Review of Social Economy* 37, 175–87.

Catalano, R. & D. Dooley 1983. The health effects of economic stability: a test of the economic stress hypothesis. *Journal of Health and Social Behavior* 22, 46–60.

Catalano, R., D. Dooley & R. Jackson 1981. Economic predictors of admissions to mental health facilities in a nonmetropolitan community. *Journal of Health and Social Behavior* 22, 284–97.

Catalano, R., D. Dooley & R. Jackson 1983. Selecting a time-series strategy. *Psychological Bulletin* 94, 506–23.

Catalano, R., D. Dooley & R. Jackson 1985. Economic antecedents of help seeking: a reformulation of the time-series tests. *Journal of Health and Social Behavior* 20, 141–52.

Cobb, S. & S. V. Kasl 1977. *Termination: the consequence of job loss*. Report No. 76-1261. Cincinatti, Ohio: National Institute for Occupational Safety and Health, Behavioral, and Motivational Factors Research.

Cohn, R. 1978. The effect of employment status change on self attitudes. *Social Psychology* 38, 300–14.

Cook, T. D., L. Dintzer & M. M. Mark 1980. The causal analysis of concomitant time series. *Applied Social Psychology Annual* 1, 93–135.

Dear, M., G. Clark & S. Clark 1979. Economic cycles and mental health care policy: an examination of the macro-context for social service planning. *Social Science and Medicine* 13, 43–53.

Dohrenwend, B. S. & B. P. Dohrenwend 1974. *Stressful life events: their nature and effects*. New York: Wiley.

Dooley, D. & R. Catalano 1979. Economic, life, and disorder changes: time-series analyses. *American Journal of Community Psychology* 7, 381–96.

Dooley, D. & R. Catalano 1984a. The epidemiology of economic stress. *American Journal of Community Psychology* 12, 387–409.

Dooley, D. & R. Catalano 1984b. Why the economy predicts help seeking: a test of competing explanations. *Journal of Health and Social Behavior* 25, 160–75.

Dooley, D., R. Catalano & A. Brownell 1981. Economic, life and symptom changes in a nonmetropolitan community. *Journal of Health and Social Behavior* 22, 144–54.

Dooley, D., R. Catalano & A. Brownell 1986. The relation of economic conditions, social support and life events to depression. *Journal of Community Psychology* **14**, 103–19.

Eyer, J. 1977. Does unemployment cause the death rate peak in each business cycle? a multifactor model of death rate change. *International Journal of Health Services* **7**, 625–61.

Feather, N. T. & P. R. Davenport 1981. Unemployment and depressive affect: a motivational and attributional analysis. *Journal of Personality and Social Psychology* **41**, 422–36.

Ferman, L. A. & J. Gardner 1979. Economic deprivation, social mobility, and mental health. In *Mental health and the economy*, L. A. Ferman & J. P. Gordus (eds.), 193–224. Kalamazoo, Mich.: Upjohn Institute.

Frank, J. A. 1981. Economic change and mental health in an uncontaminated setting. *American Journal of Community Psychology* **9**, 395–410.

Garbarino, J. & A. Crouter 1978. Defining the community contact for parent–child relations: the correlates of child maltreatment. *Child Development* **49**, 604–16.

Gil, D. 1971. Violence against children. *Journal of Marriage and Family* **33**, 637–57.

Gurney, R. M. 1980. The effects of unemployment on the psycho-social development of school-leavers. *Journal of Occupational Psychology* **53**, 205–13.

Hammermesh, A. S. & N. M. Soss 1974. An economic theory of suicide. *Journal of Political Economy* **82**, 83–98.

Hartley, J. F. 1980. The impact of unemployment upon the self-esteem of managers. *Journal of Occupational Psychology* **53**, 147–55.

Hepworth, S. J. 1980. Moderating factors of the psychological impact of unemployment. *Journal of Occupational Psychology* **53**, 139–45.

Holmes, T. H. & R. E. Rahe 1967. The social readjustment rating scale. *Journal of Psychosomatic Research* **II**, 213–18.

Hoyt, H. & A. Weimer 1939. *Principles of urban real estate*. New York: Ronald Press.

Isard, W. 1976. *Introduction to regional science*. Englewood Cliffs, N.J.: Prentice-Hall.

Korper, S. P. 1976. *Utilization of community mental health services: further consideration of the implications of socio-economic class and related variables*. Unpublished doctoral dissertation, Yale University.

Liem, R. & P. Rayman 1982. Health and social costs of unemployment: research and policy considerations. *American Psychologist* **37**, 1116–23.

Light, R. 1973. Abused and neglected children in America. *Harvard Education Review* **43**, 556–98.

Mark, M. M. 1979. The causal analysis of concomitancies in time series. In *Quasi-experimentation: design and analysis issues for field settings*, T. D. Cook & D. T. Campbell (eds.), 321–39. Chicago: Rand McNally.

Marshall, J. R. 1978. Changes in aged white male suicide: 1948–1972. *Journal of Gerontology* **33**, 763–8.

Marshall, J. R. & D. P. Funch 1979. Mental illness and the economy: a critique and partial replication. *Journal of Health and Social Behavior* **20**, 282–9.

Marshall, J. R. & R. W. Hodge 1981. Durkheim and Pierce on suicide and economic change. *Social Science Research* **10**, 101–14.

Michenbaum, D. & M. Jaremko 1983. *Stress reduction*. New York: Plenum.

Parnes, H. S. & R. King 1977. Middle-aged job losers. *Industrial Gerontology* **4**, 77–95.

Pearlin, L. I., M. A. Lieberman, E. G. Menaghan & J. T. Mullan 1981. The stress process. *Journal of Health and Social Behavior* **22**, 337–56.

Pierce, A. 1967. The economic cycle and the social suicide rate. *American Sociological Review* **32**, 457–62.

Rahe, R. & J. Paasikivi 1971. Psychosocial factors and myocardial infarction: an outpatient study in Sweden. *Journal of Psychometric Research* **15**, 33–9.

Ruch, L. O. 1977. A multidimensional analysis of the concept of life change. *Journal of Health and Social Behavior* **18**, 71–83.

Sclar, E. D. & V. J. Hoffman 1978. *Planning mental health service for a declining economy*. Final report to the National Health Services Research. Waltham, Mass.: Brandeis University, January.

Selye, H. 1946. The general adaptation syndrome and the diseases of adaption. *Journal of Clinical Endocrinology* **6**, 117–230.

Selye, H. 1962. *The story of the adaptation process*. Montreal: Acta, Inc.

Selzer, M. L. 1969. Alcoholism, mental illness and stress in ninety six drivers causing fatal accidents. *Behavioral Science* **14**, 1–10.

Selzer, M. L. & A. Vinokur 1974. Life events, subjective stress and traffic accidents. *American Journal of Psychiatry* **131**, 903–6.

Stack, S. 1981. Divorce and suicide: a time series analysis, 1933–1970. *Journal of Family Issues* **2**, 77–90.

Steinberg, L., R. Catalano & D. Dooley 1981. Economic antecedents of child abuse and neglect. *Child Development* **52**, 260–7.

Sternlieb, G. & J. W. Hughes 1977. New regional and metropolitan realities of America. *Journal of the American Institute of Planners* **43**, 226–41.

Steuart, J. 1767. *An inquiry into the principles of political economy*. London: Millar and Cadell.

Stokes, G. 1985. Epidemiological studies of the psychological response to economic instability in England: a summary. In *Health Policy Implications of Unemployment*, G. Westcott, P. G. Svensson & H. F. K. Zöllner (eds.), 133–42. Copenhagen: World Health Organization.

Theorell, T. 1974. Life events before and after the onset of premature myocardial infarction. In *Stressful life events: their nature and effect*, B. S. Dohrenwend & B. P. Dohrenwend (eds.), 101–17. New York: Wiley.

Theorell, T. & R. Rahe 1971. Psychosocial factors and myocardial infarction. *Journal of Psychosomatic Research* **15**, 25–31.

Theorell, T., E. Lind & B. Floderus 1975. The relationship of disturbing life changes and emotions to the early development of myocardial infarctions and other serious illness. *International Journal of Epidemiology* **4**, 281–93.

Thurow, L. 1980. *The zero-sum society*, New York: Basic Books.

Vigderhous, G. & G. Fishman 1978. The impact of unemployment and social integration on changing suicide rates in the U.S.A., 1920–1969. *Social Psychiatry* **13**, 239–48.

Watkins, H. E. & M. R. Bradbard 1982. Child maltreatment: an overview with suggestions for intervention and research. *Family Relations* **21**, 323–33.

8 Psychological distress, and the wellbeing of workers in distressed communities

TERRY F. BUSS and
F. STEVENS REDBURN

The relationship between changes in the economy and the mental health of the general public has long been of interest to observers of society. Failure to obtain a first job, periodic episodes of unemployment, long-term jobless-ness, poverty, plant closings, mass unemployment, and other factors associated with cyclical swings and permanent restructuring in the economy have been studied extensively to determine how they affect mental health (Brenner 1973, Buss & Redburn 1983a, Catalano & Dooley 1979, Hayes & Nutman 1981, Horwitz 1984, Jahoda 1982, NIMH 1985).

Although economic change and mental health have been of wide interest, special attention has been focused on communities that have lost many jobs due to plant closings or workforce retrenchment (see Buss & Redburn 1983a, Hansen 1980, Jahoda et al. 1933, Strange 1978). Youngstown, Ohio, provides a typical example of urban distress in Western industrial countries. In 1973, Youngstown was a world-class basic steel producer, employing nearly 80,000 workers in that industry alone. One decade later, 42,000 basic steel jobs had vanished, leaving the area with a chronically high unemploy-ment rate, averaging about 18% over the past five years. In a community where, in the past, workers shunned any form of public assistance, nearly one in nine people now receive welfare transfer payments.

Survey research methodology has been a major technique for gathering data on the relationship between economic change and mental health[1]. In using survey research, two separate controversies have periodically surfaced. First, many widely used mental health assessment methodologies are intended only to identify the most severe instances of psychological disorder or disability. Because there are relatively few psychologically disabled among the general population (5–10%), such instruments are not useful for studies focused on variations short of the extreme. Secondly, even when more discriminating mental health instrumentation is used, capable of identifying less severe forms of mental illness, studies exploring the psychological effects of economic change have often assigned people to very broad laborforce categories (employed, unemployed, or not in the labor force) without taking into account the possibility that some categories of job holders may be worse off economically than those without jobs. Such catch-all categories may further obscure important differences in psychological status due to economic circumstances.

In this chapter, more discriminating measurements of psychological status, along with more refined laborforce concepts, are used to explore more precisely the relationship between economic change and mental health. Youngstown's metropolitan area, in many ways a prototypical distressed community, provided the context in which nearly 500 personal interviews were completed during March and April 1985 with a representative sample of the labor force.

Measurement of mental health

The conceptualization of mental illness or mental health in the general population has been the subject of continuing debate (e.g., Cassimatis 1979, Veit & Ware 1983)[2].

One school of thought, which dominates inquiry in this field, employs a "medical model" of mental illness and mental health (e.g., Cassimatis 1979). Mental illness is viewed as the presence of observable or imputed signs or symptoms which mental health professionals believe are indicative of disease. Mental health, by contrast, represents the absence of disease. Physical health, which is defined as the absence of corporal illness or disease, therefore provides the basis for an analogous definition of mental health. The medical model, in a survey research context, utilizes respondent self-perceptions and self-evaluations to construct psychiatric rating scales (Warheit et al. 1979) which indicate the likely presence or absence of psychopathology and its accompanying symptoms.

A major criticism of the medical model is that members of the general public "rarely or never report occurrences of even the most prevalent psychological distress symptoms" (Veit & Ware 1983: 730). Consequently, estimates of the incidence and prevalence of psychological and emotional problems in the general public are probably understated.

A competing view of mental health applies a social–psychological perspective (Bradburn 1969, Warr 1978). The social–psychological view is not concerned with the identification of psychopathological symptoms and, in extreme cases, the diagnosis of "psychiatric cases." Instead, analysis focuses on the problems the average person contends with—the stresses and strains of everyday life. Mental health is understood as a general sense of wellbeing in which a person has both "positive" states (i.e., happiness, job satisfaction, self-esteem), and "negative" states (i.e., worry, unhappiness, dissatisfaction). Positive and negative states for individuals, importantly, are not represented as polar opposites on a single continuum, but are thought to exist independently of one another. For example, a person may be happy with life generally (a positive state) while being distressed over problems on the job (a negative state). Overall mental health is a function of the extent to which a person achieves positive and eliminates negative states. The model is not "psychopathology-seeking," but instead attempts to separate out those persons who are successfully coping from those who are not.

Perhaps the most-often cited shortcoming of the social–psychological approach is that measurements which capture positive and negative states have not been fully developed, tested, and validated at least to the same degree as many psychological rating scales (Veit & Ware 1983). This being the case, it is difficult to reach agreement on what constitutes an appropriate response—effective coping—to life's circumstances.

The intent of this study is not to attempt to resolve measurement issues in mental health. Instead, our perspective is that the psychopathology-seeking survey instruments, which tend to identify the most severe psychiatric cases, do not allow for sufficient variation in the general public to adequately assess the effects of economic change. This analysis will test the use of an alternative, social–psychological instrumentation, in exploring the relationship between economics and mental health.

Defining the labor force

Many studies treat employment status as a variable likely to explain variations in psychological status within the general population. Employment status is frequently measured by asking respondents such questions as: "Are you employed, unemployed, retired, disabled, a student, housekeeper or what?" or "What is your employment status?" Such gross measures of employment status tend to obscure important differences. To better understand some of the interpretive problems thus created, it is useful to review how labor-market economists view employment status (Levitan, Magnum & Marshall 1981). The labor force is the total number of employed and unemployed people. In order to be "employed," a worker must be directly remunerated in the marketplace for either pay or profit. "Unemployed" workers are defined as those who are available for work and are engaged in any job-seeking activity, or waiting to be called back from a layoff, or will be reporting to a new job. Anyone who is neither employed nor unemployed is considered to be "not in the labor force." Although these basic categories are useful, they do not isolate some employment status groups that may have a distinct psychological profile. The following employment status groups deserve separate examination:

(1) *Discouraged workers.* Discouraged workers are those who are not

looking for work, either because they believe that no jobs are available or because they believe that they are unqualified. By standard definition, these workers are not in the labor force.

(2) *Short-hours or part-time.* Those who work as little as one hour per week (e.g., babysitters, after-school lawn-care specialists, etc.) are considered to be employed. They are included in the same employment classification as those who work 40 or more hours.

(3) *Part-time seeking full-time.* Workers who have lost full-time jobs and have been successful only in finding a part-time replacement job, as well as part-time workers who have never had a full-time job but desire one, are included as employed workers in the labor force in the same way as full-time workers.

(4) *Labor disputes.* Workers out on strike are considered employed, but absent from work. This classification does not take into account that wages were lost and that, potentially, the strike may lead to long-term or even permanent unemployment[3].

(5) *Forced early retirees.* Workers who are considered retired, but who would have continued to work until legal retirement age 62 or 65 if they had not lost their jobs because of a plant closing or business failure, are not counted among the unemployed. Although they would be working had they not lost their jobs, they are assigned to the "not in the labor force" category.

(6) *New entrants and re-entrants.* Persons attempting to enter the labor force for the first time or to re-enter after having left are considered to be unemployed so long as they are actively searching for work.

Placing such people in the catch-all categories of employed and unemployed may lead to misinterpretations of psychometric data taken from surveys of the general public. For example, it seems indiscriminate to classify a full-time, well-paid factory worker or physician in the same category as the babysitter or itinerant worker who only could find one hour of employment during an average week; yet, depending upon the kinds of employment status questions asked, they may be lumped together.

Linking employment and psychological status

At least three constructs are useful in producing a more refined scheme of employment status classification (Levitan, Magnum & Marshall 1981): (1) "economic hardship," which attempts to capture quality-of-life aspects of work (for example, working at a job below the US-government-defined poverty level is less desirable than having a well-paid white-collar job); (2) labor market "attachment," which concerns the degree to which people desire to search for or hold a job (for example, a person who has held a full-time job for 30 years is more attached to the labor force than one who refuses to even look for work unless his or her special needs, which might be very special, are met); (3) laborforce "utilization," which reflects the extent to which groups not working are available for work (for example, discouraged workers are a surplus labor pool not being utilized in the marketplace).

Each dimension may be viewed as existing along a continuum reflecting more hardship, detachment, or nonutilization at one end (or pole) and less hardship, detachment, or nonutilization at the other. Alternatively, the three dimensions can be combined into a single continuum of employment status. On one end of this continuum are those who have difficulty finding or keeping jobs, are unskilled or inexperienced, have obligations (such as family responsibilities) which prevent them from taking available jobs, are disabled or in poor health, are poor, or just do not want to work (e.g., vagrants, "hobos"). People so classified are relegated to the *labor reserve* and are often referred to as the "secondary labor force," "sub-employed," "difficult to employ," or "not in the labor force." Toward the continuum's other extreme are those who have always worked at full-time jobs, earn decent salaries, enjoy an acceptable working quality of life, are skilled or easily trainable, *and*, when unemployed, have a high probability of becoming re-employed. People at this end of the continuum are the *core* or "primary labor force" (Jakubauskas & Palomba 1973, Levitan, Magnum & Marshall 1981).

With the increased concern for economic problems in the social sciences, some analysts have begun to use more refined labor economics constructs, such as hardship, attachment, and utilization, to help explain differences in psychological status. Warr (1978), for example, separated adults into those who were oriented toward the labor force (core workers) and those who were not (reserve workers). The results of his study, conducted on redundant steelworkers in Manchester, England, showed that psychological wellbeing (as measured by Bradburn 1969) was related to employment status and work orientation, but in complex ways. Other studies have found similar patterns (Warr 1978).

This analysis thus builds on the work of others by continuing to refine employment status measures to include workers who may be assigned to groups along the core–reserve laborforce continuum. The hypothesis central to this study is that increased economic hardship, lessened attachment, and lower utilization in the labor force will be associated with more negative psychological states.

Other labor-economic constructs may also be related to psychological status. The analysis described in this chapter sought to explore some of the following relationships:

(1) *Length of unemployment.*   Length of unemployment refers either to

the amount of time which has passed since a worker has been without a job, or to the amount of time which has passed since a worker initially began to look for a job. The latter case includes workers who are "new entrants" to the labor market and have never held a job, or workers who have temporarily dropped out of the labor force and have sought to "re-enter." It is hypothesized that the longer a worker is unemployed, the more negative will be the worker's mental health (Cobb & Kasl 1977).

(2) *Job change.*   Change in employment status, whether this involves moving to a better or worse job, making a lateral transfer, or losing a job, may be a traumatic experience. Generally, it is expected that the more changes in employment status, the less positive will be the worker's psychological status. Qualitative aspects of change could also be important in understanding mental health. Positive change in status should improve mental health, while negative status change should be associated with more negative states (Warr 1978).

(3) *Cause of unemployment.*   The way in which a worker becomes jobless varies greatly according to life circumstances. Unemployment may occur for many reasons: voluntary layoff, workforce retrenchment, mass layoffs from a plant closing, termination of seasonal work, involuntary layoff, forced early retirement, and so on. The greater the extent to which loss of work is attributed to one's self, rather than to external factors, the more negative may be the impact on mental health (Buss & Redburn 1983b).

The study

This study serves two purposes. First, it replicates recent work which attempts to assess psychological status using a measurement which includes not only the construct "psychological distress," but also "psychological wellbeing." In so doing, the study furthers our knowledge of mental health from a social–psychological perspective. Secondly, this analysis uses more rigorous concepts of employment status as explanatory or causal variables to account for differences in mental health scores. The research thus is intended as a contribution both to methodology and to substantive work on mental health and the economy.

The Youngstown/Warren SMSA was selected as the geographic unit of analysis. Personal interviews with 1,775 adults (16 years of age and older) were conducted, in June 1984, from a multistage sample of households in the SMSA (Buss 1986). Respondents answered labor-market questions about themselves and all other adults in the household so that a total of 3,855 questionnaires were completed. Some 91% of those contacted answered all questions. The survey followed the precise methodology used by the US

Bureau of the Census in its national Current Population Survey (CPS) (Bureau of the Census 1978).

In March and April 1985, a random subsample of respondents in the labor force, plus discouraged workers and forced early retired, were re-interviewed in person, using not only questionnaire items concerning labor-market participation but also the Rand Corporation's Mental Health Inventory[4]. Some 500 personal interviews were completed, representing 85% of those contacted. By conducting a panel study in two waves, it was possible not only to develop a profile of psychological status of people in the labor force, but also to determine how short-term employment status change (from June 1984 to March–April 1985) affected mental states.

To illustrate the complexity of the labor force classification, the sample for the first wave is detailed in Figure 8.1: a more detailed presentation of the sample can be found in Buss (1986)[5].

The sample for the second wave included 140 core employed workers, 51 part-time workers seeking full-time jobs, 35 working poor, 111 discouraged workers, 35 forced early retired workers, and 128 unemployed workers actively seeking jobs. (Details of this sample are given in Buss & Redburn 1985.)

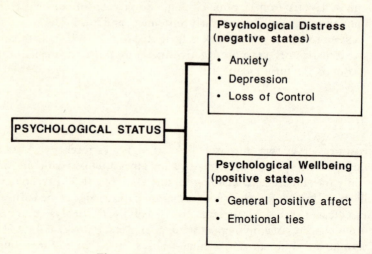

Figure 8.1   The laborforce profile.

PSYCHOLOGICAL STATUS

Psychological wellbeing has been measured in many ways (see Bradburn 1969, Health Resources Administration 1977, Warr & Wall 1975). For this study, the Mental Health Inventory (MHI) developed by the Rand Corporation was selected because it represents a widely accepted approach in this line of inquiry (Veit & Ware 1983, Ware, Johnston, Davies-Avery & Brook 1979).

Mental health is treated as having two components: psychological well-being (positive states) and psychological distress (negative states), as shown in Figure 8.2. Wellbeing is composed of two scales or indices: general positive affect, based on 11 items, and emotional ties, having 2 items. Distress encompasses three scales: anxiety, with 9 items; depression, with 4; and loss of behavioral or emotional control, with 9[6]. The statistical properties of the items and scales are described in Veit & Ware (1983)[7].

The results: economic change and mental health

Analysis began by relating employment status as frequently measured in other studies with psychological status[8]. At the aggregate or group level, findings suggested that employment is associated with less distress and greater wellbeing than is the case with either unemployment or forced early retirement. For many in the labor force, working is directly associated with mental health.

EMPLOYED, UNEMPLOYED, OR RETIRED

The psychological status of employed, unemployed[9], and forced early retired workers[10] is related to employment circumstances as hypothesized, with only a few exceptions for the individual psychological measures in the study (see Table 8.1). The composite measures of psychological distress, including its components (anxiety, depression, and loss of control) showed that employed workers were, in every case, less distressed than those who were unemployed, and the unemployed were more distressed than the forced early retired.

Table 8.1   Mental health scales by simplified employment status.

Scales	Employed	Unemployed	Forced retired	F ratio	p
Psychological distress	40.0	45.4	40.8	9.408	0.000
anxiety	18.8	20.8	19.1	5.353	0.005
loss of control	8.2	9.7	8.1	16.363	0.000
Psychological wellbeing	46.9	42.3	44.5	12.399	0.000
general positive effect	37.4	33.5	35.9	12.564	0.000
emotional ties	9.5	8.8	8.7	6.206	0.002
(*n* =)	(261)	(186)	(44)		

A vast body of traditional literature suggests that the relationship between employment and mental health reflects the greater stability and meaning that employment provides (Sinfield 1981). The forced early

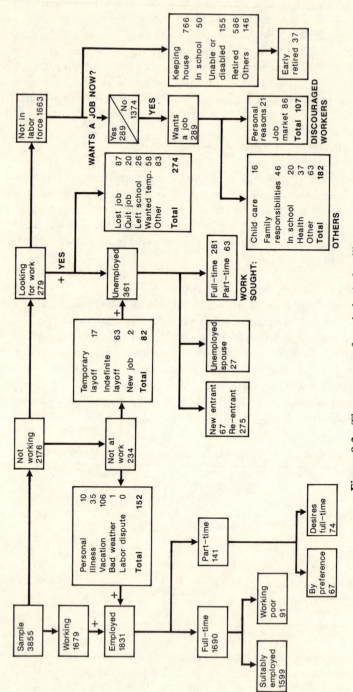

Figure 8.2 The structure of psychological wellbeing.

retired may not have wished to retire but, for most, retirement may have been an unexpected positive event (Sinfield 1981). At the very least, most forced early retired persons have more resources than most unemployed (Buss & Redburn 1983a).

Although the employed and forced early retired were less distressed than the unemployed, the retired were not noticeably more distressed than the employed as predicted. The forced early retired were slightly more anxious and showed a little less control than the employed, but were somewhat less depressed. This finding also supports the notion that although forced early retirement is feared by many workers, once retired, most workers appear to adjust to their new lifestyle in positive ways.

The composite measure of psychological wellbeing, as well as its components, general positive affect and emotional ties, paralleled the above findings for psychological distress. For all three measures, the employed perceived themselves to be better off than the unemployed. The employed were also better off than the forced early retired. The forced early retired were only slightly better off on measures of general positive affect.

MORE REFINED LABORFORCE CONCEPTS
As argued earlier, psychological status is directly related to employment status, but the labor force is much more complex than the dichotomous classification of workers as employed or unemployed would suggest. In order to look more closely at key groups making up the labor force within the employed and unemployed groups, employed respondents have been subdivided into full-time workers, working poor, and part-time workers seeking full-time jobs; and the unemployed have been subdivided into those currently (within the last month) looking for work, discouraged (not looking for work), and forced early retired. It was expected that these groups would have different levels of wellbeing and distress, depending on their degree of hardship, attachment to, and utilization by the labor market.

Findings suggest that psychological status is determined at least in part by the labor economics constructs under study; but the relationship between economics and mental health is more complex than our original hypothesis suggested.

Table 8.2 reveals that the employed full-time workers scored lower on every distress measure (i.e., anxiety, depression, and loss of control) and higher on every wellbeing measure (i.e., general positive effect, emotional ties, life perception) than either of the other employed groups, working poor and part-timers. Similarly, the employed full-time worker group had a more positive psychological status than any unemployed group. This suggests, once again, that having a job is better than being jobless; but that having a good job is preferable to having one with low pay, less prestige, limited benefits, unacceptable working hours, and so on (Jahoda 1982).

Of special interest is the comparison between unemployed people who

Table 8.2   Mental health scales by laborforce categories.

Scales	Employed	Unemployed[a]	Working poor	Part time	Discouraged[b]	Forced retired	F ratio	p
Psychological								
distress	38.1	45.5	43.8	44.4	42.1	39.5	5.055	0.000
anxiety	18.0	20.9	19.8	21.5	19.4	18.4	3.980	0.002
depression	7.6	9.5	9.1	8.9	9.2	7.8	6.351	0.000
loss of control	12.4	15.1	15.0	14.0	13.5	13.3	4.609	0.000
Psychological								
wellbeing	48.3	42.8	44.4	43.0	44.6	45.3	5.106	0.000
general positive								
effect	38.8	33.9	35.4	34.0	35.5	36.5	5.924	0.000
emotional ties	9.5	9.0	9.1	9.0	9.1	8.7	1.219	0.299

[a] Looking for work.
[b] Not looking for work.

are seeking work and those who have given up looking for a job. Job-seeking behavior may be thought of as a surrogate measure of level of "attachment" to the labor force: the greater the attachment, the less psychologically distressed a worker is expected to be. Contrary to expectations, the unemployed who are seeking work are somewhat worse off psychologically, both on distress and wellbeing, than those who have given up looking. Apparently, those who have given up looking for work have become resigned to long-term joblessness; while job seekers, who have not found work, experience negative psychological effects (Warr 1978).

Because the working poor are perceived to be only one step away from joblessness, there may be little difference in the psychological status of the working poor[11] and unemployed people. The psychological status of the working poor is very similar to that of the discouraged worker, but dissimilar to unemployed workers still seeking a job: the working poor and discouraged worker are somewhat better off than job seekers (as Table 8.2 shows). This finding suggests that the working poor may be somewhat resigned to their fate, i.e., working at subsistence levels, in the same way that discouraged workers may be resigned to joblessness.

As has been observed already, the forced early retired are more like full-time employed workers than not. As a corollary, the forced early retirees are somewhat dissimilar to the underemployed or unemployed.

EMPLOYMENT STATUS CHANGE

Laborforce status in the immediate past (i.e., the last 6–7 months) has some effect on psychological status measured in the present (Warr 1978, as suggested in Table 8.2). In order to see how short-term changes in employment might affect psychological distress and wellbeing, employment status at the first wave interview (June 1984) was compared with the status at the second wave (March–April 1985).

For measures of psychological distress and wellbeing, those whose employment status changed for the better were less distressed and had higher levels of wellbeing than those who had experienced negative changes (see Table 8.3)[12].

Table 8.3   Mental health scales by change in employment status.

Scales	Positive	Negative	No change	F ratio	p
Psychological distress	40.1	45.3	40.5	8.684	0.000
anxiety	18.8	20.8	19.0	4.989	0.007
depression	8.2	9.7	8.0	15.731	0.000
loss of control	13.0	14.8	13.5	7.005	0.001
Psychological wellbeing	46.8	42.4	44.8	11.385	0.000
general positive effect	37.4	33.6	36.0	11.619	0.000
emotional ties	9.4	8.8	8.8	5.359	0.005
(n =)	(256)	(183)	(42)		

Frequent employment status change, regardless of direction, may also be related to psychological status. In order to test this hypothesis, respondents were asked two questions: (a) "How many times have you lost or quit a job since 1974?" and "How many employers have you had since 1974?"

The results show that the number of job terminations (lost or quit) is unrelated to psychological status[13]. However, a strong relationship does exist between the number of previous employers and levels of psychological distress and wellbeing. Workers with larger numbers of employers are more distressed and express less wellbeing (see Table 8.4). This is the case not only for composite measures, but also for the component measures

Table 8.4   Mental health scales by number of employers worked for since 1974.

Scales	Number of employers				F ratio	p
	1–2	3–5	6–9	>9		
Psychological distress	41.1	44.4	47.3	47.9	3.151	0.025
anxiety	19.1	20.7	22.0	21.7	2.633	0.050
depression	8.5	9.1	10.3	10.6	3.472	0.016
loss of control	13.3	14.6	15.0	15.6	2.603	0.052
Psychological wellbeing	45.8	44.0	39.7	41.6	3.237	0.022
general positive effect	36.5	34.9	31.3	33.2	3.407	0.018
emotional ties	9.3	9.1	8.4	8.4	1.167	0.322
(n =)	(321)	(109)	(18)	(7)		

as well. The only exception to this was one wellbeing scale—emotional ties.

This ambiguous finding might be the result of measurement artifact or sampling error. An alternative explanation might be found in the questions themselves. The initial question concerned terminations which may place the individual at fault or in a socially undesirable position, i.e., lost or quit; while the latter question measures only job change, which could be either positive or negative. Therefore, job terminations for more negative reasons (e.g., being fired) may be counterbalanced by those for more positive reasons (e.g., quit to take a better job). The question concerning employer changes is not biased in this way.

TIME SINCE LAST WORKED

For the jobless, the passage of time may affect psychological status (Buss & Redburn 1983b). It would seem that the longer a worker is unemployed, the more distressed and less well-off he or she is likely to become. This may be the case not only for those who experience unemployment following job loss but also for those who have never worked.

Table 8.5   Mental health scales by "recent unemployed" (less than one year) and "never worked".

Scales	Recent unemployed[a]	Never worked	F ratio	p
Psychological distress	45.8	40.6	4.425	0.038
anxiety	21.3	18.1	7.893	0.006
depression	9.2	8.7	1.164	0.283
loss of control	15.2	13.8	1.970	0.163
Psychological wellbeing	43.2	45.3	1.114	0.294
general positive effect	34.0	36.4	2.306	0.132
emotional ties	9.2	8.8	0.647	0.423
(n =)	(53)	(51)		

[a] Less than one year.

Surprisingly, no statistically significant differences were observed between the length of time unemployed and psychological status[14]. One explanation for this finding might be that, after a certain period of time following unemployment, most workers become adjusted to their life circumstances, as reflected in a fairly narrow range of wellbeing and distress scores (Hayes & Nutman 1981, Jahoda 1982).

Next, the recently unemployed were compared with those who have never worked in an effort to understand the effects of joblessness over time. Those recently unemployed are much more distressed than those who have never worked (see Table 8.5). Anxiety appears to account for much of the distress among the recently unemployed. On the other hand, no differences in psychological wellbeing were found between the recently unemployed and those who had never worked.

These findings suggest that in the short term (one year or less) the unemployed tend to be anxious about finding a replacement job. In contrast, those who never worked appear to be much less distressed, perhaps indicating that many are not interested in working now; or they may not yet grasp the full implications of remaining jobless.

Implications for service delivery

Using advanced social–psychological conceptions of psychological status and labor economics categories of the labor force, the relationship between mental health and economic change begins to look more complex than suggested by many previous studies. The analysis confirms what has been shown on innumerable occasions, that unemployment and mental health are associated; unemployment is linked to lower levels of psychological wellbeing and to higher levels of psychological distress. However, it also

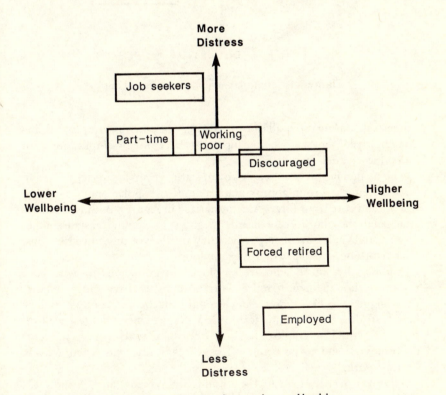

Figure 8.3   The labor force and mental health.

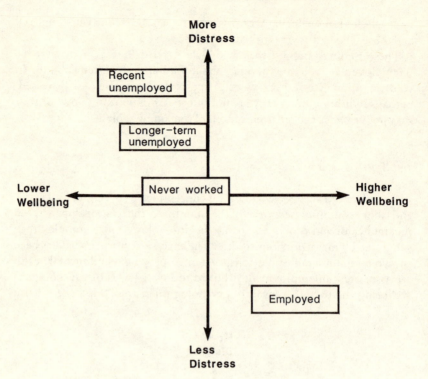

Figure 8.4   The time component in mental health.

suggests that using catch-all laborforce categories such as "employed" and "unemployed" masks relationships that have major implications for human service delivery.

The mental health of an employment status group is directly related to how closely the group approximates one of two polar opposites: labor reserve and core labor force. As summarized in Figure 8.3, those strongly attached to the labor force will suffer negative psychological states, either more distress or less wellbeing, when they are not working and desire jobs, or are working at low-pay or low-status jobs.

Additionally, those who are employed in good jobs or who have resources, though forced to retire, will report positive psychological states. Discouraged workers who are not strongly attached, in contrast, will be better-off than those seeking jobs or low-wage earners, but less well-off than the retired or employed. Once laborforce attachment wanes, the unemployed tend to be better off psychologically than when actively seeking work.

Time is also related to mental health and employment status. As indicated in Figure 8.4, among people in the labor reserve, those unemployed for long periods of time and those who have yet to hold down a job, psychological status is more positive than among those who are recently unemployed and presumably strongly attached and more closely associated with core labor.

Taking the findings in Figures 8.3 and 8.4 together, it seems clear that once workers give up looking for work and once they have been out (or never in) of the labor force for a time, their psychological status either improves or at least does not worsen. Given relatively positive psychological states, these workers appear to become more complacent about their life circumstances and less likely to initiate activities to improve their situation.

Most communities face chronic shortages in human service programs. At the same time, it is not always clear how to reach those in need of services. Some service providers, influenced by limited budgets, seek to maximize the numbers helped, by serving those easiest to reach and to serve (Lipsky 1980). The rationale for this strategy, sometimes referred to as "creaming," is that it is better to provide services to many people who can readily profit from them than it is to offer a few people help who are much less likely to benefit. On the other hand, this strategy often means that services are provided to those who would prosper without them, while being denied to others who would truly benefit.

Because of this bias in the human service delivery system, some service providers look for ways to identify those with the greatest prospect of benefiting. In this context, our analysis has the following tentative implications for human service planners[15]:

(1)   If those who are strongly attached to the labor force (job seekers, part-timers seeking full-time jobs, and working poor) become weakly attached, then they could be more difficult to place in jobs, because they may not perceive themselves as that much in distress. That is, a person who has become accustomed to life as a government dependent may never wish to return to the insecurity and stress of the labor market, especially if this means working at a low-status, low-paying job. Early service interventions that forestall this process of detachment may prove cost-effective. Programs which assist workers in locating and applying for jobs may be useful in focusing worker attention on re-employment. In the mental health field, counseling programs which promote self-esteem and self-motivation might be useful.

(2)   Those who have never worked also are more likely to become detached from the labor force the longer they remain without work experience. This group may also be an appropriate focus of public interventions which would increase their likelihood of employability. For instance, the federal Job Corps program, which prepares disadvantaged youth for work, has enhanced the employability of many

at risk of dropping out of the labor force by providing work experience and schooling, along with psychological counseling and motivational training, in a residential context[16].

(3) In a world of scarce public resources, discouraged workers perhaps merit somewhat less attention than others affected by economic change because, although they *want* jobs, many probably do not *need* jobs. Our analysis supports evidence from other research that many in this group have learned to cope in a world outside the labor force. Other studies (e.g., Finegan 1978, Flaim 1984) have found that discouraged workers are composed largely of three groups: youths living at home, or dropouts; housewives with child-rearing responsibilities; and retired people. These groups tend to enter the labor force only under very limited circumstances (e.g., wages are so high, work schedules are so flexible, or job status and prestige are so good, that staying at home becomes less attractive than working). If "discouraged" workers are not as discouraged as many of the working poor and part-time employed, there is at least some reason to believe that public resources would be better invested in improving the job status of the latter two groups than in chasing down jobs that meet the special requirements of the former group[17].

This analysis suggests the value of further efforts to refine measures of psychological and employment status, and to understand how these two statuses are related. Even the limited insights provided by this first use of a more complex set of categories point to possible changes in the focus of service programs for the unemployed. On the other hand, those recently out of work are shown to be under greater stress than other groups of unemployed, making them a potential target group for community mental health programs. On the other hand, many of those who have never worked or have become progressively more detached from the labor force appear a less promising target for interventions that ignore their relatively comfortable adjustment to not working.

Acknowledgments

The research reported here was supported by separate grants from the Office of Program Evaluation and Research, Ohio Department of Mental Health and the Division of Labor Market Information, Ohio Bureau of Employment Services. The authors would like to thank Dee Roth and Dixie Sommers for their encouragement, counsel, and continuing support. The authors assume sole responsibility for the views, interpretations, and conclusions in this chapter.

Notes

1 Other methodologies not discussed here include: a social indicator approach (e.g., Brenner 1973), worker case studies (e.g., Slote 1969, Marsden 1982, Seabrook 1982), clinical evaluations (Seligman 1974), and studies focused on physical health effects (e.g., Cobb & Kasl 1977, Curtis 1979).

2 It is important to note that surveys of the general public are not intended to provide data for individual-level analyses, that is, research cannot be, or is not, used to identify psychiatric cases. Instead, the methodology focuses primarily on differences across groups (e.g., males and females).

3 Because few workers in the local economy were on strike at the time of this study, the impact of labor disputes is not addressed.

4 The study focused on the labor force, which included discouraged workers and forced early retired. As such, those not in the labor force—retired (exclusive of those forced to retire early), household workers, students, disabled, and others—were not included.

5 Demographics (i.e., age, race, sex, education) are not reported here but will appear in subsequent analyses of these data.

6 Measures of wellbeing and distress may be combined in an overall index of mental health. We have elected not to focus analysis at this abstract level, but instead have concentrated on individual measures of wellbeing and distress.

7 Because of space limitations, detailed analyses of the mathematical properties of the scales are not reported.

8 We included forced early retired people in this initial analysis because they represent a major group in the "not in the labor force" category.

9 For purposes of this analysis, discouraged workers were classified as unemployed.

10 We included the forced early retired worker in the laborforce group in this case because all were recently compelled to withdraw from the labor market. We believe that this recent deep attachment to the labor force argues for their inclusion here as a separate group.

11 These are defined as families with earned income below the federal poverty line.

12 The only exception to this pattern was that the unemployed, and those with no change in status score identically on the wellbeing measure of emotional ties.

13 Tabular results are omitted because of space limitations.

14 Tabular results are omitted because of space limitations.

15 For an overview and evaluation of human service programs for the unemployed, see Buss & Redburn.

16 The Job Corps model has been described and evaluated in Mallar et al. (1982). This program could be expanded to include others, e.g., the homeless (Redburn & Buss 1986).

17 For a review and analysis of the discouraged worker phenomenon as a public policy issue, see Buss & Redburn 1987b.

References

Bradburn, N. M. 1969. *The structure of psychological well-being*. Chicago: Aldine.

Brenner, M. H. 1973. *Mental illness and the economy*. Cambridge, Mass.: Harvard University Press.

Brenner, M. H. 1978. A study of psychological well-being. *British Journal of Psychology* **69**, 111–21.

Bureau of the Census 1978. *The current population survey: design and methodology*. Washington, D.C.: US Department of Commerce.

Buss, T. F. 1986. Assessing the accuracy of BLS local unemployment rates: a case study. *Industrial and Labor Relations Review* **39**, 241–50.

Buss, T. F. & F. S. Redburn 1983a. *Shutdown at Youngstown: public policy for mass unemployment*. Albany, New York: State University of New York Press.

Buss, T. F. & F. S. Redburn 1983b. *Mass unemployment: plant closings and community mental health*. Beverly Hills: Sage.

Buss, T. F. & F. S. Redburn 1985. *Work and mental health*. Columbus, Ohio: Ohio Department of Mental Health.

Buss, T. F. & F. S. Redburn 1987a. *On the rebound: a human service response to plant closings*. Washington, D.C.: Council of State Planning Agencies.

Buss, T. F. & F. S. Redburn 1987b. *Hidden unemployment: discouraged workers and public policy*. New York: Praeger.

Cassimatis, E. 1979. Mental health viewed as an ideal. *Journal of Psychiatry* **42**, 241–54.

Catalano, R. & D. Dooley 1979. Does economic change provoke or uncover behavioral disorder. In *Mental health and the economy*, L. A. Ferman & J. P. Gordus (eds.), 321–46. Kalamazoo, Mich.: Upjohn Institute.

Cobb, S. & S. V. Kasl 1977. *Termination: the consequences of job loss*. Cincinnati, Ohio: National Institute for Occupational Safety and Health.

Curtis, G. C. 1979. Psychophysiology of stress. In *Mental health and the economy*, L. A. Ferman & J. P. Gordus (eds.), 235–54. Kalamazoo, Mich.: Upjohn Institute.

Ferman, L. A. & J. P. Gordus (eds.) 1979. *Mental health and the economy*. Kalamazoo, Mich.: Upjohn Institute.

Finegan, T. A. 1978. *The measurement, behavior, and classification of discouraged workers*. Washington, D.C.: National Commission on Employment and Unemployment Statistics.

Flaim, P. O. 1984. Discouraged workers: how strong are their links to the job market? *Monthly Labor Review*, August, 8–11.

Hansen, G. B. 1980. *Hardrock miners in a shutdown*. Logan, Utah: Economic Research Center, Utah State University.

Hayes, J. & P. Nutman 1981. *Understanding the unemployed*. London: Tavistock.

Health Resources Administration 1977. *A concurrent validated study of the NCHS general well-being schedule*. Washington, D.C.: US Department of Health, Education, and Welfare.

Horwitz, A. V. 1984. The economy and social pathology. *Annual Review of Sociology* **10**, 95–119.

Jahoda, M. 1982. *Employment and unemployment: a social–psychological analysis*. Cambridge: Cambridge University Press.

Jahoda, M., P. F. Lazarsfeld & H. Zeisel 1933. *Marienthal: the sociography of an unemployed community*. London: Tavistock.

Jakubauskas, E. R. & N. A. Palomba 1973. *Manpower economics*. Reading, Mass.: Addison-Wesley.

Levitan, S. G., L. Mangnum & R. Marshall 1981. *Human resources and labor markets*. New York: Harper and Row.

Lipsky, M. 1980. *Street-level bureaucracy*. New York: Russell Sage Foundation.

Marsden, D. 1982. *Workless*. London: Croom Helm.

National Institute of Mental Health (NIMH) 1985. *Unemployment and mental health*. Washington, D.C.: NIMH.

Redburn, F. S. & T. F. Buss 1986. *Responding to America's homeless: public policy alternatives*. New York: Praeger.

Seabrook, J. 1982. *Unemployment*. London: Quartet.
Seligman, M. E. 1974. Depression and learned helplessness and research. In *The Psychology of Depression*. R. J. Friedman & M. M. Katz (eds.). New York: Wiley.
Sinfield, A. 1981. *What unemployment means*. Oxford: Martin Robertson.
Slote, A. 1969. *Termination: the closing of Baker Plant*. Indianapolis: Bobbs-Merrill.
Strange, W. G. 1978. *Job loss*. Unpubl. manuscript.

Veit, C. T. & J. E. Ware, Jr. 1983. The structure of psychological distress and well-being in general populations. *Journal of Consulting and Clinical Psychology* **51**, 730–42.

Ware, J. E., S. A. Johnston, A. Davies-Avery & R. H. Brook 1979. *Conceptualization and measurement of health for adults in the health insurance study*, vol. 1. Santa Monica, Cal.: The Rand Corporation.
Warheit, G. J., R. A. Bell & J. J. Schwab 1979. *Integrated needs assessment approaches*. Gainesville: University of Florida (mimeo).
Warr, P. 1978. A study of psychological well-being. *British Journal of Psychology* **69**, 111–21.
Warr, P. & T. Wall 1975. *Work and well-being*. Harmondsworth: Penguin.

PART III

The provision and impact of community care

9 Locating mental health facilities: a case study

ANDREW J. SIXSMITH

Introduction

The objective of this chapter is to shed some light on how and why mental health facilities are located where they are, and to evaluate how British health service planners have dealt with the problem of where to locate these facilities. The issues are illustrated by a case study of services for the elderly, severely mentally infirm (ESMI) in Lancashire. The study area coincides with the now-defunct Lancashire Area Health Authority and is part of the North Western Regional Health Authority (NWRHA) in northern England.

Since the late 1970s the NWRHA has embarked on an extensive program of investment to expand their services for the mentally ill in the region. An explicit aim in planning these services has been to provide community services to replace the old large mental hospitals. In the case of ESMI services, this required the construction of new purpose-built units. Unlike long-established health services, the planning and development of the ESMI system involved decisions about where new facilities should be located.

The problem of locating ESMI facilities is a function of two competing considerations (Teitz 1968). In the context of a constrained budget, planners tend to maximize efficiency, possibly through economies of scale and service concentration. Alternatively, this trend is offset by the opposing need for easy and equitable access to facilities. However, this perspective is somewhat simplistic, and ignores the wider social and political contexts within which decisions are made; spatial outcomes are understandable and significant only ". . . as an expression of social process" (Dear 1978: 98). For example, the recent move toward a more accessible, community-based system of care for the mentally ill implies a small-scale service based on a large number of local facilities, rather than the few large centralized facilities that have characterized mental illness provision in the past. However, the impetus behind community care is not simply a matter of access. Instead, Dear & Wills (1980) suggest that community care can be interpreted as a function of social attitudes, social control, and increasing professionalism and state intervention.

In the light of these arguments, Dear & Wills (1980) have advocated an historical–hermeneutic perspective rather than the empirical-analytical

Table 9.1   Changes in the elderly population in the UK

	1961	1971	1981	1991
all ages	51,284	53,979	54,285	55,188
pensionable age	7,554	8,810	9,459	10,136
	(14.7)	(16.3)	(17.4)	(18.4)
from pensionable age to 75	—	6,274	6,406	6,325
		(11.6)	(11.8)	(11.5)
over 75	—	2,534	3,053	3,811
		(4.7)	(5.6)	(6.9)

Notes: population figures are in thousands; percentages of total population are given in brackets; pensionable age is 60 for women and 65 for men.
Sources: Census reports, 1961, 1971 and 1981; 1991 projection, Office of Population Censuses and Surveys, *OPCS Monitor*, November 1984.

approach that has characterized much of the research in health service planning (Dear 1984: 8). Nevertheless, there remains the problem of how to link spatial outcomes with the underlying structural processes. In this respect, the empirical–analytical approach offers powerful and rigorous methods of spatial analysis, and any suggestion that only an historical–hermeneutic or an empirical–analytical approach should be used seems restrictive (Bernstein 1976, Beaumont & Sixsmith 1984). Certainly, both approaches must be involved if any transition is to be made between what is and what should be, in respect to facility location.

Thus, the present chapter is in two main sections, reflecting the two approaches to the problem. The first identifies the significant factors that contributed to the evolution of the ESMI system in Lancashire. This involves an examination of the major policy initiatives on the part of the UK National Health Service (NHS) and the NWRHA, and a detailed description of ESMI service provision in the region. The second section is a detailed evaluation of ESMI services in terms of facility location and user access. Although access is only one of a number of competing issues, it is an important one, given the community-care rationale of ESMI services. The evaluation is based on the use of location–allocation models to optimize facility location, and the allocation of patients to them (Beaumont 1981). These models are also used prescriptively, to outline possible alternative patterns of provision.

Policies for the elderly mentally ill

Traditionally, health care for the elderly has been a "Cinderella" branch of the NHS. The inadequacy of services in the UK has become a matter of concern with the rapid growth of the elderly population in recent times (Table 9.1). By 1981, 17.4% of the population were of pensionable age, compared with 14.7% in 1961. From the point of view of health care, a more significant trend is the growth of the over-75 population, which could increase by as much as 50% in the 1971–91 period.

The elderly have now become a major focus of social and health care policy in the UK. For example, major policy statements by the Department of Health and Social Security (DHSS) in 1976 and 1977 established the elderly as a priority group for an improved and expanded service. These general statements were supplemented by *A happier old age* (DHSS 1979) and *Growing older* (DHSS 1981b), providing detailed evaluations of the particular service needs of the elderly. In the specific case of the elderly mentally ill, specialized services in the UK have been at best very limited and at worst nonexistent. This inadequacy is perhaps related to the failure of various health and welfare agencies to accept responsibility for care (Pasker *et al.* 1976), result-ing in inadequate provision in widely differing institutions. The type of environment and care has often been inappropriate to the needs of patients, causing distress to all concerned. It is also evident that the elderly mentally ill do not form a homogenous group. Their ailments may range from dementia due to organic deterioration, to problems such as clinical depres-sion. Psychological disorders in old age fall into three main groups: functional psychosis; reversible organic psychosis; and irreversible organic psychosis (Pfeiffer 1977; Ward 1979: ch. 2). The last disorder is essentially incurable and requires long-term care. However, the first two disorders are treatable. Consequently, ESMI services must be able to cope with a diverse range of needs. Care for the elderly mentally ill is thus problematic in some respects: the contradictory goals of long-term care and active rehabilitation may be difficult to reconcile. Moreover, services need to be sensitive, flexible and personalized; yet efficient enough to cope with a rapidly growing demand.

A better service is not just a matter of *more* services; a number of other qualitative issues have become components of policy. First, recent trends in treatment of the mentally ill (Klerman 1977) and public attitudes toward the mentally ill (Rabkin 1974, Dear & Taylor 1982) indicate a growing desire for community-based care. The community is seen as the proper focus for care for the elderly mentally ill. This would involve a dual program of deinstitu-tionalization, along with the establishment of local service outlets, and the expansion of primary, domiciliary and preventive services. A move towards community-based care may also involve a shift in responsibility from the NHS to local-authority social services for groups such as the elderly (DHSS 1981b: 1). Secondly, there is a consensus that elderly people should be maintained in their own homes as far as possible, placing emphasis on primary health and welfare services. Thirdly, services need to be flexible, as no single approach to care could cope with all the various needs of the elderly mentally ill. Finally, it is important that cases are adequately diagnosed and that appropriate care is given. Without this, potentially treatable illnesses may go undetected (Office of Health Economics 1979). These principles have been broadly incorporated into a number of influential DHSS policy documents, notably *Care in the community* (DHSS 1981a), *Services for mental illness related to old age* (DHSS 1972), and the recent *Government response to the Second Report from the Social Services Committee: community care with special reference to adult mentally ill and mentally handicapped people* (Great Britain 1985).

A change in emphasis toward community care would have considerable spatial ramifications. A move away from a hospital service, with the expansion of primary and domiciliary services, would mean decentralization and the provision of local services. The use of local facilities would mean relatively easy access for patients, and for families and visitors of patients in long-term care. The *Communtiy hospitals* document (DHSS 1974) indicates that long-stay patients would be most appropriately cared for in small local hospitals, supported by general practitioners. This would introduce a local, community orientation in the hospital system, and would help to maintain the family and community links that may be essential to the wellbeing of long-term inpatients.

Although the principles behind the concept of community care are generally accepted, the development of such a service has been constrained by a number of problems. In particular, the reorganization needed to achieve this type of régime would be extensive. Obviously, existing patterns of care are entrenched within the NHS, and the transfer of resources has not always proved easy.

POLICIES IN LANCASHIRE

The inadequacy of specialist care for the elderly mentally ill has long been recognized by health authorities in the North West of England (Manchester RHB 1961, 1967). However, the first major policy recommendations were made only in 1973, generally following earlier DHSS circulars. Given the absence of hospital services, emphasis was placed on the development of specialized assessment units, the expansion of long-stay facilities at local hospitals for patients with severe dementia, and the development of domiciliary and day-patient services.

These initial proposals were never put into practice, and it was not until 1977 that the present system of psychogeriatric care was first outlined in the original Regional Strategic Plan (NWRHA 1977). The new proposals differed from those in 1973 in that provision would be based on standard purpose-built ESMI units, rather than conventional hospital wards. The proposals required a very large capital investment program, and new facilities were to be developed in all seven of the Lancashire health districts. A standard unit provides ward accommodation of 56 beds, along with a day hospital for up to 50 patients. The services offered within a unit reflect the particular needs of individual patients and are designed to provide both long-term and short-term rehabilitative care. For example, the Beechurst unit at Chorley and District Hospital reserves half its beds for long-stay patients, while the rest are for assessment purposes and holiday relief accommodation. The day center caters for all types of ESMI patients who live at home with support from family, friends and social services, as well as for some of the residential patients.

Details of a comprehensive ESMI scheme were given in the 1979 Regional Plan. The principles underlying the provision strategy were simple: the establishment of a standard norm of provision; the calculation of district requirements based on this norm; and the outline of a system of units to meet this requirement. Each health district was seen as being self-sufficient with regard to ESMI care, and the actual level of service was determined by applying norms to the projected resident population aged 65 and over. Following DHSS guidelines (DHSS 1977), norms were established at three beds and day places per 1000 of the over-65 population, and it was a straightforward exercise to calculate the service requirement for each district (Table 9.2 and Fig. 9.1). As with any major capital project, the timescale involved was

Figure 9.1   Health districts in Lancashire.

Table 9.2   ESMI requirements in Lancashire (1979 plan).

Health district	Resident population in 1991 (over 65s)	Required level of service (beds or day places)
Lancaster	23.7	71
Blackpool	68.8	206
Preston & Chorley	45.7	137
Blackburn	38.7	116
Burnley	33.4	100
Ormskirk	14.2	43
Lancashire	224.5	673

Source: NWRHA Regional Strategic Plan, 1979.

long, but it was thought that shortfalls would be met by the late 1980s. Most ESMI services were to be provided in standard units, though some services were to be offered in conventional hospital wards. Specific details of the 1979 proposals are given in Figure 9.2 and Table 9.3.

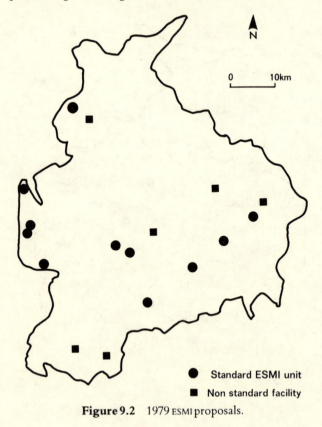

Figure 9.2   1979 ESMI proposals.

Table 9.3 Planned ESMI facilities in Lancashire (number of beds and day places).

Health district	Hospital	1979 plan		1983 plan	
		Bed	Day	Bed	Day
Lancaster	Victoria	56	50	24	—
	Lancaster Moor	?	?	—	—
	Lancaster Royal (DGH)	—	—	38	—
Blackpool	Fleetwood	56	50	—	—
	Devonshire Road (DGH)	56	50	56	50
	Lytham	56	50	56	50
	New hospital (DGH)	56	50	—	—
	Wesham Park	—	—	35	—
Preston &	Ribbleton	56	50	56	50
Chorley	Preston Royal (DGH)	56	50	56	50
	Chorley (DGH)	56	50	56	50
Blackburn	Accrington	56	50	56	50
	Queens Park (DGH)	56	50	56	50
	Clitheroe	?	?	—	—
	Ribchester	?	?	—	—
Burnley	Burnley	56	50	56	50
	Pendle	28	—	—	—
	Rossendale	—	—	38	—
Ormskirk	Ormskirk (DGH)	28	50	42	50
	Skelmersdale Community	28	—	24	11
Lancashire		700	600	649	461

Source: NWRHA Regional Strategic Plans, 1979 and 1983.

Since 1979, 9 of the 17 proposed facilities have been completed (Fig. 9.3). However, this period has been characterized by extensive spending cutbacks in the NHS as a result of current government economic policy. Obviously, the present economic situation could have had serious consequences for an ambitious program of capital development such as the ESMI scheme. The NWRHA response to cash limits has been to adopt a "realistic" approach to service provision, recognizing that "the NHS cannot meet all the demands made upon it and that some health needs of the population go unmet" (NWRHA 1983). In terms of service planning, the result of this has been twofold:

(1) *Priorities.* Who gets what is to be strictly dependent on a system of priorities covering all aspects of service provision. In the most recent Regional Plan (NWRHA 1983), long-term care for the elderly has been

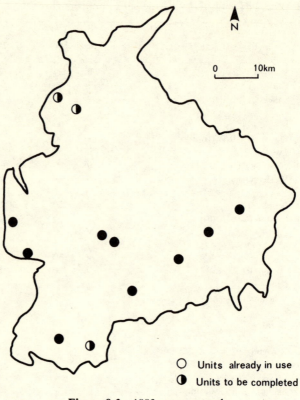

Figure 9.3   1983 ESMI proposals.

accorded a fairly low priority, representing a reorientation in policy. All things being equal:

> . . . considering benefits in terms of additive years of improved quality of life and likelihood of success in bringing this about results in ranking children's services before the elderly, emergency services before elective services, life-saving services before comfort-enhancing ones, and so on (NWRHA 1983: 38).

(2)   *Standards*. The level, quality and appropriateness of a service is to be relative rather than absolute. Explicit provision norms have been replaced by the idea of service "standards". For example, the standard for any service is the highest national level at the current time, providing a target for provision that has already been achieved somewhere and can be used as a model. In these relative terms, the NWRHA has attained a reasonably high level of ESMI service:

In 1979 many deficiencies in provision existed, but major

schemes to increase and improve facilities have been implemented. This has resulted in a level of provision which is more
closely related to the target requirement, in the right locations,
and in adequate accommodation, often in new purpose-built
units (NWRHA 1983: 156).

These two issues put a new perspective on care for the elderly mentally ill in
the region. In effect, the elderly mentally ill are not accorded an "inherently"
high priority, and the outcome of this new perspective in the context of cash
limits has been to reduce the scope and extent of the ESMI system in Lancashire
(Fig. 9.3, Table 9.2). In the latest Regional Plan, the proposed number of
standard units has been reduced from 11 to 9, while no specific mention is
made of the nonstandard provision outlined in 1979. Certainly the NWRHA
are justified in pointing to their relative success in providing ESMI services.
However, this should not obscure the fact that the identified normative
requirements in the 1979 plan will not be attained in four of the Lancashire
health districts, and that residential and day-hospital provision will be
considerably below the 1979 targets.

ASSESSMENT OF POLICIES
The NWRHA has been committed to providing a comprehensive ESMI care
service in Lancashire by the end of the present decade. The measure of
success they have had to date must represent a major planning achievement,
given the whole range of demands made upon NWRHA resources in the
present climate of cutbacks. However, the ESMI scheme in Lancashire is
open to a number of criticisms.

In terms of planning ESMI facilities, the major objectives of the NWRHA has
been to fulfil service requirements at a district level. Although consideration
is given by planners to facility location, this aspect of provision has never
been rigorously governed by established planning practices and objectives.
Given that a motivating factor behind ESMI provison is the idea of community care, factors such as location and access would seem to be pertinent
considerations. However, there has been no explicit statement about siting
ESMI units, except for an assertion in the 1979 Regional Plan that:

. . . For ESMI beds, apart from those in the District assessment unit,
to be located away from the District General Hospital, though this is
not the case at present in the Region, and indeed because of local
factors, several new units have been sited at District general hospitals
(NWRHA 1979: 103).

This follows the general belief that the best place for elderly people who are
hospitalized is in small, local hospitals. However, the siting of ESMI facilities
is closely linked to the system of District General Hospitals (DGHs) in the

region and, despite stated policy, over half the proposed facilities in Lancashire will be located at DGH sites. The availability of building space at DGH sites is one possible reason for this, but other factors may be involved. For example, the proximity of DGH facilities for assessment purposes is an essential part of ESMI care. The use of standard units is somewhat inflexible in this respect, because a whole unit would have to be sited at the DGH site, even though assessment beds do not account for all the 56 beds in a unit. Nevertheless, none of these considerations need to be crucial in determining the spatial pattern of provision. The extensive use of DGH sites for ESMI services would seem anomalous given the recent policy move towards the decentralization of hospital services (DHSS 1974, 1980).

A further observation is that all ESMI units are located at hospital sites, whether DGH or otherwise. Despite the notion of community care and its emphasis on noninstitutional care, the greater proportion of available resources has gone into a scheme of capital investment in hospital accommodation. This can be justified by the perceived need for an adequate infrastructure in an area where few facilities existed previously. However, is the enormous expense justified by the benefits? Some critics believe that the new service may only cater for a small proportion of the needs of the community and that the money would have been better spent on less capital intensive projects (MIND 1979). Moreover, the use of segregated facilities may not be in the best interests of the patients. There is evidence that severely impaired patients would fare better in mixed residential environments (Wilkin & Jolley 1979). Furthermore, there is always the problem of the fear, stigma, and institutionalization generated by separate mental illness facilities (Goffman 1961, 1975; Denzin 1969; Cohen & Taylor 1972). Hence, the ESMI unit concept may be inappropriate to the real needs of the client group:

> It is quite possible to provide humane, sensitive, therapeutic and non-segregated, non-stigmatised hospital and local authority services without a massive and expensive building programme or impossibly large increases in trained staff. This type of expensive, segregated, residential provision is neither cost-effective nor at all suited to the needs of the inmates for whom it is proposed (MIND 1979: 3).

There are advantages in providing ESMI care separately from more general facilities, because there are often behavioral problems associated with confused old people. Moreover, in many respects, mentally ill older people form a distinct group, and services may be more effectively delivered within the context of an ESMI unit. But these advantages need to be weighed against the needs of the patients: in particular, the benefits of community care may be compromised if ESMI patients are effectively isolated within these facilities.

In view of these criticisms, it is interesting to examine the evolution of the ESMI unit as the basis of psychogeriatric care in the region. The design originated from a mental illness facility built at Stepping Hill Hospital in Stockport, Greater Manchester, in the early 1970s. At the time, the DHSS was requesting that regional health authorities (RHAs) should draw up plans for providing services for mental illness, and the Stepping Hill unit was adopted as the model for subsequent developments. Units were to be built in all the health districts, and these proposals were eventually embodied in the 1977 Regional Plan. The ESMI unit design had rather a fortuitous origin, and owed more to the availability of land at the Stockport hospital than any defined rationale. Certainly, great care was taken over the internal design, and the accommodation was far better than the overall physical standards of the hospital stock in the region. Nevertheless little, if any, evaluation of the facility design has been undertaken, either before or after its general adoption as the basis of the ESMI scheme.

The criticisms of the ESMI scheme in Lancashire are significant, but should be placed within the context of an almost complete absence of hospital services for the elderly mentally ill prior to 1979. Given that some hospitalization is necessary, then these services needed to be provided, and this was the starting point for service planning in the region. However, all the regional plans also indicate a commitment to a comprehensive, district-based service. Care is not seen solely as a matter of more hospital beds, but also day-care facilities, preventive services, rehabilitation, and the whole range of primary, local-authority and voluntary care that comprise a community-based service. Whether or not this end will be achieved in practice is open to speculation; the emphasis on hospital care is deeply entrenched within the NHS, and the transfer of resources and initiative into a community context has not proved to be easy.

Notwithstanding these fundamental issues, there are still questions that need to be addressed. This section has indicated that the ESMI system in Lancashire is primarily centred on DGH sites, despite stated policy, and that little planning consideration has been given to issues beyond the fulfilment of service requirements at the district level. Given the basic need for a hospital service, one needs to ask whether the present scheme represents the most effective use of resources, particularly from the perspective of community care? There is an important spatial dimension to this issue: community involvement and integration imply physical proximity and accessibility. The next section presents a more detailed examination of this issue of facility location and user access.

Access to ESMI facilities

If ESMI care is seen primarily as a community-based service, then one might expect a system of small, local facilities. In fact, the pattern of ESMI provision in Lancashire is more spatially concentrated than the planned system of hospitals as a whole as outlined in the 1979 Strategic Plan. The large scale of provision could result in problems of access for nonresidential users, such as day patients and visitors. In the case of day patients, long ambulance journeys to and from ESMI units are a particular problem. One must consider whether the NWRHA scheme fulfills its community-care rationale, or whether the units are merely another form of mental illness ward with little chance of community integration. There is an explicit spatial dimension to this:

> Where residential services may have to cater for a wide catchment area, a specialist home or unit may have to draw on an even wider area, thus distancing some elderly people considerably from their relatives and local community. Separation from what is familiar to them may in turn increase confusion and disorientation (MIND 1979).

It is important that the issue of facility location and user access is fully evaluated in the light of such criticisms. In this paper, location–allocation models are used to examine this problem (see Beaumont & Sixsmith 1984).

LOCATION–ALLOCATION MODELS

The rationale of location–allocation models is to jointly optimize the location of facilities and the spatial allocation of users to them. This approach now forms an extensive literature on facility location (e.g. Beaumont 1981, Hodgart 1978, Leonardi 1981). Exactly what optimizing criteria are used in the model depends on the problem. In the present context of ESMI care provision, a relevant approach is to minimize the aggregate distance traveled by users to units. This formulation is consistent with the community-care idea, the current pattern of patient referral, and with the priority of maximizing benefits for the greatest number of people. This location–allocation problem can be written as:

$$\text{minimize} \quad D = \sum_{i=1}^{n} \sum_{j=1}^{p} O_i \lambda_{ij} C_{ij} \qquad (1)$$

subject to:

$$\sum_{j=1}^{p} \lambda_{ij} = 1, \quad i = 1, \dots, n \qquad (2)$$

where D represents aggregate distance traveled; O is an index of need at location $(x_i \, y_i)$; C is a generalized measure of distance between demand point i and supply point j, such as euclidean distance; λ is a binary variable which equals 1 if patients at i are allocated to facility j, and 0 if not.

This formulation can be said to be uncapacitated, in that facilities have no maximum capacity in terms of available bed space. With the ESMI unit problem, it is also interesting to look at a model which assumes that all facilities have an equal capacity. This capacitated problem can be written as:

$$\text{minimize} \quad D = \sum_{i=1}^{n} \sum_{j=1}^{p} O_i P_{ij} C_{ij} \tag{3}$$

subject to:

$$\sum_{i=1}^{n} O_i P_{ij} \leqslant k, \quad j = 1, \ldots, P \tag{4}$$

where P is the proportion of patients at i allocated to a unit at j, and k is the upper capacity constraint. The data demands of these problems are not excessive. The computer program which performs the optimization requires the location of demand points and calculates euclidean distances automatically. The measure of need is based on the number of people aged 65 years and over at each supply point, Figure 9.4 shows the distribution of

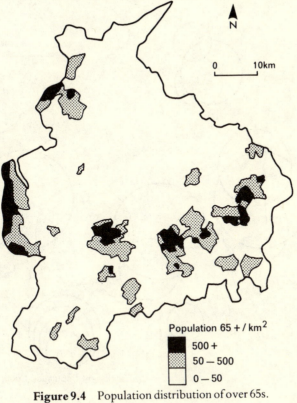

Figure 9.4 Population distribution of over 65s.

the elderly population in Lancashire, based on a Lancashire County Council survey in 1979. The distribution is uneven, with concentrations in coastal areas of Fylde and Lancaster, and the inland urban areas of Preston and east Lancashire. The only other information required is the number of facilities to be located. In the 1979 Strategic Plan around 14 units were proposed, while the number has been reduced to about 12 facilities in the most recent plan. It is useful for comparative purposes to use the location–allocation models to examine both of these schemes.

UNCAPACITATED PROBLEM
Figures 9.5a and b show the optimum locations for 12 and 14 units, based on the uncapacitated formulation of the location–allocation model. It is assumed that any number of people can be allocated to any particular unit, and people are allocated to their nearest facility. Figure 9.5 shows a large variation in the optimum size of units, reflecting the uneven population distribution in Lancashire. All the units are located in the major urban

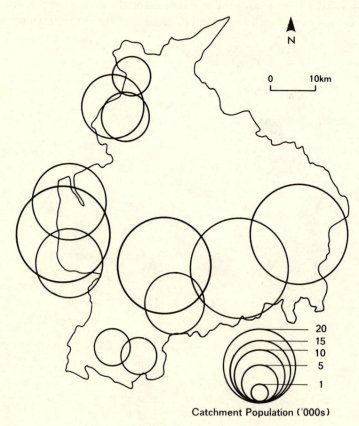

Catchment Population ('000s)

Figure 9.5a   Twelve units uncapacitated.

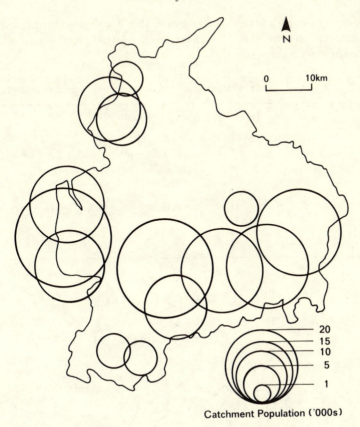

Figure 9.5b   Fourteen units uncapacitated.

centres and none are located in the more sparsely populated areas, such as north-eastern Lancashire. A comparison of the two optimal solutions shows only a few differences: in the 14-facility solution one of the large units in the 12-facility solution has been split into three smaller units.

The planned systems of ESMI provision (Figs 9.2 & 3) are broadly similar to the optimal solutions. This emphasizes the importance of the major urban centers in defining the priority for locating facilities on the basis of maximizing access for the greatest number of people. However, there is still the problem of servicing the rural areas. Figures 9.6a and b show that the catchment areas defined by the location–allocation model can be as great as 25 km across. This is even more marked with the catchment areas for the planned systems (Fig. 9.6c), because of the practice of referring patients to facilities within their own health districts.

This outcome cannot be seen as independent of the number of units used. That is, the scale of provision has a significant impact on the levels and variations of people's access to facilities. Table 9.4 shows that the mean distance between patients and their nearest unit is an indirect function of the number of units in the system.

Table 9.4   Uncapacitated problem: mean distances for a given number of units.

No. of units	Mean distance (km)
6	5.52
7	4.96
8	4.56
9	4.5
10	4.38
11	4.28
12	4.0
13	3.84
14	3.5

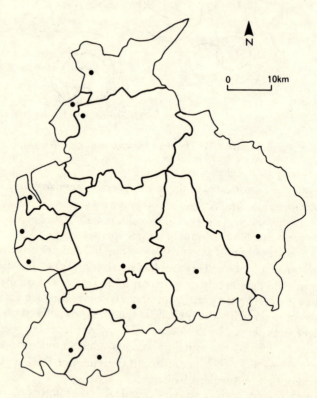

Figure 9.6a   Twelve units uncapacitated—catchment areas.

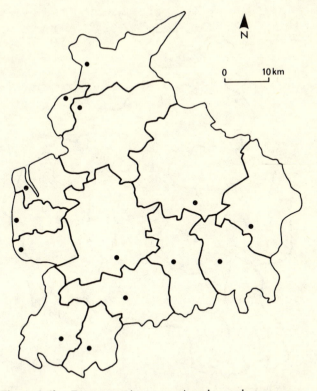

Figure 9.6b   Fourteen units uncapacitated—catchment areas.

As an alternative to the planned scale of provision, Figures 9.7a and b show the optimal locations for 20 and 24 units. The most obvious outcome is an increase in the scatter of units, with many more located away from the major urban centers. Moreover, a distinct hierarchy of unit size is apparent, with larger units in the densely populated areas and smaller units in rural centers and small towns.

It is evident that there is no access gain to be made by concentrating all services into a few urban centers. On the contrary, a single large unit will service an entire town with optimal access, while the residue of services could be located in less densely populated areas. Such a provision strategy would fulfill the requirements of maximum access for the greatest number of people, while also satisfying the desire for more equal levels of access between users.

EQUAL CAPACITY PROBLEM
Figures 9.8a and b show the optimal solutions when the model is subject to an equal capacity constraint. This even further emphasizes the urban pattern, with all units being located in places with the highest concentrations of

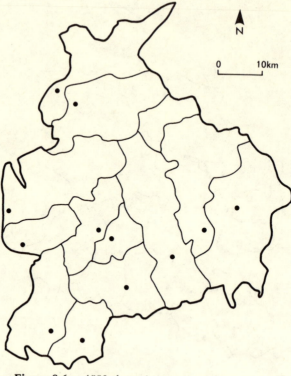

Figure 9.6c   1983 planned system—catchment areas.

elderly people. For example, the 14-unit solution locates four units on the Fylde coast in Blackpool Health District, which has the highest concentration of elderly people in the study area. Without the capacity constraint, the 14-unit solution (Fig. 9.8b) only requires 3 units in order to maximize access. The main implication of the finite capacity constraint on a facility is that it is not always possible to allocate people to their nearest facilities. Figure 9.9 shows that the catchment areas for 12 and 14 units of equal size involve a large variation in the distances traveled by patients. For example, the mean distance of travel to a unit in Lancaster Health District would be three times the mean for the system as a whole, and 15 times more than the district with the smallest mean (Table 9.5). On the whole, the equal capacity constraint involves larger average travel distances than the uncapacitated problem (Table 9.4). Also, the wide variation of distances traveled is illustrated by the standard deviation values for a given number of facilities.

SERVICE IMPLICATIONS

The results of both location–allocation problems suggest that the policy of providing services in large standard units is a little insensitive to the spatial variation in the distribution of the user population. The scale of ESMI service provision is large, with facilities having to cater for large catchment areas. Is this appropriate to the needs of the patient? From a community-care perspective the answer is likely to be no, especially in the case of districts that include large rural areas, such as Lancaster Health District.

Table 9.5 Capacitated problem: mean distances for a given number of units.

Number of units	Mean distance (km)	Standard deviation
6	12.82	7.12
7	12.08	9.14
8	7.86	4.38
9	7.4	5.4
10	7.4	5.28
11	6.5	3.4
12	6.33	4.2
13	5.5	3.4
14	5.89	3.94

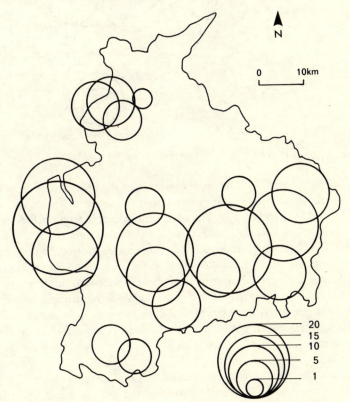

Catchment Population ('000s)

Figure 9.7a Twenty units uncapacitated.

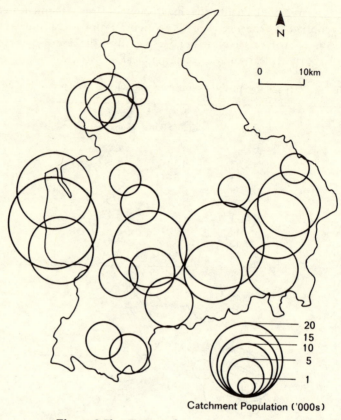

Catchment Population ('000s)

Figure 9.7b   Twenty-four units uncapacitated.

The need for smaller-scale provision seems to be borne out in an evaluation of the impact of large-scale provision on access to the ESMI unit at Chorley and District Hospital. Access is a considerable problem for patients attending the day hospital, and is recognized as such by most of the staff in the unit. The large majority of day patients are transported by ambulance, and the demands on the available resources are heavy. This causes a number of problems. For example, journeys of over two hours to and from the unit are not uncommon. Moreover, at times of heavy demand on the ambulance service, the patient list may be cut. All this means fewer hours spent at the hospital and fewer hours of occupational therapy and rehabilitation. These are examples of access problems which have a direct bearing on the quality of service.

A second user group affected by the scale of provision are visitors. This is an important issue, as a community-based service seeks to maintain the links between residential patients and their families and friends. Table 9.6 summarizes the results of a questionnaire survey of visitors to the Chorley ESMI

Table 9.6 Access to the Chorley ESMI unit.

	Car %	Bus %
type of transport used	84	16
visitors who experienced problems getting to the unit	0	48
visitors who felt that the unit was difficult to get to	0	50
visitors who would visit more often if unit was easier to get to	20	75

unit. Visitor perceptions of access to the unit fall into two clear groups, defined by the mode of transport to the unit. None of the visitors who traveled by private means experienced any problems associated with access, nor did they feel that the unit was difficult to get to. This can be compared with visitors who used public transport, half of whom expressed difficulties associated with travel. Moreover, a large majority of visitors using public transport said that they would attend more frequently if the unit was easier to get to. This is compared with a figure of only 20% for car users. These results show that problems of access are restricted to visitors who use public transport to get to the unit. Indeed, 25% of visitors with a car also said that they would experience access difficulties if a car was not available to them. Most of these respondents came from outlying districts of the study area, over 9 km from the unit, indicating that public transport would present particular difficulties for visitors from the more distant rural areas.

Given that these visitors are often the only tangible link between in-patients and their previous lives outside the hospital, the question of access is significant. Two issues should also be borne in mind. First, the difficulties in getting to the Chorley unit occur in a fairly small health district. These problems are likely to be even more severe in larger districts. Additionally, it was impossible to conduct a survey of people who did not visit the facility as a result of access difficulties. With these considerations in mind, it appears that the use of large-scale facilities may effectively isolate some older people from their familiar surroundings.

An obvious solution to problems of access to ESMI units is to enhance the mobility of the users. In the case of day patients, a possible solution is to employ outside contractors rather than to rely on the ambulance service. This would seem a logical step in the case of ESMI patients who are generally physically fit and may not require the services of fully trained ambulance crews. This alternative has been adopted for some of the ESMI units in Lancashire. Increases in car ownership also mean that visitors are now more

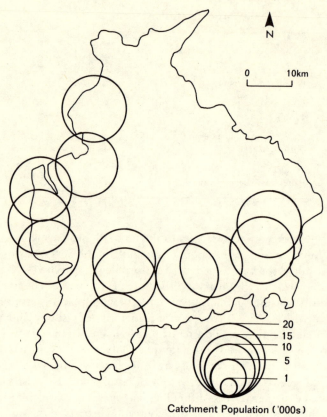

Figure 9.8a   Twelve units capacitated.

mobile. However, many people still rely on public transport, where cut-backs are likely to make access increasingly difficult.

Conclusion

This chapter has raised a number of doubts as to whether a system of care based on standard ESMI units is appropriate to the needs of users. A possible alternative to the present strategy could be the use of standard units in areas with a high density of elderly people, with smaller, nonstandard facilities in other areas. Specifically, ESMI units could be used in the major urban centers, with smaller facilities serving the smaller towns and rural centers. Hope-fully, this would help to maintain the necessary "local" character of services that is implied by the community-care concept.

Obviously, planners and decision-makers have to consider many factors besides location and access. However, it is noted that the alternative system

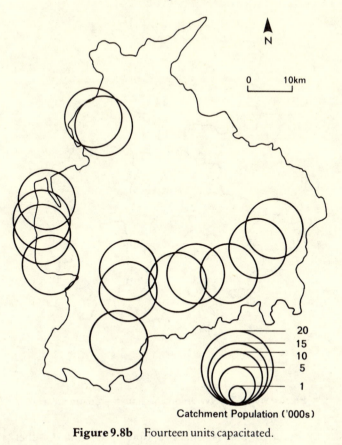

Figure 9.8b   Fourteen units capacitated.

of large centralized units and smaller, local facilities would be appropriate for a whole range of reasons. For example, Sixsmith's (1984) analysis of people's attitudes towards ESMI facilities found a distinction between attitudes toward patients with behavioral problems and those that were only mildly disturbed. The latter were generally acceptable, while the former generated consistently high levels of opposition. If community facilities are to be made as acceptable as possible, then it may be expedient to segregate patients on this basis. Purpose-built units would be appropriate to seriously disturbed patients, with more domestic facilities serving other patients. This strategy has clear parallels with the recommendations made in the present chapter.

Also, other research has identified a significant client group of elderly, mentally infirm (EMI) patients, lying between those who can be looked after in local-authority homes and those who need long-term hospital care (Copeland *et al.* 1986, de Zoysa & Blessed 1984, Royal College of Psychiatry 1978). This group could benefit from a smaller-scale and more

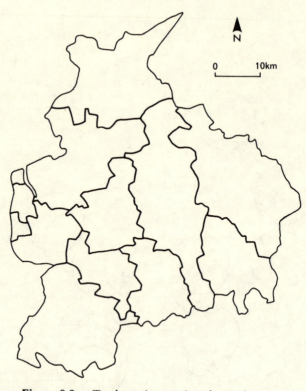

Figure 9.9a   Twelve units capacitated—catchment areas.

domestic environment than is usual in hospital provision. Godber (1977) stresses the need for alternative residential provision that would both reduce physical scale and promote community integration and personal indepen- dence. For example, small nursing homes with a domestic atmosphere for those who are physically fit, but not well enough to live alone, would be a valuable alternative (Howells & Hallas 1981). A provision strategy based on these assumptions would again match the recommendations in this chapter. This type of policy was outlined for Blackburn Health District in the 1979 Strategic Plan, where ESMI services were to be provided at two hospitals in rural centers. However, these do not appear in the most recent plan and there are no concrete proposals for this type of accommodation and care at the present time. The elderly mentally ill in Lancashire will be cared for in ESMI unit accommodation for the forseeable future.

From the earlier evaluation of the health authority's approach to planning ESMI services, it is hard to escape the conclusion that established practices rather than defined objectives count for more in determining who gets what where. For instance, the criticism of hospital and capital-oriented provision is a common one (cf. Garner 1979, Navarro 1978). In the end, is the type of care and mode of delivery appropriate to the requirements of the client? On the issue of location and access, established planning procedures may not be sensitive enough to cope with the problem at hand. ESMI service planning has been focused on fulfilling district requirements; a principle that is enshrined within the approach to service allocation outlined by the NHS Resource Allocation Working Party (RAWP) (DHSS 1976b). This approach must contribute to more equitable patterns of access, but the final outcome depends upon whether the administrative spatial structure (health districts) is the appropriate level to address the issue of accessibility. The results of the location allocation problems indicate that the NWRHA system, based on RAWP principles, may not be the most suitable.

Admittedly, issues of access and facility location are not always appreciated or understood, particularly in a planning environment such as the NHS, where there is no great tradition of expertise in spatial analysis. If locational matters are to be adequately dealt with, then such expertise needs to be available. As Beaumont & Sixsmith (1984) note, the use of interactive microcomputers could be valuable in this respect. Software including

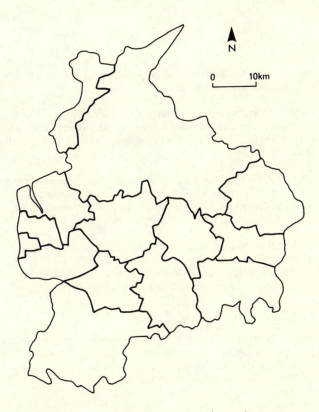

Figure 9.9b   Fourteen units capacitated—catchment areas.

location–allocation models and graphics could provide a framework for tackling location problems in a continuous decision-making process.

From a more theoretical perspective, there is also a need for a deeper understanding of the implications of spatial issues for the success of community care in community mental health services. Many studies have looked at issues of access and utilization, in respect to community hospitals (cf., Haynes & Bentham 1979, Mohan 1984) and primary care services (cf., Knox 1978, Wood & Barr 1982). However, few studies have examined access to health services from the specific perspective of community care. As already emphasized, community care has an explicit spatial dimension. In the present chapter, a fairly simple view of this relationship has been taken, equating access with proximity. However, significant issues such as the effects of accessibility on the links between residential patients and the wider community are not well understood. It is likely that these sorts of analyses would fall within the historical–hermeneutic perspective outlined earlier. Nevertheless, the outcomes of this type of research could eventually provide the parameters for defining spatial systems of community care on a more rigorous basis.

References

Beaumont, J. R. 1981. Location–allocation problems on a plane: a review of some models. *Socio-economic planning sciences* **15** (5), 217–29.

Beaumont, J. R. & A. J. Sixsmith 1984. Elderly severely mentally infirm (ESMI) units in Lancashire: an assessment of resource allocation over space. In *Planning and analysis in health care systems*, M. Clarke (ed.) 163–93. London: Pion.

Bernstein, R. J. 1976. *The restructuring of social and political theory*. Oxford: Basil Blackwell.

Cohen, S. & L. Taylor 1972. *Psychological Survival*. Harmondsworth: Penguin.

Copeland, J. R. M., C. Crosby & J. Stilwell 1986. *District experimental care schemes for elderly mentally ill people*. Research review, Liverpool University, Department of Psychiatry and Institute of Human Ageing.

Dear, M. J. 1978. Planning for mental health care: a reconsideration of public facility location theory. *International Regional Science Review* **3** (2), 93–111.

Dear, M. J. 1984. Health services planning: searching for solutions in well-defined places. In *Planning and analysis in health care systems*, M. Clarke (ed.), 7–21. London: Pion.

Dear, M. J. and S. M. Taylor 1982. *Not on our street: community attitudes to mental health care*. London: Pion.

Dear, M. J. & T. Wills 1980. The geography of community mental health care. In *Conceptual and methodological issues in medical geography*, M. S. Meade (ed.), 263–81. Chapel Hill: University of North Carolina Press.

Denzin, A. 1969. Collective behaviour in local institutions: the care of the mental hospital and the prison. *Social Problems* **15** (3).

DHSS (Department of Health and Social Security) 1972. *Services for mental illness related to old age*. London: HMSO.

DHSS 1974. *Community hospitals: their role and development in the NHS*. London: HMSO.
DHSS 1976a. *Priorities in the health and social services*. London: HMSO.
DHSS 1976b. *Sharing resources for health in England: report of the Resource Allocation Working Party*. London: HMSO.
DHSS 1977. *The way forward*. London: HMSO.
DHSS 1979. *A happier old age*. London: HMSO.
DHSS 1980. *Hospital services: the future pattern of hospital provision in England*. London: HMSO.
DHSS1981a. *Growing older*. London: HMSO.
DHSS 1981b. *Care in the community*. HC (81) 9. London: HMSO.
de Zoysa, A. S. R. & G. Blessed 1984. The place for the specialist home for the elderly mentally infirm. *Age and Ageing* **13**, 218–23.

Garner, L. 1979. *The NHS: your money or your life*. Harmondsworth: Penguin.
Godber 1977. *Age and Ageing* **6**, 100–3.
Goffman, I. 1961. *Asylums*. Harmondsworth: Penguin.
Goffman, I. 1975. *Stigma*. Harmondsworth: Penguin.
Great Britain 1985. *Government response to the second report from the social services committee, 1984–85 session: community care*. Cmnd 9674. London: HMSO.

Haynes, R. M. & C. G. Bentham 1979. *Community hospitals and rural accessibility*. Farnborough: Saxon House.
Hodgart, R. L. 1978. Optimising access to public services. *Progress in Human Geography* **19** (2), 17–48.
Howells, C. & J. Hallas 1981. *Policy analysis project on health, housing and social services for the elderly*. Nuffield Centre for Health Service Studies, University of Leeds.

Klerman, G. L. 1977. Better but not well: social and ethical issues in the deinstitutionalisation of the mentally ill. *Schizophrenia Bulletin* **3**, 617–31.
Knox, P. 1978. The intra-urban ecology of primary medical care: patterns of accessibility and their policy implications. *Environment and Planning A* **10**, 415–35.

Leonardi, G. 1981. A unifying framework for public facility location problems, part one. *Environment and Planning A* **13**, 1001–28.

Manchester Regional Hospital Board 1961. *Establishment of geriatric units in psychiatric hospitals*. Manchester: MRHB.
Manchester Regional Hospital Board 1967. *The care of the elderly in the Manchester RHB*. Manchester: MRHB.
MIND 1979. *Mental health of elderly people*. Leeds: MIND.
Mohan, J. 1984. Hospital planning and new town development: examples from North East England. In *Planning and analysis in health care systems*, M. Clarke (ed.), 142–62. London: Pion.

Navarro, V. 1978. *Class struggle, the state and medicine*. New York: Prodist.
NWRHA (North Western Regional Health Authority) 1977. *Regional strategic plan*. Gateway House, Manchester: NWRHA.
NWRHA 1979. *Regional strategic plan*. Manchester: NWRHA.
NWRHA 1983. *Regional strategic plan*. Manchester: NWRHA.

Pasker, F., I. Thomas & J. Ashley 1976. The elderly mentally ill: whose responsibility. *British Medical Journal* **164** (3).
Pfeiffer, E. 1977. Psychopathology and social pathology. In *Handbook of the*

psychology of aging, J. Birren & K. W. Schaie (eds.), New York: Van Nostrand Reinhold.

Rabkin, J. G. 1974. Public attitudes toward mental illness: a review of the literature. *Schizophrenia Bulletin* **1**, 9–33.
Royal College of Psychiatry 1978. Memorandum, cited in Copeland *et al.* (1986), op. cit.

Sixsmith, A. J. 1984. *Attitudes towards community-based mental health facilities*. Paper presented to the Institute of British Geographers Medical Geography Study Group Conference, University of Leeds, 19–20 July.

Teitz, M. B. 1968. Towards a theory of urban public facility location. *Papers of the Regional Science Association* **21**, 35–51.

Ward, R. A. 1979. *The ageing experience: an introduction to social gerontology*. New York: Lippincott.
Wilkin, D. & D. Jolley 1979. *Behavioural problems among old people in geriatric wards, psychogeriatric wards and residential homes 1976–1978*. Research report Department of Psychiatry and Community Medicine, University of Manchester.
Wood, J. & R. Barr 1982. *Inequalities in urban primary care*. Paper presented at the conference of the Institute of British Geographers Medical Geography Study Group, University of Liverpool, July.

10 "Is there one around here?"— investigating reaction to small-scale mental health hostel provision in Portsmouth, England

GRAHAM MOON

Introduction

It is now over a decade since the seminal work of Wolpert and Dear first placed the location of facilities for people with mental health problems on the geographical research agenda (Dear 1976, Wolpert, Dear & Crawford 1975, Wolpert & Wolpert 1976). Research has progressed significantly since these early papers, reaching an empirical high point in Dear & Taylor (1982). Yet, for all this achievement, the study of the geographical aspects of deinstitutionalization has been curiously deficient in two respects. First, in spite or perhaps because of a singular success in generating empirical research, there has been a comparative lack of theoretical underpinning to published work. Secondly, while extensive research has been conducted in Canada and the USA, there has been little comparable work elsewhere.

The lack of theoretical underpinning to work on deinstitutionalization has not gone unnoticed. Indeed, Dear himself has addressed the issue (Dear 1978, 1981), arguing that the location of facilities for the mentally ill reflects the wider distribution of power relations within society and the socio-economic derivation and operationalization of public policy. For Dear, and for others (e.g., Mair 1984), facility-location issues are essentially political issues; theory becomes politics. This perspective is wholly correct within its own terms, and has proved a fruitful research direction indicating the structural constraints guiding, inhibiting and affecting deinstitutionalization. However, its focus on the macroscale is a limitation, as it has led to a lack of research on more humanistic issues, such as the way in which the reaction to deinstitutionalized care is socially constructed.

Legislative and academic history perhaps provide the reasons for the North American domination of the research literature on the siting of mental health facilities. Certainly the 1963 Community Mental Health

Centers Act in the USA proposed a more comprehensive program than the 1959 UK Mental Health Act although, later yet, more radical initiatives, such as the mass deinstitutionalization program pursued in Italy, were subsequently developed (see Bean, this volume). The results and geographical impacts of the closure of asylums began to be evidenced much earlier in the USA and Canada than in Britain. In addition, the development of a core of academic interest in the topic was an undoubted catalyst to research. The work conducted by researchers originating from McMaster University and by selected others (e.g., Smith 1977) provides a large proportion of current geographical knowledge concerning deinstitutionalization.

It was primarily a desire to investigate the lessons posed by the North American work which led to the development of the research which provides the subject matter for this chapter. In an empirical analysis of the neighborhood impact of facilities, explicit attention was given to both positive and negative impacts, and to the variation between fears of impacts prior to the opening of a facility and their actual incidence once a facility began to function. Through the latter focus, the project also aimed to address the theoretical deficiencies, regarding the social construction of opposition to deinstitutionalization, which were identified in earlier research. The project ran initially for a period of one year, while a pilot study was developed using a case study of hostel provision for homeless men. Following on this work, the project was extended and its methodological approach replicated in a study of community-based facilities for people with mental health problems, hostels for persons on bail from the courts, and women's refuges (Burnett 1983, 1984).

The purpose of this chapter is not merely to report on the elements of a UK case study of deinstitutionalization which were concerned with people with mental health problems; rather, it is intended to draw out selected issues of interest from the research. These issues will be of both a theoretical and an empirical nature, and will essentially be concerned with the fears and experiences which have been engendered by community care for mental health. After a brief review of the current status of community care in the UK, attention will shift to a consideration of geographical perspectives on care. Particular attention will be given to developing UK parallels with the North American facility impact studies. In the following sections, attention will turn to an empirical consideration, drawing on the Portsmouth work, of the disjunctions between people's vague feelings concerning people with mental health problems, their fears concerning what they believe will happen when a community-based facility is opened, and their actual experience of living in the vicinity of such a facility. An examination of attitudes to community-based provision for mental health care will be therefore followed by considerations of perceptual and experiential externality.

Mental health care in England & Wales

The policy context within which mental health care in England & Wales is sited has been clearly summarized in several of the basic texts on UK health care policy (Ham, 1985). Here, only a brief overview of the route which led to community care will be presented, before attention shifts to identifying how policy developments have been translated into outputs in the form of facility provision.

The effective genesis of a mental health community care policy in the UK can be traced to developments in the early 1950s. Conditions in the large mental asylums were perceived as being in need of substantial improvement as the asylum system was apparently functioning as a repository which removed the mentally ill from the sight of the general population (Iliffe 1983). Poorly funded, understaffed and overcrowded, the asylums appeared to have ceased to offer a suitable service. The 1957 Percy Report and the subsequent 1959 mental Health Act addressed these difficulties and put forward the idea of community care. People with mental health problems were to be cared for wherever possible in "the community", although what this meant was not defined. The Act passed the control of these community services to local government; the NHS was not, at this time, expected to bear the funding burden of the new mode of care, although changes took place following subsequent reorganizations of the NHS.

The planned replacement of the asylum system by community care was confirmed by the 1962 Hospital Plan, which projected a halving of mental illness beds by 1975 (Ham 1985). Replacement services were to include out- and day-patient facilities, and the social services authorities were to provide hostels, group homes and day centers. A White Paper, *Better services for the mentally ill* (DHSS 1975), consolidated this aim, suggested provision norms, and recommended that all hospital psychiatric services could be provided in District General Hospitals (DGHs).

The arguments concerning the causal origins of this policy shift towards community care are well known (Scull 1978). Basically they involve the counterposing of theories arguing for the importance of changing public attitudes and advances in drug therapy with perspectives suggesting that community care was used as a smokescreen for financial cutbacks. In fact, with regard to the latter argument, community care for people with mental health problems, if delivered effectively, would involve little financial gain over the asylum system, and there would also be a need to run both an institutionally- and a community-based service during the changeover period. Whatever the explanation, it remains that the practise of mental health care is currently in a state of flux, with the rundown of institutions proceeding, but the replacement community services not being developed to the extent required because of fiscal restrictions and imperfect joint planning between health and social services authorities.

Present provision, in a formal sense, for people with mental health problems can be considered under three headings. First, there are the institutional forms of provision. These comprise the remaining traditional asylums catering, on a residential basis, for a full diagnostic range of mental health problems and the smaller generally newer departments of psychiatry in DGHs. Secondly, these are what can be termed quasi-community forms of provision. These are services provided in a specialized or specially adapted facility away from a person's home, usually by either health or social services, but increasingly in the UK by the private sector. Included in this category are hostels, group homes, halfway houses for former patients, and homes for the elderly mentally infirm. These facilities are community-based and (usually) small in scale. Also included in this category is day-patient and outpatient provision, involving the attendance of a mentally ill person at a center attached to a hospital or held in a local community facility. A third category of service is that which is strictly domiciliary. Perhaps constituting the essence of community care in that recipients live and are cared for in their own homes, formal domiciliary services are provided predominantly by community psychiatric nurses, social workers, and general practitioners.

Because of inadequate financing and shortcomings in developmental programs underlain by governmental fiscal constraints, the formal mechanisms of community care are severely stretched. In consequence, a considerable amount of the care which is required is either delivered informally or not at all. Informal care can be taken to imply that the primary responsibility for caring belongs with the community in which the person in need resides. In practice, this means that when a person with a mental health problem has a family, care is a family responsibility; the family should be prepared to provide a large amount of the care required by a relative with a mental health problem. This view clearly corresponds with the prevailing ideology of the current UK government; care should reflect self-help and the centrality of the family—and it is cheaper (see Eyles, this volume). Care can therefore be delivered not only in but also by the community. This interesting and profoundly geographical aspect to policies for mental health care is paradoxically much neglected by geographers. Too often it also means that care, in practice, equals care by women relatives, without involving any element of choice on the part of the care-giver (Finch & Groves 1980, Walker 1982). The imperfections in the practice of community care can thus have considerable specific consequences for the role of women in society (Lupton 1985).

Where a family does not exist, or is unwilling to provide care, the shortcomings of community care become most clearly focused. In this situation, people with mental health problems are forced onto the open housing market. Typically, they gravitate to the private renting sector or to common lodging houses, bed-and-breakfast accommodation, or hostels for the homeless. Nationally, some 30% of residents of hostels for the homeless have some form of history of mental illness, while one such hostel in Portsmouth averaged a 15% occupancy rate by people with mental health problems in 1982 (Moon & Burnett 1983a,b). Once in this volatile and highly mobile housing market, people with mental health problems become increasingly difficult to trace, and contact with community psychiatric services is often lost.

This discussion of mental health care illustrates the variety of modes of care delivery and nondelivery in the UK. Although the replacement of institutional by community care has now been a policy goal for many years, and has become firmly fixed on the academic and practitioner agendas, there remains a pressing need for research recognizing the diversity of provision. In particular, there is a need to recognize that care has undergone a shift from a model based on containment to one based on deinstitutionalization. The social construction of general attitudes to mental health care has, in general, been slow to recognize this shift and a broad subscription to containment, fostered by a lack of knowledge concerning mental illness, still prevails. A second aspect of contemporary mental health care which should be emphasized is the need to consider residential settings other than those specifically labelled for people with mental illness: given the piecemeal progress towards community care it is probable that a majority of cases of mental illness are to be found in the informal sector.

Geographical perspectives

The post-war changes in models for the organization and provision of mental health care in the UK have had consequences beyond the aspatial concerns of sociology and social policy. There have been precise identifiable geographical dimensions to the changes which have been taking place. These have been of two types: those concerned with the description of changes in the spatial pattern of facility provision, and those reflecting a deeper concern with the spatial consequences of the change in the emphasis of service delivery. The former is essentially concerned with changes in *where* facilities are located; and the latter with effects and issues consequent upon a service distribution differing radically from what had previously been available.

To take, first, the changing locational pattern of mental health care; the situation which has evolved can be characterized as one of the "urbanization of care". The enactment of community-care policies in the UK has seen the locus of mental health care shift from the often isolated green-field sites of the asylums to the inner city. This shift in itself is indicative of the changing emphases of care policies, with isolation from society being replaced by integration within the predominantly urban society of the late 20th century

UK (Walker 1982). The successful achievement of this aim of integration depends largely on the adequate funding of community care. As argued in the previous section, such funding has not been forthcoming. Accordingly, it may be suggested that the isolation of the asylum has been replaced by the alienation and equal isolation of residence in an unsupportive inner-city environment with inadequate resource levels to provide the necessary comprehensive care. It is in such situations that "ghettoization of the mentally ill" has developed in the USA; people with mental health problems concentrate into particular neighborhoods where the nature of the housing market facilitates their presence (Wolch 1980).

In the UK, examples of this rural–urban shift in the residential location of mentally ill people can be readily identified. In the area covered by the Portsmouth case study there are two large hospitals catering for the mentally ill, Knowle and St. James, the former in an isolated rural location, the latter in the city fringe. Between 1971 and 1979, the numbers of patients resident in these facilities fell from 687 to 482 (St. James) and 1032 to 505 (Knowle) (DHSS 1973, 1981). The decline in patient numbers is predominantly a reflection of the transfer of patients from the asylum to the community and to day care. Ultimately, St. James hospital is scheduled for closure, its patients will be completely served in the community, and most of the land and buildings comprising the hospital will be sold. This scenario has already taken place elsewhere; Banstead hospital, Surrey, was closed in November 1986 (Alleway 1986). Both St. James and Knowle hospitals occupy urban-fringe locations, although St. James is now in a far more urbanized position than when it was initially developed at the end of the 19th century. Both also occupy substantial sites and undoubtedly constitute realizable assets in an area of southern England where land prices and land demand are high. The small–scale community-based hostels, and the day-care provision which has progressively been replacing St. James and Knowle, is generally located in more urban situations. At the time of the research six small hostels, housing a maximum of six persons each, and a single group home where residents could prepare for independent living, were being operated by St. James hospital within the City of Portsmouth. Further hostels were located beyond the city boundaries, but all were within the built-up area of Greater Portsmouth or the surrounding small towns; none of the facilities were visually or physically isolated from the local community in which they were sited.

The growth of hostel provision in Portsmouth raises the question of the extent to which ghettoization may be occuring in that city. It is difficult to investigate this possibility in the absence of accurate data concerning the addresses of mentally ill people residing in the informal sector. For reasons of confidentiality, these were withheld in the case of people registered with the local psychiatric service, and accurate estimates of nonregistered mental illness were also not forthcoming. However, an assessment is possible of the social status of the immediate environments of the hostel facilities. In a parallel to North American findings (Joseph & Hall 1985), the facilities were highly localized, being concentrated in the southern part of Portsea Island (Figure 10.1). It would be expected that the facility neighborhoods would be stereotypically those of the "zone in transition"; characterized by high proportions of private renting, poor housing and mobility (Wolch 1980). The Portsmouth case appears to substantiate this North American

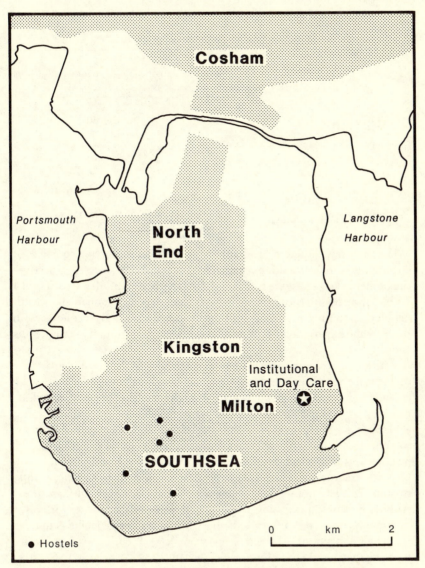

Figure 10.1   Hostel provision in Portsmouth.

expectation. Table 10.1 examines the social status of census enumeration districts within 400 meters of each facility, and suggests that the hostels are located in areas characterized by below-average numbers of children and high levels of private renting. The one exception is a hostel on the periphery of an inner-city local-authority housing estate. The defined hostel neighborhoods overlap substantially, and a core area of "hostel territory" can be identified comprising six census enumeration districts where 42.5% of households were in the private renting sector.

Table 10.1   The characteristics of hostel catchments.

Hostel	Population	% population	% local-authority housing	% owner-occupied	% private renting
A	5,024	5.6	67	18	14
B	4,329	4.6	19	50	31
C	4,394	2.6	1	38	61
D	4,764	3.8	2	56	42
E	5,561	4.4	4	58	38
F	3,997	3.4	1	56	43
city average	—	5.4	22	59	19
core hostel area		3.8	0.7	56.8	42.5

If attention is shifted to geographical approaches to the consequences of community care, it would appear that two interlinked research perspectives can be identified. These are concerned, first, with the attitudes of society as a whole, and potential host groups in particular, to people with mental health problems and the concept of community-based care; and, secondly, with the fears and experiences of communities in which community-based care is sited.

Attitudinal research suggests that mental health facilities are one of a class of a service which can be categorized as "noxious" and which provoke considerable opposition from potential neighbors. Similar facilities include prisons, airports and sewage disposal plants (Hodge & Gatrell 1976). Smith & Hanham (1981a) provided an empirical insight into the nature of attitudes to people with mental health problems in their study of the comparative noxiousness of a selection of facilities. Community-based mental health facilities emerged as only marginally less noxious than sewage plants, prisons, halfway houses for former patients and, interestingly, asylums. Although people professing to be liberal were relatively supportive of community mental health care, being willing to tolerate facilities in their own neighborhoods, conservatives were less accepting, being unsure whether they would be willing to have a facility in the same town. Clearly, such attitudes are gross generalizations, yet they indicate very real problems for health care planning, particularly when policy presumes that there will be an increasing number of such facilities. To move forward it is necessary to theorize the formation of such attitudes. This entails the identification, both theoretical and empirical, of the reasons underlying the construction of particular attitudes, and it is linked to the second broad theme; that of fears and experiences.

The concept of externality provides useful insights to this end. A relatively minor, yet significant concern in many fields of human geography, externality fields constitute the spatial manifestation of the unpriced byproducts of the production and consumption of goods and services (Knox 1981). An externality effect exists where the presence of a mental health care facility impinges on neighboring people's welfare. In some cases, such externality effects can be positive; for example, the price of accessibility (Harvey 1975) may influence people with mental health problems to live close to their treatment facility. For them, adjacency carries with it financial advantages. For other residents, however, proximity is a cost; having a mental health facility in the neighborhood may incur "public behavior" externalities (Cox 1973) in so far as local societal norms of cleanliness, sobriety, tidiness, and behavior may be offended. Externalities are therefore essentially hybrid; they may be negative or positive according to the social relations prevailing in the impacted neighborhood.

Although externality provides a means of examining facility impact, it is not without problems. The formation of externality fields entails the social construction of particular sets of attitudes concerning people with mental health problems. This process is seldom realized to be twofold. Attitudes, and thus externalities, may be constructed on the basis of perception or experience. The former is grounded in fear and imagination, and typically reflects socially determined antipathy towards "the mentally ill" as outsiders, offending social norms, who are expected to prove troublesome. In terms of facility location and locational conflict theory, the perceptual externality field is most clearly manifested prior to a hostel opening during the site-search process, when public opposition to the awesome possibility of a hostel in the neighborhood is at its greatest (Burnett & Moon 1983; Taylor, this volume). After the facility opening, the perceptual basis to externality is likely to persist for a period and perhaps initially even to be fueled by rumor and folk myth. Eventually, however, the experiential externality field will assume dominance. This form of externality is based on the reality of facility impact, and thus constitutes a true assessment of the effect of a facility on a particular neighborhood. With its basis in experience, it is less extensively socially determined, although concrete experiences of incidents or impacts may in part be a reflection of the lifestyles of local residents, and the earlier perceptual externality field will undoubtedly occasion some self-fulfilling expectations concerning impact. In addition, it is unlikely that any single individual or group alone will be aware of the full extent and nature of the experiential externality field. Impacts which are known to a hostel management or an agency such as the police, health care or social service providers, may not be known to a local public, who are unaware of precisely who is resident at a hostel. Conversely, the public may assume that some incidents or effects are the work of the hostel or hostel residents when in fact they are not. Dear & Taylor (1982) provide an example of this situation in their discussion of the relative unimportance of hostels in influencing property prices. Experiential externality is therefore comprised of an interlocking set of subfields which together constitute the reality of a hostel impact (Fig. 10.2).

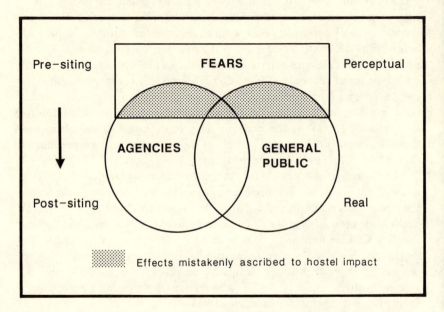

Figure 10.2   Perceived and real externality.

Attitudes to mental health provision

The study of attitudes to mental health provision has, as suggested above, been clearly shown to be both important and relevant (Smith & Hanham 1981a,b). Positive attitudes toward, and support for, community-based facilities from local residents enhance the therapeutic impact of care and increase the effectiveness of treatment. Negative attitudes, in contrast, can lead not only to alienation of both patients and staff, but also to difficulties in finding suitable sites where community opposition is minimal.

In the Portsmouth research, two separate exercises were conducted with the aim of replicating the Smith & Hanham studies in a UK situation, and comparing the differential noxiousness of community-based mental health facilities with regard to other forms of hostel facility. The first exercise involved the comparative evaluation of a large number of hostel-type facilities, while the second focused more closely on the cases of probation hostels, women's refuges, and hostels for people with mental health problems. In the first study, a sample of 102 households living in a neighborhood containing a number of different examples of hostel provision were asked where, ideally, they felt that various forms of community-based residential accommodation should be sited. In the second study, the sample size was 139, selected randomly from hostel and nonhostel neighborhoods, and respondents were simply asked if they would be opposed to a hostel being opened in their street.

Figure 10.3 portrays the replies to the first exercise. In practice, there was some difficulty in administering this question to the survey sample, because the respondents, who were interviewed in their own homes, often required quite lengthy explanations of the nature and function of the facilities concerned. Once they were aware of what was being referred to, they were often loath to offer hypothetical evaluations of their reactions, and insisted instead on airing their knowledge concerning the actual location of the facilities in question. Nevertheless, some generalizations are possible. It appears that there is a generally favorable disposition towards most hostels, with a location in the same neighborhood being acceptable. As far as mental health was concerned, the survey focused on handicap rather than illness and revealed a particularly positive attitude. It is likely that findings would have been more negative in the case of mental illness. As it was, negative attitudes were evident concerning women's refuges, bail hostels, hostels for homeless persons, and hostels for drug addicts. It should be noted that, as previously suggested, significant numbers of residents of hostels for homeless persons have been found to suffer from, or have a history of, mental illness.

In the second investigation, there was a specific focus on mental health, and 29% of respondents intimated that they would oppose the development of a hostel on their street for people with a mental health problem. While this result should not be taken to suggest that 71% of respondents would *support* the opening of a nearby hostel, it nevertheless indicates that opposition is by no means extensive. Indeed, the level of opposition was significantly lower than that for bail hostels; facilities which were, in the earlier research, found to be unwelcome. Women's refuges, opposed by approximately one quarter of the population, were another facility which generated rather less opposition than expected.

In addition to not automatically indicating general support for facilities for people with mental health problems, the survey results should similarly not necessarily be taken to indicate active opposition. While putative or potential opposition is a possible consequence of negative attitudes, it need

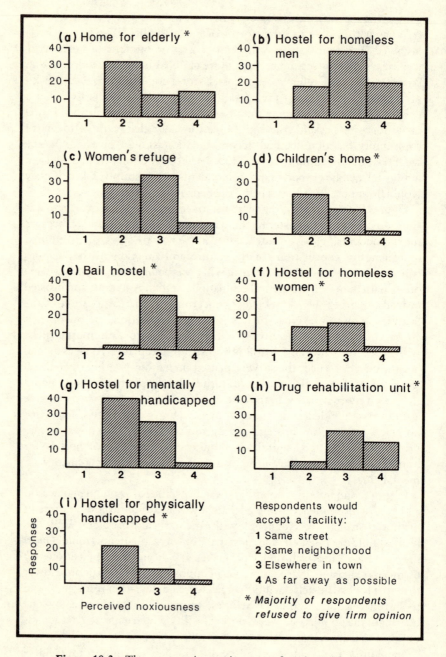

Figure 10.3   The comparative noxiousness of residential facilities.

not be an inevitable result. Indeed, a process somewhat contrary to this situation may actually be the case. The stereotypical reaction to potential developments of facilities for people with mental health problems is the oft-cited "not on our street . . .," ". . . my doorstep," "not round here" etc. This attitude, while undeniably negative in itself, is usually qualified by "but don't think I'm biased against them". It is probable that the internal contradictions of this position are not fully captured by the simple survey questions of the sort used above and by other workers (Smith & Hanham 1981b). Indeed, it is not unlikely that a significant proportion of actual opposition to facilities for mentally ill people comes from individuals or groups who, in a hypothetical situation, would claim to support such developments. Only cross-matching of survey data with case studies of location decisions can really begin to address this question (Burnett & Moon 1983).

Clearly, however, attitudinally based opposition is an important issue in the consideration of the siting of facilities for people with mental health problems. It can materially influence the availability of sites, not only through providing an underlying catalyst to public reactions and their expression, through public participation exercises, against proposed developments, but also through its more direct involvement in the formulation of planning law. In the UK, planning law, reflecting the political input of public opinion together with the ideology of the prevailing government, is quite specific concerning community-based residential provision. Local planning authorities are required to "be aware about local feeling about significant proposals", to advertise the proposals for such development, and to give opportunities for public opposition to be taken into account. In general, these opportunities are usually ignored but, in the case of noxious facilities such as hostels, opposition is usually forthcoming and trenchant in nature (Burnett & Moon 1983). A Government Development Council Policy Note issued by the Department of the Environment sets out the kernel of current policy:

> Such hostels need to be sited where they can form part of a mixed community and have ready access to employment and leisure facilities. Ideally hostels should be unobtrusively sited in areas which are residential or mixed residential and other uses, with reasonable transport and shopping facilities nearby . . . houses of the size needed are most often found in areas of older residential property or in the older areas of the City Centre (DoE 1975).

This nationally derived policy statement, while open to some interpretation, and regularly revised as government attitudes toward community-based hostels change, is made more specific by local planning practice, zoning, and tradition. For example, in Portsmouth, there is a strong presumption against development in the vicinity of schools or in areas of the town popular with tourists.

In effect, what links planning policy to individual attitudinal opposition to provision for community-based mental health care is an official recognition, by the former, of the status of the latter as legitimate political protest. However, both are based on perceptual assessments of the nature of the client group involved: neither is necessarily grounded in experience. Both seem likely to involve an assessment, rational or irrational, of what *might* happen when a facility is opened.

The perceived impact of deinstitutionalized mental health care

The fears of what might happen when a facility is opened are not easy to elucidate. The Portsmouth project approached the task through the use of hypothetical questions, asking residents if they could conceive of good or bad impacts which the development of a local hostel might bring. Using open questions, this tactic provided considerable detail about perceptions. The information was elaborated by a consideration of the contents of letters of objection to the local planning authority concerning applications for new hostels. These letters, often held to be one of the more effective means of protest in planning decisions (Moon & Burnett 1984), outlined individuals' fears about hostel developments.

In general, local residents proved marginally more able to articulate negative rather than positive feelings. Hostels were felt to be problematic as they were perceived to lead to groups of residents congregating outside the facility, pestering and frightening people; the "tone" of an area would be lowered; there would be noise; and the peace would be shattered. Particular emphasis was laid on already high housing densities, "encroachment" on conservation areas, and the impact on local, predominantly elderly, populations. Perceived positive impacts, although present, were not without self-interest. One shopkeeper suggested that the opening of a hostel would prove good for business, while another respondent claimed that it would be better than having people roaming the streets.

Letters of objection to planning proposals tended to substantiate the overall indications of the general survey. Additional factors which emerged were fears concerning noise and cooking smells, dangers to children, dangers to hostel residents from traffic, and dangers to local residents from the (presumably erratic) driving of car-owning hostel residents. Supervision was an important worry for many opponents; a worry which was particularly enhanced when it was known that a facility would have no resident staff. It was only in letters of opposition that the issue of the putative impact of developments on property values was mentioned. It may be that, as developments were all proposed in areas dominated by either local-authority housing or private renting, opponents were less likely to be affected by this issue, and those who were would be among those more likely to use the letter as a means of registering objection.

Although some applications for hostel development are withdrawn because of the level of opposition, some eventually reach the Council Chamber where they are debated often at length. At this stage, fears concerning impact are given official voice and recorded in minutes or reported in local papers. The outcome of these deliberations, though usually predetermined by party-political or local coalitions of interest, are important in that they may affect subsequent decisions. The support of a councillor, preferably the local ward councillor, is therefore crucial in overcoming the official advocacy of perceptually based fears. If such support is not forthcoming, statements such as were found in a study of siting hostels for homeless men may occur:

> We know there is good in many of these men, but we know some of them are not particular angels and incidents do occur . . . you don't put a major social problem into a tourist area.

> If you live in a situation where inadequacy becomes a privilege we will be in trouble. We live in a trendy liberal country where trendy liberals are fashionable. I hope members uphold the feelings of the public.
>   (Burnett & Moon 1983)

The same study of hostels for homeless men also suggested that the geography of these perceptual externality fields is relatively confined (Fig. 10.4). In overall terms, objections exhibit distance decay along adjacent streets, with a majority being found within 100 m of a hostel; relatively few come from beyond 200 m, and those that do tend to be isolated personal contacts of nearer residents.

The reality of hostel impact

Once hostels are actually opened, researchers are able to gauge effectively the truth behind the fears which structure both attitudes and perceptual impacts. It is this reality which forms the true impact of deinstitutionalized mental health care on the community and which, perhaps idealistically, should form the basis for reasoned future planning decisions.

Past research gives some indications of the likely nature of real or experienced impacts. Dear & Taylor (1982) cover many of the issues from a North American perspective. In the Portsmouth study, given the relatively static nature of the property market in hostel neighborhoods, it was impossible to replicate Dear & Taylor's focus on the impact of

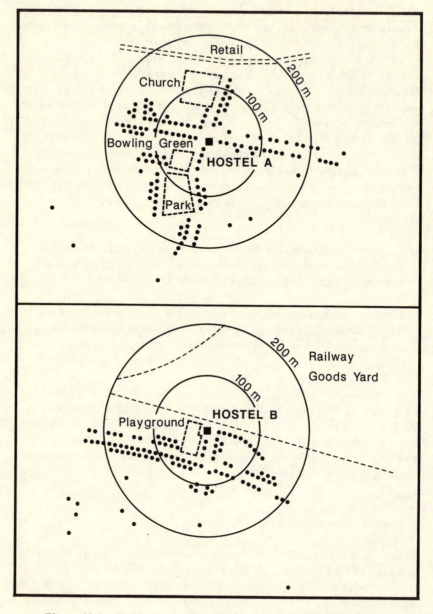

Figure 10.4   Written complaints about proposed hostel developments.

deinstitutionalized care on property prices; instead of this, attention was given to the more humanistic assessment of individuals' experiences of living in the vicinity of hostels. This information was acquired through interviews, questionnaire surveys, and examinations of incidents reported as complaints from the public in hostel management committee minutes.

In spatial terms, experienced impacts tended to be most frequent in the immediate vicinity of the hostels. The management committee minutes suggested that four further general locations could be identified where negative externalities might be experienced. First, a considerable concentration of complaints from shopping areas could be identified, where the behavior of hostel residents offended the mores of the general public. Secondly, a similar situation was evident with complaints from public parks. Thirdly, confrontations with seemingly truculent, obstructive or even impenetrable bureaucracy, and an inability to cope, occasioned complaints from staff and other claimants at offices of the Department of Health and Social Security. Finally, residents' continuing association with hospital facilities, either as a day patient or through some psychological attachment to a facility, caused some complaints to be received from nonpsychiatric staff at these institutions. In total, incidents near the hostel were far fewer than in these other locations.

A relatively low proportion of respondents to the interview and questionnaire surveys were able to cite any experienced impact, either positive or negative, from a local hostel. Positive impacts, where they were identified, comprised two types. First, some respondents discerned a positive impact which related to the hostel *per se* rather than to the behavior of its residents. Hostel developments in old buildings were seen as ensuring that a use was available for an otherwise empty building. Hostels were also seen as beneficial because they tended to be maintained in an above-average state of repair. A second form of positive impact concerned what can only be described as the adoption of harmless and eccentric residents by the local populace. A single resident at one hostel for homeless men, an outpatient at a local mental hospital, was referred to by 21 separate respondents. This resident was a kind of unofficial mascot to the local community, until a disagreement with hostel staff forced him to move elsewhere. Among his more interesting pastimes were talking to traffic, sweeping a nearby roundabout, and cautioning drivers for traffic offences!

Negative experiences which were identified in interviews tended to substantiate the fears which the development of deinstitutionalized care engenders. It should be emphasized, however, that few local people were able to cite any negative experiences, and those which could be identified were of a mild nature. For example, incidents were mentioned involving loud music, the presence of unsavory characters, cooking smells, and the emptying of a dustbin in a front garden. While undeniably unpleasant for the individuals concerned, these incidents hardly constitute an insufferable negative externality; indeed they might be argued to be an integral part of inner-city life.

A problem with the analysis of experiential impacts is that a firm knowledge of the commission of the impacts is required. It is necessary to separate out incidents which the public believe have been committed by hostel residents from those which actually have. In many cases, given the relatively mobile nature of the deinstitutionalized mentally ill, this task is impossible. Therefore, it seems likely that even the relatively low experienced impact of facilities in Portsmouth may be an overestimate. Perhaps the most startling indication of this possibility is that, when a 10% sample of residents living within 400 m of a hostel for people with mental health problems were asked where the nearest hostel to them was, 90% were unable to identify or name any hostel; only 3% of these local residents had ever formally complained about the impact the hostel had on their lives. Clearly, at least in the limited case of the Portsmouth study, the community impact to date of deinstitutionalized hostel–based care has been minimal.

Conclusions

For the purposes of future planning for deinstitutionalized mental health care, it is instructive to consider some of the reasons which may lie behind the surprisingly low community impact of facilities in Portsmouth. Traditional approaches to research of the type evident in North America would indicate the importance of the neighborhood setting of a hostel. Although the Portsmouth research did not directly focus on this issue, its relevance was undoubtedly confirmed. The hostel neighborhoods were transient and low in status; furthermore, the prevailing housing tenure was such that a low proportion of local residents had a financial stake in the neighborhood as owner–occupiers. A second explanation for the low impact may be related to the design and repair of hostels. All the facilities were small in scale, housing, at the most, six residents, and kept in good external repair. This situation means that there was not a large body of "outsiders" which could be identified within the wider, densely populated neighborhood and, in addition, the facilities were not distinguishable from other properties by being in a poor state of repair. Indeed, the reverse situation was largely the case, in that the hostels actually enhanced the neighborhood. Thirdly, and perhaps most importantly, although the hostels did not have resident staff to look after the people with mental health problems, they were closely monitored, and a resident's position in the hostel was under constant review. This flexible monitoring and support system ensured that any negative externalities could be dealt with prior to their escalation.

It would seem that the approach used in the Portsmouth research provides useful insights which could, with advantage, be incorporated into the planning process as far as the siting of hostels for people with mental health problems is concerned. By decomposing a facility impact into attitudinal, perceptual, and experential components, it can be shown that, in fact, the enormity of fear obscures the reality of impact. When taken together with the associative analyses usual in North American research, which have sought to relate ecological and individual characteristics to opposition, this approach should enable mental health care planners to approach the site-search process with a greater hope of success. A longer-term strategy would of course demand that the reasons why communities reject those with mental illness be addressed.

In conclusion, albeit on the basis of a case study in a single city, it appears that the impact of deinstitutionalized care for people with mental illness in the UK may not yet pose the problems that are found in North American cities. However, such a situation is unlikely to persist if adequate funding for support services is not forthcoming, and those in need are forced in quantity into private rented ghettos.

Acknowledgments

I should like to record my personal thanks and indebtedness to Alan Burnett, with whom the research reported here was conducted. Finance was provided by the Economic and Social Research Council, and cooperation was gratefully received from Portsmouth and South East Hampshire District Health Authority, St. James Hospital Social Work Department and a number of voluntary organizations.

References

Alleway, L. 1986. Community care—a story of great expectations. *Health Service Journal* **96**, 1478.

Burnett, A. 1983. *The effects of community based residential facilities on neighborhoods—a case study of hostels for single homeless men*. End-of-Grant Report to Economic and Social Research Council. London: ESRC.
Burnett, A. 1984. *The spatial impact of contrasted residential facilities*. End-of-Grant Report to Economic and Social Research Council. London: ESRC.
Burnett, A. & G. Moon 1983. Community opposition to hostels for single homeless men. *Area* **15**, 161–6.

Cox, K. 1973. *Conflict, power and politics in the city*. Chichester: Wiley.

Dear, M. 1976. Spatial externalities and locational conflict. In *London papers in regional science*, vol. 7, D. Massey & P. Batey (eds.), 152–67. London: Pion.
Dear, M. 1978. Planning for mental health care: a reconsideration of public facility location theory. *International Regional Science Review* **3**, 93–111.

Dear, M. 1981. Social and spatial reproduction of the mentally ill. In *Urbanisation and urban planning in capitalist society*, M. Dear & A. Scott (eds.), 481–500. London: Methuen.

Dear, M. & S. M. Taylor 1982. *Not on our street*. London: Pion.

DoE (Department of the Environment) 1975. *Development control policy note 15: hostels and homes*. London: HMSO.

DHSS (Department of Health and Social Security) 1973. *The facilities and services of mental illness and mental handicap hospitals in England and Wales, 1971*. London: HMSO.

DHSS 1975. *Better services for the mentally ill*. London: HMSO.

DHSS 1981. *The facilities and services of mental illness and mental handicap hospitals in England and Wales*. London: HMSO.

Finch, J. & D. Groves 1980. Community care and the family. *Journal of Social Policy* **9**, 487–511.

Ham, C. 1985. *Health policy in Britain*. London: Macmillan.

Harvey, D. 1975. *Social justice and the city*. London: Arnold.

Hodge, D. & A. Gatrell 1976. Spatial constraint and the location of urban public facilities. *Environment and Planning A* **8**, 215–30.

Iliffe, S. 1983. *The NHS: a picture of health*. London: Lawrence and Wishart.

Joseph, A. & G. B. Hall 1985. The locational concentration of group homes in Toronto. *Professional Geographer* **37**, 143–54.

Knox, P. 1981. *Urban social geography*. London: Longman.

Lupton, C. 1984. Community care: the role of informal networks. In *Into the community?*, Social Services Research and Intelligence Unit (eds.). Portsmouth: SSRIU.

Mair, A. 1984. Locating shelters for the homeless. *Area* **16**, 338–40.

Moon, G. & A. Burnett 1983a. *The impact of a hostel for single homeless men on its surrounding neighborhood*. Hostels Impact Project Working Paper 3, Portsmouth Polytechnic, Department of Geography.

Moon, G. & A. Burnett 1983b. *The analysis of a natural survey for hostels for single homeless men*. Hostels Impact Project Working Paper 2, Portsmouth Polytechnic, Department of Geography.

Moon, G. & A. Burnett 1984. Locating shelters for the homeless: a reply to Mair. *Area* **16**, 340–2.

Scull, A. 1978. *Decarceration, community treatment and the deviant*. London: Prentice-Hall.

Smith, C. 1977. *Geography and mental health*. Association of American Geographers Commission on College Geography. Washington, D.C.: AAG.

Smith, C. & R. Hanham 1981a. Any place but here: mental health facilities as noxious neighbors. *Professional Geographer* **33**, 326–30.

Smith, C. & R. Hanham 1981b. Proximity and public attitudes towards mental illness. *Environment and Planning A* **13**, 147–65.

Walker, A. 1982. *Community care: the family, the state and social policy*. Oxford: Blackwell.

Wolch, J. 1980. The residential location of the service dependent poor. *Annals of Association of American Geographers* **70**, 330–41.

Wolpert, J. & E. Wolpert 1976. The relocation of released mental hospital patients into residential communities. *Policy Sciences* **7**, 31–51.

Wolpert, J., M. Dear & R. Crawford 1975. Satellite mental health facilities, *Annals of Association of American Geographers* **65**, 24–35.

11   *Community reactions to deinstitutionalization*

S. MARTIN TAYLOR

Introduction

When policies to deinstitutionalize the mentally ill were introduced in North America about 25 years ago it did not require a prophet to predict that they would meet with a mixed reaction in the community. In fact, there was good reason to expect considerable reluctance on the public's part to accept the role of host to a population which had, in its memory, been safely institutionalized and thereby excluded from mainstream society. For many, no doubt, the attitude was "out of sight and out of mind." Therefore, the prospect of encountering the mentally ill on the street, in the store, perhaps at work, or even next door was unlikely to be widely received with enthusiasm.

At the time that deinstitutionalization came into effect there was some empirical evidence to suggest that mental illness, and perhaps the mentally ill, were more sympathetically perceived than in earlier decades. Some commentators (see Rabkin, 1975) attributed this positive shift to the increased acceptance of the medical model of mental illness, that, in the words of the dictum, "mental illness is an illness like any other," a message that professionals had actively propagated in the post-war period. However, deinstitutionalization was, in a real sense, the acid test of public opinion, a basis on which to judge whether increased tolerance in principle would translate into acceptance in practice. There was some reason to be skeptical, not least because the rate at which patients were moved out into the community rapidly accelerated to the point where there was little opportunity or effort given to preparing the community for the patients' return. Equally, the demand for community services almost immediately outstripped the resources, financial and otherwise, available to provide the required support. Therefore, the scene was set very quickly for what has now become a familiar outcome in the cities of North America, the inner-city psychiatric ghetto, the "asylum without walls" (Dear & Wolch 1986).

The question addressed in this chapter is: What has been the public's reaction to the deinstitutionalized mentally ill? There have been several recent studies which provide an empirical basis for making informed judgements. There are various ways in which the evidence could be organized. The approach taken here is to lay out an agenda of research questions which it seems useful to ask, and to review the evidence with respect to each of them.

A research agenda

The research agenda proposed here comprises the following seven questions:

(1) What are the attitudes of the community towards the mentally ill and mental health facilities?
(2) How can these attitudes be explained?
(3) How can they be predicted in an efficient and useful way?
(4) How, if necessary, can attitudes be changed?
(5) What are the neighborhood impacts of facilities and how do they compare with community expectations or fears?
(6) What are the implications of community attitudes for facility location decisions?
(7) What are the implications for the ability of clients to cope in community settings?

Before turning to a detailed consideration of these questions, some prefatory remarks about the evidence available to answer them is justified. The amount of evidence varies considerably among the questions. The issue of community attitudes toward the mentally ill, for example, has been the subject of extensive past research. In contrast, the question of attitude change has received little attention despite the volume of theoretical literature on the topic, and despite the various media and other programs devised to promote positive changes in public opinion.

The strength of the evidence is just as important as the amount. Most of the empirical studies have used cross-sectional survey designs. Data have been collected from samples of varying size and representativeness, and results have been presented in terms of standard measures of statistical association. There is clearly much to recommend this approach and there is often not an obvious alternative. However, the inherent weakness of the design cannot be ignored, particularly with respect to the types of inference that can be made from the data. Sample size and representativeness directly affect the generalizability of the findings. But more fundamental is the inability to make causal inferences about the relationships examined. This issue is especially relevant to questions two, four, and five on the research agenda.

An additional issue pertinent to the strength of the evidence of several of the questions on the agenda arises from the dependence on self-report data.

The measurement of perceptions, beliefs, and attitudes typically depends on self-report methods. The attendant validity problems are not easily resolved. Internal validation of the measures can be achieved by careful construction of questionnaire items and by the use of multiple-item scales. External validity is more problematic and is ultimately the criterion which governs the credibility of the results. One aspect of external validity has to do with the correspondence between measured and "true" attitudes. This becomes an especially relevant concern in the measurement of attitudes towards controversial issues to which strong social norms are attached. Self-reported attitudes may be biased toward socially acceptable responses. The normal absence of independently collected nonself-report measures means that the degree of bias present is very difficult to estimate.

Reference to these methodological issues at the outset is not intended to cast a negative light on the studies conducted to date on community attitudes toward the mentally ill. The purpose is to emphasize the need to go beyond a simple description of the results which have accumulated on each of the research questions, bearing in mind that the confidence that can be placed on the findings has to take account of both the amount and strength of the evidence.

Attitudes toward the mentally ill and mental health facilities

The social psychology and psychiatry literature provides quite a large legacy of research on attitudes toward the mentally ill. Previous reviews (Rabkin 1972, 1974, 1975, 1980) have effectively classified and summarized this work, and only the relevant main points need to be mentioned here.

Early studies tended to concentrate on professional rather than public attitudes. This is hardly surprising since institutional treatment was the norm for those diagnosed as mentally ill. A guiding question for those few studies focusing on public attitudes (e.g., Nunnally 1961) was whether there was evidence to suggest a positive shift in public opinion in response to the post-war emphasis on the medical model of mental illness. Most commentators agree that opinion did soften, but they differ on the degree to which this occurred. Echoing some of the concerns about the validity of self-reported attitudes already mentioned, Rabkin (1975: 452) points out that although people generally accepted the medical model as the "correct" thing to believe, they still tended to avoid close contact with the mentally ill. With the advent of deinstitutionalization, some have suggested, on the basis of labeling theory (e.g., Scheff 1966, 1967), that there is the potential for public opinion to harden because of the increased likelihood of contact between those labeled mentally ill and the general public.

This argument perhaps gained added strength because deinstitutionalization had proceeded so rapidly with the result that residents had had little opportunity to adapt to the changing philosophy of treatment, and to understand and accept the implications for their role as host. Anticipating this type of public response, Rabkin (1980: 15) comments that increased contact between the mentally ill and the public may engender friction and argues that if the force of public attitudes is not taken into account, the eventual outcome may be exacerbation of public fears accompanied by a retreat to custodial care and removal from the community. Less than a decade later, there is mounting evidence from California, New York, and other states of reinstitutionalization (Dear & Wolch 1987). While this is a response to a complex of political, economic, and social factors, public attitudes are certainly a component of the process.

Recognition of the potentially important effect of public attitudes on the outcomes of deinstitutionalization (e.g., Dear et al. 1977) has spawned several studies which explicitly deal with public reactions to the mentally ill in a community context (Smith & Hanham 1981, CTI 1984, Dear & Taylor 1982, Rabkin et al. 1984). In seeking to measure beliefs and attitudes, researchers immediately faced two methodological needs: the need to develop items and scales relevant to community-based mental health care; and the need to choose a label to apply to the mentally ill in the community. The approach to meeting both needs has been somewhat ad hoc; the first has been dealt with rather more systematically (e.g., Taylor & Dear 1981) than the second.

Although much of the earlier work on attitudes toward the mentally ill focused on the opinions of professionals about institutionalized patients rather than public opinions about deinstitutionalized (or never institutionalized) clients in the community, some of the methods developed provide a very valuable basis for the construction of the types of measures currently required. This is clearly shown in our Toronto-based work. We modified the opinions about Mental Illness (Cohen & Struening 1962) and Community Mental Health Ideology (Baker & Schulberg 1967) scales to construct the Attitudes toward the Mentally Ill (AMI) scales (Taylor & Dear 1981). We retained the labels of several of the original scales (authoritarianism, benevolence, social restrictiveness, and community mental health ideology) but revamped the items so that the content domain was consistent with a focus on public attitudes toward the mentally ill in community settings.

A variety of labels has been applied to the mentally ill in attitude studies, without any systematic assessment of their possible differential effects on responses. Uncertainty surrounds the appropriateness of attaching the prefix "ex" to the label, as in "ex-patients" or "ex-psychiatric patient," when referring to the mentally ill in the community. Since most of the client group remain on some form of treatment régime, there is reason to question this practice. Professional caseworkers commonly apply the term "chronically mentally ill" to a large proportion of their caseload of community-based clients, a term which, at least superficially, would seem to convey a very different impression to a questionnaire respondent. While we can do little more than speculate on the possible effects of these variations in label in the absence of good empirical evidence, it seems fair to conclude that, for measures of public attitudes, the label should accurately reflect the type of (ex-)patient the public is likely to encounter. Otherwise, we would have good reason to suspect the external validity of the measures obtained. One device for reducing ambiguity is to elaborate the label by adding a definition statement. For example, in the Toronto study (Dear & Taylor 1982), the "mentally ill" were defined as "people needing treatment for mental disorders, but who are capable of independent living outside a hospital." Moreover, it was emphasized that the mentally retarded were not included in the definition. Our earlier tests had shown this to be a common source of confusion.

The results obtained in recent studies using different measures of attitude toward the mentally ill have been consistent in showing quite a high level of public sympathy and tolerance. The most detailed findings are from our Toronto research. In the 1978 study, data were obtained from a stratified random sample of 1,090 respondents, representative of different socio-economic status groups, and of suburban and central-city populations. Scores on the four AMI scales, each of which comprised ten Likert statements, were skewed toward the positive end of the response scale. Mean scores on the four scales were: authoritarianism 3.6, and social restrictiveness 3.7 (maximum tolerance equals 5.0); benevolence 2.2, and community mental health ideology 2.4 (maximum tolerance equals 1.0). A subsequent survey (Dear *et al.* 1985) showed that similarly positive attitudes were shared by an Ontario-wide sample. In this case, a subset of 16 of the 40 AMI statements were used. The means on the four scales were: authoritarianism 3.3, and social restrictiveness 3.9; benevolence 2.3, and community mental health ideology 2.3. In short, the sample groups could be characterized as neither authoritarian nor socially restrictive; rather, they appear generally benevolent and supportive of community mental health care. Several studies in progress are using the AMI scales, and the results should provide a standardized basis for a comparative analysis of attitudes toward the mentally ill in the community, in a variety of urban and regional settings.

Generally sympathetic responses to community-based mental health care are also evident in reported attitudes toward mental health facilities. Here again, there is an issue of definition in that response is likely to vary depending on such factors as the type of facility (e.g., group home or clinic), the type of client, and level of supervision. The tendency has been to elicit reactions to relatively unspecific facility types. For example, Rabkin *et al.* (1984) measured attitudes toward "a home for former mental patients" and a "psychiatric clinic." Dear & Taylor (1982) elicited attitudes toward "community mental health facilities," defined as including "outpatient clinics, drop-in centres, and group homes which are situated in residential neighborhoods and serve the local community," and as excluding "mental health facilities which are a part of a major hospital." This remains a very broad definition, especially as most respondents are reporting attitudes toward a hypothetical facility rather than one they are aware of in their own neighborhood. A more specific approach was adopted in the later study by Dear *et al.* (1985). Three facilities were presented as "vignettes," in which the number and type of clients were described as well as the level of supervision. Attitudes were measured for locations at three distances from the respondent's home; in the neighborhood, on the block, and next door.

The findings of the different studies of attitudes toward facilities are consistent in showing that opposition is limited to a minority. Rabkin *et al.* (1985) found that 75% of respondents in their New York study would not object to having a mental facility "set up near home." Dear & Taylor (1982) showed that the percentage in their Toronto sample rating a community mental health facility as undesirable varied with the distance of the hypothetical location from the respondent's home. At 7–12 blocks, 12% rated a facility as undesirable. This rose to 24% at 2–6 blocks, and to 39% on the same block. A major study by the Canadian Training Institute (CTI 1984) examined the attitudes of residents ($n = 1,696$) in three Ontario cities, Toronto, Ottawa, and London. Using Dear & Taylor's facility rating scale, it was found that the percentage rating a facility as undesirable rose from 8% to 15% to 23% with increasing proximity to home. The Ontario-wide study by Dear *et al.* (1985) provides the most detailed results. Three different facilities, two group homes and an outpatient clinic, were rated, again for three distance zones. For all three facilities, there was a clear distance decay in opposition. The percentage rating a facility undesirable ranged from a low of 16% for a small group home with 24-hour supervision located in the neighborhood, to a high of 46% for an outpatient clinic with about 200 clients located next door.

Taken together, these findings on attitudes toward the mentally ill and community mental health facilities imply a relatively high level of public tolerance and support. At first sight, this may seem difficult to reconcile with the apparent strong community opposition frequently encountered in attempts to locate facilities in neighborhoods. In part, an explanation may lie in the exaggeration of opposition due to the tendency of conflict situations to become media events. Situations in which facilities are introduced without conflict do not attract media and, thereby, public attention. Consequently, a disproportionate weight is given to the degree of opposition. On the other hand, the potential opposition to facilities represented in the various survey results should not be underestimated. The percentage rating facility locations as undesirable approaches 50% in some instances. If we accept that this may be a somewhat conservative estimate due to a bias toward more positive ratings in response to social norms, then the data indicate that quite a large proportion of the population are to some degree resistant to community mental health care. As we have suggested elsewhere (Dear & Taylor 1982: 117–18), even if opposition is limited to a small minority, we cannot conclude that facility locations will meet with easy acceptance in the community. We have to recognize that the opponents, though in the minority, can determine community response to facilities if they have political power and influence, and if the nonopponents remain silent and voice no clear support. This combination of circumstances does not seem uncommon, and makes sense out of assertions that as many as half of all psychiatric facilities planned for residential areas may have been blocked by community opposition (Piasecki 1975).

Toward an explanation of attitudes

As is true for most attitudes, those related to community mental health care are not easily explained. To date, analyses have been based mainly on an inductive approach; tests of association between attitude measures and various plausible correlates have been conducted leading to a fairly piece-meal set of findings. In some instances, multivariate methods have been used in an effort to estimate the relative strengths of different independent variables, but this has not advanced understanding beyond quite a pre-liminary level. Previous studies provide reviews of the sets of factors related, in varying degrees, to attitudes toward the mentally ill (Rabkin 1974, 1975; Smith & Hanham 1981) and mental health facilities (Taylor et al. 1979), and only a brief overview is necessary here. Attenton will be focused on a possible theoretical framework for seeking an explanation, and on the analytical methods that might usefully be employed to advance beyond the limited conclusions attained so far.

Conceptual models of attitudinal determinants identify three sets of factors: facility and client characteristics, sociodemographic attributes of residents in host communities, and the physical and social structure of host neighborhoods. Normally, individual studies have selected subsets of variables and examined their relationship with particular attitudinal out-come measures. Rabkin (1975), for example, classifies studies on correlates of attitudes toward the mentally ill and mental illness under the headings of patient characteristics and treatment situation, personal characteristics and social context. In Segal & Aviram's (1978) research on factors affecting the community integration of the mentally ill, the determinants considered were community, client, and facility characteristics. Smith & Hanham (1981) concentrated on the sociodemographic attributes of host residents in their work on attitudes toward mental illness. With few exceptions, a fairly simple correlational approach has been adopted for analysis, with the results showing that most factors are to some degree associated with the dependent attitude variables, but none sufficiently strongly to lead to firm conclusions about determinants. All of us who have conducted work in this area lie open to the criticism of being somewhat naïve empiricists, operating largely in the absence of a guiding theoretical model. As a consequence, there has been a tendency to duplicate, rather than to dovetail, research effort.

The clearest attempt to date to embed the analysis of attitudes toward community mental health care within a theoretical framework is to be found in our work based on Fishbein & Ajzen's (1975) theory of reasoned action (Dear & Taylor 1982). Within their framework, attitudes play a central role, linking external variables, beliefs and subjective norms to specific social behaviors which can include, in this context, reactions to the mentally ill in the community. Adopting this approach, we attempted to incorporate the findings of earlier work, in defining the specific components of a theoretical model of community attitudes to mental health care (Fig. 11.1). Three sets of external variables were included: facility and user characteristics, personal sociodemographics, and indicators of neighborhood structure. These linked directly to three categories of beliefs, regarding facility impacts, the mentally ill, and the neighborhood. These in turn linked to attitudes toward facilities and, then, to behavioral intentions and to behavior, with the ultimate outcome variable being facility acceptance or rejection. The empirical test of the model, using the Toronto data set, incorporated all the links in the model up to and including behavioral intentions. The link to behavior was excluded by the absence of sufficient respondents reporting having taken action either in support of or opposition to a facility. Within these limits, the findings confirm the relationships in the model between external variables and beliefs, between beliefs and attitudes, and between attitudes and behavioral intentions.

While grounded within a theoretical framework, and in that sense an advance over previous studies, the Toronto analysis was limited in furthering the explanation of attitudes because each set of relationships within the model was treated separately. Subsequent re-analysis of the same data (Hall & Taylor 1983) went a step further by testing an analytical model which examined the relationships simultaneously. This approach, using path analysis, permits estimation of the direct and indirect efforts of each independent variable, and a more precise assessment of the overall power of the model to explain attitudes to facilities. The results show beliefs about the mentally ill, and beliefs about facility impacts, as having the strongest effects on facility desirability. According to the structure of the path model, more positive beliefs about the mentally ill lead to more positive perceptions of facility impacts which, in turn, give rise to more favorable judgements of facility desirability. By comparison, both the direct and indirect effects of external variables, including facility, personal, and neighborhood characteristics, on attitudes to facilities were weak and in most cases not significant.

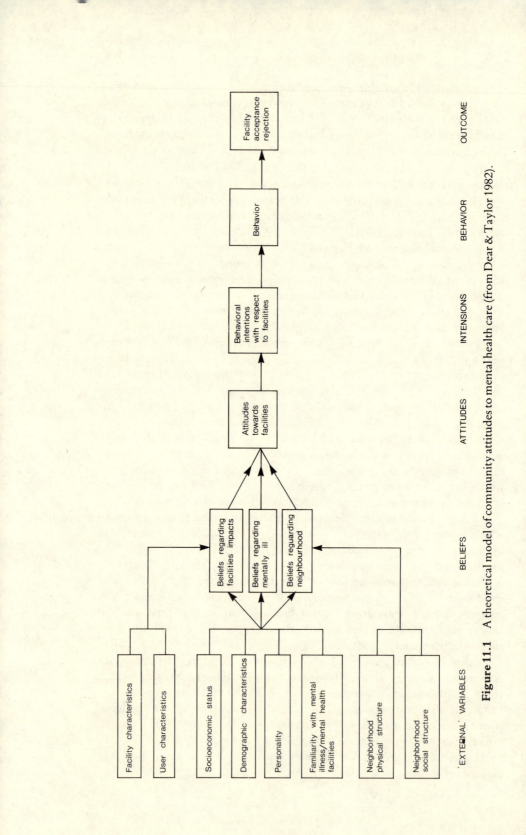

Figure 11.1 A theoretical model of community attitudes to mental health care (from Dear & Taylor 1982).

'EXTERNAL' VARIABLES   BELIEFS   ATTITUDES   INTENSIONS   BEHAVIOR   OUTCOME

Facility characteristics

User characteristics

Socioeconomic status

Demographic characteristics

Personality

Familiarity with mental illness/mental health facilities

Neighborhood physical structure

Neighborhood social structure

Beliefs regarding facilities impacts

Beliefs regarding mentally ill

Beliefs regaurding neighbourhood

Attitudes towards facilities

Behavioral intentions with respect to facilities

Behavior

Facility acceptance rejection

Smith & Hanham (1981) also used path analysis in seeking to clarify the strength and pattern of effects of various sociodemographic variables on attitudes toward mental illness. The outcome measures, based on a ten-item social rejection index, were the respondent's reactions to vignettes describing a serious and a moderate case of mental illness. Attitudes toward other social problems had the strongest effect on attitudes toward mental illness. Consistent with others' findings, homeowners were more likely to reject the mentally ill. Proximity emerges as a "two-edged sword." Residents in the neighborhood close to a mental hospital reported more positive attitudes toward serious mental illness, but this result was tempered by the finding that previous contact with mental illness, and acquaintance with workers at the facility, were not positively related to acceptance of the mentally ill. This implies that the effects of locational and social proximity are not necessarily consistent. As Smith & Hanham are careful to point out, the effects of contact may well depend on the characteristics of the individuals involved and the frequency with which contact occurs.

It is clear that the determinants of attitudes toward community mental health care clients and facilities are multiple and interacting, and that studies to date have only begun to uncover the complex structure among the salient variables. Path analysis provides a powerful statistical tool for doing this. However, its application requires a theoretical basis on which to construct a path model. The statistical measures only form a meaningful basis for inference about the strength and pattern of effects when interpreted with reference to the theory used to develop the path model. It follows that combining path analysis with a theoretical model of attitudes, such as the Fishbein & Ajzen framework, holds the most promise for advancing understanding of the factors underlying public reaction to community mental health care.

Predicting community attitudes to mental health facilities

In contrast to the disaggregate, behavioral approach to the explanation of attitudes toward community mental health care, predicative models are sensibly based on an aggregate, ecological approach. What are sought are useful "markers" of expected degrees of reaction (positive or negative) to mental health clients and facilities in potential host neighborhoods. The emphasis is therefore strongly applied in seeking to aid and inform planning decisions regarding facility location and the assignment of clients to community settings. A word of caution is immediately necessary. The ability to develop predictive models which are useful in statistical terms (i.e., high R^2 values and low standard errors) does not provide a panacea for planners, a failsafe tool for selecting optimal facility sites. To suggest this would be to

grossly oversimplify the complex of factors necessarily involved in locational decisions. A realistic assessment of the utility of a predictive model is
as a significant aid to the reduction of important elements of uncertainty that
contribute to the current complexity surrounding those decisions.

We have argued elsewhere (Taylor *et al.* 1984) that the utility of a predictive model, in this context, is maximised if it is as parsimonious as
possible, so that accurate predictions of community response can be derived
from information on a small number of independent variables. Further, the
independent variables should be drawn from existing data sets, such as
census data, to reduce time and cost in model use. Ease of accessing existing
data on community characteristics also has implications for the choice of a
geographical unit as the basis for operationally defining "community." The
most obvious choice is the census tract, given the immediate availability of
census and other data at this level, and given its reasonable correspondence
in area and population with urban neighborhoods.

Earlier studies informed our selection of variables to include in a predictive model. The work of Trute & Segal (1976) was particularly relevant.
They examined the characteristics of supportive communities for the
severely mentally disabled, and showed that support was strongest where
there was neither strong social cohesion nor severe social dislocation. The
former type of community tends to "close ranks" against the client; the
latter tends to be too chaotic and threatening.

Building on this and other findings, we developed a model of community
reaction to mental health facilities comprising six dimensions of neighborhood structure: land-use mix, demographic characteristics, socioeconomic
status, community homogeneity, community stability, and population
density. Indicators for each dimension were extracted from census and
land-use data for metropolitan Toronto, using the census tract as the unit of
observation and analysis. The statistical reproducibility of these six dimensions was examined using factor analysis, and the results led to some
revision and relabeling with the following seven neighborhood factors
forming the basis for the subsequent regression analysis; neighborhood
transience, scarcity of children, economic status, ethnic heterogeneity, sex
ratio, residential land use, and institutional land use.

Multiple regression analysis was used to predict community reaction to
facilities. Reactions were measured as the percentage of respondents in each
census tract reporting negative attitudes to facilities; these data came from
our 1978 Toronto survey. The percentage of variance explained ranged
from 16% to 37% and was highest for reactions to facilities closest to home
(i.e., within one block). Three of the seven neighborhood factors were
consistent and significant predictors: transience, scarcity of children, and
economic status. Greater opposition to facilities was associated with stable
neighborhoods with relatively large proportions of families with children
and relatively higher economic status. A typology of neighborhoods was

developed, using cluster analysis to group the census tracts on the basis of
scores on the facility attitude scale and the three neighborhood factors
shown to be significant in the regression analysis. Mapping the groups
showed a clear spatial pattern with a marked distance-decay in facility
desirability away from the center of the city. One interpretation of the
pattern is an "intolerance surface" with the topography described by
contours of intolerance (Fig. 11.2). Consistent with common belief,
suburban neighborhoods emerged as more resistant to facilities.

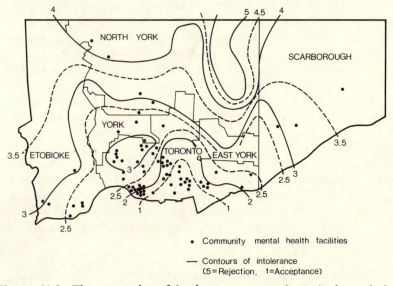

· Community mental health facilities

— Contours of intolerance
(5 = Rejection, 1=Acceptance)

Figure 11.2 The geography of intolerance: community attitudes and the
distribution of mental health facilities in metropolitan Toronto (from Dear & Wolch
1986).

These results are indicative of the practical utility which may be achieved
through the estimation of aggregate predictive models. Obviously, they
can only serve as an aid in planning the location of facilities but, in this
restricted role, they are a significant advance over anecdotal evidence and
personal opinion which otherwise have to be relied upon in evaluating the
relative merits of alternative sites.

Attitude change

The issue of changes in public attitudes toward the mentally ill and mental
health can be approached from two time perspectives. In the long term,
change can be studied by examining historical trends; for example, changes

in attitudes since 1945 in response to the medical model of mental illness. The literature on historical trends, referred to briefly on pages 224–5, has been effectively reviewed by Rabkin (1972, 1974, 1975, 1980). In the short term, change can be examined as a response to specific interventions or events. These may be of a planned variety, such as educational programs designed to foster more positive attitudes, or they may be unplanned, such as a local dispute over a facility location which may prompt opinion changes in either direction.

Research on attitude change to specific initiatives is sparse, despite the numerous programs which have been attempted to promote positive public opinion. Baron (1980) has classified the initiatives into two general categories, collaborative and structural.

> The collaborative approach asks communities to openly examine prevailing attitudes and opinions and gambles that this will lead to an enlightened course of action. By contrast, the structural approach dictates the utilization of social, legal or media levers to promote community integration despite public sentiment (Baron 1980: 9).

Baron points to the lack of systematic evaluation of past approaches, which leaves us with little idea whether collaborative or structural methods are most effective. There have been numerous public education campaigns, and yet we are relatively uninformed about the types of messages which are most effectively disseminated. Outlining future research directions, he argues that:

> What is needed, ideally, is a number of ambitious public education projects with dual goals to improve public acceptance and to evaluate their impact. At a quasi-experimental level, the success of any individual public change in a single community on a pre-post basis . . . (Baron 1980: 10).

An isolated example of this type of study was an assessment of the impact of the documentary film "Back wards to back streets." Using a pre–post design, Bridge & Medvine (1980) evaluated the impact of the film on public attitudes toward the mentally ill. Questionnaires were administered to participating audiences (in New York City, Albany, Hartford, and Bridgeport) immediately prior to and immediately following special screenings of the film. There were a number of positive findings suggesting that media initiatives can effectively promote more accepting attitudes, but it is important to note that this study measured only immediate public response to the film.

The literature is devoid of studies that systematically evaluate long-term impacts of persuasive messages aimed at encouraging greater public acceptance of the mentally ill. It was partly in response to this research void that we recently completed a pre–post study of the impacts of the Information and Action Program in Ontario (Dear *et al.* 1985).

The information and Action Program was a media-based campaign designed to increase public awareness of the needs of the mentally ill in the community, and to foster more positive opinion. The campaign involved two flights of advertising messages; the first took place between October and December 1983, and the second in July 1984. The advertising involved television, radio, and newspaper campaigns, and reached all parts of the province. The impacts were evaluated by comparing the responses of the same people to telephone surveys conducted six months before the first flight of advertising and six weeks after the second flight. Survey data were obtained from random samples selected from 12 communities that represented different regions in the province and different-sized cities or towns. A separate sample was drawn from metropolitan Toronto. In total, 992 questionnaires were completed in the baseline survey. The number dropped to 481 in the follow-up survey due to difficulties recontacting the same respondents, despite repeated call-backs.

The questionnaire contained various indicators of attitudes towards the mentally ill and mental health facilities, including items from the AMI scales developed in our 1978 study, and ratings of facility acceptance based on the vignettes described earlier in this chapter. The baseline survey showed generally positive attitudes for all indicators, suggesting that the role of the IAP was to consolidate grassroots sympathy, and to help translate it into active support for the needs of the mentally ill in the community. At the same time, the campaign could serve to counter potentially negative influences resulting from concurrent specific issues and controversies related to community mental health care.

Responses to the follow-up survey showed very few significant changes in attitudes. This was interpreted as a positive result, indicative of the success of the IAP to sustain positive opinion in the face of potentially negative extraneous influences. The follow-up also provided encouraging results about the penetration and positive lasting impression produced by the IAP. Those reporting attitude change perceived a positive change toward greater awareness of, and sympathy for, the problems of the mentally ill, implying that the IAP had succeeded in consolidating positive opinion. Most felt that the media messages were effective, primarily on the grounds that they served to further educate the public about the problems and needs of the mentally ill in the community. There was a strong consensus that further promotional initiatives such as the IAP were needed, stemming from the conviction that education promotes greater understanding, acceptance, and support. Both surveys were consistent in showing that respondents with greater familiarity or contact with the mentally ill hold more positive attitudes. This lends added support to the value of educational campaigns which aim to increase public familiarity with the needs and problems of the mentally ill.

This Ontario study illustrates the approach that can be taken to systematically evaluate the effects of an intervention designed to produce changes in public attitudes toward the mentally ill. It highlights some of the difficulties involved in accumulating strong evidence in studies of this sort. Two particular problems merit comment. The first is the problem of sample attrition in a longitudinal study design. In this case, over half of the sample was lost between the first and second surveys, which were conducted about 18 months apart. This attrition rate was higher than expected and is probably partly attributable to the use of volunteer groups of interviewers. The second problem involves the lack of control over extraneous factors that can influence attitudes over time, and thereby weaken the inferences that can be drawn about the strength of effect of the interventions. This is a difficulty inherent in all field experiments, and one not fully surmountable even in the most rigorous study designs. These problems inevitably compromise the strength of evidence. Nevertheless, recalling Baron's comments about the paucity of research on attitude change in response to public education programs, some evidence is better than no evidence at all.

Facility impacts

The media attention given to conflict over the siting of selected mental health facilities can easily lead to the impression that their impacts on local neighborhoods are profound and widespread. The research evidence leads to a different conclusion. In many instances, the impacts of facilities have been negligible, to the point that the majority of local residents are completely unaware of the presence of a facility in their neighborhood. In cases where the facility has been more visible, it is common to find that advance fears about negative effects have dissipated in light of experience devoid of incident. In short, expectations and events are typically quite different. In this brief review of the evidence, three issues are considered; facility awareness, perceptions of facility impacts, and property-value effects.

The findings recently reported by Rabkin et al. (1984) are typical of other results on facility awareness. Survey respondents were selected from 12 matched neighborhoods in Manhattan, six with a local psychiatric facility and the other six without. Despite the fact that, in the first six neighborhoods, respondents lived in immediate proximity to a facility, 77% of them were totally unaware of any program serving mental patients in their neighborhood. Rabkin comments that "this is probably our most noteworthy finding" (p. 309). A reasonable reaction to this particular result is to suggest that it may be an artifact of the study location. The complex social and physical character of Manhattan might well be regarded as an ideal environment in which to "hide" facilities. However, this objection cannot be sustained in light of similar findings from other and quite different locations. For example, in our 1978 Toronto study, only 21% (83 out of 388) of the respondents selected from neighborhoods with mental health facilities were aware of the presence of a facility. Furthermore, of these, only 40% (33 out of 83) could accurately identify the location of the facility near their home.

The obvious question is why there is such a low level of awareness. The most likely explanation has to do with the invisibility of many of the facilities. In the case of residential care facilities, the group homes or commercial boarding homes are typically indistinguishable from neighboring housing and, therefore, unless specific incidents have occurred to draw public attention, it is very likely that their existence could remain unknown except to those living very close by. Equally, many of the nonresidential facilities are inconspicuous. Social–therapeutic services, for example, are commonly incorporated within existing facilities such as churches and community centers, and again easily go unnoticed. The only high-profile facilities are clinics and drop-in centers which use store-front operations, but these are relatively few in number and are usually located in commercial areas where their presence could easily be overlooked.

Information on perceptions of facility impacts has been collected in the form of very general judgements, as well as in terms of ratings on specific impact scales. In the former category, Rabkin *et al.* (1984) found that approximately half their sample perceived the presence of a home for former mental patients as having a bad effect on the neighborhood. A smaller fraction, approximately one third, believed a psychiatric clinic would have a negative effect. In neither case were there significant differences between residents in neighborhoods with and without facilities or between residents aware or unaware of the presence of a facility. However, overall, the responses to various questions suggest that those aware of facilities had more positive perceptions of facility effects.

In our Toronto study (Dear & Taylor 1982), beliefs about facility impacts were measured by ratings on 12 semantic differential scales. For those unaware of facilities, the ratings were beliefs about the impacts a mental health facility *would have* on the neighborhood, and for those aware, they were beliefs about the impacts a facility *had had*. For all 12 scales the modal response was neutral, showing that many respondents perceived facilities as having little or no effect. For the unaware group, the percentage perceiving negative effects exceeded the percentage perceiving positive effects on all 12 scales, ranging from a high of 46% perceiving a negative effect on property values, to a low of 20% for effects on the visual appearance of the neighborhood. For the aware group, the percentage reporting negative impacts was higher on 10 of the 12 scales, the exceptions being for the perceived effects on residential character and property *taxes*, where opinions were evenly divided. In general, the percentage expressing negative perceptions was lower for the aware group suggesting that, inasmuch as awareness had any effect on perceived impacts, it was in the direction of softening rather than hardening residents' views. However, cause and effect between awareness and facility perceptions could not be inferred, because awareness covaried with other potentially salient variables; for example, with residential location within the city.

These results, together with common knowledge based on local conflicts over facility locations, show that a primary concern regarding facility impacts centers on possible property-value effects. While much of the debate in local situations is based on speculation, there are several studies which provide an empirical basis from which to draw conclusions.

Measuring the effect of an externality such as a mental health facility on property values presents a very difficult research design problem. This is because the magnitude of the effect of the facility is likely to be small and localized relative to the effects of other property-value determinants. We have discussed the design implications of these complications elsewhere (Dear & Taylor 1982). In summary, a strong design requires: a valid *a priori* definition of the impact area of a facility; a well defined causal model of property values; the specification of an adequate control sample; and property discounting procedures to account for temporal variations in house prices. These requirements are not easily met nor are detailed data sets easily obtained. Ideally, comprehensive information is needed on individual housing transactions over an extended period of time. Typically, this is privileged information, not released into the public domain and requiring a special right of access for research purposes. Even if access is secured, there is no guarantee that the data are sufficiently comprehensive or complete to meet the design and analysis requirements. With these quite stringent constraints in mind, it is important that the conclusions of property-value studies be very carefully evaluated to ensure that they are justified in light of the strength of the design and data used for analysis.

Several studies have attempted to measure the effect of mental health facilities on property values (Breslow 1976, Dear 1977, Wolpert 1978, Boeckh *et al.* 1980). They differ considerably in their design and data, and yet all arrive at the same basic conclusion that facilities have no measurable effect on the housing market in their impact areas. Different possible indicators of effects have been used. They fall under two general headings, those related to sales activity and those related to selling price. In our study (Boeckh *et al.* 1980), we had access, through the Toronto Real Estate Board, to detailed information on all transactions in five selected facility areas and five matched control areas, for a period covering two years before and two years after the opening of each facility. There was no evidence that the volume of sales activity was either greater or less in facility than in control areas before, during, or after facility introduction. Nor was there evidence that the property market in the facility areas had "bottomed out" because of lack of demand, as there was no measurable decline in selling prices. In facility areas, house prices tended to increase at a comparable rate to those in the control areas. Overall, we concluded that property-market changes in our Toronto neighborhoods were due mainly to such traditional factors as neighborhood desirability and the characteristics of housing units. The introduction of a mental health facility had no significant effect on property values.

Taken together, the results of these empirical studies provide consistent evidence that facilities have no effect on property values. However, this conclusion has a specific sphere of reference; it pertains to prices averaged over a set of transactions and as such cannot be used to make inferences about the effect of a facility on any single transaction. This becomes an important distinction when the claim is made, sometimes in a legal case, that a facility has had a detrimental effect on the value of immediately neighboring properties. The evidence from statistical analyses such as our own cannot be used either to support or refute such a contention. This is not a convenient side-step, but simply an honest statement of the inferences that can and cannot be made from statistical comparisons using average selling prices of properties, in an impact area which necessarily extends well beyond the houses next door to the facility.

Implications for the future of community mental health care

It seems appropriate to conclude this chapter by considering very briefly the implications for the future that are suggested by the precediing sections. In so doing, it is important to consider the implications from the perspectives of both the providers and users of community mental health care facilities.

From the providers' standpoint, the evidence presented seems to lead to a generally positive conclusion. There appears to be strong grassroots sympathy, in principle, for the mentally ill and for the provision of community-based facilities. Despite media reports to the contrary, facilities are often introduced into neighborhoods with minimal effect, to the point that the majority of local residents remain ignorant of the facility's presence. While there is evidence of negative perceptions of facility impacts in advance of their introduction, these tend to be reduced somewhat if and when a facility is actually located. The absence of evidence of any detrimental effect on property values is perhaps the clearest example of the anticipation being worse than the event. Furthermore, there is some, albeit quite weak, evidence to suggest that positive attitudes can be sustained in the face of potentially negative influences by educational campaigns and messages. Together, all this seems to give the green light to the provision of the much needed additional community facilities for residential and non-residential care. At first sight, there appear to be no major obstacles to an expansionist policy in terms of strong public opposition.

However, there may be storm clouds on the horizon because of the likely locations of future facilities. Up to now, facilities have concentrated in inner-city neighborhoods. There are several reasons for this, including the availability of suitable properties, especially low-cost housing for residential care services. However, another factor has been resistance on the part of suburban municipalities to share the burden of providing care for service-dependent groups in general, and the mentally ill in particular. In some cases, this resistance has translated into exclusionary zoning practices prohibiting the introduction of facilities. Such practices are now being removed and replaced by fair-share zoning policies which, in principle at least, open up the suburbs and permit a decentralization of services. The issue immediately arising from the adoption of a policy of decentralization is that of the potential reaction to facilities in communities which, to date, have not had to accept them. From our analysis described earlier in this chapter and summarized in the map of the "geography of intolerance" (Fig. 11.2), it is clear that the existing concentration of facilities corresponds quite closely with the inner-city zone of highest tolerance. Efforts to achieve a more equal distribution of facilities are therefore likely to create more opposition than has been experienced to date. The extent to which educational programs can offset and overcome negative attitudes is not certain, but becomes an important consideration in evaluating the costs and benefits of dismantling the psychiatric ghetto.

The implications from this review for facility users, the mentally ill in the community, also appear to be generally positive. The gradual shift in public opinion away from authoritarian and restrictive beliefs about the mentally ill toward a more benevolent and community-focused view of mental health care implies a growing tolerance, sensitivity to needs, and perhaps willingness to support facilities and services. However, there remains a gap between sympathy in principle and support in practice. The evidence presented would suggest that narrowing the gap involves a combination of positive first-hand experience with the mentally ill in the neighborhood, thereby reducing the fear of the unknown, and continuing public education to promote and reinforce an understanding of needs. In this latter respect, the activities of groups such as the Canadian Mental Health Association are especially important, since they are well placed to initiate, coordinate and evaluate efforts to communicate community mental health needs and priorities to the public at large. The recent Information and Action Program in Ontario is one good example of the type of outreach that is possible.

The likelihood of a gradual decentralization of services has important implications for users. The current concentration of facilities of all types in inner-city neighborhoods correlates strongly with the distribution of clients. Clearly, there is circular causation involved; services are located to respond to needs, and users locate to have access to services. Decentralization implies some fracture of these close ties, at least in the short run, with potential costs to users in terms of decreased access to care. If users are able to follow facilities and move out of the inner city, then other implications arise; specifically, the dismantling of the ghetto, which some regard as a supportive environment, not easily reproduced once the mentally ill are more widely distributed throughout the city. However, these concerns are largely speculative, and imply an understanding of the factors that influence the coping performance of the mentally ill in the community. This understanding is rudimentary at best and is only now beginning to attract the research attention it deserves (see Ch. 5 and Kearns 1986). As this review indicates, community reaction to the deinstitutionalized mentally ill has been a major research theme. The time is right for a complementary focus on the reactions of the mentally ill to the community.

References

Baker, F. & J. Schulberg 1967. The development of a community mental health ideology scale. *Community Mental Health Journal* 3, 216–25.

Baron, R. C. 1980. Assessing attitude/behaviour linkages: new directions for mental health public education research. In J. G. Rabkin, K. Gelb & J. Lazare (eds.). *Attitudes toward the mentally ill: research perceptives*, 56–8. Washington: NIMH.

Boeckh, J. L., M. Dear & S. M. Taylor 1980. Property value effects of mental health facilities. *Canadian Geographer* 24 (3), 270–85.

Breslow, S. 1976. *The effect of siting group homes on the surrounding environments*. Unpublished paper, School of Architecture and Urban Planning, Princeton University, Princeton, N.J.

Bridge, R. G. & L. G. Medvine 1980. *Back wards to back streets impact study*. Research report. New York: WNET/Thirteen TV.

CTI (Canadian Training Institute) 1984. *The effect of locating correctional group homes in residential neighborhoods*. Research report, Canadian Training Institute, York University, Downsview, Ontario.

Cohen, J. & E. L. Struening 1962. Opinions about mental illness in the personnel of two large mental hospitals. *Journal of Abnormal and Social Psychology* 64, 349–60.

Dear, M. 1977. Impact on mental health facilities on property values. *Community Mental Health Journal* 13, 150–7.

Dear, M. 1981. Social and spatial reproduction of the mentally ill. In *Urbanization and urban planning in capitalist society*, M. Dear & A. J. Scott (eds.), 481–500. London: Methuen.

Dear, M. & S. M. Taylor 1982. *Not on our street: community attitudes to mental health care*. London: Pion.

Dear M. J. & J. Wolch 1987. *Landscapes of despair: from deinstitutionalization to home-lessness.* Oxford: Polity Press.

Dear, M., R. Fincher & L. Currie 1977. Measuring the external effects of public programs. *Environment and Planning A* **9**, 137–47.

Dear, M. J. & S. M. Taylor, D. Bestvater & B. Breston 1985. *Evaluation of the Information and Action Program.* Research report, Department of Geography, McMaster University, Hamilton, Ontario.

Fishbein, M. & I. Ajzen 1975. *Belief, attitude, intention and behavior: an introduction to theory and research.* Reading, Mass.: Addison Wesley.

Hall, G. B. & S. M. Taylor 1983. A causal model of attitudes toward mental health facilities. *Environment and Planning A* **15**, 525–42.

Kearns, R. 1986. *Unravelling the web: the influence of environment upon the coping ability of psychiatric clients.* Paper presented at the 2nd Annual International Symposium in Medical Geography, July 14–18, Rutgers University, New Brunswick, New Jersey.

Nunnally, J. 1977. *Public attitudes about mental illness: literature review and recommendations.* Paper presented for Task Panel on Attitudes and Use of Media for Promotion of Mental Health, President's Commission on Mental Health, Washington D.C.

Piasecki, J. 1975. *Community response to residential services for the psychosocially disabled.* Paper presented at the First Annual Conference of the International Association for Psychosocial Rehabilitation Services, Horizon House Institute, Philadelphia.

Rabkin, J. G. 1972. Opinions about mental illness: a review of the literature. *Psychological Bulletin* **77**, 153–71.

Rabkin, J. G. 1974. Public attitudes toward mental illness: a review of the literature. *Schizophrenia Bulletin* **1**, 9–33.

Rabkin, J. G. 1975. The role of attitudes toward mental illness in evaluation of mental health programs. In *Handbook of evaluation research*, vol. 2, M. Guttenberg & E. L. Struening (eds.), 431–82. Beverly Hills: Sage.

Rabkin, J. 1980. Determinants of public attitudes about mental illness: a summary of the research literature. In *Attitudes toward the mentally ill: research perspectives*, J. Rabkin, K. Gelb & J. Lazare (eds.), 15–26. Washington: NIMH.

Rabkin, J. G., G. Muhlin & P. W. Cohen 1985. What the neighbours think: community attitudes toward local psychiatric facilities. *Community Mental Health Journal* **20**, 304–12.

Scheff, T. 1966. *Being mentally ill.* Chicago, Ill.: Aldine.

Scheff, T. 1967. *Mental illness and social progress.* New York: Harper and Row.

Segal, S. & U. Aviram 1978. *The mentally ill in community-based sheltered care.* New York: Wiley.

Smith, C. J. & R. Q. Hanham 1981. Proximity and the formation of public attitudes towards mental illness. *Environment and Planning A* **13**, 147–65.

Taylor, S. M. & M. Dear 1981. Scaling community attitudes toward the mentally ill. *Schizophrenia bulletin* **7** (2), 225–40.

Taylor, S. M., M. Dear & G. B. Hall 1979. Attitudes toward the mentally ill and reactions to mental health facilities. *Social Science and Medicine* **13D**, 281–90.

Taylor, S. M., G. B. Hall, R. C. Hughes & M. J. Dear 1984. Predicting community reaction to mental health facilities. *American Planning Association Journal* **50**, 36–47.

Trute, B. & S. Segal 1976. Census tract predictors and the social integration of sheltered care residents. *Social Psychiatry* **11**, 153–61.

Wolpert, J. 1978. *Group homes for mentally retarded and investigation of neighboring property impacts*. Woodrow Wilson School of Public and International Affairs. Princeton University, Princeton, New Jersey.

PART IV

Stigma and rejection in the community: the continuing search for a home for the mentally ill

12 No place like home: reflections on sheltering a diverse population

STEVEN P. SEGAL and JIM BAUMOHL

Introduction

A home exists where sentiment and space converge to afford attachment, stability, and a secure sense of personal control. It is an abiding place and a web of trustworthy connections, an anchor of identity and social life, the seat of intimacy and trust from which we pursue our emotional and material needs.

A home may be ready-made or it may be self-created and sustained. In our society, it is customary for an individual to leave the ready-made home of his or her family and establish a new home founded upon his particular desires and expressing his or her autonomy. Indeed, the establishment of such a home is a hallmark of full-fledged adulthood.

However, the expression of autonomy is not the same for all people. The importance of certain personal prerogatives varies enormously and, as the expression of these prerogatives affects social relationships and requires secure control of physical space, various dimensions of a home, which is both social and spatial, assume differential importance.

No matter what hierarchy of prerogatives prevails for each person, though, it is at home that this expression is most fully allowed and protected from intrusion. A home provides a bulwark for the protection of identity and personal order. In this sense, a home is a highly personalized environment that is secure against the world. It is cathected space, an extension of self.

In sum, if a house is not a home, neither is a home a house. A home is a place, narrowly or expansively conceived, which is a secure representation of important relationships with family, friends, and even institutions. In this sense, a home is a matrix of desirable and highly valued attachments. Emphasizing this affiliative dimension of home, Caplow *et al*. (1968) define homelessness as "a condition of detachment from society characterized by the absence or attenuation of the affiliative bonds that link settled persons to a network of interconnected social structures."

It is often assumed that mental patients chafe at the bit while waiting for release from the hospital, and that once released they return to communities and residences they regard as home. In fact, large numbers of chronic patients have no home, except insofar as the mental hospital has served as one. They have no stable abode, no circle of kin, no network of friends, and no role to fill from which such connections might naturally emerge. Upon release they are homeless persons, physically and socially displaced.

Further, chronic mental patients are not just like others seeking a home. They are likely to be poor and dependent upon public aid, and they are likely to exhibit some symptomology or "residual deviance" (Scheff 1966) that distances them from their fellows. They cannot readily purchase a secure tenure on property, and they lack the charm to surround themselves with friends. Chronic mental patients are often rather unsavory strangers to whom no one outside the hospital beckons.

It is not surprising, then, that every mental hospital is well aware of a population of chronic patients who periodically seek voluntary readmission, or present themselves with symptoms meeting the criteria necessary for involuntary admission. Whether the latter presentation is feigned or real is often undeterminable; however, chronic patients, caught between the rock of poverty and the hard place of enduring disorder, well understand the hospital's attractions. There is, after all, something to be said for a roof, three squares, a captive social audience, and relief from the stresses of a tenuous existence in an urban slum.

However, the comforts of the hospital as ready-made home are not without a price in personal autonomy. Long-term or episodic patienthood is not for everyone. Still, the findings of Braginsky et al. (1969), that many of their research participants "vacationed" at the hospital, and the long history of findings illustrating the ability of homeless people to use custodial institutions on their own terms (cf., Anderson 1923, 1940; Wiseman 1970; Segal, Baumohl & Johnson 1977; Segal & Baumohl 1980; Lewis & Hugi 1981), are clear indications of the hospital's value to materially and socially impoverished, disconnected persons, whether they are mentally ill, exhausted, or simply out of acceptable options.

Similarly, the environments of community-based sheltered care and mental health and social support agencies offer, at times, the material security and the social connectedness associated with a home. These institutional relationships are not without demands either, and tolerance of their expectations is often short-lived. Indeed, despite acknowledged benefits, some chronic patients avoid formal services altogether. These individuals forgo security for what they consider to be a purely autonomous relationship with the world.

Let us consider these matters in more detail. We will begin with the hospital setting and examine what it offers in the way of a home. Subsequently, we will discuss community-based sheltered care, and we will consider free-living chronic patients who have ostensibly rejected all dependence and personal compromise. Finally, we will argue that only a diverse and flexible system of community care can accommodate the ambivalent autonomy of chronic patients, while still fulfilling the state's obligation to provide them with an opportunity to find a home.

The hospital as home

Reasonably competent, self-sustaining adults find it difficult to imagine making a home in an institution such as a mental hospital. Although the hospital may provide shelter and afford sociability, and even a measure of control over a restricted environment, mental patients are symbolically and often legally under the control of their caretakers, benevolent or otherwise. Thus, while a mental hospital may be orderly and comfortable, it is not a setting which, for most of us, allows sufficient autonomy for the expression of our personal tastes.

To be sure, a great many chronic patients feel the same way about the mental hospital. They experience its care as confining and coercive, and while in residence feel like the perennial child in the father's house. For them, hospitalization is involuntary or undertaken only in desperation, or with the ambivalence of resignation to an undesirable fate. On the other hand, there is a small group of chronic patients who, like the fictional character, Oskar Matzereth in *The tin drum* (Grass 1961), are in love with symbols of shelter and care and find, in the "perfect symmetry" of a hospital bed, an answer to their longing for order and acceptance. For those who seek some stability in chaos, the adoption of the patient role and presence in the ambience of safe care can be restorative. Hospitalization can be a home-coming of a kind. Thus, the hospital may become a temporary sanctuary or, on a more permanent basis, a home after the fashion of a cloister. This does not imply resignation to the syndrome of apathy and passive compliance referred to as institutional dependency (Martin 1955, Wing 1962), but rather integration within a secure and secluded community where participatory roles exist, but where strong dependency needs are more readily satisfied than elsewhere.

Numerous studies have illuminated the problems associated with the rigidity of institutional routine, regimentation, and increased social distance between staff and patients (Bettelheim & Sylvester 1948, King *et al.* 1972, Moline 1977, Zigler & Balla 1977). As a result, hospital programs have sought to balance institutional order with personal autonomy, by emphasizing patient choice and responsibility in the matters of activity, treatment, and ward governance. Studies of individuals in these "patient-centered" environments report significant improvements in alertness, active participation, and general sense of wellbeing (Langner & Rodin 1976, Phares & Lamiell 1977).

Still, while the hospital environment may provide adequate sociability and a comfortable balance between security and autonomy for some, it has inevitable limitations that alienate many others.

First of all, the hospital is socially discontinuous. Today, especially, patients come and go rapidly, and hospital social life is transient. If the hospital serves a large metropolitan or regional area, there is little likelihood that relationships initiated in the hospital will be sustained on the outside.

Secondly, the hospital is a public place, lacking the "backstage" or private areas of most dwellings (Goffman 1961). In this respect, it shares many of the characteristics of hostels and barracks. Although patients manage to create privacy for themselves, to do so often dramatizes otherwise commonplace behavior or invites conflict with authority. The recreational use of alcohol and drugs, and the expression of sexuality, severely tax the hospital's commitment to upholding the law, and bring about the enforcement of ambiguous notions of propriety in order to protect itself from the worst possible case and its potential consequences of litigation and scandal.

In sum, the hospital provides an ambience of security and care which, for some chronic patients, are the necessary and sufficient conditions of a home. Indeed, it appears that the hospital ambience has been cathected by these patients and suits them like a warm comforter. However, for other chronic patients, the hospital environment is too confining; its demands for conformity conflict with a highly desired autonomy in matters of lifestyle. These patients are not invested in being objects of care except insofar as that care comes without demands. Many resist hospitalization under any circumstances, while others occasionally seek readmission only to regret the decision shortly thereafter.

Realistically, it is most accurate to describe chronic patients as ambivalent about the hospital in the same way that they are ambivalent about their dependency needs; for the hospital, actually and symbolically, is an environment where one accedes control to others and loses, however temporarily, a place in the outside world of autonomous and reciprocal relations. Hospitalization implies an authoritative judgment by others or a painful admission by oneself that such autonomous and reciprocal relations are going miserably. Thus, although chronic patients may view a stint in the hospital as necessary, and perhaps even welcome, it is a blow to their sense of competence and is, to that extent, a threat.

Recent history has loosened this ambivalent bond between chronic patients and the hospital environment. Deinstitutionalization in many states has greatly restricted the possibility of the hospital becoming a home and, instead, has substituted the nursing home and community-based sheltered care industries to replace the long-term shelter function of the mental hospital. The advent of Aid to the Permanently and Totally Disabled (APTD), first widely extended to the mentally ill in the mid-1960s, and the subsequent development of Supplemental Security Income (SSI) has also allowed chronic patients to purchase more independent and private living space, albeit with great difficulty. Thus, it is in local areas that chronic patients must make a home, whether in supervised or unsupervised surroundings.

Home in community-based sheltered care

The intended goal of deinstitutionalization, and its oft presumed but hardly necessary consequence of community care, is the return of formerly dependent individuals to independent functioning in the human community. This presumes that these individuals will have, or will develop, the skills and personal attributes necessary to negotiate relationships that permit participation in the social and economic flow of life. It presumes, in short, that former mental patients can and will become competent friends, employees, consumers, and so on. To do so, ex-patients must not only possess such skills and attributes, or the capacity for them, but they must be perceived as having them, or the potential for them. In other words, they must not be written off by their audience.

As the literature on community reaction to the mentally ill amply attests, former patients face a skeptical audience that expects them to be incompetent, disruptive, dangerous, and incurable. They suffer a stigmatized status which is, with the addition of attributes other than a history of mental disorder, such as large stature, maleness, youth or minority racial status, easily generalized into the additional stigmata of untrustworthiness, incompetence, criminality, shiftlessness, sexual perversion, physical disablement, and the like. The general public, whether or not it believes in the culpability of former patients in these shortcomings, whether it finds them pitiable or contemptible, expects them to be insufferable neighbors.

Unfortunately, the public's misgivings are not entirely unfounded. Many former patients exhibit the sort of residual deviance that makes normal interaction difficult, and the rehabilitative potential of the chronically mentally ill does not appear to be great. Most disturbingly, as the number of mental patients with criminal records has increased over the years, the post-discharge rates of arrest and conviction of former patients for serious crimes have increased accordingly (Rabkin 1979). Thus, although it may be mean-spirited and uncharitable to avoid former mental patients and prefer them to be excluded from ordinary social life, it is not an unreasonable desire. Indeed, the history of community care has been marked by attempts of the politically potent middle class to temper with "reasonable restraints," a charitable but somewhat unpopular impulse of organized social welfare. The nature of these restraints, especially as they are perceived by chronic patients as implied or explicit terms of residence, have a great deal to do with whether or not chronic patients come to feel at home anywhere; and if they do come to feel at home, where in the geocultural scheme of things that home happens to be (Segal, Baumohl & Moyles 1980). The geographical development of community-based sheltered care and its institutional demands upon its consumers are instructive in this respect.

Formal community care began primarily with a "family care plan." Small family-oriented homes in lower-middle-class areas were used by hospitals to board out patients thought to benefit little from the hospital regimen, and to be amenable to ordinary, if not altogether respectable, settlement in the community. This boarding-out process was safeguarded by the hospital's guarantee of close supervision and careful patient selection. At this time, hospital social workers could move patients back to the hospital at a moment's notice. Patients who were boarded out were generally older, docile, and easily controlled by a family care home manager (Segal & Aviram 1978). These were chronic patients, thoroughly at home within the ambit of institutional control, and whose great dependency needs could be satisfied by assuming even a second-class role in a surrogate family.

With the advent of deinstitutionalization and the accompanying emphasis on civil rights, former patients could no longer be moved around at the discretion of hospital staff. The concept of the conditional "probation" or "parole" of mental patients, which in California has been codified in legislation in 1913, was abandoned. Instead, upon release, mental patients became free-living individuals. Further, with the release of large numbers of patients with greatly varied characteristics, and with the growing need for sheltered care for young adults and single men in middle age, the limitations of the family-care system became obvious. In its uniformly lower-middle-class, family-dominated world, former patients without family ties or skills in family relationships were poorly integrated (Trute & Segal 1976). They remained black sheep, their social failures more apparent than any competence in social relationships they possessed. In addition, research in the UK on the "emotional arousal hypothesis" strongly suggested that family placement could often be countertherapeutic. It appeared that many former patients in group quarters, who did not have to respond to demands for intimacy and who could balance social interaction with some degree of withdrawal, fared better than many in family settings (Brown, Birley & Wing 1972). With a simple extension of family care, a great many chronic patients would have been square pegs fitted to round holes. They were not family people, and they were never likely to be very conventional people. They would not be at home in family care.

As an entrepreneurial response to this lack of fit between the large and variegated population of released patients and the existing system of family care, a private system of community-based housing flourished, providing a much greater variety of settings in which chronic patients might find a home. This was facilitated by APTD, and then SSI, which enabled former patients to become purchasers of sheltered care. In addition to the lower-middle-class and family-oriented neighborhoods in which family care was located, many community-based sheltered-care facilities situated themselves in locales openly tolerant to offbeat beliefs and behaviors, or at least not openly hostile to such deviation. Typically, facilities located in areas with a notable degree of transience, and that had experienced a significant economic decline, or were traditional enclaves of bohemianism and poverty. Sheltered-care facilities often located in vacation areas that no longer attracted a tourist population, or areas where hotels, motels, and residential properties were beginning to become run down. Here, sheltered care provided an economic alternative for the owners of such property, and the relatively low property values allowed the entrance of human service entrepreneurs who were not intensely capitalized (Segal & Aviram 1978).

During the 1960s, university-supervised housing—especially boarding homes, fraternities and sororities—lost their appeal to a generation of students bent on pursuing their own particular prerogatives, and requiring greater control of their living space in order to do so. These facilities needed a new population of residents and some became available for the purposes of sheltered care.

Finally, homeowners and individuals living in and around communities that already housed mental hospitals, communities in which attitudes toward the mentally ill are significantly more positive than elsewhere (Smith & Hanham 1981), expanded their own homes to provide sheltered care, or purchased large, older homes on the borders of commercial areas which could be easily converted for group occupancy.

Not only has this private system of sheltered care expanded the variety of neighborhoods in which released patients can find supervised housing, but it has provided a greater variety of residential settings ("facility types") ranging from highly controlled, medically oriented settings reminiscent of the traditional mental hospital, to those which are little more than boarding houses (Segal & Aviram 1978, Segal & Moyles 1979). Although the so-called halfway houses and therapeutic communities have received the bulk of academic and journalistic attention, they constitute a tiny fraction of community-based sheltered-care settings (Segal & Aviram 1978, Segal & Baumohl 1981).

This greater variance in community and facility types seems to be of substantial benefit to chronic patients, for it allows them a much wider latitude of choice in their homeseeking. Research to date suggests that the type of community in which a sheltered-care facility is located has a significant bearing on the social integration of its residents (Segal, Baumohl & Moyles 1980), and that facility characteristics influence social integration and the development of institutional dependency (Segal & Aviram 1978, Segal & Moyles 1979). In addition, research indicates that unique and complex interactions among community, facility, and resident characteristics will differentially affect the social integration of sheltered-care residents (Segal & Baumohl 1981). There is, then, every reason to believe that a variegated system of community-based sheltered care offers chronic patients more opportunity to find some community–facility combination in which they feel at home. This may require some shopping around or some degree of transience, but the probability of finding the right environment seems to be much greater than before.

Having said this, we must now hedge our praise somewhat. In spite of its greater variance in settings, contemporary sheltered care still requires accommodation to norms of group living. Although the expectations of sheltered care are considerably more flexible than those obtaining in the mental hospital, or which prevailed in family care, and although there is less potential for antagonistic captor–captive role relations in sheltered care, there are nonetheless basic matters of cooperation and public health which cannot be ignored. Belligerent, disruptive, and unhygienic residents rapidly become ex-residents and are left to fend for themselves.

Also, residents of sheltered care, like patients in mental hospitals, must conduct their private lives in what are essentially public places. Sheltered-care operators are bound to uphold the law, and since they are faced with maintaining a use permit, are concerned with matters of propriety that fall short of legal codification. Drug users and sexually active residents often have a difficult time making a home in sheltered care, preferring the privacy of independent living. Similarly, sheltered care may prove uncongenial for intensely private people who desire little or no social interaction.

Home and independent living

Typically, chronic patients attempting to make a home on their own are faced with the multitudinous problems of an independent life of poverty. Where they attempt to make this life is constrained by their lack of social and material resources, and by their disreputability and their self-consciousness of it. They seek an inexpensive haven in which they will be tolerated on their own terms; a community that shrugs off a disreputable and burdensome past and a rather eccentric self-presentation. As a young former patient of our acquaintance put it:

> The United States is a resting place for the weird. California is for those who are too weird for the United States. Berkeley is the end of the line; if you're too weird to live here, you're too weird to live on this earth (*Daily Californian*, June 6, 1980: 4).

There are spatial areas where impoverishment and a rough toleration overlap more than elsewhere. These are the skid rows, tenderloin districts, and youth ghettoes of our cities, areas which have become open asylums of a sort. The distinctive quality of these areas derives not only from their landmarks and customary institutions, but from the appearance, style, and characteristics of their residents, largely people who live, to one degree or another, outside the webs of relations that emanate from family, employment, and settled living. Their character is formed by poverty and disaffiliation together.

In these areas, social expectations and demands are relatively few, and all sorts of idiosyncrasies are tolerated to a much greater extent than elsewhere. However, the price of this toleration and freedom from institutional and interpersonal constraint is a lack of reliable and stable relationships. The minimal expectations of street life or life in a single-room-occupancy (SRO) hotel are liberating only in the sense that an individual may choose withdrawal. The suspicion and diffidence that pervades the social life of disaffiliate areas, and to some extent protects their residents from further emotional loss, simultaneously begets a lonely kind of autonomy. While it is easy to choose withdrawal, it is difficult to achieve affiliation, especially for the chronic patient who exhibits symptomology (Segal, Baumohl & Johnson 1977).

It is extraordinarily difficult for these chronic patients to develop the supportive and protective relations associated with a home. Often, they are surrounded by people whom they appraise as fundamentally untrustworthy, and their autonomous existence is filled with loneliness, the fear of victimization, and boredom. In their interpersonal relations, these individuals maintain a sense of control by practising avoidance. It is not, however, a cool and detached avoidance of all sentiment and affection, but rather an ambivalent, hot-and-cold cycle of "pseudo-kinship" and rejection wherein relations are alternately affectionate and hostile, intimate and distant, as though some threshold of sentiment and commitment is breached, resulting in the re-establishment of distance and the often brutal reaffirmation of noncommital ties.

As chronically poor people, former patients have difficulty purchasing secure tenure on living space that could fulfill the spatial requirements of a home. They must make do with whatever they can find, and what they can find is infrequently secure. Indeed, when homelessness is measured, it is usually rendered in terms of some number of "undomiciled" individuals; that is, those without a regular abode who live in various transient shelters—box cars, well concealed shrubbery, or under bridges. This, of course, is merely one important indicator of the disaffiliation of which homelessness is comprised, but it allows some rough estimate of its magnitude. Baxter & Hopper (1981), summarizing the reports of social welfare and mental health agencies in five large Eastern USA cities, report that acknowledged underestimates of the homeless are 36,000 in New

York, 5,000–10,000 in the District of Columbia, 4,000–8,000 in Boston, 8,000–9,000 in Baltimore, and over 3,000 in Philadelphia.

Some unknown, but presumably very high, percentage of this population consists of chronic mental patients. A one-month survey of lodgers in a Berkeley, California, shelter found that upwards of 40% had been hospitalized for psychiatric problems at some time (Berkeley Support Services 1977), and a week-long survey of 295 patrons of a Berkeley food-line found that 22% had been psychiatric inpatients at some point (Baumohl & Miller 1974). Tabler (1982) reported 31% ($N = 269$) of Baltimore's City Shelter residents, and Lewis (1978) reported 60% ($N = 76$) of San Francisco Travelers Aid applicants, as having psychiatric histories. Using psychiatric exams, Chmiel *et al.* (1979) reported 43% ($N = 35$) of transient migrants in Charlottesville, Virginia, and Arce *et al.* (1983) reported 40% ($N = 179$) of Philadelphia city-run shelter residents, to be mentally ill. Finally, using interview ratings of mental disorder, the New York State Office of Mental Health (1982) found positive indications of mental illness in <25% ($N = 107$) of the men using the city shelter, and Brown *et al.* (1983) found 20% with positive indications of mental illness among Phoenix foodline users.

These figures do not include the large numbers of chronic patients living in rooming houses, single-room-occupancy hotels, and other housing which both affords and compounds social isolation. Schwartz & Goldfinger (1981), summarizing an unpublished study by Chafetz, report that:

> In a study of 420 randomly selected patients seen in the same emergency services and similarly diagnosed, 20.9 per cent were found to have no local residence. An additional 52.5 per cent claimed residence in a district of San Franciso noted to have no single-family residential homes, with 89 per cent of the residences hotel rooms or "studio apartments" (p. 471).

Redevelopment, in the form of tourist hotel and condominium conversion, or by conversion to nonresidential use, is proceeding at an ominous pace, and seriously threatens this form of housing. The San Francisco Department of City Planning (1980) concluded: "If conversion continues at the same rate as the past five years, vacancies in hotels will disappear within one or two years." The Department further noted that:

> Given the limitation of social and economic resources, residential hotel tenants will be severely affected if their current homes are converted to non-residential uses. . . . Aside from low rental . . ., the proximity of the hotels to the downtown area, and the accessibility to a host of service agencies which are situated close to the hotels all provide an opportunity for the tenants, particularly the elderly and the handicapped, to live a relatively independent life.

At one point during the years of our research, we observed an unsuccessful tenant action by the residents of an SRO hotel, many of them chronic patients who were attempting to preserve their homes against the redevelopment plans of the owner. One tenant explained his feeling this way:

> This is the way I see it, and fuck him [the owner] if he don't agree. I rent this box. Four walls. About 8 by 8 by 8. And when I pay him, it's mine. I put my stuff on the walls, I play my radio, my music. I lock the door and space out and nobody comes in here I don't want. If he can take this away from me, what else have I got? I'm back on the street. Or back in that goddamned hostel listening to all those assholes cough and snore all night long, and I gotta be out at 8 in the morning. He might as well just come busting in here and strip off my clothes and kick me in the head. I'll burn this motherfucker down first. Before he does that to me I'll torch this sucker.

The hotel still stands and the tenants are gone, back to the transient hostel, the street, or to another SRO where, in all likelihood, the cycle of dispossession will be repeated. Impoverished chronic patients pay dearly for their autonomy, their freedom from supervision and group living. As Berkeley street poet Julia Vinograd wrote in "Downhill" (1971):

> I don't have a home,
> And I live there all the time.

Conclusions

Since the codification of the Mann/Dix doctrine in the New York State Care Act of 1890, which guaranteed complete state care for the seriously mentally ill, the state has been in the business of providing a home for chronic patients. From the outset, the terms of this obligation have focused upon the rudiments of survival: food, shelter, clothing, and of course, "humane care" or simple human kindness. In the mental hospital, in the bosom of *parens patriae*, the children of chaos were to find an orderly parental household where the bills were paid and brows were cooled with kind attention. Such a relationship between the state and the mentally ill has, until very recently, assumed a degree of ready dependence on the part of the patient who, by forfeiting his autonomy, could be assured of stability and security through the medium of a ready-made home.

In this chapter we have contended that this sort of solution has been workable for some, perhaps many, of the chronically mentally ill, but that it has inherent limitations common to all institutional care, no matter how "patient-centered" and benign, for it is in the exercise of personal autonomy, in the expression of individual tastes and desires, that social life and physical place come to form the sense of home that is an egosyntonic extension of self.

The state's role in providing homes for the chronically mentally ill has changed in accommodation to the patient's autonomy. By and large, the state is no longer principally an overseer of large, segregated "total institutions," but has become, instead, a provider of financial assistance to independent consumers of community-based sheltered care or various unsupervised arrangements. Similarly, the nature of sheltered care has changed. The family care system's reliance upon family atmosphere and lower-middle-class settings was unrealistic, failing to provide sufficient diversity to accommodate the broad range of preferences in a hetero-geneous chronic patient population. Today's diverse sheltered-care industry is a vast improvement on the provincialism of family care, but it is still limited by inevitable attention to law and propriety and by the constraints of group living. In general, sheltered care wrings fewer com-promises from its residents than did hospital or family care, but its demands are still sufficiently stringent to exclude or drive out many chronic patients.

Consequently, thousands of chronic patients, many of them young, have turned up in precisely those areas that have traditionally housed the impoverished and disconnected, the various "skid-row"-like areas of our cities. Here, social expectations are minimal and institutional constraint is largely evaded. At the cost of intimacy and security, here, finally, is the hole in the wall where life is tough but nominally free.

It is in this group that we see the full-blown symptoms of the ambivalent relationship between chronic patients and the system of care that surrounds them, for the psychological and material underpinnings of their autonomy are fragile. They are vulnerable to prolonged social isolation, periodic dispossession, and occasional victimization. They are often made dependent by circumstance, and failing to cope, are confronted with those institutions they fear will engulf them. While they may need what such institutions have to offer, they are wary of the price.

In this connection, Wiseman (1970) and Lewis & Hugi (1981) have described what we believe to be a typical pattern of service utilization among impoverished, free-living chronic patients: the selective use of "therapeutic stations" for purposes that differ from the stated mission of the institution. For example, the hospital is not viewed as a site of treatment, but as a site of temporary refuge; the aftercare clinic not as a site of therapy but as a safe place to make contact; the mental health worker is not a therapist, but a mailbox, telephone, or automatic banking teller. This modest manipulation of the system of care enables chronic patients to fulfill dependency needs, or simply needs for sociability, without sacrificing control of their circumstances for long or without opening their homes, whether hotel room or ventilator shaft, to intrusion by strangers.

Increasingly, this pattern has been recognized for what it is and ironically institutionalized, after a fashion. A number of drop-in programs, most of them store-fronts, have deliberately adopted the function of a community living-room, and have dispensed with most therapeutic and institutional formalities (cf., Segal & Baumohl 1980, 1985). Hospital psychiatric emergency rooms, while hamstrung by limited bed space in their ability to provide refuge, have nonetheless begun to assume responsibility for getting chronic patients to other respite settings. For those chronic patients who approach the hospital involuntarily or in desperation, and who are not gravely disabled or a danger to themselves or others, this is a constructive development. For those who desperately want the trappings of inpatient care and security, who want to be completely dependent for a time, the current system seems a bit over-weaning.

Quite simply, what we advocate for community care is diversity. If chronic patients are ever to be at home anywhere, they must find environments consistent with their varying tastes. Thus, appropriate variance in environments must be created where it does not exist, and must be preserved where already present. Rising property values and the failure of government subsidies to keep pace with inflation in operating costs threaten diversity in the sheltered-care industry. Urban renewal, largely in the form of condominium and tourist-hotel conversion, seriously threatens the existence of inexpensive rooming houses and residential hotels. The residential displacement of the chronically mentally ill is therefore a compelling matter. We must pay serious attention to the erosion of their resources or face a return to the use of long-term hospitalization, or the evils of some resurrected poorhouse in which the mentally ill are abused and exploited.

Acknowledgments

The research on which this chapter is based was supported in part by Grant no. 1-R03-H504564 from the National Center for Health Services Research, and a Faculty Research Grant from the Committee on Research, University of California, Berkeley.

References

Anderson, N. 1923. *The hobo*. Chicago: University of Chicago Press.
Anderson, N. 1940. *Men on the move*. Chicago: University of Chicago Press.
Arce, A. A., M. Tadlock & M. J. Vergare 1983. A psychiatric profile of street people admitted to an emergency shelter. *Hospital Community Psychiatry* **34**, 812–17.

Baumohl, J. & H. Miller 1974. *Down and out in Berkeley*. Berkeley, California: City of Berkeley–University of California Community Affairs Committee.

Baxter, E. & K. Hopper 1981. *Private lives/public places*. New York: Community Service Society.

Berkeley Support Services 1977. Internal memorandum. November.

Bettelheim, B. & E. Sylvester 1948. A therapeutic milieu. *American Journal of Orthopsychiatry* **18**, 191–206.

Braginsky, B. M., D. D. Braginsky & K. Ring 1969. *Methods of madness: the mental hospital as a last resort*. New York: Holt, Rinehart and Winston.

Brown, C., S. MacFarlane & R. Paredes 1983. *The homeless of Phoenix: who are they? And what should be done?* Phoenix South Community Mental Health Center.

Brown, G. W., J. L. T. Birley & J. K. Wing 1972. Influence of family life on the course of schizophrenic disorders: a replication. *British Journal of Psychiatry* **121**, 241–58.

Caplow, T., H. M. Bahr & D. Sternberg 1968. Homelessness. In *International encyclopedia of the social sciences*, D. Sills (ed.), vol. 6, 494–9. New York: Macmillan.

Chmiel, A. J., S. Akhtar & J. Morris 1979. The long-distance psychiatric patient in the emergency room. *International Journal of Social Psychiatry* **25**, 38–46.

Goffman, E. 1961. *Asylums*. New York: Doubleday.

Grass, G. 1961. *The tin drum*. New York: Pantheon.

King, R. D., N. V. Raynes & J. Tizard 1971. *Patterns of residential care: sociological studies in institutions for handicapped children*. London: Routledge & Kegan Paul.

Langner, E. J. & J. Rodin 1976. The effects of choice and enhanced personal responsibility for the aged: a field experiment in an institutional setting. *Journal of Personality and Social Psychology* **34**, 191–8.

Lewis, D. A. & R. Hugi 1981. Therapeutic stations and the chronically treated mentally ill. *Social Service Review* **55**, 206–20.

Lewis, N. 1978. *Community intake services for the transient mentally disabled* (TMD). Travelers Aid Society of San Francisco.

Martin, D. V. 1955. "Institutionalism," *Lancet* **1,** 6942, 1188–90.

Moline, R. A. 1977. The therapeutic community and milieu therapy: a review and current assessment. *Community Mental Health Review* **2**, 1–13.

New York State Office of Mental Health 1982. *Who are the homeless? A study of randomly selected men who use the New York City Shelters*. Albany, New York, May.

Phares, E. J. & J. T. Lamiell 1977. Personality. *Annual Review of Psychology* **28**, 113–40.

Rabkin, J. G. 1979. Criminal behavior of discharged mental patients: a critical appraisal of the research. *Psychological Bulletin* **86**, 1–27.

San Franciso Department of City Planning 1980. *The conversion and demolition of residential hotel units*. San Francisco: Board of Supervisors of the City and County of San Francisco, November.

Scheff, T. J. 1966. *Being mentally ill: a sociological theory*. Chicago: Aldine.

Schwartz, S. R. & S. M. Goldfinger 1981. The new chronic patient: clinical characteristics of an emerging sub-group. *Hospital and Community Psychiatry* **32**, 47–74.

Segal, S. P. & U. Aviram 1978. *The mentally ill in community-based sheltered-care.* New York: John Wiley.

Segal, S. P. & J. Baumohl 1980. Engaging the disengaged. *Social Work* **25**, 358–66.

Segal, S. P. & J. Baumohl 1981. Toward harmonious community care placement. In *New directions for mental health services: issues in community residential care*, R. Budson (ed.), 49–61. San Francisco: Jossey-Bass.

Segal, S. P. & J. Baumohl 1985. The community living room. *Social Casework* **66**, 111–16.

Segal, S. P. & E. W. Moyles 1979. Management style and institutional dependency in sheltered care. *Social Psychiatry* **14**, 159–65.

Segal, S. P., J. Baumohl & E. Johnson 1977. Falling through the cracks: mental disorder and social margin in a young vagrant population. *Social Problems* **24**, 387–400.

Segal, S. P., J. Baumohl & E. W. Moyles 1980. Neighborhood types and community reaction to the mentally ill: a paradox of intensity. *Journal of Health and Social Behavior* **21**, 345–59.

Smith, C. J. & R. Q. Hanham 1981. Proximity and the formation of public attitudes towards mental illness. *Environment and Planning A* **13**, 147–65.

Trute, B. & S. P. Segal 1976. Census tract predictors and the social integration of sheltered care residents. *Social Psychiatry* **11**, 153–61.

Vinograd, J. 1971. *Street feet.* Berkeley, Calif.: Thorp Springs Press.

Wing, J. 1962. Institutionalism in mental hospitals. *British Journal of Sociology and Clinical Psychology* **1**, 38–51.

Wiseman, J. 1970. *Stations of the lost: the treatment of skid row alcoholics.* Englewood Cliffs, N.J.: Prentice-Hall.

Zigler, E. & D. A. Balla 1977. Impact of institutional experience on the behavior and development of retarded persons. *American Journal of Mental Deficiency* **82**, 1–11.

13 *To back wards?—prospects for reinstitutionalization of the mentally disabled*

JENNIFER R. WOLCH,
CYNTHIA A. NELSON, and
ANNETTE RUBALCABA

Introduction

Professional and public commitment to the community-based care philosophy that has guided mental health policy for the past three decades may be waning. Most experts now acknowledge, albeit often reluctantly, that community care is an ideal that may never be fully realized in practice. Community mental health advocates, spurred by genuine concern over the worsening plight of the mentally disabled, are enjoying a renewed public interest in their efforts; yet simultaneously, there are significant signs of retrenchment from community care theory and practice. The emphasis on provision of shelters as an expedient response to the burgeoning problem of the homeless mentally disabled; growing concern about upgrading or expanding institutions such as jails and state mental hospitals; and the increasing number of mental health professionals who are aligning themselves with the "new asylum movement" all point towards growing support for reinstitutionalizing the mentally disabled.

We explore this potential here, beginning with an overview of the deinstitutionalization movement and its outcomes. We review the factors leading to its "failure," and the ghettoization of the mentally disabled in urban core areas; the destabilizing impacts of gentrification, urban redevelopment, and social-service spending cuts on these fragile coping environments; and evolving outcomes for the mentally disabled. These outcomes include transinstitutionalization to inappropriate treatment settings such as jails and nursing homes, and homelessness which, ironically, has been instrumental in raising public consciousness concerning the mentally disabled and has fueled pressures for their reinstitutionalization.

In the final sections of the chapter, we draw on California's experience, beginning with a review of state mental health policy, often regarded as innovative and progressive. We document the crisis of California's mentally disabled in the wake of deinstitutionalization, and explore public and professional responses to this crisis, characterized by efforts to expand institutional capacity (in both traditional hospital and nonhospital settings), increase the degree of social control over the mentally disabled, and shift the intergovernmental, sectoral, and spatial pattern of responsibility for the mentally disabled, all of which signal a movement toward reinstitutionalization.

Finally, we consider the extent to which signs of retrenchment, spurred perhaps by a small but zealous vanguard, presage a far-reaching philosophical and ideological realignment among professionals and the public versus a temporary setback for the community care movement. We conclude with a discussion of successful litigation and legislative initiatives designed to redress present inadequacies of mental health care programs, and thereby move us closer to a comprehensive and sustainable community care system, and explore their implications for future trends in services delivery for the mentally disabled.

The unfulfilled promise of deinstitutionalization

With the advantage of hindsight, we can see that the era of deinstitutionalization was ushered in with much naivete and many simplistic notions . . . The importance of developing . . . supportive living arrangements was not clearly seen, or at least not implemented. Community treatment was much discussed, but there was no clear idea as to what it should consist of, and the resistance of community mental health centers to providing services to the chronically mentally ill was not anticipated. Nor was it foreseen how reluctant many states would be to allocate funds for community-based services (Lamb 1984: 900–1).

Excluded from affluent suburbs, [the mentally disabled] clustered in fading inner-city zones, drawn by cheap housing and access to public and commercial services. By the mid-seventies, the exodus from large-scale institutions had produced a new kind of urban ghetto . . . (Wolch & Gabriel 1985: 53).

Since its implementation three decades ago, deinstitutionalization policy has failed to live up to the expectations of politicians, professionals, the public, and the mentally disabled. Although legislative initiatives creating a system of community-based mental health care represented a positive step towards improving and protecting the rights of the mentally disabled, what emerged were "awkward" and "underdeveloped" systems that, for a number of reasons, were unable to provide the long-term care and support services needed by the chronically ill (Nickerson 1985a).

Among the most frequently cited factors responsible for this disappointing performance was the lack of financial support for community mental health networks. In many cases, mental health funds continued to be targeted to state facilities while cities, already financially burdened, tried to cope with the influx of ex-patients. Lacking sufficient resources, localities found it nearly impossible to construct community-care systems that provided the full range of cash and in-kind income supplements, health care, mental health, and rehabilitation services needed by this group (Nickerson 1985a).

Community mental health programs were also plagued by lack of planning and coordination. As Bassuk (1984) notes, community centers failed to coordinate their activities with state institutions. Furthermore, state hospitals provided treatment and services under one roof, whereas no analogous entity was created to oversee the numerous services required by clients living in the community (Lamb 1984).

Finally, the concept of deinstitutionalization was flawed by the notion that serious, chronic mental disorders could be minimized, if not totally prevented, through care provided within the local community. The community care paradigm was never sufficiently validated, despite its emergence as the conceptual and ideological basis for mental health policy nationwide (Lyons 1984: ch. 4). Consequently, community mental health centers failed to fully address the needs of the mentally disabled, particularly those with chronic illnesses: rather, programs offered by outpatient clinics emphasized counseling and other therapy aimed at people suffering from anxiety or mild depression (but without identifiable mental disorders), those whose mental problems were not incapacitating, and those who showed the most "promise" for recovery (Nickerson 1985b).

Studies from the mid-1970s have shown that, as a result of inadequacies in the community-based service network coupled with urban social and economic conditions, the mentally disabled (along with such other service-dependent populations as the physically handicapped, the needy elderly, and the retarded) become ghettoized in decaying central-city areas. In these zones, property values were low, and community opposition to service facility entry was weak (Wolpert, Dear & Crawford 1975, Wolpert & Wolpert 1976, Lamb 1979). Housed in group homes and board-and-care facilities, as well as "transinstitutionalized" to nursing homes, mentally disabled ex-patients typically subsisted near the povery line, and—often heavily medicated—"shuffle[d] to oblivion" (Reich & Siegal 1973). Nonetheless, most clients preferred to stay out of large-scale institutions community, even though they remained unaccepted by and inadequately cared for in the community.

By the late 1970s and early 1980s, their prospects had worsened. As documented in several metropolitan areas, pressures to gentrify and redevelop the urban "zone of dependence" had begun to push mentally disabled and other service-dependent residents and their support facilities out (Wolch & Gabriel 1985). Suburban housing price escalation, led by the no-growth movements of the 1970s, along with continued regional and central-city job expansion, had led middle-income households to inner-city neighborhoods. There, new residents joined city politicians to revitalize their downtown areas and improve sagging local tax bases, in an increasingly successful attempt to dismantle the meager community-based service network. At the same time, however, pressure on state hospitals to keep patient counts to a minimum, as well as policies which protect client rights by limiting powers of involuntary commitment, foreclosed a retreat back to state mental hospitals as a service option.

Evolving outcomes for the mentally disabled: transinstitutionalization and homelessness

As one mental health professional put it, "mentally ill persons . . . are thought to be too dangerous to be accepted for treatment [at community health centers] but not dangerous enough to be committed [to mental hospitals] . . . the criminal justice system [has become] the system that can't say no . . . they are becoming the . . . poor man's mental hospital" (Nickerson 1985a: 1).

Now we see thousands of [homeless] people on the streets, under bridges, on river banks and along railroad tracks (Bronzan, in Jacobs 1985a: I: 1).

Urban renewal and gentrification in the inner city, coupled with cutbacks in social services in the urban core, have led mentally disabled persons to seek shelter and treatment in even less adequate community settings. Although few studies have attempted to systematically track their mobility, many mentally disabled persons have been found living in single-room-occupancy (SRO) hotels or flophouses, which offer only the most meager of living accommodation and limited access to needed health care and social services. Others have dispersed to adjacent communities which have yet to mount significant opposition to their presence (US General Accounting Office 1983).

However, a number of trends indicate growing rates of "trans-institutionalization" to inappropriate treatment settings such as skilled nursing facilities, which offer custodial care and limited health care but no mental health programming. In the USA in 1977, 350,000 out of 1.3 million nursing-home residents nationwide were diagnosed with either a primary or secondary level of mental disorder; in 1984, the National Institute of Mental Health estimated that the number had increased to 750,000 (US General Accounting Office 1977, Ahr & Holcomb 1985, Nickerson 1985a). In Massachusetts, for example, a survey found that the number of former mental patients residing in nursing homes ranged from 30% to 90% of facility clients (Nickerson 1985a). Many of these individuals were released from state hospitals, bypassing the community mental health system to "follow the beds." Others have undoubtedly been placed in such facilities due to the absence of more appropriate community settings.

The lack of adequate community supports has also led to incarceration of the mentally disabled within the criminal justice system for crimes which are more indicative of their mental health disabilities than criminal intent. Systematic evidence for this trend is only now emerging, as policy makers call for studies of mental disorder among the criminal justice population, in response to mounting problems in detention facilities associated with disordered offenders (such studies are currently under way in Canada and in the state of California, for instance). Recent media reports are more abundant. They suggest that this type of transinstitutionalization has reached alarming proportions. In Virginia, for example, at least 12,000 mentally ill persons were estimated to have been jailed annually due to the lack of appropriate community-based residential and psychiatric facilities (Boodman 1985). This problem is exacerbated by pressure on state hospitals to keep patient counts to a minimum, by policies which protect client rights by limiting involuntary commitment, and by society's limited tolerance of the behavior patterns manifested by the mentally ill.

Transinstitutionalization of the mentally disabled has been recognized as a problem since in the mid-1970s, although rates seem to have been increasing dramatically since then. But perhaps an even more disturbing outcome of deinstitutionalization is the recent and widely publicized increase in the number of homeless mentally disabled persons. Although estimates of the size of the homeless population vary widely, ranging from 250,000 to 2.5 million, most analysts agree that numbers have been increasing, in large part, due to an expansion in the homeless mentally disabled population (Bassuk 1984).

For years, the homeless population was typified by the familiar Skid Row transient: male, alcoholic, averaging 50 years of age. Now young persons are found among the homeless and are frequently diagnosed as schizophrenic, or as suffering from affective and personality disorders and substance abuse (Bachrach 1984, Nickerson 1985b). Bachrach also cites "the existence of impoverished and highly stressed social networks, revolving-door utilization of the mental health service system, revolving-door involvement in the criminal justice system, a high prevalence of physical illness, and a high degree of resistance to traditional treatment interventions, as "characteristic of many homeless mentally disabled persons" (Bachrach 1984: 12).

Media accounts, and the few existing demographic studies of the shelter population, reveal the extent to which the crisis of the homeless mentally disabled has reached into communities nationwide. Despite problems of defining "mental disability" and obtaining representative samples, there is a growing consensus that a significant share of the homeless suffer from some form of mental disability. In Boston, for example, most guests at the sample of homeless shelters studied by Bassuk are young (in their thirties) and have a history of mental illness (Nickerson 1985b: 12). In St. Louis, roughly half of the clients using homeless services were judged to be mentally disabled, showing symptoms of paranoid ideation and psychosis (Morse *et al.* 1985). A staggering 97% of all guests at a homeless shelter in the Washington, D.C. area were found to suffer from some form of mental disability (Huguenin 1984). Using more restrictive definitions of mental disability, Farr & Koegel (1986) found lower but still significant proportions (33%) of the Los Angeles Skid Row population to be mentally disordered.

The growing number of young adults in age groups most at risk for chronic mental disability has, in part, been responsible for recent increases in the number of homeless mentally ill (Bachrach 1984). Drastic cutbacks in public spending for social services and the absence of fully developed, coordinated and funded community-based programs for the chronically mentally disabled are perhaps more significant factors. In fact, evidence shows that increasing numbers of the homeless mentally disabled have had little or no contact with state hospitals or the ostensible "safety net" of the community mental health system (Lamb 1984, Bachrach 1984).

Responses to public outcry and professional pressure: the Californian experience

It will take a long time and many more restorations to get the (California) program back to where we were in the mid-1970s. And we were not in good shape then (Elpers, in Jacobs 1985c: 11).

Research on community-based care problems in California in general, and in Los Angeles County in particular, enables a preliminary assessment of the policy response to mounting public and professional pressure to ameliorate the crisis of the mentally disabled. California is frequently a "bell-weather" state, at the forefront of social policy trends, and so examination of the Californian experience may be indicative of future events in other areas. In this section, we first review the history of mental health care policy in California, then describe the outcomes of both policy and urban change for community-based clients and, finally, identify the major elements in the political response to the mounting problems of the state's mentally disabled population.

BACKGROUND OF MENTAL HEALTH POLICY IN CALIFORNIA

Like other states in the nation, California began to release large numbers of mentally disabled clients from its state hospital system during the 1960s. From an all-time high of 37,500 residents in 1959, state hospital capacity had fallen to under 2,500 by the mid-1980s (Wolch & Gabriel 1985, Dear & Wolch 1986). In addition to establishing federally-funded Community Mental Health Centers in urban areas, the state government also acted to promote deinstitutionalization. The first legislative step along the path of transition from an institution-based mode of service to community-based care was the 1957 Short–Doyle Act, which set up a system of state funding for county-level programs. Later, the Lanterman–Patris–Short (LPS) Act of 1967 made it far more difficult to involuntarily commit mentally disabled persons to state mental hospitals and keep them there (Anderson 1984: 215—18).

As elsewhere, local governments (in this case counties) were not prepared to establish comprehensive mental health treatment programs, many were not particularly committed to the notion of community-based care, and coordination between the state hospital system and fledgling local programs was minimal. Most significantly, state funds were inadequate; then-Governor Reagan signed the LPS Bill, but authorized far less money than the authors of the bill deemed necessary. Funds from the shrinking state hospital system did not "follow" clients into the community.

Not only were initial funding levels dangerously low, but subsequent fiscal policies at all levels of government exacerbated the situation. During the Brown administration of the 1970s, fiscal conservatism and the local impacts of Proposition 13 "sent the system into a tailspin" (Anderson 1984: 215). Finally, the dramatic reductions in social spending under President Reagan have had severe implications, particularly for the state's community-based mentally disabled who must rely on cash benefits such as Social Security Disability Insurance and SSI, which are ever-more difficult to obtain; on county hospitals squeezed by medical cuts; on diminishing Foodstamp resources; and on social services resources such as Title XX, depleted by major cuts (for a numerical example of the extent of cuts in one county, see Wolch & Gabriel 1985). Federal cuts have not been offset by increased state or local spending; during his first year in office, Governor Deukmejian vetoed $30 million for mental health, following the trend of curtailing mental health budgets set by his predecessor, Governor Brown. While, during the past fiscal year, Deukmejian has requested increases in state funding for mental health, state financial support will still be less than it was before he took office, even if increases are appropriated (Jacobs 1985a: I: 1).

POLICY OUTCOMES FOR COMMUNITIES AND THE MENTALLY DISABLED
What were the results of this haphazard transfer of care to the community level for California's mentally disabled?

California's experience in this regard was similar to that of other urban areas across the nation. With the advent of deinstitutionalization, the mentally disabled were ghettoized in deteriorating central cities, only to be later displaced in increasing numbers due to social spending cutbacks coupled with gentrification and urban renewal. What our work has uncovered are deteriorating living conditions for the mentally disabled in the community; mounting transinstitutionalization (most frequently, to the criminal justice system); and increased homelessness. In response, there have been distinct moves in the direction of reinstitutionalizing the mentally disabled in traditional facilities and new institutional forms; the imposition of increasingly stringent social controls on the mentally disabled; and dramatic attempts to shift responsibilities for the "knotty problem" of the community-based mentally disabled from one level of government to another, from one public department to another, and from one locale to another.

Community living arrangements   The plight of mentally disabled residents of congregate living quarters seems to have grown substantially worse, primarily due to heightened competition for a shrinking supply of adequate facilities.

On the supply side, competition for adequate community living situations has grown due to demolition of facilities in the path of redevelopment, and re-conversion of properties back to family residential use (Wolch & Gabriel 1985). Moreover, although not well documented, continued neighborhood opposition to group-care facilities has frustrated attempts to establish new community-care capacity.

On the demand side, changes in relative payment schedules for retarded versus mentally disabled has led to provider preferences for retarded clients. In 1977, the state began to increase reimbursements for the board and care of retarded adults, while holding down levels for the mentally disabled; the disparity is now almost $500 per month ($945 for retarded adults versus $503 for mentally disabled) (Jacobs 1985d: I: 3). As a result, few home operators are willing to take in the mentally disabled, particularly the most severely disturbed who require extensive supervision.

Increasing competition has effectively forced mentally disabled residents out of higher-quality board-and-care homes. Many reside in substandard facilities; one-third of the 22,000 licensed board-and-care homes, housing 150,000 people, are considered substandard (California State Commission on California Government Organization and Economy 1983). Others have wound up in rundown apartments and rooming houses, and in unlicensed facilities which offer little supervision or activity programs, in frequently brutalizing conditions (*Los Angeles Times* 1985a: I: 33).

Homelessness   The rate of homelessness in the state has grown dramatically since 1980, according to both formal and informal estimates (all very imperfect); the most recent figure cited by state mental health officials is 75,000 (Jacobs 1985d). State mental health officials corroborate findings of the few research reports that have been published, as well as informal estimates of service operators: a large share of the homeless in California are mentally disabled. Estimates for Los Angeles, for instance, range from 20% to 40%; if drug and alcohol abusers are included (many of whom suffer mental disabilities), the proportion is considerably higher (Jacobs 1985d, Farr & Koegel 1986, Robertson, Ropers & Boyer 1985). Los Angeles in particular has become a "mecca" for the homeless; dubbed the "homeless capital of the nation," the Department of Housing and Urban Development estimates that up to 30,000 are homeless in Los Angeles County (US Department of Housing and Urban Development 1984). Again, local estimates indicate that a high proportion of the homeless population is mentally disabled, either ex-patients released from state mental hospitals or, as is increasingly common, part of the "young chronic drifter" population receiving growing attention in the psychiatric literature (Lamb 1982).

Transinstitutionalization   The problem of misassignment (or trans-institutionalization) of the mentally ill to either medical facilities lacking psychosocial supports, or to criminal justice facilities, has been a recurring problem since the advent of deinstitutionalization. However, while placement in skilled nursing facilities and other medical units was once the predominant type of transinstitutionalization (US General Accounting Office 1977), according to state and local mental health and criminal justice officials, prisons and jails are now being deluged with mentally disabled persons drawn particularly from the ranks of the homeless. In California, this trend has exacerbated an explosion in the incarcerated population brought about by the imposition of stiffer sentencing laws and the Administration's "law and order" stance. Like criminal justice systems in many other parts of the country, the state prison system is now severely overcrowded (by 60%) (Lyons 1984: III: 1; Paddock 1985: I: 16). In Los Angeles County, the daily jail population has leapt from 9,000 inmates in 1980 to the current total of 17,000, 6,000 more than the design capacity of local facilities (Paddock 1985: I: 16). While estimates of the mentally disabled proportion of the criminal justice population are scarce (pending state legislation calls for a study of this very issue), state officials acknowledge that poor community living opportunities and the homeless-ness crisis have resulted in a dramatic upsurge of mentally disabled in the criminal justice system[1].

POLICY RESPONSES AND PROBLEM SHIFTING
The crisis of deinstitutionalization has not gone unnoticed by politicians

and public officials, psychiatric professionals, community groups, or community mental health advocates. Although just emerging and not yet well documented, several responses in the direction of reinstitutionalization of the mentally disabled can be identified. These include:

(1) public policy to increase and protect state and local institutional capacity;
(2) attempts to strengthen social control measures; and
(3) state and local policies, and community opposition movements, to shift the intergovernmental, sectoral, and spatial division of responsibility for the mentally disabled.

Increasing institutional capacity   The state and local governments are seeking to expand the institutional capacity available to handle the mentally disabled. These efforts include:

(1) construction of and increased funding for shelters for the homeless;
(2) the upgrading of the state mental hospital system, and expansion of local inpatient facilities; and
(3) expansion of criminal justice beds, along with segregation of mentally disordered offenders.

Together, these policies represent an effort toward reinstitutionalization of a growing proportion of the mentally disabled.

The construction and expansion of existing shelters for the homeless has occurred across the state, in urban areas burdened with increasing numbers of the hungry and homeless. While these shelters are designed to be temporary or transitional lodging, residents frequently have extended lengths of stay, or they move in and out of shelters on a continuous basis. The result is that these facilities have become yet another way in which the mentally disabled are institutionalized, and hence spatially and socially isolated.

In an effort to increase the number and capacity of shelters, new state legislation has been initiated to supply emergency shelters for the homeless, and for veterans, and to develop transitional housing. The initial state augmentation proposed for shelters was $20 million. Public shelter capacity in Los Angeles County, which stood at about 1,500 bed spaces as of spring 1984, received a boost with the construction of a 19,000 square foot, 138-bed "temporary" plywood shelter, built by union volunteers in the Skid Row zone of Los Angeles. There have also been various initiatives to construct new additional shelters in the cities of Santa Monica and West Hollywood, as well as in San Pedro and San Fernando Valley districts of the city of Los Angeles (Los Angeles County Department of Mental Health 1985; *Los Angeles Times* 1985b: II: 4; Clayton 1985: 12).

This trend toward erection of shelters mirrors the pattern across the country. For example, the City of New York opened a shelter on an isolated and uninhabited island, which now houses an average of 500 to 600 persons daily (Baxter & Hopper 1982: 30); the City also began a $64 million shelter-building program (Boodman 1985). In Boston, the State Department of Mental Health converted a gymnasium into a shelter exclusively for the homeless mentally disabled (Nickerson 1985a: 22). Bergen County (New Jersey) opened a shelter in 1984 (Parisi 1985: I: 36); and Massachusetts, in the 1984/5 fiscal year, allocated $5.3 million for a total of 1,500 shelter beds in 17 public and 60 private shelters for the homeless (Parisi 1985).

California has also led the way in funding increased resources for the state mental hospital system, in an effort to upgrade staffing levels and improve seriously deteriorated physical facilities. The Deukmejian administration has committed $133 million over the next five years to accomplish this goal, designed to permit the hospital system to meet national professional standards, and be reaccredited for receipt of federal reimbursements; but no specific long-term commitment has been made to community-based service delivery—a pattern similar to that found in other states (Jacobs 1985b: I: 3; Boodman 1985: A: 16; Nickerson 1985a: 22).

Although efforts to upgrade the state mental hospitals have been supported by the state's psychiatric workers union, which is concerned with state hospital safety problems (Hernandez 1985: I: 24), reaccreditation is also the objective of many mental health professionals influenced by the "new asylum" movements in psychiatry. Advocates of this movement see an upgraded state hospital system as a necessary and valuable resource for the most severely disabled. Proponents point to the number of acutely ill and often dangerous persons who require a more "structured" environment (Lamb & Lamb 1984, Krauthammer 1985, Lamb & Peel 1984, Rosenblatt 1984, Boffey 1984, Talbott 1984). Long-term asylum may be the necessary and humane option, although involuntary placement in asylums may infringe on client rights; "asylum means taking people away to be cared for, whether they like it or not. That means taking control—and that means violating their rights, as currently defined" (Krauthammer 1985: A15a). But some suggest that the only solution to the problem of rights violation is to limit the rights in question (Lamb 1984).

The plans to upgrade the system do not increase the bed capacity of the state hospital system; but increasing the quality of care may reduce existing disincentives for utilization of these facilities. Moreover, long-range plans for the mental health system, still in the initial design stage, do include proposals to increase hospital capacity along with expansion of community-based service capacity: instead of the 2,200 short-term care beds now in place in the state mental hospital system, a new model plan for mental health service system development (dubbed the "California Model") calls for increasing that number to 3,900, and instead of the current

1,800 long-term rehabilitation beds in existence, suggests the need for more than 10,000 (Jacobs 1985b).

In addition to targeting funds for improvement of the state mental hospital system, the state has adopted a renewed policy of transfering responsibility for the mentally disabled to the county level, this time with some additional resources. The new state budget calls for a 14% ($40 million) augmentation in local mental health programs, to be allocated to individual counties for the buy-out of state hospital beds (according to initial proposals), as well as a 4% cost-of-living increase for local programs. However, the majority of the funds are to be used by counties in developing state-approved community programs that can range from long-term hospital beds to independent living arrangements and day-treatment services (California Legislative Analyst 1985).

While seemingly supportive of community-based services, there is indication that local discretion in the utilization of augmentation funds will lead to the development of more extensive inpatient facilities. This may come about as a result of professional pressures for more acute-care beds, as well as from community pressures to remove the mentally ill from their midst. In Los Angeles County, for example, the Director of County Mental Health proposes to use most of the $13.8 million state allocation to build new or support existing residential capacity: for psychiatric beds ($5.1 million); to support shelters for the homeless ($857,461); for children's inpatient beds and services ($2 million); and for mentally ill in the jails ($791,251) (Los Angeles County, Department of Mental Health 1985). This leaves approximately $5 million for other services; after deducting cost-of-living adjustments, and administrative services, community-based out-patient, outreach, and other support programs are left with only $1.5 million—or about 11%—for the community-based system. This is a substantial increase over initial proposals by the department made earlier in the year.

One of the factors underlying this emphasis on beds is the vocal opposition of many local politicians and community leaders to any further reductions in state-hospital bed capacity, and their demands that the indigent mentally disabled be removed from the streets. During this year's hearings on the state mental health budget, for example, the Department of Mental Health advised that 399 beds at a hospital in the Los Angeles vicinity be "bought out" by counties, meaning that these beds would be closed, and the funds redirected to counties on the basis of local proposals to meet mental health needs via alternative, community-based service provision. This proposal was vehemently quashed by legislators, led by a state senator from the Los Angeles area. Policy makers questioned whether proposed community-based programs had the demonstrated ability to substitute for state mental hospital beds. Moreover, they emphasized that political pressure from business and community leaders (the "ruling class," in the words of one legislator) to curb and control the homeless population was so strong, that proposals to reduce the state's capacity to isolate the mentally disabled from society would be soundly defeated[2].

Finally, the state response to the exploding prison population is to build more bed capacity. The Deukmejian administration has won voter approval for a $1.2 billion bond issue to add capacity for 19,000 inmates by 1989. In addition, abandoned facilities will be drawn into service, instructional and recreation rooms (day rooms, classrooms, and gymnasiums) in existing prisons may be used for temporary bed spaces, and minimum security facilities will be upgraded to house a wider range of offenders (*Los Angeles Times* 1985c: II: 4).

In addition to building more beds itself, however, the criminal justice system is increasingly attempting to segregate mentally ill offenders and transfer them to state mental hospitals (*Los Angeles Times* 1985c: II: 4; California Legislative Analyst 1985). The Department of Corrections budget request for the 1985/6 fiscal year includes funds for additional state mental hospital bed spaces over past years, a 250% increase in contracted space since 1982/3 (California Legislative Analyst 1985: 999).

Increasing social control In addition to policies related to institutional capacity, state administrators and legislators have initiated policies which dramatically increase the degree of social control over the mentally disabled, particularly offenders. These initiatives are designed to reduce the prison overcrowding problem by transferring mentally disordered prisoners to the mental health system, and to prevent the release of potentially violent offenders at the end of their terms. Furthermore, pressure to revise basic commitment laws (the Lanterman–Petris–Short Act) is growing and likely to result in legislative action; professional groups, such as the Los Angeles Psychiatric Association, are behind such initiatives (Jacobs 1985a: I: 1).

Two bills currently under discussion in the state Legislature are indicative of the new efforts to alter involuntary commitment procedures as they affect mentally disordered offenders. Although they have been amended and weakened during legislative debate, both bills have a similar agenda— to circumvent indeterminant sentencing laws, and to require state hospital treatement of mentally disordered offenders coming out of the criminal justice system. One bill (SB 1054), as originally drafted, would have blocked the release of as many as 300 prisoners per year. According to this bill, a new condition of parole would be acceptance of mental hospital treatment unless the State Department of Mental Health certifies that the offender will not be a danger to the health and safety of others while on outpatient status, and will benefit from outpatient status. Once an outpatient, treatment would be compulsory; failure to submit to treatment could result in immediate return to the state hospital. The other bill (SB 1296) is similar; it introduces special provisions for one-year commitment of mentally disordered violent offenders after their sentences have been completed, without a court hearing. This would essentially extend their incarceration in either prison or state mental hospital until deemed "sufficiently improved." In the absence of any improvement in condition, commitment can be extended, subject to court hearing, every year. And again, once on parole, parolees are subject to compulsory treatment and the threat of return to prison or hospital should they refuse such treatment.

These efforts are related to those of other states to overhaul involuntary commitment procedures. For example, the State of Virginia has doubled funding for commitment systems, providing for greater ease in making commitments, and introducing a "provisional discharge" program similar to parole, which would compel the discharged individual to agree to outpatient treatment and medication, with noncompliance resulting in reinstitutionalization without hearing or ability to appeal (Boodman & Moore 1985: D4).

Shifting the problem The crises of homelessness and the jail population explosion have in many ways become "political footballs," with parties responsible for solving some aspect of the crises attempting to pass that football to one another, and thereby avoid the burden of solution or failure. These concerted efforts to foist the "knotty problem" onto others include: (1) attempts to alter the intergovernmental division of responsibility for the mentally disabled; (2) attempts to change the sectoral division of labor between mental health and criminal justice departments; and (3) to shift the spatial distribution of caring responsibilities among urban districts and communities.

At the level of intergovernmental relations, the state has clearly followed a policy of reducing state provision of services, instead providing counties with funds and administrative supports of various types, and "local control" to develop their own systems of mental health care. However, this is also a way to situate the burden of failures at the local level, and protect the Deukmejian administration from attacks on the state's mental health program. At the same time, local governments, faced with major budgetary dilemmas due to soaring relief costs, have begun to attack the state for lack of attention and action on the homelessness question, and for past failures in mental health policy. For instance, Los Angeles County blamed $21.7 million of their $37.5 million deficit on expansion of home-lessness and poverty relief program costs (Vollmer 1985a: II1), and has reported that over half of the continually increasing number of relief requests are from the homeless (Vollmer 1985b: II6). In response, the Los Angeles Grand Jury charged that the state is "shirking its responsibility" for the homelessness problem by requiring localities to provide relief programs but not providing funds for them (Connell 1985a). In their report to the

County Board of Supervisors, the Jury also claimed that the state has sent the mentally disabled back to counties, and failed to send sufficient funds to meet their needs (Connell 1985a). Politically, this has been a (successful) strategy to pressure the state to expand its local funding for the homeless.

Continuing struggles between the State Departments of Mental Health and Corrections reveal the sectoral dimension of problem shifting. Due to differences in professional orientation as well as differences in the political pressures to which each unit is subject, there have been several attempts to transfer responsibility for care of mentally disordered offenders between mental health and criminal justice. The Department of Mental Health favors the development of a continuum of treatment settings for mentally disordered offenders within (and by) the criminal justice system, given their growing numbers in prisons and jails. In contrast, the Department of Corrections is under severe pressure to expand prison capacity and relieve overcrowding; transfer of mentally disordered offenders to state mental hospitals is an attractive way to help alleviate the need for new prison construction. The Mental Health Department response, on the basis of both theory and practice, is to reserve the use of asylums for the noncriminally insane[1].

Finally, business groups, residential communities, and local governments have all attempted to shift the problem of hosting facilities for the homeless and mentally disabled to other locales. The Los Angeles case is particularly revealing. The homeless population there is concentrated in "Skid Row", directly east of the central business district. Here, single-room-occupancy hotels, emergency-service agencies, temporary-employment agencies, missions, and public parks provide support and space for the population. This concentration is the historical legacy of explicit policy strategies by the City of Los Angeles and its Community Redevelopment Agency (CRA), to "contain" the homeless via spatial segregation and isolation. However, like other service-dependent ghettos, Skid Row is being dismantled; currently, CRA plans for the central business district are impeded by Skid Row, leading to an effort to "move" the district further east, as evidenced by city decisions to move a major mission/shelter, and to relocate a "temporary" shelter (to become permanent) further east than initially intended.

In response, a new association of eastern downtown businesses (mainly light industry) has been established to fight this move, and to demand concessions from CRA, claiming that they are unable and unwilling to bear even greater burdens of proximity to the ghetto. As a result, CRA has doubled security forces in the area (Ackerman 1985: 1). The agency also struck a compromise on the issue of relocating its "temporary" shelter, promising to make the relocated shelter also "temporary" instead of permanent—it now has a one-year life (Connell 1985b). The councilman for the Skid Row district reportedly has no intention of allowing a "total concentration" of homeless shelters there, and has proposed the creation of an "outdoor home" for street people in Saugus, a distant semirural part of city's fringe (Connell 1985b).

The call for an outdoor home in Saugus is ironic. The site is the same one as proposed for a new state prison by Los Angeles Mayor Tom Bradley. His selection of the Saugus location came after an earlier proposal to site the prison close to downtown was defeated by neighboring community groups, who claimed that their area was already saturated with criminal justice facilities. The residents of Saugus, however, have launched a vociferous attack on the Mayor's new site selection, jeopardizing the proposal's success.

The problem of the homeless has become increasingly visible, even to residents of better-off neighborhoods heretofore unaccustomed to the sight of homeless persons. In Santa Monica, a mounting homelessness problem has been blamed both on the state and on the City of Los Angeles for not providing adequate services for the homeless, who are then encouraged to migrate from downtown to Santa Monica. Waiting for others to take action, the city has not proposed concrete local policy solutions or programs to meet the needs of the homeless.

Back to back wards?

> To some, reinstitutionalization seems like a simple solution to the problems of deinstitutionalization such as homelessness. But activity and treatment programs geared to the needs of long-term patients can easily be set up in the community, and living conditions, structured or unstructured, can be raised to any level we choose—if adequate funds are made available (Lamb 1984: 904).

Our research on the prospects for reinstitutionalization of the mentally disabled indicates that there are indeed clear signs of renewed professional emphasis, societal willingness, and increased legal authority to isolate the mentally disabled in traditional and new institutions. From our perspective, this is a retrograde step, away from fulfilling the promise of deinstitutionalization, back toward the repressive incarceration so familiar to students of social welfare history. We would like to conclude, however, with some evidence of new program development in California and other parts of the nation which represents an alternative and more positive response to the problems of the mentally disabled.

In California, pressure for reinstitutionalization and tighter social controls on the mentally disabled have put community mental health advocates on the defensive. Amid accusations that deinstitutionalization was a failure, community mental health leaders have attempted to show that the policy itself was not misguided, but its implementation was faulty. In addition, advocates have been active in resisting local efforts to target augmentation funds for inpatient facilities, insisting on more funds for community-based residential alternatives and outpatient services (*Los Angeles Times* 1985b: II: 4). Along with the American Civil Liberties Union, they have also fought changes in involuntary commitments and treatment procedures for mentally disordered offenders, succeeding in substantially weakening proposed legislation (Jacobs 1985c).

In addition, progressive efforts to reform and support the community-based mental health system have been advocated by community mental health organizations and parent associations. As a result of a lengthy review study of the system by Assemblyman Bruce Bronzan (D-Fresno) which incorporated their input, legislation has been passed which seeks to dramatically augment the community-based resource pool. The bill provides for additional funds for the homeless mentally disabled, isolated elderly, and the mentally disabled in jail; increases payments to board-and-care operators for the mentally disabled; establishes local treatment programs for mentally disabled jailed for minor offenses; doubles the number of therapy sessions allowed under Medical (California's version of Medicaid), presently limited to two per month; and launches a model program to monitor potentially dangerous mentally ill offenders after their release from prison to make certain they receive adequate treatment in the community (Jacobs 1985c). The Bronzan–Mojonnier Bill (AB 2541) has met with remarkable success, despite the increased spending inherent in the bills proposals; $20 million has been authorized for the current fiscal year (Los Angeles County, Community and Senior Citizen Services Department 1985).

Other proposed bills are also encouraging. For instance, one bill (SB 667) would require that homeless persons who are detailed under the provision of the LPS Act receive special attention at the time of discharge, instead of simply being released. A second bill (SB 822) requires the Department of Mental Health to set up $1.5-million pilot programs in three large urban counties to provide case management services to homeless chronically mentally disabled persons. Amendments to the 1957 Short–Doyle Act in a third bill (AB 2381) provide additional financial incentives for new and more innovative programs at the county level, and streamlined relationships between counties and the state (Bronzan 1984).

In addition to legislation, the development of a model continuum of mental health care has begun, although it is still in the research and financial analysis stages, and has not been officially endorsed by the Department of Mental Health (the "California Model" referred to earlier). The proposal, developed by a group including legislative staff, county and state mental health officials, professionals, and patient and family advocate organizations, describes a continuum of mental health care that should be available in each community. The mix of services specified in the model makes concessions to demands for more institutional capacity, as mentioned earlier; however, community-treatment facilities are heavily emphasized. Preliminary cost estimates suggest that such a model system would require a doubling of mental health expenditures, to $1.8 billion. While not likely to become official policy in the immediate future, the California model does provide the well articulated vision of an adequate community-based mental health system (Jacobs 1985b).

In other parts of the nation, positive steps are also under way. For example, Massachusetts has planned to spend $10.8 million in 1985 for expansion of income, medical, and mental health care to homeless persons in the community, while also allocating $13.6 million in programs to prevent homelessness (rental assistance, utility payments) (Henshaw 1984: I: 36). New Jersey has committed to spend an additional $7 million on mental health centers and residential development projects for the mentally disabled. Bergen County has used these funds to build scattered-site facilities in upper- and middle-income areas (Henshaw 1984). In western Massachusetts, a model community-based care plan similar to other plans in Madison, Denver, and Rockland County, New York, has been created which offers a rich continuum of services (Goleman 1984: III 1). Finally, all across the country, public-interest lawyers have gone to bat for the homeless and mentally disabled, putting barriers in the way of reinstitutionalization and obtaining increased and improved services in the community.

So, are we on our way back to back wards? There are clear indications that reinstitutionalization has once again become a politically acceptable alternative to the community-based model. In the current political–economic climate, strenuous efforts of progressive professionals, clients themselves, and their families may be required to stave off the pressures for reinstitutionalization. But that effort is well under way in some parts of the country. And it is clearly worthwhile. As Lamb (1984) notes, the development of a caring yet least-restrictive support system for the mentally disabled is entirely possible, as successful efforts on the part of some communities have shown. Fulfillment of the promise of deinstitutionalization is only dependent upon the collective will to commit sufficient resources.

Acknowledgments

The authors extend their thanks to Virginia Westbrook, and the School of Urban and Regional Planning at the University of Southern California, for administrative support.

Notes

1 Richard Mandella, Chief, Forensic Services, California State Department of Mental Health, pers. comm., March 1985.
2 William De Risi, California Department of Mental Health, Division of State Hospitals, pers. comm., March 1985.

References

Ackerman, T. 1985. Hired guns for an East Side patrol. *Downtown News*, July 17.
Ahr, P. & W. Holcomb 1985. State Mental Health Directors priorities for mental health care. *Hospital and Community Psychiatry* **36**, 39–45.
Anderson, T. 1984. Thousands released; few treatment facilities. *California Journal* **15**, 215–18.

Bachrach, L. 1984. Research on services for the homeless mentally ill. *Hospital and Community Psychiatry* **35**, 910–13.
Bassuk, E. 1984. The homeless problem. *Scientific American* **251**, 40–5.
Baxter, E. & K. Hopper 1982. The new mendicancy: homeless in New York City. *American Journal of Orthopsychiatry* **52**, 393–408.
Boffey, P. 1984. Community care for the mentally ill termed a failure. *New York Times*, September 13.
Boodman, S. 1985. Ex-patients struggle to adjust on outside. *Washington Post*, May 12.
Boodman, S. & M. Moore 1985. Virginia panel approves involuntary commitment change. *Washington Post*, January 18.
Bronzan, B. 1984. State leaders fad the treatment problem. *California Journal* **35**, 220.

California Legislative Analyst 1985. *Analysis of the 1985–86 budget bill*. Sacramento, Calif.
California State Commission on California State Government Organization and Economy 1983. *Community residential care in California*. N. Shapell, Cahir. Sacramento, Calif.
Clayton, J. 1985. City's skid row shelter will set up on new site. *Los Angeles Times*, July 7.
Connell, R. 1985a. State accused of shirking its duty on the homeless. *Los Angeles Times*, June 18.
Connell, R. 1985b. L.A., firms on skid row OK 1-year plan on shelter for the homeless. *Los Angeles Times*, November 2.

Dear, M. & J. Wolch 1986. *Deinstitutionalization and the north American city*. Cambridge: Polity Press.

Farr, R. K., P. Koegel & A. Burnam 1986. *A study of homelessness in the skid row area of Los Angeles*. Los Angeles County Department of Mental Health.

Goleman, D. 1984. Lawsuits try to force care for the mentally ill. *New York Times*, April 24.

Henshaw, C. 1984. Communities caring for their mentally ill. *New York Times*, May 31.
Hernandez, M. 1985. Workers at 11 state mental hospitals sue over safety. *Los Angeles Times*, June 6.
Huguenin, E. 1984. "Homeless": a new name for the mentally ill. *Washington Post*, November 18, C8.

Jacobs, P. 1985a. Mental case law: matter of rights. *Los Angeles Times*, March 18.
Jacobs, P. 1985b. Model mental health plan seeks to double spending. *Los Angeles Times*, March 20.
Jacobs, P. 1985c. Panel OKs major reforms in aid for state's mentally ill. *Los Angeles Times*, May 18.
Jacobs, P. 1985d. Parents' groups decry inequities in state aid for the mentally ill and the retarded. *Los Angeles Times*, May 19.

Krauthammer, C. 1985. For the homeless: asylum. *Washington Post*, January 4.

Lamb, H. 1979. The new asylums in the community. *Archives of General Psychiatry* **36**, 129–34.
Lamb, H. 1982. Young adult chronic patients: the new drifters. *Hospital and Community Psychiatry* **33**, 465–8.
Lamb, H. 1984. Deinstitutionalization and the homeless mentally ill. *Hospital and Community Psychiatry* **35**, 899–907.
Lamb, H. & D. Lamb 1984. A nonhospital alternative to acute hospitalization. *Hospital and Community Psychiatry* **35**, 728–30.
Lamb, H. & R. Peele 1984. The need for continuing asylum and sanctuary. *Hospital and Community Psychiatry* **35**, 798–801.
Los Angeles County, Community and Senior Citizen Services Department 1985. *Report of the Countywide Task Force on the homeless*. August. Los Angeles, Calif.
Los Angeles County, Department of Mental Health 1985. Memo to Board of Supervisors on allocation of 1985–86 state augmentation dollars. July 2. Los Angeles, Calif.
Los Angeles Times 1985a. Mental care home hit with stiffest fine. June 20.
Los Angeles Times 1985b. Shortchanging mental health. June 28.
Los Angeles Times 1985c. Prisons: making room. September 2.
Lyons, R. 1984. How release of mental patients began. *New York Times*, October 30.

Morse, B., N. Schields, C. Hanneke, R. Calsyn, B. Burger & B. Nelson 1985. *Homeless people in St. Louis: a mental health program evaluation, field study, and follow-up evaluation*. St. Louis: Missouri Department of Mental Health.

Nickerson, C. 1985a. Reformers' dream that went astray. *Boston Globe*, March 10.
Nickerson, C. 1985b. Young and mentally ill, they drift to the fringes of society. *Boston Globe*, March 2.

Paddock, R. 1985. Governor tours prison, denies that trip is campaign related. *Los Angeles Times*, July 23, 116.
Parisi, A. 1985. Bergen County dedicates home for homeless. *New York Times*, April 24.

Reich, R. & L. Siegal 1973. Psychiatry under siege: the chronically mentally ill shuffle to oblivion. *Psychiatric Annals* **3**, 35–55.

Robertson, M., R. Ropers & R. Boyer 1985. *The homeless of Los Angeles County: an empirical evaluation*. Los Angeles, Calif.: Basic Shelter Research Project, Document no. 4, School of Public Health University of California, Los Angeles.

Rosenblatt, A. 1984. Concepts of the asylum in the care of the mentally ill. *Hospital and Community Psychiatry* **35**, 244–50.

Talbott, J. 1984. The need for asylum, not asylums. *Hospital and Community Psychiatry* **35**, 209.

US Department of Housing and Urban Development 1984. *A report to the Secretary on the homeless and emergency shelters*. Washington: US Government Printing Office.

US General Accounting Office 1977. *Returning the mentally disabled to the community: government needs to do more*. Washington: US Government Printing Office.

US General Accounting Office 1983. *An analysis of zoning and other problems affecting the establishment of group homes for the mentally disabled*. Washington: US Government Printing Office.

Vollmer, T. 1985a. County hit for big bite by soaring relief costs. *Los Angeles Times*, July 9.

Vollmer, T. 1985b. County hopes to modify aid for homeless. *Los Angeles Times*, July 17.

Wolch, J. & S. Gabriel. 1985. Dismantling the community-based human service system. *Journal of the American Planning Association* **51**, 53–62.

Wolpert, J., M. Dear & R. Crawford 1975. Satellite mental health facilities. *Annals, Association of American Geographers* **65**, 24–35.

Wolpert, J. & E. Wolpert 1976. The relocation of released mental hospital patients into residential communities. *Policy Sciences* **7**, 31–51.

14 Homelessness and mental illness in America: emerging issues in the construction of a social problem

JOSEPH P. MORRISSEY and
KOSTAS GOUNIS

Since the early 1980s, homelessness in urban America has been identified as a social crisis of major proportions. As each new winter sets new post-Depression records in the numbers of individuals and families who seek emergency shelter, the plight of the homeless population is forced to the forefront of public consciousness. Media coverage of people living on the streets, in terminals, and in crowded shelters has heightened the visibility of homelessness and created a demand for answers from politicians, administrators, and other experts (Shipp 1986). Although local responses vary, including many instances in which "Americans are becoming less tolerant of street people" (Abrams 1984), there seems to be agreement among informed observers on three things: (a) that the size of the homeless population is enormous; (b) that it is growing; and (c) that existing interventions, primarily in the form of providing emergency shelter, are neither sufficient to accommodate the ever-increasing numbers of homeless, nor are they appropriate for addressing the diverse needs of this extremely hetero-geneous population (Lamb 1984a, b; Bassuk 1984a; Roth *et al*. 1985; Morse & Calysn 1985; General Accounting Office 1985; Hyde 1985).

Homelessness, whether as a media spectacle, a partisan political forum, or a challenge to traditional boundaries between human service agencies, has stirred a highly polemicized debate, and there is an abundance of studies, journalistic accounts, testimonies, and reports which attempt to provide explanations and to champion solutions. In many instances, these debates have centered around numbers. "Counting the homeless," aside from being a necessary first step in order to establish the scope of the problem and the dimensions of need, has often generated controversy due to the varying political implications of these numerical exercises. A case in point is the nationwide estimate arrived at in a study commissioned by the US Department of Housing and Urban Development (HUD 1984). The HUD report was partly an effort to play down the estimate provided by the Community for

Creative Non-Violence (Hombs & Snyder 1982), an advocacy group based in Washington, D.C. which conducted a national survey of local shelter providers. Respondents in that survey estimated that an average of 1% of the population in their localities were homeless; extrapolated to the nation as a whole, this estimate meant that the homeless numbered 2–3 million people (General Accounting Office 1985). In contrast, HUD reported that some 250,000–350,000 persons were homeless on an average night in the winter of 1983–4. The HUD report has been discredited as numerical sorcery (Conason 1985), designed more to sustain a particular political viewpoint rather than a serious effort to enumerate the true scope of the problem. Questions have been raised about its methodology to the point where the House Subcommittee on Housing and Community Development held hearings on the report (Snyder 1985, *Safety Network* 1986).

Politics aside, the various attempts to survey the homeless population have invariably encountered many difficulties, ranging from the logistical problems of locating undomiciled individuals to more conceptual issues such as defining homelessness (Bachrach 1984a, b; Lovell *et al*. 1984; Milburn & Watts 1985). Despite the problems in establishing a reliable base-line, it is widely accepted that homelessness is increasing: "The rates of increase nationwide vary from a HUD estimate of 10 percent per year between 1980 and 1983, to a U.S. Conference of Mayors estimate of 38 percent during 1983" (General Accounting Office 1985: 10).

On another level, numbers have also been debated at length when the focus shifts into questions of causality and the needs of the homeless population. It has been argued that the most compelling fact about homelessness is the function of today's skid rows as "psychiatric dumping grounds" (Reich & Siegel 1978) and of public shelters as "open asylums" (Walsh 1985). The undeniable presence of significant numbers of mentally disturbed persons among the homeless has been the subject of continuous and as yet un-resolved controversy and dilemma. The perception that mental illness is rampant among the homeless becomes, for some, an indication that mental health policies are the cause of homelessness and a reason to press for mental health solutions to the problem (Bassuk 1984b, Morganthau 1986). In a parallel vein, the perception that psychopathology, as opposed to social and economic processes, explains the phenomenon is being reproduced and reinforced in the public imagination by the inevitable appeal of "the impaired capacity model of homelessness" (Hopper 1985) as an explanation and a guide for designing solutions. When the sources of homelessness lie in the homeless themselves, i.e., when individuals "choose," either on the basis of psychopathology or deviant lifestyle, to be homeless, the appropriate interventions become service-oriented, with the most extreme proponents of this view calling for "reinstitutionalization" or their return to the asylum (Perkins 1985).

The growing expectation that mental health interventions can solve the problem of homelessness originates in a combination of misperceptions concerning both the efficacy of mental health technologies as well as the phenomenology itself. To the extent that homelessness is defined as a mental health problem, it represents the latest example of alchemy in the mental health policy arena (Goldman & Morrissey 1985). Alchemy in this context calls attention to the transformation of social problems into mental health problems. By "psychiatrizing" social problems, alchemy deflects public attention away from fundamental causes (usually political and economic in nature), builds public expectations that service-based interventions will remedy the problem and, thereby, sets the stage for failure and yet another cycle of reform in mental health policy.

In this chapter, we will analyze homelessness in the USA from the alchemy perspective. The presentation will be organized into four parts. First, we will present a brief historical review of mental health policies in the USA. Secondly, we will review the basic findings from several reports as to the causes of homelessness and the numbers of homeless who are mentally ill. This will then provide a basis for describing the similarities and differences between homelessness and earlier instances of alchemy, in terms of the coalition of interests which support this definitional magic. Finally, we will present an alternative view of homelessness as a structural embodiment of current political and economic policies. From this point of view, which we will call the *survival economics* perspective, homelessness is a new niche in the urban ecology of the 1980s.

Alchemy and mental health policy: a retrospect

The history of public mental health policy in America is characterized by a cyclical pattern of institutional reforms (Morrissey *et al.* 1980, Morrissey & Goldman 1984). Each cycle was marked by a new environmental approach to treatment, and a new type of facility or locus of care. The first cycle in the early 19th century introduced moral treatment and the asylum; the second cycle in the early 20th century was associated with the mental hygiene movement and the psychopathic hospital; and the third cycle in the mid-20th century developed out of the community mental health movement and its spawning of community mental health centers. Each reform promised that it would prevent chronicity by the early treatment of acute cases, yet each failed to eliminate chronicity or to alter the care of the chronically mentally ill in a fundamental way. As a result, the optimism of reform was soon replaced by pessimism about the ever-growing numbers of incurable chronic patients, and public support turned to neglect.

The reform movements that stimulated these cycles often gained momentum by transforming social problems (e.g., dependency, senility, criminality, poverty, and racism) into mental health issues. Failure to address the basic social problems themselves resulted in a repeating cycle of reforms which only partly accomplished the goals of their activist proponents.

The dynamic behind these reform–neglect cycles, in large part, has been a combination of the strivings toward professionalization by psychiatry, and the concerted efforts of activists and lobbyists to secure resources for their proposed reforms. Professionalization involves the development of expansive claims by practitioners that they have specialized knowledge and expertise which uniquely equips them to solve problems of particular importance or concern to society (Freidson 1970). Claims for special competence are advanced so as to obtain the public "license and mandate" (Hughes 1958) to have exclusive jurisdiction over a problem area such as illness, contracts, or religious beliefs. Although the claims are advanced on behalf of clients, the prime beneficiary of this process is often the professionalizing group itself, which gains in social status, income, and power *vis-à-vis* competing occupational specialists.

The professionalization basis for mental health reform is well illustrated by the development of psychiatry during the late 19th and early 20th centuries, and the resource acquisition component by the so-called "psychotropic drug revolution," which fueled the community mental health movement in the 1950s and 1960s. Since each of these stories has been described and analyzed in some detail elsewhere (Grob 1973, 1983; Lyons 1984; Gronfein 1985), only the highlights need be recounted here.

Throughout the latter half of the 19th century, organized psychiatry was virtually coterminous with the group of medical superintendents of public and private asylums (Grob 1973). Following the demise of the moral therapy movement and the social transformation of American society which began in the 1850s and 1860s, the medical superintendents passively accepted the redefinition of asylum functions from treatment to custodial care and community protection. As cure rates dropped precipitously, and as chronic patients began to accumulate, state legislatures placed increasing emphasis on the custody of the largest number of patients at the lowest cost. The small, pastoral retreats that marked the moral therapy era were transformed into general-purpose solutions to the welfare burdens of a society undergoing rapid urbanization, industrialization, and stratification along social class and ethnic lines. The medical superintendents turned to a variety of trade-union interests concerning the proper construction and equipping of asylums, the operation of farms, and qualifications of asylum staff. These interests deflected attention away from quality of care in the asylums toward topics which advanced psychiatry's exclusive claims over superintendency of the mentally ill.

In the early 20th century, the mental hygiene movement was ushered in with promises of asylum reform and a renewed emphasis on the treatability of mental illness (Deutsch 1944, Sicherman 1980, Grob 1983). This movement had a broad base of support from neurologists, social workers, and lay reformers who were critical of asylum psychiatry and united in their desire to break the stranglehold of medical superintendents over the care of the insane. Mental hygienists advocated creating a "psychopathic hospital," an acute treatment or reception facility affiliated with university training and research institutes. Psychiatric dispensaries and child-guidance clinics were also among the innovations spawned by this movement. Although these facilities provided high-quality care for a few, they were unable to eliminate chronic illness, and patients continued to accumulate in state institutions.

As the movement matured, its original goal of improving mental-hospital care fell by the wayside. In its place, reformers began to champion the relevance of psychiatry in the care of the feeble-minded, eugenics, control of alcoholism, management of abnormal children, treatment of criminals, prevention of prostitution and dependency, and even the problem of industrial productivity (Rothman 1980, Grob 1983): yet little of this was supported by any innovations in effective treatment techniques. Once again, the professionalizing thrusts of psychiatry broadened its functions and roles by expanding its boundaries into the community, and claiming expertise relevant to a range of new social problems. In the process, the locus of power within psychiatry gradually shifted from state mental hospitals to universities and private office practice. The exhilaration of forging a marriage between psychiatry and social activism deflected the attention of many psychiatrists from the custodial and managerial origins of their discipline, and the state mental hospitals became defined as the back-water of the profession.

World War II marked the transition from the mental hygiene to the community mental health movement. Wartime experiences in the number of selective service rejectees and combat casualties associated with mental illness, coupled with front-line successes of brief psychiatric interventions, stimulated renewed interest in prevention and new optimism for treatment. The community mental health movement was born out of this enthusiasm for brief treatment techniques, which avoided the removal of patients to faraway hospitals. Psychiatrists returning to state mental hospitals from military service experimented with brief hospitalization and new psycho-social treatment techniques. In the mid-1950s, the new psychotropic drugs came into widespread use in the state mental hospitals. These treatment and policy innovations led to the development of new community-based aftercare clinics to serve a growing number of discharged mental patients. At the same time, there was a growth in the number of outpatient clinics and acute psychiatric inpatient units in general hospitals. Again, reformers offered the promise that early intervention in a community setting could prevent chronicity and long-term disability, rendering the state mental hospital obsolete.

The symbol of the new reform was the community mental health center (CMHC), a comprehensive array of inpatient and outpatient services organized under a single administrative entity that would assume treatment responsibility for all persons in a delimited catchment area. To finance these centers, community mental health reformers called for the massive support of the federal government, which finally occurred in 1963 with the passage of the Community Mental Health Centers Act (Musto 1975). Over the next decade, the goals of community mental health were coupled with the "Great Society" attack of the Kennedy–Johnson administrations on a variety of social problems including poverty, racism, delinquency, and urban disorganization.

To develop governmental support for the CMHC program, mental health advocates championed the role of the new psychoactive drugs in treating and controlling mental disorders in the community and, ultimately, as the vehicle whereby state mental health authorities could avoid the massive costs of the state hospitals. As Lyons (1984) notes: "The picture is one of cost-conscious policy makers, who were quick to buy optimistic projections that were, in some instances, buttressed by misinformation and by a willingness to suspend skepticism. . . . The records show that the politicians were dogged by the image and financial problems posed by these State hospitals and that the scientific and medical establishment sold Congress and the state legislatures a quick fix for a complicated problem that was bought sight unseen." Although a variety of other legal and political–economic factors played a prominent part in the policy of deinstitutionalization (Morrissey et al. 1980), it was this emphasis on prevention of chronicity via early drug treatment in the community that was presented as the "scientific" basis for deinstitutionalization. Many of the psychiatrists who played a key role in securing governmental support for this policy now acknowledge that the benefits of community care, and the efficacy of psychoactive drugs, were oversold to secure governmental funding for community programs (Lyons 1984).

The point of this brief retrospective, then, is to highlight the history of alchemy in mental health policy. Social problems have been transformed into mental health issues, both as a result of professionalization activities and as a way of securing resources for the implementation of reform agendas. The consequences of these efforts is that they are formulas for failure: exaggerated claims of success cannot be sustained, and this leads to pessimism and retrenchment. The result is a cyclical pattern of reforms and retrenchment in mental health care (Morrisey & Goldman 1984).

Alchemy and homelessness: a prospect

In the late 1970s, as the failures of mental hospital deinstitutionalization policies were receiving widespread attention in the media, reports began to appear which characterized urban skid rows and other transient areas as "psychiatric dumping grounds" (Reich & Siegel 1978, Siegel *et al*. 1977). In subsequent years, a variety of efforts were made to assess the prevalence of mental disorders among the urban homeless. In order to appreciate the context in which alchemy is now being played out with regard to urban homelessness, it will be useful to review the findings from a number of recent studies.

What the literature clearly indicates is that prevalence varies, depending upon the sampling site and the population studied (Fischer & Breakey 1985). Studies which report a *high* prevalence rate of mental disorders among the homeless tend to be those based upon a small preselected or nonrandom sample from a single service program, or from a single type of service site. This genre is well represented by recent studies in Philadelphia (Arce *et al*. 1983), New York (Lipton *et al*. 1983), and Boston (Bassuk *et al*. 1984). The Philadelphia study (n = 193) was based upon a retrospective review of psychiatric examinations performed in a specialized shelter; the New York study (n = 100) entailed a record review of persons admitted to a psychiatric service in a municipal general hospital; and the Boston study (n = 78) was based upon clinician interviews of the residents at one shelter. Each study reported that almost all of their homeless subjects had a mental disorder (Philadelphia 84.4%, New York 100%, and Boston 91%).

In contrast, studies which report a relatively *low* prevalence rate tend to be those based upon a random sample of shelter users, using standardized diagnostic and assessment schedules. Such data have recently been reported for St. Louis (Morse & Calysn 1985), Baltimore (Fischer *et al*. 1986), and New York City (Struening 1986). The St. Louis study (n = 248) was based on a random sample of users in 13 of 16 emergency shelters, using the Brief Symptom Inventory (BSI) as a case-finding instrument. The Baltimore study (n = 51) was based on a random sample of males from shelters, using the Diagnostic Interview Schedule (DIS). The New York study (n = 832) was based on a random sample of residents in 17 of the 19 municipal shelters, using a variety of standardized rating scales.

The St. Louis study found that 25% of the respondents had a prior psychiatric hospitalization (another 16% had received outpatient mental health services), and that 46.9% scored above the screening cutoff on a global severity index from the BSI. The Baltimore study found that 33% had a prior psychiatric hospitalization history, and that 37% had a current DIS diagnosis. The New York study, in turn, reported that only 17% of the residents had a prior psychiatric hospitalization, and that 22% had a history of serious mental disorders (another 12% were found to have moderately severe depressive symptoms).

These studies illustrate the methodological problems involved in interpreting the current research literature on homelessness and mental illness. The lack of standardized sampling and diagnostic methods makes it difficult to compare rates across studies. Nonetheless, it is clear that broader-based studies relying upon standardized (if not identical) assessment instruments yield a much *lower* prevalence rate than single-site, nonrandom samples. The broader-based studies also suggest, to varying degrees, that there is a greater proportion of persons who are currently symptomatic than there is of persons who have had a prior psychiatric hospitalization. In other words, it would appear that the homeless mentally ill population is not coterminous with the minority who have been previously hospitalized in a state or other mental hospital.

A recent study conducted in Ohio (Roth *et al.* 1985) provides the clearest statement to date of this relationship. Approximately 30% of the respondents reported a prior psychiatric hospitalization, while 30% were currently symptomatic; however, there was only about a 50% overlap between the two groups. In other words, less than one-half of the persons with a prior hospitalization history were currently symptomatic, and less than one-half of those currently symptomatic had no prior hospitalization history.

Given such data, to what extent is homelessness a mental health problem? This question is central to the alchemy thesis and it has been much debated over the past decade. The issue has revolved around competing explanations as to the causes of homelessness; specifically, the role that mental health deinstitutionalization policies have played in creating homelessness over the past two decades. Despite the importance of this question, it has not been examined to date in a rigorous way. As Fischer & Breakey (1985: 20) note:

> The published literature does not include any studies specifically designed to document the role of deinstitutionalization in homelessness. Though the widespread dissatisfaction with its implementation in the United States in recent years may well be justified, there is a danger that the deinstitutionalization movement and shortcomings in community mental health services may become scapegoats for the various other forces in society that have contributed to the homelessness problem.

Although the multiple causes of urban homelessness have been documented in a number of reports (Hombs & Snyder 1982, General Accounting Office 1985, Roth *et al.* 1985), the work of Kim Hopper and his colleagues represents the most thorough review and assessment of the issue now available (Baxter & Hopper 1981, Salerno *et al.* 1984, Hopper & Hamberg 1984, Hopper 1985). These assessments indicate that the primary causes of homelessness are to be found in the changes and interactions among a variety of economic and political factors:

(1) *Household income and income sources.* The decline in real wages through-out the 1970s and 1980s; the loss of middle-income unionized jobs in the manufacturing sector; recurrent high levels of unemployment and underemployment; erosion of benefit levels in welfare entitlements and restrictions in eligibility; and an upward climb in official poverty rates.

(2) *Household composition.* The accelerated formation of single-parent households, and a rapid increase in the divorce rate.

(3) *Housing.* The sharp decline in the percentage of families who could afford to purchase homes and decreasing household size, both of which intensified competition for rental housing; the increases in proportion of total income paid for rent; and the loss of low-income single-room-occupancy (SRO) units from the nation's housing stock.

(4) *Regional population shifts.* The migration of unemployed workers and their families from the industrialized northeast to sunbelt areas in search of new job opportunities.

These trends combined to move more and more households to the brink of subsistence during the 1970s. In the early 1980s, the brink was crossed by thousands of individuals as a consequence of the recessions of 1979 and 1982 and the Reagan budget cuts (Hopper 1985). The number of people officially living in poverty grew by 40% between 1978 and 1983 (from 11.4% to 15.2% of the population). Many of the unemployed remained jobless for extended periods, but fewer than 50% of those who lost jobs in 1982 received unemployment benefits. In addition, means-tested assistance programs were reduced, and new eligibility rates meant that 50% of the working poor were dropped from aid to families with dependent children (AFDC) rolls, while another 40% of such families had their benefits reduced. Nearly 500,000 (one-sixth of the total) recipients of disability benefits (SSDI) were also dropped from the rolls. The reduction in food-stamp programs also forced many households to resort to soup kitchens and food pantries to supplement their income.

A characterization of the current debate over homelessness as a mental health versus a social welfare problem as the latest form of alchemy in the mental health arena must be qualified in terms of its similarities and differences with earlier instances of this phenomenon. Today, no professional group is seeking to make homelessness an exclusive domain of practice and intervention. While individual psychiatrists are prominent in the debate over the causes and remedies for homelessness (Lamb 1984b), the profession has yet to embrace the issue in the way that its 19th century and early 20th century adherents did with regard to moral therapy and mental hygiene. Indeed, psychiatry is well along the route of remedicalizing itself, and forging a much closer alliance with general medicine in the context of the general hospital. In this new position, psychiatry has retreated from the social activism which characterized some of its more radical members during the 1950s and 1960s (Group for the Advancement of Psychiatry 1983).

As in the past, however, the alchemy process has been displaced from its professional context into an intergovernmental context. One of the under-lying issues in the effort to pin homelessness on mental health policy has been the question of which level of government is ultimately responsible for finding and funding a solution to the problem. Much of the "numbers game" in New York City over the past decade, for example, has revolved around this issue. To the extent that deinstitutionalization could be defined as the culprit, city and county governments throughout the country were absolved from providing a long-term solution, as the state had ultimate responsibility for discharged patients in the community. Similarly, coupling homelessness with mental health problems also served the Reagan administration's policy of phasing down the role of the federal government in meeting health and welfare needs of the citizens. In contrast, documenting the societal-level economic and political causes of homeless-ness squarely fixes responsibility with the federal government for both the cause and relief of the problem.

Attention must also be focused on the likely consequences of this debate. Currently, the mental health system is reeling from the aftermath of deinstitutionalization in the community and is experiencing resource short-falls. It no longer represents the well endowed social movement it had been in the 1950s and 1960s. Moreover, the mental health professions have not demonstrated competence in successfully solving the range of employ-ment, housing, and social welfare problems which define urban homeless-ness today. If the mental health sector is saddled with primary responsibility for the cause and relief of homelessness, this may undermine an already precarious resource base for the long-term care of the chronic mentally ill in the community settings (Goldman & Morrissey 1985).

Homelessness: a survival economics perspective

The debates between elected officials and administrators, advocates and mental health professionals are highly politicized. The emphasis is on allocating blame and developing particular, "crisis-intervention" responses which often obscure the fact that the "homeless" constitute a *heterogeneous* population that stubbornly defies classification. Service inter-ventions—even when they are attempted for a particular subgroup, the mentally ill for instance—invariably encounter immense difficulties in engaging and responding to the needs of the targeted population (Morrissey *et al.* 1985, 1986). Relief efforts in general, when they have been mounted, seem to teach more by their failures than by their successes (Hopper & Hamberg 1984).

The manner in which the contraction of the public relief system serves the function of "regulating the poor" has led Piven & Cloward (1982) to describe the emergence of a "new class war". The idea that people have a right to subsistence and, subsequently, to the establishment and maintenance of programs which have protected the poor, has come under attack by the combined power of the state and the market. Piven & Cloward envision that, in the long run, the democratic process which has forced the state to inaugurate these programs in the past will assert itself over this combined attack: people will press for new alternatives by defying the rules and causing disruptions which will articulate their outrage.

The realization which underlies these projections is that displacement will continue and homelessness will persist because "something has gone grievously wrong with the fundamental needs-satisfying structures of our society" (Hopper & Hamberg 1984). In the short run, however, the lived reality of the population affected by the harsh allocation of resources in today's economy forces people to make choices and to perceive options for identity within the narrow constraints of a system which makes survival a full-time occupation. *Survival economics* redefines the normative system of reciprocities between the marginalized population and the formal and informal institutions, which regulate the distribution of the ever-diminishing resources which are available to the poor.

The inability to maintain or to find affordable housing is one of the areas where the poor, especially the dependent poor, have felt the impact of current political and economic processes. The lack of housing, aside from denying people the opportunity to have a home, also signifies that fundamental pre-conditions for and assumptions regarding social integration become suspended. Normal everyday activities and roles such as being a worker and a taxpayer, a tenant and a rent-payer, and a consumer of services and other market goods are all expressions of the degree to which a person participates in, and is accountable to, the normative structures which regulate social interaction. Homes as support groups, or households as socioeconomic units, provide the psychological and material support which mediates and facilitates social integration. The consensual acceptance of the given socio-economic order, and the enactment of roles allocated and reinforced by this order, become possible only to the extent that these support groups and social units remain viable. The assumptions and prerequisites for social integration have thus become rather untenable as homes and households become beyond the reach of an increasing number of people.

A brief overview of the recent history of the homelessness issue in New York City will serve to draw out this survival economics perspective. In the early 1980s, there seemed to be an explosive growth in the number of home-less persons. Reaganomics was certainly responsible for this voluminous flushing out of people. At the same time, or soon afterwards, the following also emerged: the New York City shelter system in its present scope; the increasing involvement and prominence of advocacy groups, especially the Coalition for the Homeless; the role of religious groups in providing an alternative shelter system; various entrepreneurs with schemes for housing the homeless as public monies were becoming available; and also the less frequent use of "derelict" or "bum" in favor of "homeless." On account of these developments and the efforts of these parties "homelessness" continues to be a much publicized issue.

However, there are some nuances worth noting in these developments. Under legal pressure, New York City officials signed the consent decree that requires shelter to be made available to anyone who requests it. A few years later, City officials often conveyed the feeling that this step caused the flood-gates to open, serving as an invitation to people to seek public shelter. Beginning in the winter of 1985–86, City police have also moved in the direction of rounding up, in the streets, people who refuse to accept placement in a public shelter, allegedly in order to protect them from themselves; thus equating homelessness with mental illness. And there is the familiar scenario of "temporary" shelters and other housing facilities becoming "permanent", of each new facility instantly filling up with people, the majority of whom may have no real intention or realistic chance of moving on to a permanent home, It is as if the availability of shelter causes the demand.

In many instances, homeless men interviewed in New York City shelters would accept the definition "homeless" only after arriving at a shelter; that is, after entering that whole system which is centered at East 3rd Street on the Bowery and radiates out into armories, churches, former hospital wards, and the like. Yet the majority of these men who arrived at the shelters had subsisted on the fringes long before they were recognized as "homeless" or identified themselves as such. Survival economics, which may range from narcotics trafficking to bottle-retrieving or panhandling, and from windshield wiping to mugging, including the occasional odd-job (cleaning up a bar in the Bowery, or sweeping the sidewalk in front of a fruit stand in Queens) involves strategies which make the costs of maintaining a home rather unattractive. The exigencies of this survival economics, which has been around for a while, often involve residing, over considerable periods of time, in places such as prisons or hospitals, doubling-up with friends or relatives, and now making use of shelters. Illegal and other underground economic activities foster relationships which eclipse the role of the "home" as a support group, and which imply residential arrangements which discourage the establishment and maintaining of permanent households in favor of different types of "sheltering."

In a sense, when public shelters become available they come to epitomize this need for sheltering and to give it an "institutionalized" recognition. The shelter brings under one roof all these diverse styles of subsistence, all these groups who have been without homes for a long time without necessarily being called homeless. Initially, the shelter may serve as an additional resource. Eventually, however, it becomes a permanent station, both because other resources, especially friends and family, are depleted and because the shelter system itself becomes the locus or center for the activities and exchanges regulating the survival economy of these populations. In short, the convergence of public policy (or of the lack of it), of advocacy, and of the choices the disenfranchised populations have to make results in the "homeless" being forced to or aided in forming a sense of unique identity as such.

On another level, however, even when homelessness comes close to being recognized as the predicament of an ever-increasing number of people regardless of their sanity (in other words, even when the public and various levels of government concede that not all people, not even the majority of those who have no permanent place to live, are mentally impaired), there is still resistance in acknowledging the reality of the crisis. This resistance stems from the fact that homelessness defies and offends established values of American society: "choosing" not to have a home or not being able to afford one become manifestations of social conditions which fly in the face of all that is sacred in the spectacle of the American way of life.

It should be clear by now to professionals, administrators, and observers that the massive displacement evidenced by the growing numbers of homeless populations around the USA cannot be explained on the basis of individual disability alone. More than 25 years ago, Mills (1959: 8) articulated the distinction between conditions which can be attributed to individuals, or "personal troubles," and those which must be recognized as the effect of economic and political processes, that is, "public issues of social structure":

> When, in a city of 100,000, only one man is unemployed, that is his personal trouble, and for its relief we properly look to the character of the man, his skills, and his immediate opportunities. But when in a nation of 50 million employees, 15 million men are unemployed, that is a [public] issue, and we may not hope to find its solution within the range of opportunities open to any one individual. The very structure of opportunities has collapsed. Both the correct statement of the problem and the range of possible solutions require us to consider the economic and political institutions of the society, and not merely the personal situation and character of a scatter of individuals.

By merely substituting homelessness for unemployment, Mills' observations go to the heart of the present crisis.

The term "homelessness" has come to dominate social discourse, precisely because in its ambiguity it serves only as a partial recognition of the emergence of social phenomena, which casts doubt both on the expansive-ness of the American dream as well as on the efficacy of institutional arrangements aimed at promoting or safeguarding or selling this dream. Again, as Mills (1959: 7) pointed out "An issue is a public matter [because] some value cherished by [the public] is felt to be threatened." However, Mills adds that:

> Often there is debate about what that value really is and about what it is that really threatens it. This debate is often without focus if only because it is the very nature of an issue, unlike even widespread trouble, that it cannot very well be defined in terms of the immediate and everyday environments of ordinary men. An issue, in fact, often involves a *crisis in institutional arrangements* . . . [emphasis added].

Homelessness is thus revealed as a condition that affects more and more people every day, and the label has been applied to describe the plight of these dispossessed people. The popularity of the term is undeniably warranted by the wide prevalence of the phenomenon. But once discovered and liberally applied, "homelessness" ceases to be merely a description of the absence of a home, i.e., a situational descriptor (Hopper 1985), and instead becomes an inducement towards the definition of a particular subculture and serves as a vehicle for self-identification. The "homeless" begin to form a particular constituency as the result of a process which serves both the wider public and those who are the homeless themselves. In short, what we are suggesting is that homelessness emerges as a condition which is over-determined by public reaction, and by behaviors which are intrinsic to the sphere of survival economics.

Conclusions

From all present indications, the problem of homelessness in America will intensify and expand over the next few years. The character of homelessness is also changing. Today, for example, children constitute the single largest segment of the New York City shelter system and the number of families served now number in the thousands. Efforts are being made by municipal and state-government officials (as well as by numerous private groups) to develop alternative housing and service-intervention programs, but the homelessness problem seems to grow unabated. What was first introduced as short-term emergency shelter is now becoming a long-term housing program, and in the process, the public shelter system seems to be recreating the almshouses of the 19th century (Katz 1985).

We have argued in this chapter that homelessness represents the latest instance of alchemy in the mental health policy arena, as well as a crisis of the normative constraints which regulate the moral economy of the urban poor. While no single interpretative or causal framework has yet to gain wide acceptance in the public debate, it does make a difference if homelessness is popularly defined as a mental health as opposed to a social welfare problem—as "personal troubles" versus a "public issue" in Mills' terms. The micro-issue of the extent to which mental illness is due to personal versus social causes is beyond the scope of this chapter. Here, we emphasize the macro-issues of collective definition and interventions. The notion that all of these people somehow are former state mental hospital patients is appealing both in the simplicity of its causal imagery and in the apparent ease of its preferred solution. This view is tantamount to "blaming the victim" (Ryan 1976), or at least blaming a group of misguided bureaucrats and professionals who failed either to keep the patients hospitalized or to provide them guaranteed housing upon release. The solution is equally convenient and simplistic: the homeless should be removed from the streets and returned to the state hospitals which are now nearly empty. However, both views are inconsistent with a growing body of information which clearly documents the economic and political causes of homelessness, the fact that most of the homeless have never been hospitalized in public or private psychiatric facilities, and that the majority are not now currently symptomatic.

The diversity of the homeless population, the many different pathways to homelessness, and the multifaceted reality of the experience of homelessness, all make it necessary to acknowledge that the only thing the homeless share is poverty and the absence of a permanent place to live. Indeed, advocates for the homeless have consistently emphasized the role that the unavailability of affordable housing has played in the emergence of widespread displacement and the subsequent persistence and growth of homelessness as a "captive state" (Hopper & Hamberg 1984: 5). Both advocates and liberal researchers have been emphasizing the need to examine the political economy of homelessness and to press for more affordable housing, for more responsibility on the part of government, and for a reversal in the assault launched by the Reagan administration against the welfare state. The systematic effort to dismantle the "safety net," and to withdraw the protection that the public relief system has provided against the insecurities and hardships of an unrestrained market economy, undoubtedly accounts for the massive displacement of people that we have witnessed in the 1980s.

The intense debate on homelessness and the increasing frustration encountered by agencies and groups that are attempting to either control, conceal, or correct the problem serves to exemplify the fact that, in the urban ecology of the 1980s, the terms "homeless" and "homelessness" often encompass and obscure human groups and social conditions which render the traditionally established means for regulating the poor rather ineffective and irrelevant. These groups explore and exploit the margins and crevices of the urban space very much like new hunter–gatherers or nomads, for whom survival requires transhumant lifestyles similar to those that have been encountered by anthropologists in most parts of the non-industrialized world. Given the rigidity of the rationalized, bureaucratic institutions of our society, policy makers will inevitably fail to contain the problem of homelessness as long as the reality of homelessness is that of an increasing number of people who are unable to have even their most basic needs met in socially sanctioned and acceptable ways, and through the recognized formal and informal institutions of our society.

Consequently, neither the alchemy of mental health policy nor what remains of the safety net of the welfare state appear to provide the context within which homelessness can be dealt with adequately, and in ways which capture the scope of the problem. The mental health needs of a small proportion of the homeless population notwithstanding, it can not be over-emphasized that revising mental health policy in the direction demanded by the proponents of the "homelessness equals mental illness" view (*New York Post* 1986) is, to say the least, a misguided position. And unless the structural questions of urban poverty are addressed, homelessness will persist and expand as a new niche in today's urban ecology.

Acknowledgments

The comments of Deborah Dennis and Sue Barrow on an earlier draft of this chapter are gratefully acknowledged.

References

Abrams, A. 1984. Down on the homeless. *Newsday*, November 26.
Arce, A., M. Tadlock, M. Vergare & S. Shapiro 1983. A psychiatric profile of street people admitted to an emergency shelter. *Hospital Community Psychiatry* **34**, 812.

Bachrach, L. 1984a. Research services for the homeless mentally ill. *Hospital and Community Psychiatry* **35**, 910–13.
Bachrach, L. 1984b. Interpreting research on the homeless mentally ill: some caveats. *Hospital and Community Psychiatry* **35**, 914–17.
Bassuk, E. 1984a. Homelessness: the need for mental health advocates. *Hospital and Community Psychiatry* **35**, 867.
Bassuk, E. 1984b. The homelessness problem. *Scientific American* **251**, 40–5.
Bassuk, E., L. Rubin & A. Lauriet 1984. Is homelessness a mental health problem? *American Journal of Psychiatry* **141**, 1546–50.
Baxter, E. & K. Hopper 1981. *Private lives/public spaces: homeless adults on the streets of New York City*. New York: Community Services Society.

Conason, J. 1985. Body count: how the Reagan administration hides the homeless. *Village Voice*, December 3, 25–30.

Deutsch, A. 1944. The history of mental hygiene. In *One hundred years of American psychiatry*, American Psychiatric Association (ed.). New York: Columbia University Press.

Fischer, P. & W. Breakey 1985. Homelessness and mental health: an overview. *International Journal of Mental Health* **14**, 6–41.
Fischer, P., S. Shapiro, W. Breakey, J. Anthony & M. Kramer 1986. Mental health and social characteristics of the homeless: a survey of mission users. *American Journal of Public Health* **76**, 519–23.
Freidson, E. 1970. *Profession of medicine*. New York: Dodd, Mead.

General Accounting Office 1985. *Homelessness: a complex problem and the federal response*. Washington, D.C.: US General Accounting Office.
Goldman, H. & J. Morrissey 1985. The alchemy of mental health policy: homelessness and the fourth cycle of reform. *American Journal of Public Health* **75**, 727–31.
Grob, G. 1973. *Mental institutions in America: social policy to 1875*. New York: The Free Press.
Grob, G. 1983. *Mental illness and American society, 1875–1940*. Princeton, N.J.: Princeton University Press.
Gronfein, W. 1985. Psychotropic drugs and the origins of deinstitutionalization. *Social Problems* **32**, 437–54.
Group for the Advancement of Psychiatry 1983. *Community psychiatry: a reappraisal*. New York: Mental Health Materials Center.

Hombs, M. & M. Snyder 1982. *Homelessness in America: a forced march to nowhere*. Washington: Community for Creative Non-Violence.
Hopper, K. 1985. *Rethinking the link between homelessness and psychiatric disorder: a limited goods perspective*. New York: Division of Sociomedical Sciences, Columbia University.
Hopper, K. & J. Hamberg 1984. *The making of America's homeless: from skid row to new poor, 1945–1984*. New York: Community Service Society (unpubl.).
HUD (US Department of Housing and Urban Development) 1984. *A report to the secretary on the homeless and emergency shelters*. Washington, D.C.: US Government Printing Office.
Hughes, E. 1958. *Men and their work*. New York: The Free Press.
Hyde, P. S. 1985. Homelessness in America: public policy, public blame. *Psychosocial Rehabilitation Journal* **8**, 21–5.

Katz, M. 1985. Poorhouses and the origins of the public old age home. *Millbank Memorial Fund Quarterly: Health and Society* **62**, 110–40.

Lamb, H. R. 1984a. Deinstitutionalization and the homeless mentally ill. *Hospital and Community Psychiatry* **35**, 910.
Lamb, H. R. 1984b. *The homeless mentally ill: a task force report of the American Psychiatric Association*. Washington, D.C.: American Psychiatric Association Press.
Lipton, F., A. Sabatini & S. Katz 1983. Down and out in the city: the homeless mentally ill. *Hospital and Community Psychiatry* **34**, 817.
Lovell, A. M., S. Barrow & E. L. Struening 1984. Measurement issues in services

research on the homeless mentally ill. In *Proceedings of the Eighth Annual NSIS National Users Group Conference*, J. Franks & M. S. Levine (eds.). Orangeburg, N.Y.: Informations Division, Nathan S. Kline Institute.

Lyons, R. 1984. How release of mental patients began: policy makers recall their reasoning and reflect on outcome. *New York Times*, October 30.

Milburn, N. & R. Watts 1985. Methodological issues in research on the homeless and the homeless mentally ill. *International Journal of Mental Health* **14**, 42–60.

Mills, C. W. 1959. *The sociological imagination*. New York: Grove Press.

Morganthau, T. 1986. Abandoned: the chronic mentally ill. *Newsweek*, January 6, 14–19.

Morrissey, J. & H. Goldman 1984. Cycles of reform in the care of the chronically mentally ill. *Hospital and Community Psychiatry* **35**, 785–93.

Morrissey, J., H. Goldman & L. Klerman 1980. *The enduring asylum: cycles of institutional reform at Worcester State Hospital*. New York: Grune & Stratton.

Morrissey, J., D. Dennis, K. Gounis & S. Barrow 1985. *The development and utilization of the Queens Men's Shelter*. Albany, N.Y.: New York State Office of Mental Health.

Morrissey, J., K. Gounis, S. Barrow, E. Struening & S. Katz 1986. Organizational barriers to serving the mentally ill homeless. In *Treating the homeless: urban psychiatry's challenge*, B. Jones (ed.). Washington, D.C.: American Psychiatric Association.

Morse, G. & R. Calysn 1985. Mentally disturbed homeless people in St. Louis: needy, willing, but underserved. *International Journal of Mental Health* **14**, 74–94.

Musto, D. 1975. Whatever happened to community mental health? *The Public Interest* **39**, 53–79.

New York Post 1986. Civil liberties should not bar help to those in need. May 5.

Perkins, J. 1985. New institutions for the homeless. *Wall Street Journal*, February 26.

Piven, F. & R. Cloward 1982. *The new class war: Reagan's attack on the welfare state and its consequences*. New York: Pantheon.

Reich, R. & L. Siegel 1978. The emergence of the Bowery as a psychiatric dumping ground. *Psychiatric Quarterly* **50**, 191–201.

Roth, D., J. Bean, N. Lust & T. Saveanu 1985. *Homelessness in Ohio: a study of people in need*. Columbus: Ohio Department of Mental Health.

Rothman, D. 1980. *Conscience and convenience: the asylum and its alternatives in progressive America*. Boston: Little, Brown.

Ryan, W. 1976. *Blaming the victim*, rev. edn. New York: Vintage.

Salerno, D., K. Hopper & E. Baxter 1984. *Hardship in the heartland: homelessness in eight U.S. cities*. New York: Community Service Society.

Segal, S., J. Baumohl & E. Johnson 1977. Falling through the cracks: mental disorder and social margin in a young vagrant population. *Social Problems* **24**, 387–400.

Shipp, E. 1986. Do more for homeless, say half of those polled. *New York Times*, February 3.

Sicherman, B. 1980. *The quest for mental health in America: 1880–1917*. New York: Arno Press.

Snyder, M. 1985. Testimony. In *The federal response to the homeless crisis*. Subcommittee of the Committee on Government Operations, US House of

Representatives, 309–51. Washington, D.C.: US Government Printing Office.

Struening, E. 1986. *Characteristics of residents of the New York City shelter system.* New York: Community Support Systems Evaluation Program, New York State Psychiatric Institute.

Walsh, J. 1985. Are city shelters now open asylums? *In These Times*, January 22.

Index